# Plotting Disability in the Nineteenth-Century Novel

Edinburgh Critical Studies in Victorian Culture
Series Editor: Julian Wolfreys

Recent books in the series:
*Rudyard Kipling's Fiction: Mapping Psychic Spaces*
Lizzy Welby

*The Decadent Image: The Poetry of Wilde, Symons and Dowson*
Kostas Boyiopoulos

*British India and Victorian Literary Culture*
Máire ní Fhlathúin

*Anthony Trollope's Late Style: Victorian Liberalism and Literary Form*
Frederik Van Dam

*Dark Paradise: Pacific Islands in the Nineteenth-Century British Imagination*
Jenn Fuller

*Twentieth-Century Victorian: Arthur Conan Doyle and the Strand Magazine, 1891–1930*
Jonathan Cranfield

*The Lyric Poem and Aestheticism: Forms of Modernity*
Marion Thain

*Gender, Technology and the New Woman*
Lena Wånggren

*Self-Harm in New Woman Writing*
Alexandra Gray

*Suffragist Artists in Partnership: Gender, Word and Image*
Lucy Ella Rose

*Victorian Liberalism and Material Culture: Synergies of Thought and Place*
Kevin A. Morrison

*The Victorian Male Body*
Joanne-Ella Parsons and Ruth Heholt

*Nineteenth-Century Settler Emigration in British Literature and Art*
Fariha Shaikh

*The Pre-Raphaelites and Orientalism*
Eleonora Sasso

*The Late-Victorian Little Magazine*
Koenraad Claes

*Coastal Cultures of the Long Nineteenth Century*
Matthew Ingleby and Matt P. M. Kerr

*Dickens and Demolition: Literary Afterlives and Mid-Nineteenth-Century Urban Development*
Joanna Hofer-Robinson

*Artful Experiments: Ways of Knowing in Victorian Literature and Science*
Philipp Erchinger

*Victorian Poetry and the Poetics of the Literary Periodical*
Caley Ehnes

*The Victorian Actress in the Novel and on the Stage*
Renata Kobetts Miller

*Dickens's Clowns: Charles Dickens, Joseph Grimaldi and the Pantomime of Life*
Jonathan Buckmaster

*Italian Politics and Nineteenth-Century British Literature and Culture*
Patricia Cove

*Cultural Encounters with the Arabian Nights in Nineteenth-Century Britain*
Melissa Dickson

*Novel Institutions: Anachronism, Irish Novels and Nineteenth-Century Realism*
Mary L. Mullen

*The Fin-de-Siècle Scottish Revival: Romance, Decadence and Celtic Identity*
Michael Shaw

*Contested Liberalisms: Martineau, Dickens and the Victorian Press*
Iain Crawford

*Plotting Disability in the Nineteenth-Century Novel*
Clare Walker Gore

Forthcoming volumes:
*Her Father's Name: Gender, Theatricality and Spiritualism in Florence Marryat's Fiction*
Tatiana Kontou

*The Sculptural Body in Victorian Literature: Encrypted Sexualities*
Patricia Pulham

*Olive Schreiner and the Politics of Print Culture, 1883–1920*
Clare Gill

*Victorian Auto/Biography: Problems in Genre and Subject*
Amber Regis

*Gissing, Shakespeare and the Life of Writing*
Thomas Ue

*The Aesthetics of Space in Nineteenth-Century British Literature, 1851–1908*
Giles Whiteley

*Women's Mobility in Henry James*
Anna Despotopoulou

*The Persian Presence in Victorian Poetry*
Reza Taher-Kermani

*Michael Field's Revisionary Poetics*
Jill Ehnenn

*The Americanisation of W. T. Stead*
Helena Goodwyn

*Literary Illusions: Performance Magic and Victorian Literature*
Christopher Pittard

For a complete list of titles published visit the Edinburgh Critical Studies in Victorian Culture web page at www.edinburghuniversitypress.com/series/ECVC

Also Available:
*Victoriographies – A Journal of Nineteenth-Century Writing, 1790–1914*, edited by Diane Piccitto and Patricia Pulham
ISSN: 2044-2416
www.eupjournals.com/vic

# Plotting Disability in the Nineteenth-Century Novel

Clare Walker Gore

EDINBURGH
University Press

Edinburgh University Press is one of the leading university presses in the UK. We publish academic books and journals in our selected subject areas across the humanities and social sciences, combining cutting-edge scholarship with high editorial and production values to produce academic works of lasting importance. For more information visit our website: edinburghuniversitypress.com

© Clare Walker Gore, 2020, 2021

Edinburgh University Press Ltd
The Tun – Holyrood Road, 12(2f) Jackson's Entry, Edinburgh EH8 8PJ

First published in hardback by Edinburgh University Press 2020

Typeset in 11/13 Adobe Sabon by
IDSUK (DataConnection) Ltd

A CIP record for this book is available from the British Library

ISBN 978 1 4744 5501 5 (hardback)
ISBN 978 1 4744 5502 2 (paperback)
ISBN 978 1 4744 5503 9 (webready PDF)
ISBN 978 1 4744 5504 6 (epub)

The right of Clare Walker Gore to be identified as the author of this work has been asserted in accordance with the Copyright, Designs and Patents Act 1988, and the Copyright and Related Rights Regulations 2003 (SI No. 2498).

# Contents

| | |
|---|---|
| Series Editor's Preface | vi |
| Acknowledgements | viii |
| Introduction | 1 |
| 1. A Possible Person?: Marking the Minor Character in Dickens | 21 |
| 2. At the Margins of Mystery: Sensational Difference in Wilkie Collins | 74 |
| 3. (De)Forming Families: Disability and the Marriage Plot in Dinah Mulock Craik and Charlotte M. Yonge | 116 |
| 4. Terminal Decline: Physical Frailty and Moral Inheritance in George Eliot and Henry James | 173 |
| Coda | 232 |
| Bibliography | 238 |
| Index | 253 |

## Series Editor's Preface

'Victorian' is a term, at once indicative of a strongly determined concept and an often notoriously vague notion, emptied of all meaningful content by the many journalistic misconceptions that persist about the inhabitants and cultures of the British Isles and Victoria's Empire in the nineteenth century. As such, it has become a by-word for the assumption of various, often contradictory habits of thought, belief, behaviour and perceptions. Victorian studies and studies in nineteenth-century literature and culture have, from their institutional inception, questioned narrowness of presumption, pushed at the limits of the nominal definition, and have sought to question the very grounds on which the unreflective perception of the so-called Victorian has been built; and so they continue to do. Victorian and nineteenth-century studies of literature and culture maintain a breadth and diversity of interest, of focus and inquiry, in an interrogative and intellectually open-minded and challenging manner, which are equal to the exploration and inquisitiveness of its subjects. Many of the questions asked by scholars and researchers of the innumerable productions of nineteenth-century society actively put into suspension the clichés and stereotypes of 'Victorianism', whether the approach has been sustained by historical, scientific, philosophical, empirical, ideological or theoretical concerns; indeed, it would be incorrect to assume that each of these approaches to the idea of the Victorian has been, or has remained, in the main exclusive, sealed off from the interests and engagements of other approaches. A vital interdisciplinarity has been pursued and embraced, for the most part, even as there has been contest and debate amongst Victorianists, pursued with as much fervour as the affirmative exploration between different disciplines and differing epistemologies put to work in the service of reading the nineteenth century.

Edinburgh Critical Studies in Victorian Culture aims to take up both the debates and the inventive approaches and departures from convention that studies in the nineteenth century have witnessed for the last half-century at least. Aiming to maintain a 'Victorian' (in the most positive sense of that motif) spirit of inquiry, the series' purpose is to continue and augment the cross-fertilisation of interdisciplinary approaches, and to offer, in addition, a number of timely and untimely revisions of Victorian literature, culture, history and identity. At the same time, the series will ask questions concerning what has been missed or improperly received, misread, or not read at all, in order to present a multi-faceted and heterogeneous kaleidoscope of representations. Drawing on the most provocative, thoughtful and original research, the series will seek to prod at the notion of the 'Victorian', and in so doing, principally through theoretically and epistemologically sophisticated close readings of the historicity of literature and culture in the nineteenth century, to offer the reader provocative insights into a world that is at once overly familiar, and irreducibly different, other and strange. Working from original sources, primary documents and recent interdisciplinary theoretical models, Edinburgh Critical Studies in Victorian Culture seeks not simply to push at the boundaries of research in the nineteenth century, but also to inaugurate the persistent erasure and provisional, strategic redrawing of those borders.

Julian Wolfreys

# Acknowledgements

For their financial support, I would like to thank the Arts and Humanities Research Council (AHRC) for the funding grant that initially made this research possible, and the Fellows of Trinity College, Cambridge, for the Junior Research Fellowship that allowed me to continue working on it. Along the way, I am grateful to the AHRC, Selwyn College and the Faculty of English for travel and completion grants, and to the staff of the English Faculty Library and the Cambridge University Library for their practical assistance. In this regard I would particularly like to thank Colin Clarkson, who has helped me so much over the course of my research. At Edinburgh University Press, I would like to thank the series editor, Julian Wolfreys, and my editors Michelle Houston and Ersev Ersoy, for all their encouragement and valuable editorial input. I am grateful to both of the peer reviewers who read the manuscript and made such helpful suggestions.

Earlier versions of some of the material in Chapter 3 appeared in the following essays: '"Setting novels at defiance": Novel Reading and Novelistic Form in Charlotte M. Yonge's *The Heir of Redclyffe*', *Nineteenth-Century Gender Studies*, 10.1 (Spring 2014); '"The right and natural law of things": Disability and the Form of the Family in the Fiction of Dinah Mulock Craik and Charlotte M. Yonge', in *Queer Victorian Families: Curious Relations in Literature*, edited by Duc Dau and Shale Preston (Routledge, 2015); '"The Awful Individuality of Suffering": Disabled Characterisation in Dinah Mulock Craik's *Olive* and *A Noble Life*', in *The Variable Body in History*, edited by Chris Mounsey and Stan Booth (Peter Lang, 2016); and '"Excluded from a woman's natural destiny": Disability and Femininity in Dinah Mulock Craik's *Olive* and Charlotte M. Yonge's *The Daisy Chain*', in *Reassessing Women's Writing of the 1840s and 1850s*, edited by Adrienne E. Gavin and Carolyn W. de la L. Oulton (Palgrave Macmillan, 2018). I would like to thank the editors for kindly permitting me to use this material.

My intellectual and personal debts are really too many to name, but since this book is the product of twelve very happy years spent at and around the University of Cambridge, I would like to begin by thanking the English Fellows of Selwyn College – Sarah Meer, Philip Connell and Jean Chothia – for admitting me in the first place, and for making my formative undergraduate years such happy ones. I would also like to thank Sarah, who supervised my first forays into nineteenth-century literature, for being so generous with her time and expertise, both then and ever since.

I was very fortunate to be taught by Alison Hennegan, who went on to supervise the doctoral research out of which this book has emerged. I cannot thank her enough for encouraging and assisting me at every stage of the project, and for sharing her enormous knowledge of nineteenth-century literature (especially its less well-trodden paths) with me over many years of supervision. She was a wonderful supervisor, and I hope this book captures even a fraction of the enjoyment I had in researching this topic under her direction. I would also like to thank my PhD examiners, Jan-Melissa Schramm and Martha Stoddard Holmes, for their incisive and generous reading of my work, and for their invaluable suggestions about how the project might be expanded and developed. I was truly lucky to have them as examiners, and am deeply grateful to them both.

Since coming to Trinity in 2016, I have found myself surrounded by brilliant scholars, and have had in Adrian Poole the kindest and wisest of mentors. I would like to thank him for all his encouragement and support, especially as I set about trying to write my first book, and for his great intellectual generosity in being willing to talk about Henry James with me. Here at Trinity, I am also very grateful to Anne Toner and Alex Freer, and to Anna Berman, who is one of the few people as keen to talk about Charlotte M. Yonge as I am. For many stimulating discussions about Victorian fiction, extremely generous proof reading and innumerable acts of kindness along the way, I would like to thank my friends Katherine Thompson, Kathryn Maude and Katharine Jenkins.

It is hard to know how to begin to thank my family, without whom none of this would have been possible. I am so grateful to my wonderful grandmother, Ursula Gore, and my dearest sister Hannah, who has always been my best friend and partner in crime. To my parents, Pauline Walker and Mark Gore, who first encouraged my literary interests, I owe every happy hour that I have spent reading, and every word I have written. I thank them all, more than I can say.

Finally, I would like to express my gratitude to George Bernard Owers. I first put pen to paper to write about disability in Dickens shortly before we went on our first date, and this manuscript will be in the publisher's hands just before we celebrate our second wedding anniversary. He has therefore lived with this project for as long as I have, and has been unstinting in his support and his encouragement throughout. Talking about novels with him is one of the great pleasures of my life. I do not have words to thank him for everything that he has done and continues to do for me, and so I simply dedicate this book to him, with my love.

## Illustration Acknowledgements

Figures 1.1, 1.2, 1.3 and 1.4 are reproduced by kind permission of the Syndics of Cambridge University Library. They are held at the Cambridge University Library under the classmarks Lib.7.83.10; Lib 4.84.61, p.253; Lib.4.84.61, p.168; Syn.7.84.105.

To G. B. O.

# Introduction

Any scholar writing about disability in the nineteenth-century novel is faced with an obvious and immediate problem. The term 'disabled' was not used then as it is now; when applied to characters in a nineteenth-century novel, it is necessarily anachronistic. Flicking through the pages of Henry Mayhew's *London Labour and the London Poor* (1851–61), we meet a wide variety of 'crippled', 'afflicted', 'maimed' and 'deformed' characters, but they are not collectively described as 'the disabled'.[1]

Yet Mayhew does have recourse to the adjective 'disabled', and he does use it to describe a category of persons. An old gentleman is said to be 'disabled from an accident'; some of the hot eel sellers 'have been disabled during their work'. The fate of those who fake bodily ailment to beg is contrasted to that of '[t]he men that had really been out and got disabled'; a stationery seller who has already described himself as having been 'very much afflicted' recalls a time when he 'had no use of [his] arm, was ill and disabled'.[2] In all these cases, 'disability' seems to apply to a particular kind of affliction: one that prevents the subject from working. While the modern sense of the term 'disabled' – 'having a physical or mental condition which limits activity, movement, sensations, etc.' – certainly applies in all these cases, Mayhew seems principally to draw on the older sense of the word, to mean 'rendered incapable of action or use; incapacitated; taken out of service'.[3] In the examples I have given here, and elsewhere, Mayhew mainly uses 'disabled' as an adjective that indicates an inability to work in those who are 'afflicted', 'deformed' or 'crippled', terms that would now be considered offensive when applied to a person (although their adjectival use continues to thrive in metaphor), and which have been largely replaced by the supposedly more neutral term 'disabled'. The older sense of the word 'disabled' is still dominant for Mayhew, but it already carries the suggestion of its primary modern meaning.

It is worth homing in on the slippage between the two meanings of disability in this mid-Victorian text, because it is a slippage that survives, albeit at a repressed level, in our own usage, and has a painful and sharply political charge. At the present time, the suggestion that a disabled person is 'rendered incapable of action' – is, in other words, *totally* defined by inability – would widely be regarded as offensive. Yet the linguistic overlap haunts the word: difficult as it is for me as a woman routinely described as 'disabled' to acknowledge the fact, to be called 'disabled' *is* to be defined by incapacity and inability. The term is rooted not in neutrally but in negatively conceived difference; there is very little space between the two meanings neatly separated in the dictionary, outrageous as it would be to claim that they are synonymous. Disability theorist Susan Wendell explains her preference for the phrase 'a person with a disability' rather than 'a disabled person' in exactly these terms,[4] but other scholars have urged their disabled readers to *claim* the term 'disability', to refuse what they see as a squeamishness about acknowledging our shared history of stigmatised social identity and cultural exclusion.[5]

This study delves into the literary aspect of that history, exploring the connection between disability as a social identity and disability as incapacity in novelistic characterisation. The interplay between the two senses of the word 'disabled' is considerably more complex in fiction than it is for Henry Mayhew, whose definition of 'work', at least, is relatively clear. To 'work', in Mayhew's terms, is to perform an activity for money. Despite all the difficulties he runs into as his beliefs about what kind of labour ought to be financially remunerative collide with the realities of life in the East End, he more or less retains this definition as he divides up those he meets, as his subtitle puts it, into *Those That Will Work, Those That Cannot Work, and Those That Will Not Work*. Persons who fall into the second category can, for Mayhew, meaningfully be described as 'disabled' because they cannot perform the economically productive labour that is, by his account, a person's primary function. It is notable that the 'Crippled Seller of Nutmeg-Graters', who persists in trying 'to earn his own living', is never described by Mayhew as 'disabled': for Mayhew, only those who fail to work in the economic sense fail to work *as people* and become 'disabled'.[6]

Novelistic characters do not, of course, have to 'work' in that sense. Nor do they have bodies. Indeed, the not-having of a body is perhaps the most fundamental way in which we can distinguish a character from a person. Yet imagining characters *as* people is essential to our experience of reading nineteenth-century novels, which rarely fail to describe characters' bodies, in more or less detail, and which do therefore contain characters who are 'disabled' in the social sense: those who are marked by physical difference that defines them in the social world imagined by the novel. And while a character cannot work in the sense that Mayhew uses the word – cannot perform economically productive labour – there can be little doubt, I think, that characters have work to do. Whether by performing the comic turns or pathetic set pieces that engage the reader's interest, by uttering the casual remark that provides the detective with the necessary clue to resolve the novel's mystery, or by dying at the opportune moment to clear the way for the heroine's marriage, the characters who populate novels are working all the time to keep the wheels of the plot grinding – working, in other words, to make the novel work. If the attribution of disabled identity (being 'crippled', 'afflicted', 'deformed') limits characters' ability to perform such work, then we might consider characters as disabled in the dictionary's second sense: 'incapacitated, taken out of service'. To be a disabled character might, in other words, mean being disabled *as* a character.

By investigating the narrative work performed by disabled characters in the Victorian novel, I aim to test this proposition. If plot is, as Peter Brooks suggests, 'the logic or perhaps the syntax of a certain kind of discourse . . . the principal ordering force of those meanings that we try to wrest from human temporality',[7] then which characters are able to play which roles in which plots becomes the most important question we can ask about them, especially when we are dealing with characters who are apparently defined by incapacity. Examining what disabled characters *do* in novels is arguably more important than examining what is said about them because, as Patricia Ingham puts it, plots 'make statements . . . not simply answer[ing] the question "What happened next"' but 'show[ing] "what it all means"'.[8]

Disability in the sense of incapacity and disability in the sense of identity-defining difference can never be completely disentangled: they are mutually constitutive when the stigma attached to the social identity incapacitates, and when particular physical incapacities are generalised and made the basis of a socially defining identity. Yet a focus on novelistic plot lays bare the capacities of characters defined by incapacity, and the work done by those defined as not working. Plotting disabled characters across the field of Victorian fiction, I have discovered them in the act of performing an astonishing variety of narrative work, the social identity arising from their impairments actually *enabling* them to play a host of necessary plot roles. Perhaps unsurprisingly, this is not in spite but rather because of their exclusion from certain plot-lines, and their declared unfitness to play certain narrative roles. That physical impairments can bring compensatory abilities is commonplace; analogously, I have found that the incapacitating effects of disability as a social identity are frequently enabling at the level of narrative. Attention to disability is also enabling for the literary critic: charting the positioning of disabled characters ('plotting' in a spatial sense), and examining the plots in which they participate, offer new ways to narrate the story of the nineteenth-century novel. Plotting disabled characters through Victorian fiction enables us to see that the positioning of such characters was an important marker of generic affiliation throughout the period, and has shaped the critical reception of nineteenth-century novels in hitherto unacknowledged ways.

Before delving into the texts themselves, however, it is worth pausing to consider the terms of this enquiry, which have hitherto been treated as self-explanatory. Asking what is at stake when I use the terms 'disabled' and 'characters' seems the right place to begin, and enables me to stake out the critical territory into which this discussion leads.

## Disability: Definitions and Debates

Much like feminist, postcolonial and queer theories, the academic discipline of disability studies emerged out of a political movement, in this case the disability rights movement, which re-cast disability as a socially constructed rather than a biological state. As disability rights activists made the case that disabled people are disabled by social prejudice rather than by physical impairment, and argued for the removal of the architectural, technical and attitudinal barriers that excluded disabled people from full participation in public life, scholars began to argue that disability was an identity category rather than a property of persons.[9] Rosemarie Garland-Thomson's contention that disability is 'another culture-bound, physically justified difference to consider alongside race, gender, class, ethnicity and sexuality' neatly encapsulates the theoretical shift away from seeing disability as a state of the body and towards seeing it as a social reading of the body, in Thomson's formulation 'the attribution of corporeal deviance – not so much a property of bodies as a product of cultural rules about what bodies should be or do'.[10]

Such statements force the questions: from what standard is 'difference' measured? At what point does difference become sufficiently marked to be defining rather than incidental? What level of impairment is regarded as pathological – and what impairments or abilities are being measured? These questions lead inescapably to the recognition that disability is a relative and unstable category, and that the very concept of disability is, in Lennard J. Davis's words, 'a function of the concept of normalcy'.[11] This concept is in turn totally unstable: as Garland-Thomson points out, the 'normate' position is occupied by only a minority of actual people.[12] We will all become disabled if we live long enough, and if 'disability' simply means impaired physical function, then all those of us with experience of pain, illness or injury (which is to say, everyone) can claim to have experienced disability.[13] Yet disability as a social category is not all-expansive; in fact, it exists to contain these experiences, to cordon them off and, by attributing them only to an unfortunate (or deviant) minority, to protect the 'able' from association with them. Perhaps this is why, as the most unstable of identity categories, disability has been one of the hardest to analyse or to unsettle as 'the last frontier of unquestioned inferiority', in Tobin Siebers's words.[14] Its dual basis in embodiment and in social construction has made it particularly hard to unravel as an idea, while the academy's unwillingness to engage with it can surely be explained by the fact that, as David Mitchell and Sharon Snyder explain, 'disability has undergone a dual negation – it has been attributed to all "deviant" biologies as a discrediting feature, while also serving as the material marker of inferiority itself. One might think of disability as the master trope of human disqualification.'[15]

The unpicking of this 'trope' in academic work has taken place alongside huge practical changes arising from the recognition that disability is a socially constructed category that is therefore subject to re-formulation, rather than a tragically immutable personal misfortune, as changes in the built environment, in laws, public policy, educational practice and popular culture have materially altered disabled people's lives for the better. Indeed, the social model of disability has begun to enjoy such success in these respects that academics have felt able to move away from its polemical pursuit, and articulate more complex and ambivalent theories about disability that take into account the *interaction* of physical and social experiences in disabled people's lives and histories, leading to a turn back to the body in disability studies.[16]

I attempt this potted and partial history of disability activism and theory both in order to lay out the groundwork for my own enquiry – which is underpinned by the recognition that disability is a social category as well as an embodied experience, and that its historical construction is therefore specific and subject to change – and in order to indicate what I believe is at stake in enquiries like these. Writing disabled people back into history is a political endeavour, an anti-eugenic gesture that claims space for a marginalised experience, and insists upon the personhood of those deemed 'disabled'. Reading disability back into literary history, looking not through but at disabled characters in novels, and considering them as disabled, rather than immediately translating their disabilities into something else by instantly reaching for metaphor, is, similarly, a political project.[17] I state this so emphatically because the discussion ahead is in many respects more formalist in approach than it is overtly politically oriented. This is not an attempt to shy away from the inherently political nature of writing about disability in fiction, but rather an attempt to take what I see as the next step in moving the literary critical aspect of disability studies forwards.

As I shall demonstrate below, the scholars working in this area – including authors of foundational texts such as David Mitchell and Sharon Snyder, Lennard J. Davis and Rosemarie Garland-Thomson – have performed an enormous service in writing disability back into the history of the novel, and in providing a critical framework within which it is possible to write about disability; the present study is heavily (indeed, fundamentally) indebted to their pioneering work. However, in treating fictional texts primarily as documents that can be used to reconstruct the social experience of disabled people, their reading practice inevitably sacrifices a degree of critical nuance and specificity for broader ideological gains. There is a tendency in the work of disability studies scholars to treat fictional characters very much like real people, and this leads not only to a hierarchical reading practice (whereby there are positive representations to be praised and negative ones to be condemned), but also to a falsely flattened version of literary history, which renders novels as textual evidence for what is really a historical investigation, rather than as historical artefacts that are also aesthetic works, and have to be judged to some extent on their own terms. By reading these novels for what they tell us about how disability has shaped novelistic characterisation, and how the attribution of social disability to a character narratively dis/ables them, I hope in this book to demonstrate the potential that disability holds for literary criticism: not just what novels have to offer scholars of disability, but what attention to disability has to offer the literary critic.

## Disabled Characters: A Contradiction in Terms?

The difficulty of wading into the fierce critical debate about how characters in novels ought to be read is not one to be under-estimated, but I have been greatly assisted by Alex Woloch's study of characterisation in the nineteenth-century novel, *The One Vs. the Many*, and his helpful observation that:

> Characterization has been such a divisive question in twentieth-century literary theory – and has created recurrent disputes between humanist and structural (or mimetic and formal) positions – because the literary character is itself divided, always emerging at the juncture between structure and reference. In other words, a literary *dialectic* that operates dynamically within the narrative text gets transformed into a theoretical *contradiction*, presenting students of literature with an unpalatable choice: language *or* reference, structure *or* individuality. My study recasts theoretical conflict back into literary process.[18]

This approach enables Woloch to write about character effectively without adjudicating between the claims of, for example, Martin Price, with his humanist insistence that 'characters are, within the frame of their fictional world, no less than fictional persons',[19] and a structuralist position that reads character as a semiotic sign that has no personhood at all.[20] By attending to what he calls the 'character-space', which, in his words, 'marks the intersection of an implied human personality ... and the definitively circumscribed form of the text', Woloch is able to offer a reading of different kinds of characters (in this case, major and minor) that relates literary structures to social ones – arguing that 'minor characters are the proletariat of the Victorian novel' – without claiming a flattening equivalence.[21] In linking different kinds of characters to different kinds of people, Woloch is able to explore how categories of social organisation shape novelistic categories of character, thereby bringing the mimetic and formal aspects of novelistic characterisation together.

Woloch's approach is especially useful to the present discussion because bridging the gap between the formal and mimetic aspects of characterisation is peculiarly difficult when writing about disability in the novel, which can so easily lead to the fallacy of assuming an equivalence between the way we read the bodies of characters and the way we read the bodies of people in the social world. In order to consider characters as being 'disabled' in the social sense, a connection has to be assumed between social and narrative categories of organisation, the assumption being that the social categories by which we read the bodies of those in the social world – what might be called the dis/ability system – informs the way we read the bodies of fictional characters. Yet to assume a straight equivalence, especially without paying close attention to questions of genre, is surely misleading because the relationship between embodiment and characterisation varies so much in different textual traditions. As Martin Price points out, '[i]n the realistic novel, we expect the characters to have a broad range of attributes, and we assume that the more attributes they have, the less important some may be'.[22] We may therefore assign very little significance to, in his example, the colour of the heroine's hair in a realist novel, while we might assume the golden hair of the heroine of a fairy tale to be of the utmost importance, since 'the typology of romance is such that attributes are comparatively few and are tightly coordinated'.[23] Even within the smaller field of the nineteenth-century novel, we do not read the body of a character in a George Eliot or an Anthony Trollope novel in the same way that we read the body of, say, one of Dickens's characters. In the first two cases, the novelists' commitment to a realistic depiction of character makes it likely that at least some physical attributes will be incidental, and we read in the expectation that the inner lives of characters will be revealed gradually –perhaps through free indirect speech or inner monologue – rather than written on their bodies (or, indeed, announced by their names). In contrast, as Juliet John ably demonstrates in her study *Dickens's Villains*, it is impossible to do Dickens justice without recognising the 'melodramatic aesthetics' that inform his methods of characterisation, and in a very real way render 'surfaces ... synonymous with depths'.[24] We cannot read the bodies of characters in the same way in different kinds of novels, let alone assume equivalence between how the bodies of characters and the bodies of people signify for the reader.

This point might seem too obvious to be worth labouring, except that when critics come to analyse representations of disability in the novel, and the alignment of moral deviance and physical abnormality is read as repressive or even hateful towards disabled *people*, the crucial – if complex – distinction between characters and persons is lost. Julia Miele Rodas draws attention to exactly this slippage when, arguing for the complexity of Dickens's 'relationship with disabled identity', she observes that the author 'is often criticized for his sentimental and apparently objectifying representations of characters (or people) with disabilities'.[25] The parenthesis here encourages us to pause and ponder the connection between Dickens's treatment of disabled characters and of disabled people: as Rodas indicates here, they are not completely separate, and yet they cannot be treated as synonymous. Something vitally important for literary criticism is lost in the straightforward alignment of person and character, and it can be restored most effectively, I would suggest, through close attention to the text at hand, in terms of its form and its genre – close attention, in other words, to how embodiment and characterisation interact in this specific text. Demonstrating the variety of ways in which disability works in the texts of a given period, the differences between various fictional constructions of disability in particular historical moments, from our own and from each other, is not a refusal of argumentative boldness, but a demonstration of the socially constructed and therefore changeable nature of disability as an identity and an experience – effectively, an illustration of the political argument that informs and shapes earlier critical work in the field of disability studies.

## Approaches to Disability in the Novel

Existing work on disability in the novel has tended to prioritise political boldness and teleological arguments over such critical nuance, aiming to articulate a totalising theory about how disability works in fiction. This ambition is very much evident in Mitchell and Snyder's groundbreaking study *Narrative Prosthesis*, which attempts to theorise the role of disability in Western narrative, ranging from Sophocles to Shakespeare, Melville and Nietzsche. Their arguments about the ways in which disability has been used 'as a stock feature of characterization and, second, as an opportunistic metaphorical device', which exploits 'the potency of disability as a symbolic figure, [but] rarely take[s] up disability as an experience of social or political dimensions', are provocative and suggestive, but, necessarily, impose an overarching narrative of consistency upon texts written in wildly different forms and contexts.[26] Their approach is highly effective as a challenge to further enquiry and discussion, but risks reifying disability history – and, along the way, narrative itself – into a monolithic entity.

While Mitchell and Snyder are admittedly unusual in the sheer ambition of their study,[27] the thrust of their work towards politically bold but critically questionable generalisations is shared by other major scholars in the field. In her pioneering study *Extraordinary Bodies*, Rosemarie Garland-Thomson limits the scope of her enquiry to the representation of disabled female characters in American fiction, but she still seeks to make a totalising argument about how disability works across this enormously wide field, arguing that fiction functions as a freak show, as 'literary texts necessarily make disabled characters into freaks, stripped of normalizing contexts and engulfed by a single stigmatic act'.[28] While she is relating a contemporary way of exhibiting physically disabled people to fictional representations of disabled characters in the same period, and her study is accordingly illuminating, the significant differences between different *kinds* of novels written in that period is lost. As I hope to demonstrate, not all disabled characters in Victorian novels are 'stripped of normalizing contexts', and it is very much open to question whether they are 'engulfed' by the stigmatised social identity attributed to them. Lennard J. Davis is even more trenchantly generalising when he argues in *Enforcing Normalcy* that because 'novels are a social practice that arose as part of the project of middle-class hegemony ... the plot and character development of novels tend to pull toward the normative', leading him to suggest 'not ... simply that novels tend to embody the prejudices of society towards people with disabilities ... [but] that the very structures on which the novel rests tend to be normative, ideologically emphasizing the universal quality of the central character whose normativity encourages us to identify with him or her'.[29]

Although Davis's study tends towards the summative and schematic in his treatment of individual texts, his broad argument about disability in the nineteenth-century novel is usefully provocative. For one thing, he points our attention towards a question that is central to this study: who can be a protagonist in a novel, and who has to be relegated to minor status? Disabled characters, as Davis states, tend to be relegated to the narrative margins – but is it true to say that this is because they are simply not 'normal' enough to occupy the centre of the narrative? The nineteenth-century novel throws open the question of who might be worth writing a novel about; whereas earlier forms of narrative had tended to reproduce a hierarchical social order by having noble characters as protagonists and their servants in minor or comic roles – as is broadly the case in Shakespearean and Jacobean drama, for example – the nineteenth-century novel reflects an increasingly democratic and mobile age, in which a character's possibility for advancement in social and narrative terms is greater. If a novel could have as its hero a carpenter, as did George Eliot's *Adam Bede* (1859), or a fallen woman for its heroine, as did Elizabeth Gaskell's *Ruth* (1853), then why not a 'cripple'?

Moreover, while Davis's claim that the 'normal' became the subject for the novel in the period does have much to substantiate it in the claims to probability that realist fiction repeatedly makes, the opposite claim, that narrative is primarily motivated by *ab*normality, has to be acknowledged. Peter Brooks's directly contradictory statement that it is the deviant that constitutes the 'narratable' in the nineteenth-century novel not only resonates with the detective fiction he is primarily discussing at this point, but reminds us that if plots require 'wandering' as well as resolution, character requires distinctiveness as well as the universality Davis is prioritising in his account.[30] As Jan-Melissa Schramm points out in her discussion of the definition of 'character' in Johnson's Dictionary (1755), the use of the term to mean 'a mark, a stamp' then had priority over the sense in which it indicated 'personal qualities'; in the nineteenth-century novel, the tension between the idea of 'character' as the sign by which someone can be known or recognised, and 'character' as someone's inner self, persists.[31] Moreover, 'having a character' and 'being a character' mean different things. To 'be a character' is to be distinctive, eccentric, marked out; in this sense, it is surely much easier for a disabled character in a novel to 'be a character' than an able-bodied, 'normal' character. If, on the other hand, only 'normal' people can be imagined as major characters – those who are, to borrow Garland-Thomson's phrase, 'definitive human beings'[32] – if 'having character' is actually *opposed* to 'being a character', then disabled characters are relegated to the margins by the very distinctiveness that seems to invite narration.

Tobin Siebers suggests that disability functions in cultural representations as 'a diacritical marker of difference',[33] and it is possible to imagine this as a double-edged and contradictory position in narrative. Even if it is straightforwardly oppressive in social terms, it is far less clear that Foucault's theory that 'marking' is a sign of marginalisation in modern society applies to the novel.[34] 'Difference' is a valuable narrative quality, something that enables distinctions to be made between characters, and the management (usually the suppression but occasionally the celebration) of which motivates plot. Moreover, the correlation between outer and inner selves, sign and substance, social and narrative position, so fraught in the Victorian novel, is thrown into such sharp relief by the question of how disabled characters should be written (if they should be written at all) that it is unsurprising that nineteenth-century novelists were unable to resist their creation. Examining disabled characters in Victorian fiction makes sense not just as part of a wider project of writing disability history, but because they are such a significant minority of the fictional population of the period that asking what work they do, and why they are there, is a crucial part of understanding the fiction itself.

## Reading Disabled Characters in the Victorian Novel

Disability studies and Victorian studies have a great deal to offer one another, as Jennifer Esmail and Christopher Keep argue in their introduction to a special journal issue devoted to the subject,[35] and they have already become peculiarly enmeshed, with the (few) existing studies of disability in literature mainly clustering around the Victorian period. Lennard J. Davis provides a clear indication of why this might be when he suggests that 'disability, as we know the concept, is really a socially driven relation to the body that became relatively organized in the eighteenth and nineteenth centuries'.[36] This was the period in which the New Poor Law placed added pressure on the question of who was 'fit' for work, since only those deemed unfit could gain outdoor relief as opposed to entering the workhouse; the period that saw the term 'eugenics' coined and witnessed its rise as an ideology positing the elimination of hereditary disability as a desirable goal; and the period in which many of the images of disability most familiar in present popular culture were created. There is therefore a strong argument to be made that the modern social category of disability really emerged in the nineteenth century, and this provides one important rationale for examining disability in the nineteenth-century novel, the major literary form of the era. Indeed, the argument that we are still living with the Victorians' idea of disability underpins the first (and, until quite recently, the only) book-length study of disability in nineteenth-century British literature and culture, Martha Stoddard Holmes's seminal *Fictions of Affliction*.[37]

In this study, Stoddard Holmes argues that contemporary constructions of disability are generally melodramatic, so that emotional excess 'disproportionately defines' disability 'in ways that inform not only the popular imagination, but also, as a consequence, public policy'.[38] In order 'to question, analyse, and disrupt the "natural" connection between disability and feeling, recast it as naturalized rather than natural, and suggest some of the cultural work which produced it', Stoddard Holmes goes back to texts of the Victorian period, arguing that '[t]hese texts' recurrent ways of representing bodies and feelings helped produce not only a social identity for disabled people that was significantly defined in emotional terms, but also the distinctive identity of "disabled" and its co-product, "able"'.[39] In making this case, Stoddard Holmes discusses a selection of novels, particularly examining disabled female characters' place in the marriage plot in the Victorian novel, the representation of disabled boys and men in relation to beggary and work (drawing on a variety of non-fictional texts as well as novels), and finally the negotiation of melodrama in auto/biographical writing by and about disabled subjects.

My own study builds on Stoddard Holmes's pioneering work, whilst taking a different critical approach. The sheer range of texts that Stoddard Holmes addresses, and the tight focus on one particular trope – the association between disability and excessive emotion – limit her readings of novels: she is generally able to look at only one or two works by any given author, and she selects only those that illustrate the melodramatic model at work. My own approach is both narrower and deeper, in being focused entirely on the nineteenth-century novel. Although I hope it contributes to the wider project of writing disability back into cultural history, this study aims above all to demonstrate the value of attending to disability for literary criticism. By examining disabled characters' relationship to plot in the work of six very different Victorian novelists, I hope to demonstrate that attention to disability has the potential both to offer fresh readings of familiar, canonical work, and to bring less well-known works into the critical conversation, to contribute to debates about formal questions relating to characterisation and plot, and to feminist, queer, religious and social histories of the nineteenth-century novel. In this, the present study takes up Julia Miele Rodas's call for the 'mainstreaming of disability studies',[40] accepting the principle that integrating attention to disability into literary critical practice – as feminist readings have become integrated – is the next step in the project begun by disability studies scholars of permanently changing the academic conversation to include disability. My readings also seek to bring into the discourse existing critical work concerned with ideas of health, fitness, embodiment and physical difference, but which does not engage with disability as an idea. So much of the fascinating work that has been done in this area in recent years does not explicitly consider disability as a category, but is illuminating when read from this angle.[41]

Drawing on this work, I have chosen to focus my project on six nineteenth-century novelists: Charles Dickens, Wilkie Collins, Charlotte M. Yonge, Dinah Mulock Craik, George Eliot and Henry James. The path that I trace through Victorian fiction by tracking disabled characters across the work of these six writers is just one of many that could have been taken. Melodrama, sensation, the 'feminine' domestic tradition and late Victorian realism represent four novelistic genres that seem to me important, and which offer contrasting yet related ways of plotting disability. However, this is not to say that the industrial novel, the imperialist adventure novel, the historical novel or the naturalist novel (to give just four alternative examples) would not have offered rich possibilities. Similarly, while I recognise that there is much work to be done on the depiction of intellectually disabled characters within the work of these writers, I have in this study, for reasons of space and coherence, restricted myself to their treatment of characters who are defined by their bodily difference from what the narrative constructs as a norm, and have therefore considered intellectual disability only when it is written on the body of the character in question.[42] I chose these six writers partly because of the prevalence of disabled characters across their work, which makes it possible to build up a picture of how their use of disabled characters evolved, how it varied depending on the plots being employed and the genre of the novel in which they appeared, and how the representation of disability shaped the critical reaction not only to different novelists, but to particular novels within their œuvre.

The selection and arrangement of these writers also represents an aspect of my argument, which is that literary history has been written in such a way as to distort our sense of where disability is to be found in 'the' nineteenth-century novel. Disability features centrally in didactic domestic fiction associated with women writers, and because much of this work has not been canonised, the impression persists that disabled characters are marginalised across the spectrum of nineteenth-century fiction. The first three chapters of this book therefore have a centrifugal movement, beginning at the heart of the canon, with the work of Charles Dickens, in whose writing disabled characters tend to be quite clearly marginalised, moving to the more liminal Wilkie Collins, in whose fiction disabled characters occupy a correspondingly liminal state, and lastly to the outer reaches of the canon, to the largely forgotten but once-popular novels of Charlotte M. Yonge and Dinah Mulock Craik, in which disabled characters play a central role. As the representation of disability became associated with a particularly gendered genre of work – with 'domestic' fiction, above all – in parallel with the rise of eugenics and the rise of literary critical standards that excluded popular women's fiction from the emerging novelistic canon, these works were denigrated, I will suggest, partly because of their central focus on disability. It does not, of course, follow that Dickens's work has been celebrated because it sidelines disabled characters – on the contrary, his treatment of disability was largely erased from the critical conversation – but rather that the formal qualities of Dickens's work, which *have* been celebrated, necessitate the narrative suppression of disabled characters. In my final chapter, I turn back to two centrally canonical writers, in order to track the decline of the disability plots I have traced through early and mid-Victorian fiction, arguing that the modernist turn away from these plot structures is prefigured in the realist novel as it developed in the hands of Eliot and James. Their ongoing struggle with the plot structures they inherited can be traced through sustained attention to their disability plots, which re-work and break down those explored in the first three chapters.

The first chapter explores the marginalised position of disabled characters in the overcrowded novels of Charles Dickens. Although Dickens is famous for being an anti-Malthusian champion of the dispossessed and stigmatised, I demonstrate that, in his novels, physical disability is indivisible from minor status. Building on work by Alex Woloch and Michiel Heyns, I argue that Dickens trains his readers to understand physical distinctiveness and impairment as indicators of minor status, but that he uses this connection in subtle ways to highlight the cruelties of the narrative order. By writing minorness on to his characters' bodies as disability, Dickens draws attention to the inequities of his narrative structure, and encourages us to invest attention in those characters who are ultimately marginalised by the novels' plotting. The 'scapegoating' that Heyns identifies as a crucial feature of the Dickensian plot is interrogated within the novels themselves by disabled characters who resist their narrative disablement, from the villainous Silas Wegg to the sympathetic Jenny Wren. Through heroines such as Esther Summerson and Little Dorrit, who become major characters through their very minorness – a self-understanding written upon their bodies as disability – Dickens troubles his own narrative strategies, using disability to complicate readers' response to the novels' plot-lines and final arrangements of characters.

In the second chapter, I explore the role of disability in Wilkie Collins's mystery novels. These depend for their plotting upon generating uncertainty about the true identities of the characters at hand, and encourage the reader to mistrust the signs of social and novelistic identity: it is essential that we do not correctly identify every character's place in the plot, in order that we will be surprised by the mystery's solution. The signs of the body are therefore placed under tremendous pressure. On one hand, somatic signs are represented as crucial clues for reader and detective; on the other, they must fail us at least some of the time for the mystery to be sustained. Collins uses disability as an unreliable sign in exactly this way, engaging the reader's preconceptions about a disabled character's relationship to plot so that he can perform sensational reversals at the novels' conclusions. Disability also enables Collins to put sensation to affective work, as he represents characters' disabilities in such a way as to elicit sympathy for their social and narrative exclusion. Through generating sympathy for disabled characters such as Rosanna Spearman, Limping Lucy and Miserrimus Dexter, Collins encourages us to question the justice of the social categories that structure the novels' final settlements, and of the detective plot in which they are re-established – a sensational denaturalising of the social and narrative order, which has serious political implications. My analysis builds on the seminal studies of plot in the sensation novel by critics such as D. A. Miller, Ronald Thomas and Peter Brooks, but demonstrates how attention to disability disrupts their schematic accounts of how plotting works in Collins's fiction.

I also argue that in Collins's less 'sensational' and more 'domestic' novel, *Poor Miss Finch* (1872), disabled characters are situated quite differently in relation to plot, illustrating the pivotal role of genre in shaping the representation of disabled characters, and how the treatment of disabled characters could signal generic affiliation. This paves the way for my discussion of domestic fiction in the third chapter. Here, I examine novels by Dinah Mulock Craik and Charlotte M. Yonge, in which we see disability at the heart of familial and romantic plot-lines. Both authors represent disability as a powerful state, which develops the disabled person's moral qualities, enabling them to exert an uplifting influence upon those around them, and fostering dependent relationships that are mutually beneficial. For both writers, I argue, this becomes a way of validating experiences and qualities coded 'feminine'. Moreover, the disabled character's problematic relation to the marriage plot enables these authors to experiment with alternative narrative possibilities for female characters, without overtly questioning the desirability of marriage, and to experiment with familial structures that are not based on the marriage bond. The connection between these novelists' critical fortunes and their representation of disability also makes them a crucial test-case for understanding the relationship between disability and canon formation. By examining critical reactions to their positioning of disabled characters, I demonstrate that attitudes to disability have been inextricably bound up with the reception of domestic fiction.

My fourth chapter charts the decline of the redemptive disability plot in the work of George Eliot and Henry James, demonstrating that disability provides a vantage point from which to narrate the coming apart of providential and realist plotting in the latter part of the nineteenth century. While in *The Mill on the Floss* (1860), Eliot represents disability as a monitory experience that develops crucial moral qualities of sympathy and selflessness in the crippled bystander, Philip Wakem, her refusal to allow him to act effectively disables the plot of the novel, condemning its heroine to tragedy. The idea that those who are best able morally to understand the novel's action are those who are least able practically to influence it is further developed in *Daniel Deronda* (1876). Here, the consumptive visionary Mordecai has a crucial plot role to play, both in passing on a valuable legacy of intellectual and religious heritage to Daniel, and in literally passing on, so that Daniel is able to take up his role as messianic leader. However, the darkness of the novel's 'English' plot is reflected in the terminal illness that dominates the 'Jewish' plot, while in Daniel's mother, Leonora, Eliot creates a dark double for Mordecai, a character who powerfully resents the self-sacrificial, 'transmitting' role that her terminal illness forces upon her, and whose sustained resistance to being made 'the instrument [her] father wanted' stands in stark opposition to his 'yearning for transmission'.[43]

In *The Portrait of a Lady* (published just five years after *Deronda*), James offers a grimmer reworking of the same motifs: here, the heroine's consumptive benefactor has disturbingly ambiguous motives, and the results of his bequest are disastrous. Yet through plotting Ralph's ill-fated attempt to live through Isabel, and the failure of the resultant marriage plot, James offers the reader hope for the heroine's moral growth and final triumph: Ralph's terminal illness enables a death-bed scene that is redemptive for both characters. No such hope remains in *The Wings of the Dove* (1902), in which not only is Milly Theale's material inheritance a source of fatal temptation to the hero and heroine, but her moral inheritance is refused – or perhaps simply cannot be accepted – by a 'brutal' pair of plotters whose only saving grace is that they are riven with regret for what they have done. Drawing on mid-century tropes of angelic invalidism, James shows them unfit for purpose in the modern world, disabling the disability plot to tragic effect – and, as he does so, paving the way for both modernist departures from Victorian plotting conventions, and modernist treatments of disability. Fittingly, it is James's damning verdict on Dickens's treatment of disability that provides our starting place, a jumping-off point from which to plunge into the bewilderingly populous world of Dickens's fiction, and from which to consider the anti-realism of his disabled characters.

## Notes

1. These terms occur repeatedly in Mayhew's writings, but all these examples are taken from a single page (Mayhew, *London Labour and the London Poor*, vol. 4, p. 431).
2. Ibid. p. 190, p. 415, p. 270.

3. 'Disabled, Adj. and N.', *OED Online*. The second definition of the word, by which it means 'having a physical or mental condition which limits activity, movement, sensations, etc.', can reasonably be described as 'modern', since the entry notes that the adjective 'came to be used as the standard term in this sense in the second half of the twentieth century', although it had long existed.
4. Wendell, *The Rejected Body*, p. 78.
5. The political gesture that lies behind the call to use the term 'disabled' rather than the phrase 'a person with a disability' can be seen in the very title of Simi Linton's seminal polemic, *Claiming Disability: Knowledge and Identity*. The significance of claiming to 'be disabled' rather than to 'have a disability' in terms of the social model of disability will be explored further in the next section.
6. Mayhew, *London Labour and the London Poor*, vol. 1, pp. 329–30.
7. Brooks, *Reading for the Plot*, p. xi.
8. Ingham, *The Language of Gender and Class*, p. 27.
9. For a helpfully condensed history of the emergence of the 'social model' of disability, see Shakespeare, 'The Social Model of Disability', pp. 215–21.
10. Garland-Thomson, *Extraordinary Bodies*, p. 5, pp. 6–7.
11. Davis, *Enforcing Normalcy*, p. 2.
12. Garland-Thomson, *Extraordinary Bodies*, p. 8.
13. Davis, *Enforcing Normalcy*, p. xv. Susan Wendell and Rosemarie Garland-Thomson also discuss this idea at greater length; see Wendell, *The Rejected Body*, pp. 32–3; Garland-Thomson, *Extraordinary Bodies*, pp. 13–14.
14. Siebers, *Disability Theory*, p. 6.
15. Mitchell and Snyder, *Narrative Prosthesis*, p. 3.
16. Tobin Siebers's theory of 'complex embodiment', which 'views the economy between social representations and the body not as unidirectional, as in the social model, or nonexistent, as in the medical model, but as reciprocal' (*Disability Theory*, p. 25), is an excellent example of this turn to the body. I think it goes some way towards correcting the distortion of disabled people's experiences by the (necessarily) blunt earlier formulations of disability as *purely* constructed.
17. As Lennard J. Davis argues in his Foreword to a recent collection of essays on disability in *Jane Eyre*, 'before we can leap to the metaphor, we must know the object' (Davis, 'Foreword', *The Madwoman and the Blindman*, p. xi).
18. Woloch, *The One Vs. the Many*, p. 17.
19. Price, *Forms of Life*, p. 64.
20. James Phelan offers a helpful summary of these positions, which he defines as the 'mimetic' and 'synthetic' (*Reading People*, pp. 2–7), while Brian Rosenberg suggests considering these approaches as the 'representational', 'nonrepresentational' and 'revised representational',

and gives a useful outline of the critical history of what he sees as the three schools (*Little Dorrit's Shadows*, pp. 3–4).
21. Woloch, *The One Vs. the Many*, p. 13, p. 17.
22. Price, *Forms of Life*, p. 25.
23. Ibid.
24. John, *Dickens's Villains*, p. 8, p. 111.
25. Rodas, 'Tiny Tim, Blind Bertha, and the Resistance of Miss Mowcher', pp. 51–2. This essay offers a fascinating account of the effect that the protests of the real Jane Seymour Hill – a neighbour of Dickens who believed herself to be the model for Miss Mowcher – had on the plotting of *David Copperfield*, as 'her' character was allowed to voice Hill's own warning against 'associat[ing] bodily defects with mental' (Dickens, *David Copperfield*, p. 452), and given an unexpectedly heroic part to play in the capture of the villain's henchman, Littimer.
26. Mitchell and Snyder, *Narrative Prosthesis*, p. 48.
27. They are not, however, unique: the same publisher brought out a translation of Henri-Jacques Stiker's *A History of Disability* the year before. Stiker's history of disability as an idea and an experience from Classical antiquity to the present day has strengths and weaknesses similar to those of Mitchell and Snyder's work: it is provocative, suggestive and overtly politically engaged – but it has to sacrifice a degree of specificity along the way.
28. Garland-Thomson, *Extraordinary Bodies*, p. 11.
29. Davis, *Enforcing Normalcy*, pp. 41–2.
30. Brooks, *Reading for the Plot*, p. 139.
31. Schramm, *Atonement and Self-Sacrifice in Nineteenth-Century Narrative*, pp. 65–6.
32. Garland-Thomson, *Extraordinary Bodies*, p. 8.
33. Siebers, *Disability Theory*, p. 6.
34. Foucault did not apply his theory about social power being exerted in disciplinary society through 'marking' subordinated subjects to disabled people, but his claim that '[i]n a disciplinary regime, individualization is "descending"; as power becomes more anonymous and more functional, those on whom it is exercised tend to be more strongly individualized' offers a clear explanation for why those who are defined by 'difference' are necessarily oppressed in a disciplinary society (*Discipline and Punish*, p. 193).
35. Esmail and Keep, 'Victorian Disability: Introduction', p. 47.
36. Davis, *Enforcing Normalcy*, p. 3.
37. Stoddard Holmes's was not the first study of disability in the nineteenth-century novel, being preceded by Mary Klages's *Woeful Afflictions: Disability and Sentimentality in Victorian America* (1999), a study that, as its title suggests, is principally concerned with American literature and culture, although it includes a very helpful analysis of Dinah Mulock Craik's *John Halifax, Gentleman*, one of the novels I will be discussing

later. Klages's study is like Stoddard Holmes's in being primarily concerned with one way of representing and using disability – in this case, the sentimental rather than the melodramatic tradition – and in combining the study of fictional, non-fictional and auto/biographical texts.
38. Stoddard Holmes, *Fictions of Affliction*, pp. 2–4.
39. Ibid. p. 4.
40. Rodas, 'Mainstreaming Disability Studies?', p. 382. Since 2012, the publication of Karen Bourrier's study of friendship between able and disabled men in the nineteenth-century novel, *The Measure of Manliness: Disability and Masculinity in the Mid-Victorian Novel*, the appearance of the first collection of essays devoted to the idea of disability in a single Victorian novel, *The Madwoman and the Blindman: Jane Eyre, Discourse, Disability* (edited by Bolt, Rodas and Donaldson), and the central importance of disabled characters to Talia Schaffer's prize-winning study of the marriage plot, *Romance's Rival: Familiar Marriage in Victorian Fiction*, suggests that Rodas's hope for future 'mainstreaming' is already being realised.
41. For example, Miriam Bailin, Athena Vrettos and Erin O'Connor have all written enlightening studies of illness in Victorian fiction, which, like Maria H. Frawley's writings on invalidism and Holly Furneaux's recent work on queer masculinities in the Victorian novel, can usefully be read from a disability studies perspective (see Bailin, *The Sickroom in Victorian Fiction*; Vrettos, *Somatic Fictions*; O'Connor, *Raw Material*; Frawley, *Invalidism and Identity in Nineteenth-Century Britain*; Furneaux, *Queer Dickens* and 'Negotiating the Gentle-Man').
42. I have adopted an expansive definition of physical disability, which includes any deviation from a narratively constructed bodily norm that defines a character's identity in the social world of the novel. I have not attempted any clear distinction between, for example, degenerative illness that causes a character to waste away, permanent paralysis, or facial scarring that is registered as 'disfigurement' because I want to work as closely as possible with the categories the texts themselves construct, and I agree with both Martha Stoddard Holmes and Karen Bourrier that no hard-and-fast definitions are made in Victorian novels between different *kinds* of physical disability: it all depends on context (see Stoddard Holmes, *Fictions of Affliction*, p. 13; Bourrier, *The Measure of Manliness*, p. 16). Although blind and deaf characters certainly fall into this category, only one blind character is discussed at length here (see Chapter 2); in recent years, Jennifer Esmail and Heather Tilley have produced brilliant studies focused entirely on sensory impairment in Victorian literature (see Tilley, *Blindness and Writing*; Esmail, *Reading Victorian Deafness*).
43. Eliot, *Deronda*, p. 568, p. 405.

Chapter 1

# A Possible Person?: Marking the Minor Character in Dickens

What do we get in return for accepting Miss Jenny Wren as a possible person? This young lady is the type of a certain class of characters of which Mr Dickens has made a speciality, and with which he has been accustomed to draw alternate smiles and tears, according as he pressed one spring or another. But this is very cheap merriment and very cheap pathos. Miss Jenny Wren is a poor little dwarf, afflicted, as she constantly reiterates, with a 'bad back' and 'queer legs,' who makes dolls' dresses, and is for ever pricking at those with whom she converses, in the air, with her needle, and assuring them that she knows their 'tricks and their manners.' Like all Mr Dickens's pathetic characters, she is a little monster; she is deformed, unhealthy, unnatural; she belongs to the troop of hunchbacks, imbeciles, and precocious children who have carried on the sentimental business in all Mr Dickens's novels; the little Nells, the Smikes, the Paul Dombeys.[1]

In the damning review of *Our Mutual Friend* (1865) from which this passage is taken, Henry James singles out Jenny Wren as the personification of everything that is wrong with Dickensian characterisation. She appears doubly to offend him as 'a little monster', departing from the 'natural' both in her disability and in the anti-realist elements of her characterisation. Her distinctive speech patterns and gestures, her sentimental pathos and her grotesque aggression all mark her out for James as belonging to a 'class of characters' within Dickens's work who betray him as a 'superficial' novelist.[2]

It has been well established that Dickens fared badly at the hands of critics for whom, in Brian Rosenberg's words, 'psychological verisimilitude [was] the central criterion for judging the effectiveness of character',[3] and it would be all too easy to dismiss James's reading of Jenny on those grounds, and additionally as representing a knee-jerk revulsion from disability, which leads him to reject anyone 'deformed, [or] unhealthy' as a 'possible person'.[4] Yet in yoking together Jenny's disability and 'monstrosity' as aspects of her inadmissibility as 'a possible person' and thereby connecting her disability to her anti-realist characterisation, James does a valuable service. His attempt to construct an anti-realist school of characterisation, of which Jenny is the 'type', strains at the seams as it attempts to accommodate the characters who 'carr[y] on all the sentimental business', and yet it does point to a crucial feature of Dickens's minor characters. They are all to some extent marginalised within the novels they enliven by their failure as realist characters, more or less disabled in narrative terms by their embodiment. We know upon meeting a minor character in Dickens that they *are* minor because their bodies betray them as such. All of them are marked out from the major characters they meet by their distinctive, distorted bodies; all of them depart from the 'normal' standard set by the characters who occupy the narrative centre. It is telling that when E. M. Forster, in Jamesian mode, is lamenting Dickens's failure to create 'round' characters, he singles out David Copperfield and Pip as 'attempt[ing] roundness'.[5] While Dickens never creates characters who would satisfy Henry James's definition of realism, his protagonists are far less distantly removed from such a standard than the minor characters whose extraordinary bodies mark them out for minorness.

To put this proposition another way, it is very difficult – perhaps impossible – to call to mind a distinct impression of Nicholas Nickleby's appearance, where Smike's is so clearly defined. We can see Smike as we cannot see Nicholas, Smike's body rendered vivid for us by its particularity, its distinctiveness and its over-determined significance. Everything that we need to know about Smike is written on to his pathetic, spectacular body, carefully described for us so that we could recognise him in any illustration, whereas Nicholas's appearance is essentially generic.[6] The opposition between Nicholas and Smike does not simply arise from the fact that Smike is disabled; it is similarly present if we contrast Nicholas with Wackford Squeers, the Infant Phenomenon or the Little Kenwigses. David Copperfield is not *physically* present for us in the same way as Miss Mowcher, Betsey Trotwood or Uriah Heep; John Harmon does not hobble before our eyes as does Silas Wegg. The minor characters of these novels are vividly present to us in their physical form because their physicality is distinguished for us, made memorable by its particularity and by its relevance. Their bodies express themselves: they are all surface, and their surface is accordingly marked. They are all disabled in narrative terms as minor characters, and while not all of them are physically disabled, all physically disabled characters belong in this marked, marginalised group.

These characters are not 'possible persons' in the same sense as their eponymous counterparts. The novels belong to their major characters; they are allotted the most narrative space and the lion's share of narrative rewards. Minor characters are not simply marked out as minor by physical distortion and physical distinctiveness, but, as Alex Woloch suggests, distorted *by* their minorness: 'highly distinctive speech patterns, emphasis on an eccentric gesture or habit, concentration on specific physical features or body parts – are all rooted in, or motivated by, the human being's constriction to an extremely reduced space'.[7] Yet, as he goes on to point out, in the overcrowded novels of Dickens, these very features enable minor characters to stick in our minds, to exceed their narrative function by commanding far more of our attention than their plot role allows, to such an extent that, as he puts it, 'the narrative process that underlies all of Dickens's work [is that of] the central, but passive, protagonist who encounters the powerful, but distorted, minor character'.[8]

Woloch's acknowledgement of the 'powerful' nature of the minor characters offers an explanation for the phenomenon that perhaps irritated James into the vehemence of his condemnation. These characters fail the critical standards that were, until recently, dominant, and yet have consistently succeeded the best with readers. E. M. Forster's rueful admission that '[Dickens's] immense success with types suggests there may be more in flatness than the severer critics admit'[9] acknowledges what James's review has to suppress: that Dickens's reputation as the great creator of character has rested upon his minor characters. A retrospective of Dickens's work in *Blackwood's* in 1871 is typical both in acknowledging Dickens's success as a creator of beloved and memorable characters, and in attributing this success to his minor characters, featuring not a single protagonist in its lengthy list of representative successes.[10] The pictures that decorate the inside covers of Claire Tomalin's bicentennial biography of Dickens attest to the longevity of this judgement; long after the criteria by which the *Blackwood's* reviewer judged Dickens have been declared obsolete, still it is his vivid minor characters – Quilp, the Marchioness, Mr Micawber, Uriah Heep – who represent Dickens in the popular imagination and personify 'the Dickensian'.[11]

Their position as minor characters therefore puts disabled characters in a contradictory position in Dickens's novels. In one sense, they neatly illustrate Lennard J. Davis's argument that 'the plot and character development of novels tend to pull towards the normative'.[12] At the same time, as Pam Morris points out, minor characters actually pull our attention *away* from the ostensible centres of Dickens's novels, and in so doing, disrupt the social and moral agenda their main plot-lines serve. Morris's call for a 'dialogic reading practice' that 'allows for some redistribution of critical focus from the central characters, at times the least imaginatively compelling, towards those at the margin of the text' alerts us to the power that the novels' disabled characters might exert from 'the margin'.[13] It also acknowledges, almost in passing, that the novels themselves prompt and encourage exactly the redistribution of attention to which, as a Marxist critic, Morris is politically committed. Similarly, Michiel Heyns's observation that 'some of Dickens's most troubling implications are generated by that which escapes the final ordering of purposeful plots', and his focus on Dickens's decision 'to admit elements hostile to his ethical design – only to expel them again in the interests of resolution', point us towards those minor characters whose embodiment marginalises them in narrative *and* social terms as crucial figures in Dickens's design.[14] Critics' increasing willingness to examine what Juliet John calls Dickens's 'externalised aesthetics' on their own terms, and not to see exaggerated embodiment or overdetermined bodily signs as aesthetic flaws, has enabled minor characters to become the objects of serious critical attention, rather than an embarrassing example of Dickens's work getting out of hand.[15]

None of the critics cited above has disability in their sights as a subject for study in itself, but their approaches illustrate the potential that 'redistribution of critical focus' (to borrow Morris's phrase) has for those attempting to plot disability through Dickens's work. Moreover, as this brief introduction has outlined, such a shift of focus towards the margins of the novels does not work against the dynamics of the novels themselves (as Morris's political metaphors imply), but rather with them. Brian Rosenberg's contention that Dickens displays 'perspicacity about his own methods of characterization ... find[ing] ways within his fiction to highlight, problematize, deconstruct, and parody his own habits as a writer'[16] is borne out by a close examination of how Dickens maps social categories of embodiment on to literary categories of characterisation. Dickens constructs and collapses these categories through his characters' bodies, and – crucially – draws our attention to the process by which he does so.

It is my contention that the dark energies that animate Dickens's novels frequently emanate from his doubly marginalised disabled characters, who pull our attention away from the ostensible centres of the novels and trouble our reading through focusing our attention on their stigmatised bodies. Moreover, whether they take on assistive roles in the novels' plot-lines, willingly acquiescing to their function as sentimental objects, grotesque performers or sacrificial victims, or whether they resist their narrative marginalisation, drawing attention to their own exclusion from the restorative conclusions, these characters force our attention towards the injustices, cruelties and ambiguities of the narrative economy of these overcrowded, under-resourced novels. While Dickens is famous as the voice of resistance against Malthusian logic, emphatic champion of the little crippled child 'who did NOT die', in fact Tiny Tim is unusual, both in his total acquiescence to his narrative fate – happy to be made a spectacle, 'hop[ing] the people saw him in the church, because he was a cripple, and it might be pleasant to them to remember upon Christmas day, who made lame beggars walk' – and in his finding space upon the Cratchits' hearth.[17]

Before Tiny Tim, Dickens had in *Nicholas Nickleby* (1839) created Smike, the nineteen-year-old who is outgrowing his status as crippled child but is unable to become a man, disabled as an agent in the mystery plot by his ignorance of his own identity, and shut out from the marriage plot he longs to join. Through Smike, Dickens troubles the generic conventions upon which the novel rests, putting Smike the sentimental spectacle on stage, juxtaposing him with the overtly theatrical in such a way that the exploitative use the melodramatic narrative makes of his body is thrown into troubling relief. In *The Old Curiosity Shop* (1841), the anti-realist elements of Dickens's novelistic methods are brought centre-stage, the heroine and villain of the piece both extraordinarily bodied, at the opposite poles of sentimental and grotesque spectacular embodiment. While Little Nell is not disabled in the social sense (unlike Quilp), she is an early prototype of the heroine whose sense of self has been so distorted by the impossible demands her author makes in the name of feminine virtue that the body upon which they are written is marked out for minorness: painful, remarked upon and ultimately stigmatised. The Marchioness acts as Nell's grotesque counterpart, a precursor to Jenny Wren as Little Nell is to Little Dorrit, but brought into tantalising proximity with her idealised other self. In *Bleak House* (1853) and *Little Dorrit* (1857), minorness becomes a condition of majorness for heroines whose self-doubt – even self-erasure – is the condition of their moral power and thus of their narrative centrality. In both novels, Dickens marks the bodies of his heroines with the signs of the suffering they cannot express – because to do so would be to disqualify themselves as embodiments of feminine virtue – and through disabling their bodies, enables them to occupy otherwise impossibly contradictory narrative positions.

By the time we encounter 'the person of the house' in *Our Mutual Friend*'s Jenny Wren (1865), I hope to have demonstrated the possibilities opened up for Dickens through writing the disabled body, and – answering James's question – to have illustrated what we have to gain from her acquaintance.[18] However, while Jenny Wren has been justly celebrated as a late, great creation of Dickens's mature period,[19] we can fully understand her narrative position only by comparing her to the novel's other disabled minor character, Silas Wegg. The girl with the wooden crutch and the man with the wooden leg occupy opposing ends of the spectrum of Dickens's treatment of minor characters, one assisting in the novel's plot and rewarded with a subsidiary marriage plot of her own, the other attempting to derail it and violently expelled from the novel as a result, but they are crucially alike in the part their embodiment plays in enabling them *both* to fulfil and to trouble these roles. It is above all the resistance of Dickens's minor characters to their own minorness, and commensurately his disabled characters' resistance to their own disabling *as* characters, that this chapter charts, beginning with the boy who cannot be a man.

## 'Be a man': Smike as Disabled Subject

The passage that describes Nicholas's first impression of the pupils of Dotheboys Hall invests their bodies with clear meanings, their 'stunted growth . . . the bleared eye, the hare-lip, the crooked foot' all telling 'of unnatural aversion conceived by parents for their offspring, or of young lives which, from the earliest dawn of infancy, had been one horrible endurance of cruelty and neglect'.[20] The boys' disabilities are clearly instrumental to their status as sentimental objects evoking a particular kind of affective response in Nicholas, and through him the reader, legible signs for anyone who knows how to feel and is thereby distinguished from the morally inadequate Squeerses. The didacticism associated with sentimentality as a genre is clearly present, as we are told how to read the boys' bodily peculiarities as over-determined affective signs. Reduced to their disabilities, summed up as 'deformities', these boys typify the sentimental subjects for whom Mary Klages coins the term 'posters' because of their status as passive stimuli of affect.[21]

This moment of clarity is immediately complicated, however, by the narrator's observation in the very next paragraph that 'this scene, painful as it was, had its grotesque features, which, in a less interested observer than Nicholas, might have provoked a smile'.[22]

Apparently, the very features that should bring a tear to our eye might also bring a smile to our lips, since they 'would have been irresistibly ridiculous, but for the foul appearance of dirt, disorder, and disease with which they were associated'.[23] The dual heritage of disability as the basis for caricature and its antidote – the deviation from normality that gives rise to humour, the deviation from normality too grave to be funny – can be seen in the illustration that Phiz produced to accompany this text (Fig. 1.1), at the centre of which is Smike, kneeling down with his head bowed, marked out by his black

Figure 1.1  Hablôt K. Browne, 'The internal economy of Dotheboys Hall', *Nicholas Nickleby* (London: Chapman and Hall, 1839), facing p. 68.

suit and white ruffled collar. This illustration not only has to balance the sentimental and grotesque elements of the description, but also to register the opposition between Nicholas and all that surrounds him. Nicholas has to be marked out as the hero, the chosen one who will bring this suffering to an end, the personification of the forces that oppose 'dirt, disorder, and disease', but also as the major character surrounded by minor figures. Rosemarie Garland-Thomson's definition of the 'normate' as the 'unmarked'[24] comes to mind when we notice that, in Phiz's illustration, Nicholas is distinguished from the characters surrounding him not only by his tallness and (over-determined) straightness, in comparison to the bent and crooked figures all around him, but by the paleness of his face, which looks lighter because it is unmarked by the caricaturist's lines, which give expression to those of the others. Nicholas is the 'normal' figure in many senses – as the respectable, socially mobile bourgeois hero opposing the backward forces of cruelty and vested interest, as the able-bodied man amidst a 'motley' crew of disabled boys, as the sole possessor of a moral standard in a scene of immorality, as the observing figure with whom the reader identifies – and they are all captured in the illustration of his blank, unmarked, generic body. Juliet John has identified the blankness of the melodramatic hero as a crucial aspect of his heroism, since in melodrama 'types are more valuable than individuals because they speak to what is shared, or typical; they have relevance, that is, outside themselves'.[25] The boys surrounding Nicholas clearly have relevance 'outside themselves', as representative victims of cruelty, but as John suggests, they do not purport to be 'typical' as Nicholas does; we identify *with* him looking *at* them, not the other way around.

Where does this leave Smike, who is to leave Dotheboys Hall with Nicholas and take up a place at his side? He is clearly represented as one of the many in the scene, not marked out as Nicholas's counterpart; he is distinguished as the first among equals by the white frill that enables us to identify him by name, but partakes of their shared identity as 'deformities'. Phiz has, in fact, correctly identified Smike's place in the novel's plot, for his minorness has been written on to his body in such a way that it cannot be erased, even by the revelation that he is in fact Nicholas's cousin, a Nickleby in his own right. Smike's traction as a character arises out of this tension between the place in the family and the plot that is rightfully his, and his identity as one of the 'deformities' who have no place in the novel's conclusion. His troubling of narrative and social categories is written on to the body that condemns him to the novel's margins.

Nicholas seems to model a straightforward reaction to Smike's 'anxious and timid' first appearance in the novel, as his disappointed hopes for a letter from home go 'to Nicholas's heart at once', as he reads in Smike's pitiful gestures 'a long and very sad history'.[26] The reader and Nicholas are drawn together by a shared affective response to Smike's suffering, which is made manifest in his 'attenuated frame'.[27] Yet when Smike attempts to join in this sentimental communion, prompted to weep at his *own* suffering, Nicholas's reaction is a partial withdrawal of his sympathy:

> ... he burst into tears. 'Oh dear, oh dear!' he cried, covering his face with his cracked and horny hands. 'My heart will break. It will, it will.'
>
> 'Hush!' said Nicholas, laying his hand upon his shoulder. 'Be a man; you are nearly one by years, God help you.'
>
> 'By years!' cried Smike. 'Oh dear, dear, how many of them! How many of them since I was a little child, younger than any that are here now! Where are they all!'
>
> 'Whom do you speak of?' inquired Nicholas, wishing to rouse the poor half-witted creature to reason.
>
> 'My friends,' he replied, 'myself – my – oh! What sufferings mine have been!'[28]

In this exchange, Nicholas does not feel able to give Smike the wholehearted sympathy he might offer a woman or child, but feels compelled to reprove Smike, to urge him to 'be a man'. The question of whether Smike *could* in fact 'be a man' is one that the text insistently raises and never resolves. The 'extraordinary mixture of garments' that Smike wears externalises the challenge he poses to categories of gender and age, since, '[a]lthough he could not have been less than eighteen or nineteen years old ... he wore a skeleton suit, such as is usually put on very little boys ... a tattered child's frill, only half concealed by a coarse, man's neckerchief'.[29] Smike's alienation from the family in which he would have been able to attain maturity and masculinity is captured in this outfit, which recalls his banishment from home and his neglected upbringing at Dotheboys Hall, where no one has bothered to acknowledge his ageing or to mark his adult status sartorially. Smike recognises that it is his isolation from 'friends' that disables him even as a sentimental subject, since unlike the fellow-pupil whose death he remembers, who was able 'to see faces round his bed', he would be unable to act in such a death-bed scene, since he has no 'friends' to wish for and no home that he can remember.[30] Smike begins the process of winning the friend who will ultimately enable him to have such a death-bed scene here, by making a tearful appeal to Nicholas – but he does so at the price of ever being considered 'a man'.

The relationship between Smike and Nicholas is founded on Smike's appeal for pity and Nicholas's answer; it is intensified by Nicholas's intervention to save him from being beaten, and then formalised by the vow of fidelity to Nicholas that Smike makes upon his knees.[31] As Angus Easson points out in his analysis of gesture in *Nicholas Nickleby*, 'Smike's behaviour [in this scene], bursting into tears, clasping a man's hands, is characteristic of a woman', and this 'point is enforced' through the wording of his promise to Nicholas, which so closely resembles that of the marriage vow.[32] More recently, Holly Furneaux has pushed this argument further, arguing that Nicholas and Smike's relationship should be understood in homoerotic terms: 'Combined with his gratitude, loyalty and deep affection is a specifically physical admiration of Nicholas's body.'[33] A relationship that is instigated by Nicholas's protection of Smike from bodily harm cannot be allowed direct bodily expression but is re-routed, Furneaux argues, through the more appropriate love-object of Nicholas's sister, whose resemblance to Nicholas is the basis for Smike's pre-emptive admiration.

Smike's feminised relationship to Nicholas can be seen clearly in the power structures of their relationship, which find expression in Nicholas's resolution to 'do enough for us both' if they go to sea,[34] an assumption of responsibility for Smike's welfare that mirrors the paternalistic stance of Nicholas's relationships with his mother, sister and eventually wife. Smike assumes this role of dependant unwillingly, but only in the sense that he regards Nicholas as his 'master': 'You will never let me serve you as I ought. You will never know how I think, day and night, of ways to please you.'[35] His adoringly subservient stance recalls that of a Dickensian heroine, and the dialectic of protective concern (and mastery) with a desire to please (and self-subordinate) mirrors the structure of Dickens's most idealised heterosexual relationships. Their mutual affection is expressed through the structures of feeling associated with marriage, and this is made possible only by the feminised subject position Smike occupies as a result of his disability. Disability becomes in this formulation a necessary condition for a particular kind of homoeroticism, by re-gendering one of the men involved in a culturally acceptable way.

This view of Smike's re-gendered identity, and the argument that it is not incidental but essential that he be feminised in relation to Nicholas, are borne out by contemporary adaptations of *Nicholas*

*Nickleby*, in which Smike was consistently played by a woman, and in which disability seems not to have been emphasised anything like so clearly as his femininity. In Edward Stirling's extremely popular adaptation, staged in November 1838 when the serial publication of the novel was less than halfway through its run, Smike was played by Mary Ann Keeley, and so successful was this casting that she revived the part in the 1840 follow-up, *The Fortunes of Smike*, which Stirling dedicated to her.[36] In this second adaptation, staged after the whole novel had been published, Smike does indeed fall in love with Kate Nickleby and die of a broken heart,[37] but in the earlier play, when Stirling was merely guessing how the novel would conclude, Smike has eyes only for Nicholas. As if to underline the significance of the scene in which Smike admits that he cannot bear to leave Nicholas, Stirling re-formulates Smike's line in the novel, 'I could not leave you without a word', as 'to-day I tried to leave you, but I could not without a word. I – I love you too much.'[38] By ensuring that on stage, the person delivering these lines to Nicholas was in fact a woman, impersonating a man, the production asserts the underlying heteronormativity of this otherwise homoerotic relationship.

In the novel, the only compelling explanation for the impossibility of a relationship between Smike and Kate is to be found in Smike's disabled identity, as 'a poor creature'.[39] It cannot be explained in class terms, since Smike turns out *not* to be illegitimate or socially remote from the Nicklebys, but in fact to be a first cousin to Nicholas and Kate. In narrative terms, his place ought to be analogous to that of Oliver Twist, saved from the den of thieves and restored to the bosom of the bourgeois family where he always belonged. Like Oliver, Smike is a persistently well-spoken, instinctively morally upright character who does not appear to have imbibed any of the vices that have surrounded him, and, like Oliver, he has passively waited for rescue. However, unlike Oliver, he is not an angelically beautiful child but a stunted adult, whose deprivation is written on his body, and is therefore inerasable. Steven Marcus relates both Smike and Nicholas to Oliver Twist, arguing that

> Smike is that part of the proto-hero, Oliver Twist, which is never allowed to reveal itself in Nicholas . . . . His suffering hav[ing] despoiled him of a sense of self, . . . witness . . . to the murderous consequences of a childhood without adequate love and protection

whereas 'Nicholas is the other side of Oliver Twist', endowed with 'mysterious grace' and improbably assisted at every turn.[40] This reading enables us to see Smike as the scapegoat both in and of the text, to borrow René Girard's terms:[41] his sufferings and death stimulate our indignation about child abuse, but they also ensure that the hero has nothing to suffer. Getting out of the way at the right moment is a crucial part of Smike's narrative work – but at this early stage in Dickens's œuvre, it seems important to the author that this scapegoating be made to seem 'natural'.[42]

This is partly achieved through Smike's own acceptance of his essential difference from others, his recognition that he can never fully participate in the Nickleby family except after death: 'In the churchyard we are all alike, but here there are none like me. I am a poor creature, but I know that.'[43] Smike's recognition of his essential difference amounts to an acknowledgement of his place in the narrative schema, and thus points to the narrative disability occasioned by the physical and mental disabilities caused by his experience of abuse and neglect. Smike briefly sees a way out of his situation, 'brightened up' by the prospect of meeting Nicholas's 'pretty sister'.[44] A romance with Kate would offer him a way into the Nickleby family and a normative plot-line that would enable him to escape his narrative marginality. This prospect is, of course, thwarted: the communality that Klages identifies as the distinguishing feature of sentimental structures of feeling[45] turns out to be located, as Smike predicted, in the graveyard. Once safely in his grave, Smike can be fully embraced by the Nickleby family; at the end of the novel, we see his tombstone being decorated with flowers by the children born of Kate's marriage to Frank Cheeryble and Nicholas's marriage to Madeline Bray, who tearfully 'speak low and softly of their poor dead cousin'.[46] The feelings Smike evokes are essential to the family but his living presence is not: the sentimental subject is most effective, in fact, when no longer living. His agency as a desiring subject, whether for Nicholas (whom he would draw away from Madeline) or Kate (whom he would draw away from Frank), is disruptive to his role as an object of affect. Smike's death is thereby useful to the Nickleby family, freeing the Nickleby siblings for the purposes of the marriage plot – and incidentally ridding the family of its wicked uncle Ralph along the way, as Smike becomes the passive agent of punishment for his father, who kills himself when he discovers Smike's true identity too late to make him any atonement. Helena Michie argues that it is 'the fundamental exclusiveness' of the bourgeois family that kills Smike, citing the 'ruthless' marriage plot as the cause of his expulsion from the narrative.[47]

In addition to being feminised to such an extent that he is unfitted to play the masculine role in the marriage plot, and is enabled to form a relationship with Nicholas that threatens Nicholas's own assumption of such a role, Smike is also the wrong *kind* of character to join the Nickleby family, even if his plot role technically accords him a place there. Minor characters cannot win the love of the major ones, as Mr Toots of *Dombey and Son* and John Chivery of *Our Mutual Friend* find out to their cost – and Smike is marked out for minorness by his grotesque embodiment. Having been introduced as one of the 'deformities' of Dotheboys Hall, and embodying the suffering caused there, he has to be expelled from the novel for its pastoral, familial idyll to be established at the end. Oliver Twist can move from the horrors of the workhouse to the comforts of the pastoral but Smike cannot, and in this sense, his disabled body disables him as a character, limiting his ability to move through the novel's plot. That he resists this reduction of himself to his body and his narrative role as a sentimental sacrifice amounts to a subtle challenge to the novel's sentimental and melodramatic plot structures, which Dickens developed much further in his later fiction.

This is not the only commentary that Smike's characterisation offers upon the novel's use and arrangement of bodies. Dickens also draws out the spectacular nature of sentimental subjectivity by bringing Smike and Nicholas into direct contact with the theatrical, in the form of the Crummleses and their troupe of actors. Their juxtaposition with Smike's anti-theatrical and yet implicitly *spectacular* sentimental characterisation is particularly complex, and is once again grounded in their responses to Smike's embodiment.

It is not surprising that *Nicholas Nickleby* has been so frequently staged, for it is one of Dickens's most theatrical novels. One of the ways in which it draws on melodramatic tradition is in the embodiment of its characters, whose physicalities and personalities are entirely consonant.[48] Ralph Nickleby's wickedness is written on his body, just as Nicholas's goodness is written on his, and the contrast between them can be seen merely by observing their physiognomies: 'the face of the old man was stern, hard-featured and forbidding; that of the young one, open, handsome, and ingenuous'.[49] Smike's body, of course, is not to be read so easily, in that its meanings are complex, but it does, nevertheless, *mean*: his gestures, his features, his costume and his impairments are the means of establishing his function in the plot far more powerfully than the dialogue or any expository account of his thoughts and feelings. To put Smike on stage, then, is the logical next step in this externalisation of his interiority.

To put Smike on stage *within the novel*, however, is to call into question the very basis of that externalisation, which is that it is involuntary. Like all sentimental subjects, Smike does not manipulate his own performance because he cannot; to do so would be to undermine the similarly involuntary affective reaction of the onlooker, who must feel that their own uncontrollably expressed emotion (their tears, their sighs) is being elicited by the subject's similarly uncontrollable affective expression. That is why the perfect sentimental subject is the suffering child, the naivety and spontaneity of whose performance is (in the sentimental tradition, at least) more safely assumed.

Yet the prospect of Smike on stage is one Dickens holds out. For Vincent Crummles, the actor–manager, there is nothing wrong with exploiting the different kinds of affect that different bodies stimulate: as he rhetorically asks Nicholas, '[h]ow are you to get up the sympathies of the audience in a legitimate manner if there isn't a little man contending against a great one?'[50] As Lillian Craton points out, '[s]mall, suffering bodies are a hallmark of Dickens' sentimentality .... Thus Crummles' tactical and unsentimental use of this sentimental imagery creates a fascinating moment of irony within the text.'[51] If Crummles's cheerfully cynical attitude towards the manipulative aspect of sentimental representation indirectly encourages us to reflect upon Dickens's own practice, his view of Smike's body explicitly challenges the one the reader has been encouraged to develop. Where Nicholas cannot see what Crummles calls Smike's 'capital countenance' without exclaiming '[p]oor fellow!', Crummles views him with what Nicholas rightly calls 'a professional eye':

> He'd make such an actor for the starved business as was never was seen in this country. Only let him be tolerably well up in the Apothecary in Romeo and Juliet . . . and he'd be certain of three rounds [of applause] the moment he put his head out.[52]

Crummles's 'professional eye' enables him to view Smike's countenance as 'capital' in a double sense: not only as praiseworthy, but as something from which Smike could make a profit. There is, of course, a pitiless quality in this assessment, as Smike's fitness for the 'starved business' comes from real starvation, and it recalls Crummles's callous treatment of his daughter, the Infant Phenomenon, who has been 'kept up late every night, and put on an unlimited allowance of gin and water from infancy, to prevent her from growing tall'.[53] At the same time, it holds out the possibility that Smike might come to be financially independent, even applauded – that Smike the 'poster' might yet become Smike the performer, if he capitalises on his 'capital' physicality.

It is not to be. While Nicholas's insistence that 'I never acted a part in my life, except at school'[54] does not prevent him from turning to and acting (admittedly with occasionally poor grace), Smike is almost wholly incapable of appearing on stage. The only aspect of his part that he can represent effectively is that which is drawn from his own experience: he 'had as yet been unable to get any more of his part into his head than the general idea that he was very hungry, which – perhaps from old recollections – he had acquired with great aptitude'.[55] Like a true sentimental subject, Smike can perform only what he really feels, thereby precluding the possibility of cheating his audience into falsely won sympathy.

Martha Stoddard Holmes has argued that this risk of being drawn to give undeserved or disproportionate sympathy accounts for much readerly resistance to sentimental fiction, and was particularly potent at the time when the New Poor Laws sought to distinguish rigidly between deserving and undeserving charitable objects, between deserved and undeserved suffering.[56] Stoddard Holmes points out that in this formulation, in which any appeal for sympathy was suspect, 'visible disability might constitute a way of being seen without being regarded as "obtruding" oneself, and of communicating without offensive clamor through the silent, modest speech of the impaired body'.[57] The legibility of this sign is potentially undermined by theatricality: the actor's performance proves that physical signs of emotion and experience can be assumed, and thereby destabilises the sentimentalist's valuing of such signs as the basis for true human connection.

The complexity of this proposition is compounded by the fact that, at the time, the idea that bodily suffering might be routinely faked in order to win false sympathy was very much current. Physical disability is as highly suspect as it is emotionally charged in the writing of Henry Mayhew, for example. His attempts to divide up the disabled beggars he encounters into the truly pitiable and deserving (the nutmeg-grater seller, unfortunate through no fault of his own) and the false or somehow undeserving (the man who became disabled through his own drunken fault, for example) have a desperate quality.[58] The idea that bodily suffering might be faked, or might not be a sign of truly blameless suffering, threatens the category of the 'crippled' that Mayhew seeks to construct, and is therefore socially menacing as well as emotionally troubling.[59] The same structure of feeling lies behind Dickens's refusal to put Smike on stage and allow him to capitalise on his impaired body as a stimulus of affect, and yet makes the possibility that he *could* do so irresistibly tempting. Dickens encourages the reader to interpret Smike's body as a reliable sign of his history, his identity and his personality – as Nicholas does in their first meeting – and yet flirts with the disruption of this relationship by *almost* allowing Smike to use the way his body is read deliberately, and to his own advantage.

This is a possibility that the text has to curtail in order for Smike's body to continue to be available for sentimental effect. Theatrical as *Nicholas Nickleby* is in one sense, it is a profoundly anti-theatrical text in another: as Angus Easson points out, 'being unable to act, in *Nicholas Nickleby*, validates not only the emotion but also the person'.[60] Clearly, Dickens was too sophisticated in his use of sentimental tropes and scenes not to have been aware of the ways in which their spectacular quality aligned them with the theatrical, and throughout *Nicholas Nickleby*, he encodes the possibility for slippage between acting and feeling, and of the possibility for sentimental subjects to exploit this potential, to control the affect they stimulate. Smike's characterisation is a particularly potent site for such slippage, and although he is destined to remain a 'poor fellow', we are confronted with an alternative view of his physicality – by which his countenance is 'capital' – to hold up against Nicholas's understanding of him as a 'poor creature'. In his next novel, Dickens was to draw out the possibilities for theatrical and sentimental uses of the body even more clearly, in his juxtaposition of the characters of Little Nell and Quilp.

### The Dwarves of *The Old Curiosity Shop*

> The child was closely followed by an elderly man of remarkably hard features and forbidding aspect, and so low in stature as to be quite a dwarf, though his head and face were large enough for the body of a giant. His black eyes were restless, sly, and cunning . . . . But what added most to the grotesque expression of his face, was a ghastly smile, which, appearing to be the mere result of habit and to have no connection with any mirthful or complacent feeling, constantly revealed the few discoloured fangs that were yet scattered in his mouth, and gave him the aspect of a panting dog.[61]

This description of the dwarf Quilp, taken from *The Old Curiosity Shop* (1841), is at the opposite pole of Dickens's use of bodily difference from that occupied by Smike. We are encouraged to stare at

Quilp, to marvel, ogle and recoil from him as 'a uglier dwarf than can be seen anywhers for a penny'.[62] This is an appellation that Quilp appears to resent – since he recalls it whenever he is persecuting its originator, Kit Nubbles – and yet one that he also claims with a kind of pride, taking malign delight in his terrifying appearance, particularly as a means of frightening his wife into submission, pulling faces at her and 'perform[ing] so many horrifying and uncommon acts' that she and her mother are completely cowed.[63] The language of performance here anticipates the descriptions of the showmen Nell joins for a while, who include 'a giant, and a little lady without legs or arms',[64] and these grotesque characters do indeed partake of some of Quilp's threatening immorality, as well as his indisputable comicality and vitality for the reader.

In one sense, our heroine Little Nell, the beautiful, angelic girl who is so radically incorruptible that she cannot live in the fallen world and dies before reaching adulthood, stands in stark contrast to these grotesques, the sentimental and the freakish representing opposite modes of being in the novel. In another sense, however, such a dichotomy is a false one; certainly, Little Nell is contrasted to Quilp and to the performers she meets on her travels, but she is also like them. Hilary Schor's suggestion that, over the course of the novel, Dickens 'moves his heroine herself close to the realm of the female freak'[65] points to this identification of Nell with the circus performers, but also resonates particularly strongly with Rosemarie Garland-Thomson's provocative definition of the freakish as that which is wholly defined by embodiment: 'When the body becomes pure text, a freak has been made from a physically different human being.'[66] Nell's body functions as 'pure text' in exactly the way Garland-Thomson suggests the freak's does, and the text seems to mark Nell's enfreaked status by forcing her – at the level of plot – into the role of spectacle, making of the supposedly domesticated daughter a performative 'other' who stands apart from the normative family she cannot enter as surely as does Smike. She is like him in being allied with the outcasts of the novel, despite existing at its narrative centre, and although she clearly prefigures Florence Dombey and Agnes Wickfield, the idealised, static child–women of *Dombey and Son* (1848) and *David Copperfield* (1850), she is also an early incarnation of those heroines whose unspeakable suffering is written on to their unusual bodies, Esther Summerson and Little Dorrit. Although Little Nell's littleness is less remarkable than Little Dorrit's, given that she is only fourteen, her body is treated as abnormal and spectacular within the text, and is marked by the contradictions and pressures of her narrative position as a heroine, until we could reasonably call it 'impaired', especially since the bodily weakness that her littleness indicates ultimately kills her.

In an essay that draws Little Nell and Little Dorrit together, Lauren Byler points out in passing that both are fundamentally like minor characters, relating this to their allegorical function and the exemplarity that 'flattens them into emblems of goodness'.[67] I read this minorness in Nell's distorted body, which garners the kind of attention ordinarily reserved for minor (or, in Forster's term, 'flattened') characters, here placed squarely at the centre of a novel of its own – a novel that, tellingly, has itself been marginalised within the Dickensian canon, no longer occupying the central place it once did.[68]

In his Preface to the 1848 edition, Dickens attempts to distinguish Nell in kind from those who surround her, stating that 'I had it always in my fancy to surround the lonely figure of the child with grotesque and wild, but not impossible companions.'[69] However, the dichotomy he seeks to create here is repeatedly collapsed within the novel itself, as Nell is brought ever closer to these 'grotesque and wild' figures, her body associated as frequently with the circus as with the sick bed, and thus with grotesque as well as sentimental traditions of bodily display. The Manichean structures of melodrama that hold Little Nell and Quilp apart point in themselves to the theatrical, spectacular nature of the novel: the concern for realism that is indicated by Dickens's caveat that his figures are 'not impossible' is a misleading, retrospective repositioning of the novel in generic terms.

Quilp is, as Paul Schlicke points out, very like the character of Punch,[70] as much an entertainer as anything else, staging his wickedness with great glee, and turning his physical abnormalities to his own uses in ways that ally him with the freaks of the circus, who also capitalise upon their physiognomies. Nell, on the other hand, appears to perform her vulnerability in a purely unselfconscious sentimental display. From the very first time we meet her, 'put[ting] her hand in [Master Humphrey's] as confidingly as if she had known [him] from a child', she is established as a character who trusts in the fellow feeling of strangers, and before the chapter is out she is modelling the reaction she is intended to draw from the reader, her eyes 'dimmed with tears'.[71] Unlike poor Smike, she has a wholly sympathetic audience for her tears: Master Humphrey's 'curiosity and interest' quickly give way to deep concern.[72] As in *Nicholas Nickleby*, however, the unselfconsciousness of the character cannot be wholly shared by the reader. Eight chapters later, as we watch Nell and her grandfather weep together, and perhaps shed a few sympathetic tears ourselves, Dickens highlights the voyeuristic nature of our observation, having Master Humphrey point out to us that '[t]hese were not words for other ears, nor was it a scene for other eyes. And yet other ears and eyes were there and greedily taking in all that passed.'[73] Before we are told that this intruder is Quilp, there is a queasy moment in which we might take it to apply to ourselves, and to our own reading practice.

Nor is this the only moment at which we are drawn into Quilp's subject position rather than Nell's. When Quilp describes her as 'chubby, rosy, cosy little Nell . . . so small, so compact, so beautifully modelled, so fair, with such blue veins and such a transparent skin, and such little feet', he evokes her bodily presence with such vividness that we can hardly help being party to its re-construction, even as we are being made aware that Quilp is performing this anatomising of Nell in a deliberate effort to discomfort her grandfather, in fact 'feigning to be quite absorbed in the subject'.[74] Quilp's perspective renders obscene even Nell's relationship with her grandfather: '"Ah!" said the dwarf, smacking his lips, "what a nice kiss that was – just upon the rosy part."'[75] As Hilary Schor points out, in scenes like this, Nell is rendered 'a kind of pornographic object'.[76] Why does Dickens force us to see his child heroine in this way? John Carey argues that Quilp acts as an avatar for the violence Dickens himself wishes to visit upon his insufferably sweet heroine, suggesting that 'Quilp is Dickens's way of avenging himself upon the sentimental set-up of *The Old Curiosity Shop*' and that, through him, 'Dickens offers violence to his own sexless heroine . . . and with aggressive enjoyment.'[77]

Compelling as this reading is, I think it is ultimately more productive to acknowledge the dialectic between the two sentimental and grotesque elements of the text and recognise Dickens's exploitation of the potential for slippage between the two, rather than allying him entirely with the latter. Rather than taking Quilp's gleefully unpleasant commentary as (or only as) an outlet for his creator's own feelings, we can also see it as making us aware of Nell's vulnerability to misconstruction, her inability to take control of how she is perceived by others, as do Quilp and his fellow grotesques. Of course, Quilp himself is not completely in control of how he is perceived by others, since he can hardly help being an 'uglier dwarf than can be seen anywheres for a penny' – but he can capitalise upon this perception, as the nameless freaks can (to a greater or lesser extent) capitalise upon theirs. By contrast, poor Nell does not have this capacity: it would be antithetical to the naivety that is her most fundamental characteristic ever to manipulate the impression she makes upon other people. Cruelly, it is this unselfconsciousness that renders her peculiarly vulnerable to Quilp's obscene misconstructions. Disabled as a performer by her naivety, Nell is also disabled as a sentimental subject when her interlocutors and onlookers refuse to partake in the sentimental contract and feel with her. Trapped in Quilp's world, Nell can never learn to play by its rules – since to learn from her experience would erode the innocence by which she is defined – and embrace her status as a curiosity, and yet it seems that she is finally too 'curious' to find a place at the cosy hearth of the Nubbles family at the end of the novel. Like Smike, she has nowhere to go but the graveyard.

In the sense that there is, finally, no place for her within the stable, insular family setting that concludes the novel, Nell has something in common not only with Smike, but also with the outcast, disabled characters and villains within the novel, against whom she is defined. Moreover, her repeatedly emphasised littleness means that, as Lillian Craton points out, 'the novel's arch villain sees eye-to-eye, physically at least, with the novel's young heroine'.[78] Quilp himself draws on this likeness when he declares his intention to move into her bedroom: 'The bedstead is about my size. I think I shall make it *my* little room.'[79] Quilp's appeal to Nell to become his 'little cherry-cheeked, red-lipped wife'[80] opens up the possibility that, despite their obvious and heavily emphasised moral and physical differences, Nell's unusually small size might play a role in Quilp's desire for her, as suggestive of some kind of compatibility between them. As Craton goes on to argue, '[b]ehind the image of the suffering child lurks the performing dwarf of the fairground':[81] for all that Nell is supposed to be at odds with the circus folk and their values, she does become something of a performer on the road, 'produc[ing] quite a sensation in the little country place'.[82] Mrs Jarley draws attention to the similarity between Little Nell's itinerant and dispossessed state and that of the show people she has joined the first time they meet: '"You don't mean to say that you're travelling about the country without knowing where you're going to?" said the lady of the caravan. "What curious people you are! What line are you in?"'[83] The 'curiosity' of the title has repeatedly been used in relation to Little Nell – the original impetus of the narrative being Master Humphrey's 'curiosity' about her,[84] surely intended to stimulate the reader's – and Nell now becomes one of the 'curiosities' of Mrs Jarley's show, her unusual appearance rendering her the perfect living advertisement for the wax-work exhibition. Although the narrator assures us that it is in fact her extreme

Figure 1.2  Hablôt K. Browne, Untitled illustration, *The Old Curiosity Shop*, in *Master Humphrey's Clock*, 3 vols (London: Chapman and Hall, 1840–1), vol. 1, p. 253.

conventionality that draws in the crowds – that it is Nell's 'beauty' and 'gentle and timid bearing' that produce the 'sensation'[85] – this is interestingly belied by the illustration that begins the chapter in which these claims are made (Fig. 1.2).

The illustrations of *The Old Curiosity Shop* are markedly inconsistent because they are produced by two different artists with very different styles,[86] but it is still noteworthy that Little Nell, who has up to this point been consistently depicted as a child, is drawn here as a miniature woman, with a distinctly adult figure and a stature so diminutive that she is only half as tall as the man standing next to her. In drawing Nell as a dwarf, the artist has made her look far more at home on Jarley's wagon than we might expect, and this resonates with the possibility held out, at this point in the story, that Mrs Jarley might act as both a care-giver and a role-model to Little Nell, offering as she does an alternative model of femininity in which a certain degree of selfishness can co-exist with generosity. Whereas

Nell starves herself to feed her grandfather and is frequently too much exhausted to nourish herself, Mrs Jarley is depicted as feasting, drinking and even sleeping with great abandon: '"it does you good," said the lady of the caravan, "when you're tired, to sleep as long as ever you can, and get the fatigue quite off"'.[87] Nell, however, does not learn self-indulgence from Mrs Jarley, sharing in none of her comical flaws and refusing to imitate her sternness towards her grandfather. She remains committed to a sentimental mode of shared feeling rather than the theatrical mode of shared performance in which Mrs Jarley could instruct her, instantiated by her desire to listen in on the conversations of the Edwards sisters, and share in their affecting reunion vicariously, rather than to remain in Mrs Jarley's comfortable caravan and eat, drink and be merry.

That Nell must *actively* resist assimilation into Mrs Jarley's world, and that we are shown the process by which she *makes* herself 'Little Nell' – essentially through starving herself, as Anna Krugovoy Silver points out[88] – complicates the statement I have made regarding the unselfconsciousness of her performance. In order to react to Nell as a sentimental spectacle, we have to believe her performance of goodness to be unselfconscious, and yet, as Lauren Byler argues, Nell does remind her grandfather of her self-sacrifice in order to bring him into line, demonstrating what Byler calls the 'cut of cuteness'.[89] Where Byler sees this as Dickens's subtle acknowledgement of his own crowd-pleasing theatrical techniques, Silver suggests that he remains totally invested in Little Nell's perfection, which extends to a celebration of her stunted embodiment, arguing that Nell's 'body becomes the symbol of her femininity so that, in Dickens's poetics of anorexia, her starved body on its deathbed is beautiful; it *must* be beautiful to represent those traits that Nell embodies'.[90] While this seems to me to be true in the case of Little Nell, the more ambiguous and troublingly disabled body of Little Dorrit is prefigured elsewhere in the text, in that of the Marchioness, another girl who has been starved into littleness – in her own doubly suggestive phrase, 'kept short'.[91] Simultaneously Nell's double and her opposite, the Marchioness captures the novel's oscillation between grotesque and sentimental treatment of the exceptional body, embodying both the disturbing and the redemptive possibilities of slippage between the two.

In his study of the work of Dickens's illustrator, Hablôt K. Browne ('Phiz'), Michael Steig draws attention to Browne's shifting portrayal of the Marchioness, which captures her transformation from comic grotesque to sentimentalised heroine.[92] In the illustration Browne

Marking the Minor Character 43

Figure 1.3 Hablôt K. Browne, Untitled illustration, *The Old Curiosity Shop*, in *Master Humphrey's Clock*, 3 vols (London: Chapman and Hall, 1840–1), vol. 2, p. 158.

drew for the 1840–1 serial edition of the novel (Fig. 1.3), he represents the Marchioness as a grotesque child–woman, with a wizened, elderly face, in distorted contrast to her small stature, emphasised by her over-sized feet resting on the table, unable to reach the floor. Yet in the illustration he drew for the novel's 1848 reprint (Fig. 1.4), the Marchioness is a conventionally pretty girl, with a burgeoning womanly figure and a modestly sweet expression. Her poverty is picturesquely captured in her mended dress, rather than embodied in hideous or risible distortion. This disjunction can be attributed to the transformation that occurs in the characterisation of the Marchioness herself, who is introduced to us as an abused child (and the child of Quilp and Sally Brass at that, in the manuscript version[93]), and then grows into a staunch friend to her ally Dick Swiveller, his capable nurse, then his ward at school and finally his wife. Yet the slippage between idealised and grotesque modes of representation is more profound than this trajectory acknowledges: the Marchioness was already Dick's nurse when Browne realised her as he did in the first

Figure 1.4   Hablôt K. Browne, 'The Marchioness', *The Old Curiosity Shop*, (London: Chapman and Hall, 1848), facing p. 293.

illustration. She could perform the most idealised of feminine roles before she became prettily picturesque, when she was still being drawn as a comic grotesque, a freakish child–woman rather than a beautiful woman–child. In her 'cunning'[94] and precocity, the Marchioness clearly prefigures Jenny Wren, but she is apparently able to perform the narrative role of Lizzie Hexham; the illustrations capture not only the character's development, but the artist's uncertainty about which aspect of her character to foreground, representing the widely divergent bodies of the two possible Marchionesses.

Moreover, in Browne's uncertainty as to how to draw the Marchioness, we can see prefigured the tension between Little Dorrit the adorable child–woman, whose littleness simply renders her maternal and moral capabilities more unthreatening, more picturesque and thus all the more desirable, and Little Dorrit the distorted grotesque, shrunken by neglect, starved of literal or metaphorical sustenance to the point that she is marked out from those who surround her by her inadequate body, capable of arousing horror rather than admiration, and yet uniquely able to fill the maternal absence at the heart of Arthur Clennam's life and the text itself. In the Marchioness's story of growing from an abused and neglected child into the perfect nurse and companion, and, as wife, the embodiment in herself of her rescuer's reward, we can see the stories of Esther Summerson and Little Dorrit captured in microcosm. Like Esther, the Marchioness is illegitimate;[95] like Little Dorrit, she has been 'kept short' by starvation and emotional neglect. In her uncertain and unstable embodiment – Is she beautiful or is she ugly? Is she an ideal child–woman or a grotesque woman–child? – she anticipates Esther Summerson's scarred face and Little Dorrit's eleven-year-old's body.

The power that Little Dorrit wields within the novel named after her is prefigured, on a small scale, by the fact that the Marchioness, another abused and neglected child–woman, is not merely the subject of transformation, but its agent. In Steven Marcus's view, Dick Swiveller re-makes the Marchioness as a character, transforming her from the unnamed 'small servant' into a 'person', arguing that, from his first visit to the kitchen, 'he then proceeds, like Prometheus, to civilize her – by teaching her to play cribbage, and giving her a name. . . . He has done nothing less than create another person; he has given her an identity, brought her up out of darkness into life.'[96] What Marcus omits to mention is that the Marchioness has, in her turn, re-made Dick. He appears in the first half of the novel as an irresponsible dandy, ranged more or less on the side of Sally Brass and Quilp, insofar as he is in their employ and failing to thwart their schemes. It is through his kindness to the starved Marchioness that we begin to recognise his latent moral worth, and through his acquaintance with her that he discovers enough of Sally and Quilp's scheme against Kit to be able to play an assistive role in bringing about narrative justice. Dick's plot role is transformed through his contact with the Marchioness, who saves his life not only by nursing him through an illness – as Dick himself repeatedly reminds us[97] – but in later consenting to become Mrs Sophronia Swiveller. As his wife, she brings about his moral reformation, making of him 'an attached and domesticated husband'.[98] Ultimately, Dick is saved through recognising what we might (*pace* James) call the possible personhood of the 'small servant'.[99] The power the minor character might have if she were drawn in from the margins – literally brought up out of the kitchen – seems in *The Old Curiosity Shop* to fascinate Dickens, and prefigures his creation of Esther Summerson and Little Dorrit, heroines who first appear at the margins of the novels that will turn out to be theirs.

### Shrunken, Scarred and Lovely: Disabling Femininity in *Bleak House* and *Little Dorrit*

Discussing the anti-realist sentimentality with which Dickens treats his most idealised characters, Fred Kaplan cites Little Nell, Esther Summerson and Little Dorrit as 'embodiments of Dickens's belief in the moral sentiments'.[100] What he does not point out is that all three characters' embodiment is highly unusual, highly marked and actually disabling within the novels they inhabit. Where Little Nell's littleness allies her with the performing freaks and grotesque dwarf who are her co-stars in the spectacular variety show that is *The Old Curiosity Shop*, in their far more muted and broadly realist novels Esther Summerson and Amy Dorrit seem marked for minorness by their physicalities, set apart from the major characters by their abnormal bodies.[101] Esther's scarred face and Little Dorrit's 'diminutive' body – so small as to enable her 'to have been passed in the street for little more than half [her] age', a prospect literalised when a prostitute mistakes her for a child – match their self-identification as minor characters.[102] Both repeatedly stress their own unimportance and see themselves as standing on the sidelines of the main action, conceiving their own role as purely assistive. In fact, they stand at the centre of the novels they inhabit, both as the figures on whom the mystery plots turn and as the moral exemplars who are finally recognised as such by their narrative communities and duly rewarded in the marriage plot. Why Dickens should have chosen to depart from his usual practice by marking out the bodies of these heroines as deviant, and why their physical disablement becomes narratively enabling, are the questions I now wish to take up.

Esther Summerson begins her narration in *Bleak House* (1853) by declaring her unfitness to be a narrator at all: 'I have a great deal of difficulty in beginning to write my portion of these pages,' she tells us, 'for I know I am not clever.'[103] Her connection to the novel's main plot-line – which at this point, in the third chapter, appears to concern the Jarndyce case in Chancery – seems tangential. She is brought in only as the companion to the heiress, whose position as the romantic heroine is immediately established by Esther's description of her as 'such a beautiful girl!'[104] Having begun her narration by declaring her inadequacy as a narrator, Esther tries to write herself out of the novel as a character as well, apologising to the reader for presuming to intrude into the novel at all: 'It seems so curious to me to be obliged to write all this about myself! As if this narrative were the narrative of my life! But my little body will soon fall into the back-ground now.'[105] In fact, Esther's body does no such thing, as she turns out to be not the minor character she considers herself, but the heroine of the novel, at the very centre of its plot, the figure on whom the mystery turns and upon whose body the marriage plot centres. Moreover, it is her body that registers both her right and her resistance to this role, through the traumatic scarring that corporealises both her mental suffering and her selfless service to others.

It is Esther's self-conception as minor, the total selflessness that she embraces as part of her self-confessed quest 'to do some good to some one, and win some love to myself if I could',[106] that fits her for a major role. Yet the scars that literalise this praiseworthy self-effacement are a source of almost unmitigated pain to Esther herself, who expresses the change as a devastating loss, even as a form of total erasure: 'I had never been a beauty, and had never thought myself one; but I had been very different from this. It was all gone now.'[107] Although Esther's scars do not entail any kind of physical impairment, they do constitute a disability in being a socially stigmatised form of physical difference, amounting to what she calls a 'disfigurement',[108] disqualifying her from marriageability in her own eyes – and, as if to demonstrate the accuracy of her perception at least in broadly social terms, in those of her less worthy suitor, Guppy, who is anxious to withdraw his previous proposal of marriage upon seeing her face.[109] Her scarring does not, however, render her any less attractive to the true hero of the novel, Allan, who is unchanged in his devotion, declaring her in the novel's final paragraph, 'prettier than . . . ever'.[110] Far from being pushed to the novel's margins, it would seem that the scarred woman, the woman stigmatised by illegitimacy and poverty, and convinced of her own unworthiness, is in fact the *ideal* woman, her 'disfigurement' an enhancement of her loveliness.[111]

Given the interpretive weight borne by the bodies of Dickens's characters, however, the same proposition can also be expressed the opposite way: the ideal woman is disfigured by her narrative role, the unspeakable pain of her experience written on the body that both gives form to her goodness and bears witness to the deforming weight of expectation and pathological self-hatred that Dickens demands of his heroines. That Dickens was unaware of the disabling effect his ideal of femininity had upon his heroines is a common enough charge, but in fact, the self-repression, self-distrust and total unassertiveness that has marked his heroines from Little Nell onwards *are* shown as damaging Esther's well-being. If Dickens writes beneficence, contentment and patience on to his heroines' countenances (which explains why they are always and necessarily beautiful), it is surely significant that he marks Esther's with 'disfiguring' scars.

Moreover, the relatively simple proposition that a true lover can see past outer appearance, and only the shallow and unworthy pay any attention to the beauty or otherwise of Esther's face, is greatly complicated by Esther's own feelings about her facial scarring. As John Gordon points out in his essay 'Is Esther pretty?', this question is of pivotal importance to Esther herself, who not only 'rarely meets another female without immediately assessing her relative attractiveness', but actually begins her narrative by pointing out the 'beautiful complexion and rosy lips' of her childhood doll.[112] This beginning is given retrospective emphasis by the fact that it is mirrored in the novel's concluding paragraphs, in which Esther indirectly tries to ask Allan, now her husband, whether she was pretty before her illness and whether she is pretty now. Clearly, Esther herself finds it difficult to believe her own claim that her family 'can very well do without much beauty in me', since her looks still prey on her mind, but she is not willing to answer Allan's question, 'don't you know that you are prettier than you ever were?',[113] in the affirmative. She *almost* qualifies the statement that her family 'can very well do without much beauty in [her]' by tentatively adding '– even supposing –',[114] but stops herself before she can finish. The dash with which she concludes her narrative subtly destabilises an otherwise reassuring final paragraph, taking us, nightmarishly, back to Esther's miserable beginning. We had been led to hope that, over the course of her progress from forlorn charity pupil to beloved wife and mother, her mental anguish had been assuaged, her crushing self-doubt lifted by that most conventional of narrative rewards, the love of her husband. But at the last moment, we see that Esther cannot allow herself to indulge in one moment's self-belief. We understand now that, however much she is loved, however much praise is showered upon her, Esther will *never* claim to be pretty.

Why does this matter? Because claiming to be pretty, in Esther's own world-view, would amount to self-love, and this would be antithetical to Esther's self-punishing self-conception as inadequate, which is repeatedly and insistently linked to her goodness. It is when her aunt tells her that she is 'degraded' by illegitimacy and she understands herself as having 'brought no joy, at any time, to anybody's heart' that Esther makes her celebrated vow 'to be industrious, contented and kind-hearted, and to do some good to some one, and win some love to myself if I could'.[115] Her goodness and her sense of inadequacy are never disentangled, so that it would indeed threaten the place she has won at the novel's conclusion to believe Allan's praise.

Esther is literally disfigured by her own goodness in the sense that she contracts smallpox as a result of her selfless nursing of her maid, Charley; her fear that 'Charley's pretty looks would change and be disfigured' are set at rest as she sees her 'growing into her old childish likeness again',[116] but by a cruel plot twist, the fate Esther has feared for Charley becomes her own. This twist can be seen as structurally necessary in plot terms, as the mystery of Esther's parentage can be preserved only as long as her likeness to her mother, Lady Dedlock, is not widely observed. Esther recognises the utility of her changed countenance in the moment of her first reunion with her mother: 'I felt, through all my tumult of emotion, a burst of gratitude to the providence of God that I was so changed as that I could never disgrace her by any trace of likeness.'[117] Yet her hopes are not realised, as her scars fail to protect her mother from the 'disgrace' of discovery: the plot punishes Lady Dedlock's past transgression with persecution and death, despite the pity that is doled out by both narratives.

What, then, was the point of Esther's scarring? It has been argued that her scars save her from disgrace herself, fitting her to be a heroine by separating her from her guilty mother. Miriam Bailin suggests that this erasure of the somatic bond between mother and daughter

> functions as a mark of separation from the shame of her past . . . . Her scars prevent the full identification of herself with her mother, which in the larger metaphoric context of the novel would signify the perilous convergence of guilt and shame with respectability and restored status.[118]

Hilary Schor takes this argument even further, by suggesting that Esther's place in the novel depends upon the destruction of the mother who threatens her respectability, that she has to

> seek for her own face in the wide world and never, ever, to hope of finding it again, on herself or on anyone else, for she (and the text) have killed off the one true double she had . . . the one woman whose story could drag her down (both by revealing her status and destroying her secure place in Bleak House).[119]

While Schor's reading is a powerful one, she does not address the fact that Esther's 'own face' has *already* been destroyed by the novel's plotting. Moreover, neither critic acknowledges that, in addition to being shameful, her likeness to her mother – a famous beauty – is also Esther's only inheritance. Like the maid in the nursery rhyme, Esther's face was her only fortune; in being deprived of it, she is the most radically dispossessed of all Dickens's dispossessed heroines. For Esther, the loss is absolute. As she starkly declares when she first sees her changed face: 'It was all gone.'[120]

At this point, Esther questions whether it is right for her to keep the flowers that Allan Woodcourt gave her, 'whether I had a right to preserve what he had sent to one so different'.[121] Apparently, it is not enough for Esther, or for the novel, that she should have given up the hope of being married to the man she loves, repressing even the acknowledgement of her love until the moment she gives up all hope of its return: her very right to remember it is in doubt. The pain of this constant self-denial is repressed by her narration but it is written on her ravaged face; Helena Michie calls the repeated (and compulsively recorded) first unveilings of her scarred face to her friends 'moments of painful triumph. For the first time, *Bleak House*'s cast of characters is forced to read the autobiographical calendar of distress Esther failed to reproduce in those three hundred pages of living and writing.'[122] Esther's moral success in turning her flinty aunt's injunction to '[s]ubmission, self-denial, diligent work' into a credo of selfless virtue has made her an ideal heroine,[123] but it has also forced her to repress every trace of pain – even to smile at her own reflection after accepting a marriage proposal from her guardian Jarndyce when she is still in love with Allan Woodcourt.[124] The extremity of her self-repression, and the pain it causes her, are acknowledged by the narrative in being written on to her body in her facial disfigurement, which enables this utterly (and celebratedly) unassertive heroine to declare, at last, her own suffering. This is not to say that Esther's disabling femininity is not celebrated in and by the novel. Rather, it is to suggest that Dickens acknowledges that only a woman whose sense of self has been systematically undermined in childhood and who believes herself to be worthless would be able to fulfil the angelic role his plots require, and that he acknowledges the pain she must undergo in order to perform this role by writing it on her face.

In fact, Dickens's heroines have been struggling to survive the experiences that led them to be so good, and to survive their own goodness, long before he first scarred one of them. Little Nell dies as a result of her own self-sacrificing virtue; Florence Dombey has to survive a neglected childhood and is physically marked by her father's abuse with 'the darkening mark of an angry hand'.[125] Agnes Wickfield, perhaps the most angelic of all Dickens's saintly heroines, with her perpetual pointing heavenward, has to act as her father's housekeeper, 'staid' and 'discreet',[126] when she is still a child, suffers half a lifetime of unacknowledged desire for David, and not only almost loses her place in the marriage plot as a result of her total unassertiveness (as do Esther and Little Dorrit), but actually has to befriend and mentor her usurper, Dora. Dickens indicates that all these heroines have been in some way damaged by their own goodness, but in *Bleak House* he goes a step further, literalising the idea that the heroine is scarred both for and by the novel's plot.

If Esther's scarring can be understood as an externalisation of her self-hatred, both the mark of her goodness and the price she must pay for it, then Little Dorrit's littleness serves a similarly complex function. She is first introduced to the text incidentally, in the manner of a minor character, her presence registered only retrospectively by Arthur Clennam, who recalls after leaving his mother's room that there was 'a girl . . . almost hidden in the dark corner'. Affrey immediately affirms that she is of no importance and re-directs his attentions towards his long-lost sweetheart, Flora Finching: 'Little Dorrit? She's nothing . . . . But there's another girl that's about. Have you forgot your old sweetheart?'[127] Given that Arthur has already met and been struck by the beauty of the heiress Pet Meagles, described as 'round and fresh and dimpled and spoilt . . . [with] an air of timidity and dependence which was the best weakness in the world, and gave her the only crowning charm a girl so pretty and pleasant could have been without',[128] it is unlikely that competent and colourless Little Dorrit, with her 'pale transparent face . . . not beautiful in feature',[129] would strike the reader as the romantic heroine at this point, were it not for the title of the novel, which proclaims her centrality. This title also, as Patricia Ingham points out, insists on the importance of her littleness,[130] which is stressed when Arthur first pays her sustained attention: she has 'a diminutive figure', 'small features', 'a tiny form' and 'much of the appearance of a subdued child'.[131]

Dickens's interest in child–women can be traced back to *The Old Curiosity Shop*, and clearly seen in *David Copperfield*, which features both Dora the 'child–wife',[132] still a child when she should be a woman and unable to bear a child of her own, and Agnes, the woman who was never a child and is always a mother, even appearing to David as the re-embodiment of her own mother when she is still a child.[133] While David is ultimately destined for domestic happiness with his 'good angel' Agnes,[134] it is Dora who is erotically appealing, and her childishness is an essential part of this appeal for David: 'She had the most delightful little voice, the gayest little laugh . . . . She was rather diminutive altogether. So much the more precious, I thought.'[135] This is far from being a peculiarity of David's; from Dolly Varden in *Barnaby Rudge* (1841) to Bella Wilfer in *Our Mutual Friend* (1865), a woman is practically never registered as sexually appealing in a Dickens novel without being called 'little' and endowed with the vulnerability that the adjective connotes. The exceptions to this rule are, of course, the child–woman's polar opposite, the fully adult, dangerous, dark women – Alice Marwood in *Dombey and Son* (1848), Rosa Dartle in *David Copperfield* (1850), Estella Havisham in *Great Expectations* (1860) – and, attractive as these women are, their sexuality is always threatening, and usually connected to their barely controlled, sometimes murderous rage. Sexually attractive women who are not childlike are universally terrifying, and the motherly women who represent the heroes' refuge from both dark temptress and child–woman, the competent housekeepers and angel–wives who offer domestic security and spiritual salvation – Agnes, Esther, Biddy – lack the sexual allure of their rivals.

In a sense, then, Little Dorrit's littleness clearly marks her as a wish-fulfilling figure, who brings together in one person the littleness of the desirable child–woman and the maternal capabilities of the woman–child. Yet Little Dorrit's littleness is more complex than this, for Dickens does not choose to represent her simply as adorably little, but as problematically, noticeably, even freakishly little. He draws attention to the disjunction between her age and her body by including a scene that forces us to take literally the proposition that, at 'not less than two-and-twenty, she might have passed in the street for little more than half that age'.[136] When she walks the street at night, a prostitute mistakes her for a child:

> 'Kiss a poor lost creature, dear,' she said, bending her face . . . . Little Dorrit turned towards her.
> 'Why, my God!' she said, recoiling, 'you're a woman!'
> 'Don't mind that!' said Little Dorrit, clasping one of the hands that had suddenly released hers. 'I am not afraid of you . . . let me speak to you as if I really were a child.'
> 'You can't do it,' said the woman. 'You are kind and innocent; but you can't look at me out of a child's eyes. I never should have touched you, but I thought you were a child.' And, with a strange, wild cry, she went away.[137]

Anny Sadrin suggests that the scene forces us to recognise that there is something 'truly monstrous and shocking' in Little Dorrit's embodiment, while Patricia Ingham draws attention to the 'gratuituousness of the episode', which 'enforces a reading of the passage as emphatic: a Little Dorrit/Amy, a child–woman, is a manifest horror'.[138]

It is, of course, important to set this scene alongside the many, many instances in which Little Dorrit is shown to be irresistibly attractive to others, who find nothing 'monstrous' in her extreme diminutiveness, but who are, on the contrary, charmed by her appearance of vulnerability. Yet Sadrin and Ingham's readings usefully point towards the fact that Little Dorrit's littleness is in this scene made to represent the disabling aspects of her goodness – and it is far from being an isolated instance. Early on in the novel, we are told that, when she was younger, Little Dorrit was almost refused an apprenticeship on the grounds that she is 'so very, very little', causing her 'to sob over that unfortunate defect of hers, which came so often in her way'.[139] Byler suggests that this is simply a 'lie', given how useful her littleness is to her in so many ways, but in fact there is truth in Lillian Craton's assertion that Little Dorrit 'struggles with problems of perception, the misreading of her body's unique features'.[140] Her littleness not only leads others to underestimate her capabilities, as in this early scene, but for much of the novel prevents Arthur from considering her as a romantic possibility. He expresses astonishment when he learns that John Chivery loves her, exclaiming that he has been used 'to consider Little – . . . habituated to consider Miss Dorrit in a light altogether removed from that in which you present her to me', his self-correction highlighting the connection between her sexlessness and her nickname (and by implication her littleness) in his mind.[141] Dickens draws attention throughout the text to Little Dorrit's unrecognised love for Arthur and the pain it causes her; whereas Agnes's desire for David is almost completely repressed by the text of *David Copperfield*, and Esther's feelings for Allan are only occasionally allowed to surface elliptically in *Bleak House*, *Little Dorrit* is shot through with its heroine's painful experience of unrequited love. In case we have somehow missed the many, many hints that Little Dorrit does not want Arthur to see her as a child, Dickens has Little Dorrit tell the story of her love for Arthur to Maggy, lightly disguised as a fairy story, in which she casts herself as 'the poor tiny woman' whose love is a 'shadow' she must keep secret, and which ultimately kills her.[142]

It is telling that Little Dorrit depicts Arthur himself as a shadowy presence in her allegory, for he shares her own tendency to self-effacement. His unhappy and unloved childhood has given him much of Esther's self-hatred, and while his own self-conception as minor is not physically marked, he does repeatedly try to oust himself from his rightful position as the novel's romantic hero, not merely through being drawn to the wrong woman (Pet Meagles), but also in giving her up to his rival, writing himself off as 'Nobody', as four chapter headings remind us. It seems fitting that Little Dorrit should love a man who considers himself 'nobody', and there is a kind of wish-fulfilment in these two self-doubting characters each recognising the importance of the other. At the same time, the goodness they embody has its drawbacks. Arthur's insistent belief in his own unworthiness makes him a singularly passive hero who is incapable of recognising Little Dorrit's feelings for him for most of the novel – and even then tries to prevent her from acting upon them – while Little Dorrit's insistence on propping up her father's delusions lends credence to Patricia Ingham's claim that 'Little Dorrit/Amy herself is a contradictory and disruptive figure who sustains nothing more than a sadly dysfunctional family.'[143]

After all, Little Dorrit's littleness is not – like Esther's scarring – something that is done *to her*, but something that she has done *to herself*. Her restricted growth has resulted from self-deprivation: we are told immediately after she has first been described that one of the 'moral phenomena' of Little Dorrit is her 'extraordinary repugnance to dining in company',[144] and it soon becomes apparent that she saves her food to give to her father. We repeatedly see her refuse food, go without sleep and resist any capitulation to her bodily needs – even when respite is offered to her. One of her very rare moments of self-assertion arises from Flora Finching's kindly suggestion that she is overworked and ought to rest: 'I have always been strong enough to do what I want to do,' she insists, having refused lavish offers of refreshment in favour of 'bread and butter and tea'.[145] Unlike Esther's smallpox, then, which was contracted in a straightforward act of mercy – nursing another in need – Little Dorrit chooses not to alleviate her condition when she could, and more than acquiesces in her family's neglect. This leads Byler to speak of her 'self-mutilation', and Schor of her 'willed smallness'; although it is counter-intuitive to think of a Dickensian heroine as self-harming, and the thrust of the narrative works to validate the selflessness and dutifulness that Little Dorrit embodies, I think that very embodiment does complicate our reaction to that moral drive.[146] When the body upon which her goodness is written is represented as disabled, we cannot escape the suggestion that Little Dorrit's virtue is in itself disabling.

Moreover, there are marked limitations to the happy ending the novel offers these two unwilling protagonists. Not only has Little Dorrit had to give up her fortune, but she has chosen to have Arthur burn the papers that would have released him from the undefined sense of guilt that has haunted him throughout the novel and revealed his true parentage, an action which, as Sherri Wolf points out, 'far exceeds Mrs. Clennam's request'.[147] In thwarting the possibility of full understanding for Arthur and working to disseminate guilt as much as to resolve it, Wolf argues that Little Dorrit 'functions as a counter-force to the novel's ostensible plot'.[148] To think of Little Dorrit as working *against* the novel's plot is deeply counter-intuitive when she is held up as the novel's moral exemplar, and when the resolution of its mysteries and the apportioning of its rewards are co-extensive with her marriage.[149] Yet the limitations of those values and the pain and difficulty of embodying them are written on to Little Dorrit's body, which seems to register a kind of resistance to the role she has to play for the novel to function.

The disabling aspect of Little Dorrit's embodiment is further stressed by the representation of the character with whom she is most consistently paired. As Brian Rosenberg points out, Dickens habitually 'express[es] character through images of doubleness, inversion, and opposition such as twins, shadows, and mirrors'.[150] It is therefore worth examining the purpose served by Little Dorrit's 'double', Maggy, the mentally disabled woman who calls her 'Little mother', and who is her exact opposite in having the body of a woman but the mind of a child, 'with large bones, large features, large feet and hands, large eyes, and no hair'.[151] Rather than existing alongside Little Dorrit to establish her normality – as Smike does for Nicholas, for example – Maggy actually serves to highlight Little Dorrit's extraordinariness and to suggest parallels between their experiences. Maggy's heavily laboured largeness emphasises Little Dorrit's littleness, while Maggy's experience of abuse as a child, which has arrested her mental development, reminds us that Little Dorrit's physical development has been stunted by *her* neglect. Maggy's unabashed demands for care and her repeated assertions of hunger serve to emphasise Little Dorrit's refusal to acknowledge her own needs, and the implication that these represent equal and opposite responses to neglect – excessive self-assertion on one hand, excessive self-denial on the other – casts what might otherwise be taken as Little Dorrit's straightforward goodness in a pathological light. Maggy has retained the mind of a ten-year-old, Little Dorrit the body of an eleven-year-old:[152] their pairing highlights the distortion of each, reminding us that Little Dorrit has as much in common with the minor characters (and thus the grotesques) of the novel as with the principal players. While Maggy's presence in the text works to establish Little Dorrit's virtue and underlines her maternal capacities, pairing Little Dorrit with a character who is unambiguously disabled, associated above all with 'the hospital',[153] reminds us of the possibility that we should consider Little Dorrit as belonging in the same category.

Moreover, Dickens provides Little Dorrit with a darker double in Tattycoram, another marginalised and impoverished young woman with a diminutive nickname. The text powerfully registers Tatty's resistance to her status as a minor character, adjunct to Pet Meagles rather than heroine in her own right:

> She was younger than her young mistress, and would she remain to see *her* always held up as the only creature who was young and interesting, and to be cherished and loved? No. She wouldn't, she wouldn't, she wouldn't. What did we think she, Tattycoram, might have been if she had been caressed and cared for in her childhood, like her young mistress?[154]

In Tattycoram's furious repudiation of the beautiful Pet, Dickens offers an inverted mirror-image of the doting Esther's relationship with her 'pet', Ada. The comparison with Little Dorrit is obvious but it is also troubling, for the object of Tatty's jealousy, Pet, was also Little Dorrit's rival for Arthur's affections, and it is hard to resist the sense that Tatty voices exactly the grievances Little Dorrit is not allowed to resent. The comparison between them is underlined when, at the end of the novel, Mr Meagles holds Little Dorrit up to Tattycoram as the example she should follow, as a woman who has embraced her stigmatised and marginalised position, and thus turned it to good: 'The people stand out of her way to let her go by . . . her young life has been one of active resignation, goodness, and noble service.'[155] Yet in order to become like Little Dorrit, what Tatty has to learn is self-repression: she affirms her commitment to a new life by promising not just to count five-and-twenty, as Mr Meagles has so often exhorted her, but to 'count five-and-twenty hundred, five-and-twenty thousand!'[156] By encouraging us to think of Little Dorrit as a character with something to hide, we are led to wonder whether she – like Tatty – has a rage that must be suppressed. We might even wonder whether she has put herself on the starvation diet that Mr Bumble recommended for Oliver Twist in the fear that she, too, may 'turn wicious'.[157]

By writing the restrictive and even distorting aspect of her self-erasing goodness on to her body, implying that she has shrunk herself through goodness to such an extent that her littleness is disabling, Dickens draws our attention to the disabling nature of feminine goodness, and to the complex politics of embodiment and narrative positioning. The perfect heroine, it would seem, has to conceive of herself as minor, and that self-conception can be expressed through her body because Dickens has taught us to associate minorness with physical distortion and disability. Yet if self-effacement has become the condition for narrative centrality, Dickens counter-balances the rewards these heroines enjoy, not only with their own suffering, but also by representing the resentment of those who do not get to share their limelight. This rebelliousness on the part of the marginalised minor character simmers in *Little Dorrit*, and comes to the surface in *Our Mutual Friend* in the figure of Silas Wegg. In this novel, Dickens returns to the figure of the neglected daughter with a distorted body, but allows Little Dorrit's muted resistance to become vocal aggression, creating in Jenny Wren the first of his little women who is allowed to be both 'beautiful' and 'sharp'. However, while Jenny has justly been celebrated as a disabled character who asserts her right to narrative space, her relegation to minor status, and her willingness to take on an assistive narrative role, mark the limitations of 'possible personhood' for disabled characters in Dickens's work. In the violent expulsion of her grotesque alter ego, Silas Wegg, we can see the brutality latent in Dickens's desire for an orderly narrative conclusion, in the fate of the minor character who strains against his allotted narrative role.

### The Active Crutch and the Wooden Leg: Prosthesis, Personhood and the Place of the Minor Character in *Our Mutual Friend*

There is a blend of triumph and relief in many critical accounts of Jenny Wren's characterisation in *Our Mutual Friend* (1865). When Hilary Schor gets round to Jenny at the end of her study of daughters in Dickens, for example, she concludes that Jenny

> seems to offer some other account of property and personhood for Dickens . . . one in which the heroine has a house that is less bleak, and in which she can sign her name to her own (however antic and crooked) story.[158]

The wrongs suffered by Dickens's women have piled up in Schor's account, so that by the time we meet the self-assertive Jenny, she appears as a cross between an avenging angel and a reconciliatory offering.

My own reading of Jenny's characterisation partially bears out Schor's triumphalism. By endowing her with the capacity not only to soothe and to heal suffering, but also to resent it, and with the power not only to assist others through her capacity for imaginative creativity but to name herself, her circumstances and her desires, and by doing so, to change her own story, Dickens enables Jenny to surpass her predecessors, combining the previously incompatible qualities of different kinds of characters. However, in this discussion I want not only to account for the extraordinary power of Jenny's characterisation, but also to offer a balanced reading that acknowledges the limits of her 'possible personhood'. While Jenny is an unprecedentedly flexible minor character, enabled to perform a multiplicity of roles that do indeed give us a sense of her 'roundness', the possibilities of her personhood are none the less circumscribed by her narrative positioning as a minor character. While Jenny is a refreshingly active and vocal disabled character, she is still disabled *as* a character in various important ways. Moreover, it is only by reading her happy ending alongside and against the fate of the novel's other character with 'queer legs', Silas Wegg, that a true picture of Dickens's treatment of physically disabled characters in *Our Mutual Friend* emerges.

Jenny erupts into the novel with an assertion of her right to claim recognition and space: 'I can't get up', she tells her visitors, 'because my back's bad, and my legs are queer. But I'm the person of the house.'[159] This statement is striking because it forces us to recognise *both* Jenny's impairments and her capabilities, drawing our attention as much to her assumption of an adult role and its corresponding status as to her physical suffering and limitations. She resembles Little Nell and Little Dorrit in being an abused daughter who has been deprived of emotional and material support by her inadequate (in this case, alcoholic) father, whom she has had to care for, but she is totally unlike them in claiming recognition for her work. She acknowledges, and forces others to acknowledge, the reversal of their roles by calling her father her 'child', even her 'troublesome bad child'.[160] Unlike Little Nell and Little Dorrit, she does not feel obliged to suffer in silence, but voices her anger when he spends her hard-earned money on drink: '"I wish you had been taken up, and locked up," said the person of the house. "I wish you had been poked into cells and black holes, and run over by rats and spiders and beetles."'[161] It is impossible to imagine Little Nell indulging in such a wish when her grandfather steals her money to gamble with it; indeed, Jenny more closely resembles Little Nell's adversary, Quilp, when she indulges in vengeful fantasies concerning the 'red hot liquor' with which she would choke a (hypothetical) drunken husband,[162] or in her dealings with villain Fascination Fledgeby, in which she gleefully puts pepper underneath his bandages to increase the pain of his wounds.[163]

Yet if she partakes of Quilpishness in these scenes, in others she is the 'poor little dolls' dressmaker',[164] the vulnerable crippled child deserving of our pity. Her 'ecstatic' visions of angel children and her ability to look like an angelic vision herself, a 'little creature looking down out of a Glory of her long bright radiant hair',[165] allies her to sentimental rather than grotesque representations of disabled children, recalling Tiny Tim or Paul Dombey. As well as acting as a wicked nurse to Fledgeby, she is capable of feats of nursing that ally her instead with heroines such as Little Dorrit, acting as an angelic nurse to Eugene Wrayburn, tending to him with 'softened compassion . . . as if she were an interpreter between this sentient world and the insensible man'.[166] Jenny is far from being the first minor character in Dickens to combine sharpness with benevolence – Susan Nipps (in *Dombey and Son*) or Betsey Trotwood (in *David Copperfield*) similarly conceal hearts of gold beneath prickly exteriors – but she is the first to combine sharpness with loveliness, to be both 'crooked' and 'beautiful'.[167]

Not only does her capacity for aggressive self-assertion fail to negate her capacity for pathos, but Dickens actually brings the two together in his representation of her grief for her father. When they bring his body home on a stretcher, her familiar epithet 'my bad child' becomes a piercing lament:

> The brisk little crutch-stick was but too brisk. 'O gentlemen, gentlemen, he belongs to me! . . . he's my child, out without leave. My poor bad, bad boy! and he don't know me, he don't know me! O what shall I do,' cried the little creature, wildly beating her hands together, 'when my own child don't know me!'[168]

When mourning her father's death, Jenny regrets her former harshness, but also recognises and acknowledges that she did her best in a difficult situation, responding to her friend Riah's reassurance that she is 'a good girl . . . a patient girl' with touching honesty:

> 'As for patience,' she would reply with a shrug, 'not much of that, godmother. If I had been patient, I should never have called him names. But I hope I did it for his good. And besides, I felt my responsibility as a mother so much.'[169]

Jenny is spared the dualistic approach that forced Tattycoram to choose between being a Miss Wade or a Little Dorrit, completely consumed by anger or completely repressing every vestige of it. Instead, she is able to acknowledge her anger without clinging to it, forgiving her father without denying his faults.

In her realistic self-assessment, she resembles Dickens's most knowing little woman, the dwarf Miss Mowcher in *David Copperfield*, whose self-proclaimedly 'volatile' character allows her to appear first as a confidante of Steerforth's, and later as the agent of justice who has Littimer arrested.[170] The opening description of Jenny as 'a dwarf – a girl – a something' suggests her kinship with those characters whose littleness is presented as deviant rather than adorable, and Jenny resembles Miss Mowcher in her claim to precocious worldliness, captured by her oft-repeated catch-phrase, '*I* know their tricks and their manners'.[171] However, whereas Miss Mowcher is presumed by David to be morally corrupt and unfeeling because of her performance, and has to make a direct appeal for sympathy before he changes his mind about her, Jenny's moral probity is never seriously in doubt. Moreover, while Miss Mowcher's sharpness forces David to take her seriously, and leads him to accept her reproving injunction 'not to associate bodily defect with mental',[172] it also precludes her from appearing as a sentimental spectacle: because she does not have Tiny Tim's naivety, she is also unable to access his idealised status as a sentimental object. She can name herself 'little Mowcher' but she cannot escape the comic use of her grotesque body, made ridiculous – even after her appeal for sympathy and respect – by her over-sized umbrella.[173] Jenny, on the other hand, *is* shown alternately in a comic, pathetic and even an erotic light, as the narrator draws our attention repeatedly to her beautiful golden hair, falling 'in a beautiful shower over the poor shoulders, that were in need of such adorning rain'.[174] In this image, which brings together Jenny's hunched shoulders and lovely hair, we are faced with a woman both disabled and beautiful.[175]

Moreover, unlike Esther Summerson, Jenny's attractiveness is not based upon her self-deprecation: she clearly sees herself as desirable, and makes the most of the features other people admire. When Sloppy calls on her, in her last appearance in the novel, she lets down her beautiful hair 'with an arch look' and is 'not displeased' by his 'burst of admiration'.[176] She also insists that he recognise her impairments, suggesting that if he wants to 'ornament' her crutch, he had 'better see [her] use it'.[177] Jenny's self-possession impresses Sloppy rather than intimidates him, and he leaves, promising that he will 'soon come back again'.[178] Jenny has been voicing fantasies about the 'Him' she means to marry since her first appearance in the novel, and it is heavily implied that she has found him in Sloppy. Far from being punished for having the self-assertion to claim to be 'the person of the house' and the temerity to imagine herself as the heroine of her own marriage plot, Jenny appears to be rewarded with her heart's desire.

In her ability to fulfil so many different roles and to appear in so many different lights, Jenny is a truly 'round' minor character in a distinctively Dickensian sense: she is not a 'possible person' in her mimetic likeness to a real person or in her psychological complexity (in fact, Jenny's characterisation is thoroughly externalised), but in the multiplicity of roles she is able to inhabit and in the variety of tropes she combines. This is captured in the flexibility of her distinctive catch-phrases and the varying effects of her emphasised physical features, which do represent the 'highly distinctive speech patterns, emphasis on an eccentric gesture or habit, concentration on specific physical features or body parts' that Woloch suggests are typical of the Dickensian minor character,[179] but which in Jenny's case signify so differently at different times as to make her more than the sum of her parts. Despite the small amount of narrative space she actually occupies, she stands out as a character capable of starring in a novel of her own, and in this sense, Jenny represents the acme of Dickens's use of the minor character: she is a person of possibilities who leaps from the page.

Jenny's disability plays an essential part in enabling this flexibility. In every one of the roles I have discussed, her disability is relevant: in enabling her to have her angelic visions, in giving her the experience of suffering that enables her to nurse Eugene so sensitively, in keeping her from the temptations of the streets that she suggests might have corrupted her,[180] and even in enabling her to voice her romantic desires and express a sense of her potential sexuality, as Lizzie and Bella – conventionally attractive, able-bodied women – cannot. As Helena Michie argues, 'Dickens can allow Jenny fantasies of an erotic future precisely because she is crippled, precisely because she does not function traditionally as a heroine. Fantasy and deformity open up a space for the erotic, as does Jenny's (chronological) youth.'[181] Jenny's disability enables her to fulfil the roles that would otherwise be contradictory, acting in itself as a kind of crutch for Dickens, one that is as 'active' as Jenny's own.

Yet enabling as Jenny's disability is in all these ways, Michie's acknowledgement that Jenny 'does not function traditionally as a heroine' points us to the limits of her role in the novel, as does the happy ending with which she is rewarded for her good service to the novel's protagonists. When she had first talked of having a husband, she had told Lizzie that 'He couldn't brush my hair like you do, and he couldn't do anything like you do.'[182] 'He' appeared in that fantasy as a second-best substitute for the companionship of Lizzie herself, which Jenny hopes to have at least until she is married. In fact, Jenny not only accepts Lizzie's marriage to Eugene, but promotes it; she puts her imaginative capabilities at the service of the marriage plot that marginalises her, first drawing out Lizzie's confession of love for Eugene, and then saving Eugene's life by enabling him to recognise his true desire that Lizzie become his wife.[183] Jenny has used her imaginative powers to re-name herself and those around her, naming her true relationship with her father by calling him her 'child',[184] calling Riah her 'Godmother' in recognition of his benevolence,[185] and expressing her own sense of self by abandoning her 'real name', Fanny Cleaver, and 'bestow[ing] upon herself the appellation of Jenny Wren'.[186] By naming Lizzie as Eugene's 'wife', she transforms Eugene's previously destructive and transgressive desire into redemptive love, re-fashioning the narrative of his pursuit of Lizzie – which had seemed likely to end in seduction or tragedy – into a marriage plot that also, as Melissa Free points out, turns 'her best friend into a lady . . . the working girl into a lady and wife'. Yet, as Free argues, this transformation is also a sacrifice for Jenny herself, who in giving Lizzie what she most wants, has to give up her own claim to Lizzie.[187] Even if we do not read their relationship as passionately as does Free, it is still the case that Jenny's own happy ending is made to depend absolutely upon her willingness to put her talents in the service of the novel's main plot, to what Michiel Heyns calls 'the business of a Dickens novel [which is] to arrange the marriage of its heroine, at any price'.[188]

Moreover, Jenny's own marriage puts her firmly back in her marginalised place. Those critics who have celebrated the potency of Jenny's characterisation have struggled to accept it: Stoddard Holmes comments on the 'insufficiency' of this conclusion, while for Schor it is 'inappropriate', if no worse than the marriages of other

Dickensian heroines.[189] Sloppy is a sympathetic character, whose physical strength, intellectual dullness and emotional vulnerability are clearly intended to complement Jenny's physical frailty, intellectual sharpness and emotional resilience – but he is quite definitely a grotesque, minor character, and in accepting him as a suitor, Jenny tacitly accedes to her own place in the narrative economy.[190]

The fate of the minor character who does *not* do so is clearly marked by the characterisation of Silas Wegg, the disabled character who plays a role that is a mirror-image of Jenny's in the parallel plot-line involving the Harmon fortune. Silas's disability is used in the opposite way from Jenny's. Instead of stimulating our sympathy for implied physical suffering, standing for struggle against difficult odds and endowing him with greater capacities for spirituality and imaginativeness, Silas's one-leggedness is made to stand for his moral incompleteness.[191] I am not suggesting that he is represented as monstrous because he is disabled, but rather that his disability is used to express his monstrosity, as when he is said to be

> so wooden a man that he seemed to have taken to his wooden leg naturally, and rather suggested to the fanciful observer that he might be expected . . . to be completely set up with a pair of wooden legs in about six months.[192]

This identification of man and prosthesis is underlined, as Goldie Morgentaler points out, by 'the close rhyming association between Silas's family name of Wegg and his missing body part'.[193] Where Jenny's crutch is used to express her pluckiness, Wegg's wooden leg is used to externalise inner inadequacy. Silas is as necessary to the novel as Jenny, but in the opposite way: he acts not as the reconciling, healing and assistive figure, midwife to the marriage plot, but as a scapegoat, on to whom greed, dishonesty and hollow ambition can be offloaded and expelled.

If this was all that could be said about Silas, he would be a 'wooden' character indeed, but, apparently unable to resist troubling uninterestingly still waters, Dickens invests Silas with a desire for physical – and, by extension, personal – wholeness. He is not just a one-legged character; he is a one-legged character in search of his missing limb, yearning to 'collect [him]self like a genteel person'.[194] As his use of the word 'genteel' suggests, Silas expresses this wish as part of his base desire for social advancement, linking it to his 'prospect for getting on in life', which chimes with Erin O'Connor's suggestion that since 'physical and social mobility' were frequently 'conflated' in writing of the period, 'the discourse of prosthesis [was] infused with class consciousness'.[195] Yet Silas's attempt to buy back his leg bone also resonates at a more profound level than this, representing a resistance not just to his social but also to his narrative positioning.

Silas is an irredeemable character, and it is necessary that he should be so, or we would not be able to enjoy Boffin's machinations to lead him into further villainy, nor his expulsion from the novel (and, with him, the expulsion of the corruption he embodies). We know him to be irredeemable partly because what is wrong with him, visibly, cannot be put right: he can never re-grow his missing leg. Dickens writes Silas's one-leggedness in such a way that it is made expressive of his moral incompleteness, and this incompleteness is therefore inerasable, written as it is on to his body. Silas's yearning for his missing limb therefore stands for a desire for a kind of personhood that he is denied, the wholeness that the narrative schema requires him *not* to acquire. Tellingly, the 1998 BBC adaptation of the novel, in which Silas was made a slightly more sympathetic character, included a dream sequence in which Silas dances on the dust heaps, his leg restored.[196] Adrienne E. Gavin suggests that this scene 'draws specific and empathetic attention to his loss and enables us to read behind Wegg'.[197] It would make little sense for the restoration of Wegg's leg to enable us to 'read behind' his character, unless it is instinctively recognised that Wegg's limitations as a character and his inability to win our sympathy are connected to his leglessness. Dickens uses Wegg's disability to disable him as a character – but also makes us aware of the manœuvre, so that we are not, in fact, able to accept Silas's marginalisation wholeheartedly.

For one thing, Dickens endows Silas with an attractive comic zest, and with a capacity to transform his grim circumstances through imaginative fantasy that allies him with Jenny. Selling ballads, oranges and nuts on a stall in front of a shut-up mansion – later owned by Boffin – Silas has

> not only settled it with himself in course of time, that he was errand-goer by appointment to the house at the corner (though he received such commissions not half a dozen times in a year, and then only as some servant's deputy), but also that he was one of the house's retainers and owed vassalage to it and was bound to leal and loyal interest in it.[198]

It is difficult not to enjoy Silas's capacity to give himself importance in his own eyes by imagining an entire family of employers for himself. Similarly, it is difficult not to smile at the transparency of his attempts to convince Boffin of his qualifications as a man of letters – 'know him? Old familiar Decline and Falling Off of the Rooshan? Rather, sir! Ever since I was not so high as your stick' – to secure better terms for his services – 'I never did 'aggle and I never will 'aggle. Consequently I meet you at once free and fair with – Done for double the money!' – and to help himself to Boffin's veal and ham pie on the grounds that it is 'very mellering to the organ'.[199] The narrator's condemnation of Silas's 'wooden conceit and craft'[200] seems both excessive and po-faced, as though Dickens were thrown off balance by his desire to curtail the possibility of readerly identification with or sympathy for Silas, whilst yet inviting both by making Silas seem rather harmless.

The point, of course, is that Silas is *not* harmless: he embodies the vices of acquisitiveness and ambition that the novel's plot works to expose and expel. Bella Wilfer's similar greed has to be cured through Boffin's assumption of the character of a mercenary miser, a ploy that he also employs against Wegg and his less villainous accomplice, Mr Venus. Whereas Mr Venus cannot be diverted from his honest purpose of giving up blackmail by all Boffin's tempting, Silas completely fails the test, taking advantage of what he believes to be Boffin's dishonesty and showing himself, in Boffin's words, 'artful, and so ungrateful'.[201] Yet because Silas's scheming takes place in the context of Boffin's counter-scheming, there is some basis for Silas's complaints that he has been unfairly treated, comically as these are expressed: 'it's not easy to say how the tone of my mind may have been lowered by my unwholesome reading on the subject of Misers, when you was leading me and others on to think you one yourself, sir'.[202] Boffin has deceived not merely other characters in the novel, but the reader as well: we are led to believe that Boffin really has been corrupted by his fortune, and it is harder, for that reason, to feel truly outraged on his behalf when he is being blackmailed.

Silas's desire to get above himself socially is equally a desire to escape his marginalised narrative position as a minor character; in attempting to plot against Boffin and apportion some of the Harmon inheritance to himself, he attempts to write himself into the major plot-line and appropriate its rewards, to make of himself a major character. Rather than accepting his position, as Jenny does, and working to further the fortunes of the favoured (major) characters, Silas has attempted to usurp the rightful role of the author, seeking to make of himself a major character when the novel's legitimate plotting condemns him to its margins. In the blackmail scheme by which he hopes to extort from Boffin a part of the Harmon fortune, he is motivated, as Mr Venus recognises, by a desire for revenge; when questioned as to why he should feel 'revengefully' against his patron and employer, Silas declares, 'I'm a hundred times the man he is, sir; five hundred times!'[203] Silas's resentment at the illiterate Boffin's accession to a fortune, his insistence that Boffin is a 'usurper', 'the minion of fortune and the worm of the hour', seem grounded in the fact that he and Boffin are, in class terms, much alike.[204] Boffin is Silas's 'better' in social terms only because of his money; without it, he and Silas would be equals. That Silas cannot understand the other respects in which Boffin is his 'better' is obviously a measure of his moral blindness, but it is also something that Boffin deliberately obscures at this point in the novel, tempting Silas on to cheat him by appearing to Silas as a mercenary and dishonest man. The bad taste this leaves in the reader's mouth is likely to make us wonder whether there is something wrong in the narrative order – and, by extension, whether Silas has some grounds for resentment at his marginalised narrative positioning.

The violence of Silas's expulsion from the novel – shaken by Harmon, thrown into a scavenger's cart by Sloppy – and the unvarying vehemence of the narrator's condemnation of him along the way, which appears to preclude any sympathy for his physical sufferings or material deprivation, require some additional explanation, I would suggest, besides simply his wickedness. It seems to me that both Jenny and Silas are avatars for their author, the one an idealised self-projection, the other a debased nightmare. As Hilary Schor has pointed out, Jenny 'fictionalises in much the way Dickens does: she fills imaginary gardens with flowers that defeat "mere" realism; she gives imaginary people no-names that sound like Dickens's . . . turn[ing] horror into comic relief and unexpected blessing'.[205] Silas the social climber, purveyor of literature to those he secretly despises, the man hobbled by his origins, clinging to a crutch of make-believe, seems to me the ugly mirror-image of Jenny and of his author. He *has* to be written out of the novel because of the threat he poses to the novel's legitimate plot, and perhaps even to its legitimate plotter.

Jenny Wren and Silas Wegg exemplify opposite ends of the spectrum of Dickens's treatment of minor characters, and the uses to which he puts disability. One is made a repository of the values the novel celebrates, assisting the progress of its main plot, and is duly rewarded (if put back in her place) at its conclusion; her disability enables her to perform this work, a crucial aspect of her appeal to our sympathy and admiration. The other is an embodiment of the destructive forces the novel works to expose and defeat, attempting to plot on his own account, and is violently cast out as a result; *his* disability is used to mark his non-membership of the narrative community, a measure of his stigmatised difference and sign of his moral distortion. Yet these characters are alike in exceeding their narrative function, pulling our attention towards themselves and causing the reader to resist their containment. Their physical disabilities turn out to be a crucial component of their narrative power: in both cases, disability acts as a narrative prosthesis – to borrow David Mitchell and Sharon Snyder's term[206] – enabling Dickens to put these characters to their particular kinds of narrative work, but also enabling the characters themselves to take hold of the reader's imaginations, to make a claim for space that they are not allotted. In the last analysis, Jenny and Silas demonstrate both how disabled characters enlarge the possibilities of Dickensian characterisation, and how their claim to personhood is always conditional upon their acceptance of minor status, and is subordinated where necessary to the wider demands of the novelistic plot.

## Notes

1. James, '*Our Mutual Friend*', pp. 854–5.
2. Ibid. p. 854, p. 856.
3. Rosenberg, *Little Dorrit's Shadows*, p. 4. Rosenberg offers a helpful summary of the history of critical responses to Dickens's characterisation, pp. 13–20.
4. The idea that disabled people cannot be 'persons' – and thus that a disabled character could not truly be a 'person' either – can be clearly seen in twentieth-century critical writing before the advent of disability studies. For example, when Amélie Oksenberg Rorty is trying to find a definition for 'person' and 'character', and to distinguish between them, she cites disabled people, in passing, as those whose 'personhood' is in doubt, classing them with foetuses and corporations ('A Literary Postscript', p. 322).
5. Forster, *Aspects of the Novel*, p. 49.
6. For example, see Fig. 1.1.
7. Woloch, *The One Vs. the Many*, p. 129.
8. Ibid. p. 35.
9. Forster, *Aspects of the Novel*, p. 49.
10. 'Charles Dickens', *Blackwood's Edinburgh Magazine*, pp. 673–95.
11. See the illustrations on the inside covers of Tomalin, *Charles Dickens*.
12. Davis, *Enforcing Normalcy*, p. 41.
13. Morris, *Dickens's Class Consciousness*, p. 14.
14. Heyns, *Expulsion and the Nineteenth-Century Novel*, pp. 24–5.

15. John, *Dickens's Villains*, p. 20.
16. Rosenberg, *Little Dorrit's Shadows*, p. 4.
17. Dickens, 'A Christmas Carol', p. 83, p. 50.
18. Dickens, *Mutual Friend*, p. 222.
19. For celebratory accounts of Jenny as a welcome exception to Dickensian trends, see Stoddard Holmes, *Fictions*, pp. 57–9; Michie, 'Who Is This in Pain?', pp. 199–212; and Schor, *Dickens and the Daughter of the House*, pp. 198–207.
20. Dickens, *Nickleby*, p. 88.
21. Klages, *Woeful Afflictions*, p. 56.
22. Dickens, *Nickleby*, p. 88.
23. Ibid.
24. Garland-Thomson, *Extraordinary Bodies*, p. 40.
25. John, *Dickens's Villains*, pp. 33–4.
26. Dickens, *Nickleby*, p. 79.
27. Ibid.
28. Ibid. p. 97.
29. Ibid. p. 79.
30. Ibid. p. 97.
31. Ibid. p. 159.
32. Easson, 'Emotion and Gesture in *Nicholas Nickleby*', p. 146.
33. Furneaux, *Queer Dickens*, p. 128.
34. Dickens, *Nickleby*, p. 272.
35. Ibid. p. 273.
36. Stirling, *The Fortunes of Smike*.
37. While this might seem to re-introduce a certain amount of gender trouble, the fact that Smike and Kate never have anything approaching a love scene, and Smike's love for Kate is repeatedly asserted (by Smike himself) to be impossible, may have convinced Stirling that there would be nothing overly problematic about having Smike played by a woman in this version, too.
38. Stirling, *Nicholas Nickleby: A Farce in Two Acts*, II, iii.
39. Dickens, *Nickleby*, p. 443.
40. Marcus, *Dickens: From Pickwick to Dombey*, pp. 123–4.
41. Girard, *The Scapegoat*, p. 119.
42. Michiel Heyns argues that in Dickens's late work, 'the unwaveringly unsentimental treatment of the outcast and of the favourite is more honest . . . Dickens has come to see that the favourites of fortune simply *are* favoured, whether fairly or not' (*Expulsion and the Nineteenth-Century Novel*, p. 124), a proposition that I will explore in more detail in the second half of this chapter.
43. Dickens, *Nickleby*, p. 443.
44. Ibid.
45. Klages, *Woeful Afflictions*, p. 6.
46. Dickens, *Nickleby*, p. 831.

47. Michie, 'From Blood to Law', pp. 131–3. For a similar account, see Marchbanks, 'From Caricature to Character', pp. 3–14.
48. Peter Brooks and Juliet John both treat the externalisation of character as a crucial and defining aspect of melodrama (Brooks, *The Melodramatic Imagination*, pp. 35–6; John, *Dickens's Villains*, pp. 19–20).
49. Dickens, *Nickleby*, p. 24.
50. Ibid. pp. 279–80.
51. Craton, *The Victorian Freak Show*, p. 42.
52. Dickens, *Nickleby*, p. 281.
53. Ibid. p. 290.
54. Ibid. p. 283.
55. Ibid. p. 329.
56. Stoddard Holmes, *Fictions of Affliction*, p. 4.
57. Ibid. p. 114.
58. Mayhew, *London Labour*, vol. 1, p. 329; vol. 4, p. 432.
59. Ibid., vol. 4, p. 431. For further discussion of this issue, see Hayward, 'Those Who Cannot Work'.
60. Easson, 'Emotion and Gesture in *Nicholas Nickleby*', p. 143.
61. Dickens, *Old Curiosity Shop*, p. 27.
62. Ibid. p. 53.
63. Ibid. p. 45.
64. Ibid. p. 148.
65. Schor, *Dickens and the Daughter of the House*, p. 36.
66. Garland-Thomson, *Extraordinary Bodies*, p. 59.
67. Byler, 'Dickens's Little Women', p. 228.
68. Bowen, *Other Dickens: Pickwick to Chuzzlewit*, p. 133; Marcus, *Dickens: From Pickwick to Dombey*, p. 129.
69. Dickens, *Old Curiosity Shop*, p. 6.
70. Schlicke, *Dickens and Popular Entertainment*, p. 128. John also calls Quilp a 'pantomimic' villain (*Dickens's Villains*, p. 11).
71. Dickens, *Old Curiosity Shop*, p. 9, p. 14.
72. Ibid. p. 9. Master Humphrey is the narrator of the first three chapters of the novel, who subsequently disappears from the text.
73. Dickens, *Old Curiosity Shop*, p. 79.
74. Ibid. p. 80.
75. Ibid.
76. Schor, *Dickens and the Daughter of the House*, p. 34.
77. Carey, *The Violent Effigy*, p. 26.
78. Craton, *The Victorian Freak Show*, p. 54.
79. Dickens, *Old Curiosity Shop*, p. 93.
80. Ibid. p. 52.
81. Craton, *The Victorian Freak Show*, p. 43.
82. Dickens, *Old Curiosity Shop*, p. 220.
83. Ibid. p. 207.
84. Ibid. p. 10.

85. Ibid. p. 220.
86. For a detailed discussion of the different styles of Cattermole and Browne, see Steig, *Dickens and Phiz*, pp. 53–7.
87. Dickens, *Old Curiosity Shop*, p. 213.
88. Silver, *Victorian Literature and the Anorexic Body*, p. 83.
89. Byler, 'Dickens's Little Women', p. 222, p. 227.
90. Silver, *Victorian Literature and the Anorexic Body*, p. 85.
91. Dickens, *Old Curiosity Shop*, p. 481.
92. Steig, *Dickens and Phiz*, pp. 54–5.
93. Morris, *Dickens's Class Consciousness*, p. 12.
94. Dickens, *Old Curiosity Shop*, p. 437.
95. Ibid. p. 275.
96. Marcus, *Dickens: From Pickwick to Dombey*, p. 136.
97. Dickens, *Old Curiosity Shop*, pp. 482–3.
98. Ibid. p. 552.
99. Ibid. p. 274.
100. Kaplan, *Sacred Tears*, p. 40.
101. Alex Woloch observes this in a footnote, calling Esther 'at once a startlingly major and minor character, collapsing the terms of this study in on themselves', but he does not elaborate on why or how this is the case (*The One Vs. the Many*, p. 347).
102. Dickens, *Little Dorrit*, p. 64, p. 180.
103. Dickens, *Bleak House*, p. 25.
104. Ibid. p. 38.
105. Ibid. p. 35.
106. Ibid. p. 27.
107. Ibid. p. 528.
108. Ibid. p. 639.
109. Ibid. pp. 568–9.
110. Ibid. p. 914. The same can also be said of John Jarndyce, whose 'generosity', in Esther's words, 'rose above my disfigurement' (Ibid. p. 639). The complexities and ambiguities of his ultimately abandoned attempt to marry Esther are too many to be adequately treated here, but it is worth noting that the fundamental worthiness of his love – as opposed to Guppy's – is established by his reaction to her scarred face, as indeed is the moral worth of Ada and the otherwise erring Richard.
111. Lennard J. Davis goes so far as to argue that Esther embodies the fact that, in the nineteenth-century novel, 'disfigurement and disability become a positive virtue, particularly in women', suggesting that Esther is 'disfigured by smallpox, not as punishment for her sins, but as a mark of female suffering and spiritual transcendence over the body' ('Dr. Johnson', p. 69.) While I agree that Esther's disfigurement is not punitive in any straightforward sense, I hope to complicate Davis's reading here by demonstrating the painful and troubling aspects of Esther's literalised self-effacement.

112. Dickens, *Bleak House*, p. 24; Gordon, *Sensation and Sublimation*, p. 175.
113. Dickens, *Bleak House*, p. 914.
114. Ibid.
115. Ibid. pp. 26–7.
116. Ibid. p. 460, p. 463.
117. Ibid. p. 535.
118. Bailin, *The Sickroom in Victorian Fiction*, pp. 105–6.
119. Schor, *Dickens and the Daughter of the House*, p. 121.
120. Dickens, *Bleak House*, p. 528.
121. Ibid. p. 528.
122. Michie, 'Who Is This in Pain?', p. 207.
123. Dickens, *Bleak House*, p. 26.
124. Ibid. pp. 639–40.
125. Dickens, *Dombey*, p. 718.
126. Dickens, *Copperfield*, p. 217.
127. Dickens, *Little Dorrit*, pp. 52–3.
128. Ibid. p. 30.
129. Ibid. p. 65.
130. Ingham, 'Nobody's Fault', p. 111.
131. Dickens, *Little Dorrit*, pp. 64–5.
132. Dickens, *Copperfield*, p. 627.
133. Ibid. p. 217.
134. Ibid. p. 357.
135. Ibid. p. 381.
136. Dickens, *Little Dorrit*, p. 64.
137. Ibid. p. 180.
138. Sadrin, *Parentage and Inheritance in the Novels of Charles Dickens*, p. 56; Ingham, 'Nobody's Fault', p. 112.
139. Dickens, *Little Dorrit*, p. 84.
140. Byler, 'Dickens's Little Women', p. 224; Craton, *The Victorian Freak Show*, p. 62.
141. Dickens, *Little Dorrit*, pp. 259–60.
142. Ibid. pp. 294–5.
143. Ingham, 'Nobody's Fault', p. 114.
144. Dickens, *Little Dorrit*, p. 65.
145. Ibid. p. 287, p. 283.
146. Byler, 'Dickens's Little Women', p. 236; Schor, *Dickens and the Daughter of the House*, p. 126.
147. Wolf, 'The Enormous Power of No Body', p. 246.
148. Ibid.
149. In this sense, Little Dorrit wholly fits Michiel Heyns's definition of Dickensian heroines as those who 'have their strongest reality as near-symbolic incarnations of the novel's overt teleology, foci of its legitimate designs and repositories of its official values' (*Expulsion and the Nineteenth-Century Novel*, pp. 91–2.)

150. Rosenberg, *Little Dorrit's Shadows*, p. 26.
151. Dickens, *Little Dorrit*, p. 105.
152. Ibid. p. 111, p. 64.
153. Ibid. p. 111.
154. Ibid. p. 322.
155. Ibid. p. 793.
156. Ibid.
157. Dickens, *Oliver Twist*, pp. 50–1.
158. Schor, *Dickens and the Daughter of the House*, p. 207.
159. Dickens, *Mutual Friend*, p. 222.
160. Ibid. p. 240.
161. Ibid. p. 241.
162. Ibid. p. 243.
163. Ibid. p. 724.
164. Ibid. p. 243.
165. Ibid. p. 240, p. 281.
166. Ibid. p. 739.
167. Ibid. p. 228, p. 240.
168. Ibid. p. 731.
169. Ibid. p. 732.
170. Dickens, *Copperfield*, p. 323, pp. 835–6.
171. Dickens, *Mutual Friend*, p. 222, p. 224 and *passim*.
172. Dickens, *Copperfield*, p. 452.
173. Ibid. p. 450, p. 453.
174. Dickens, *Mutual Friend*, p. 347.
175. For a contrasting reading of this scene, see Michie, *The Flesh Made Word*, p. 100.
176. Dickens, *Mutual Friend*, p. 808, p. 809.
177. Ibid. p. 810.
178. Ibid. p. 811.
179. Woloch, *The One Vs. the Many*, p. 129.
180. Dickens, *Mutual Friend*, p. 732.
181. Michie, 'Who Is This in Pain?', p. 211.
182. Dickens, *Mutual Friend*, p. 234.
183. Ibid. p. 347, pp. 741–2.
184. Ibid. p. 240, p. 731 and *passim*.
185. Ibid. p. 725, p. 732.
186. Ibid. p. 333. For a detailed discussion of the significance of Jenny's name, see Free, 'Freaks That Matter', pp. 263–268. It seems significant that Jenny names herself, rather than being re-named by her rescuer like her predecessor in *The Old Curiosity Shop*, the Marchioness.
187. Ibid. pp. 268–9.
188. Heyns, *Expulsion and the Nineteenth-Century Novel*, p. 92.
189. Schor, *Dickens and the Daughter of the House*, p. 203; Stoddard Holmes, *Fictions of Affliction*, p. 59. Talia Schaffer provides an alternative reading of this relationship, arguing that is based on a

kind of care-giving that the novel validates as the basis of every good marriage, so that 'what makes [it] viable is not [Jenny's] sexuality but her sociality'. This argument is highly persuasive but works, I think, only in the context of Schaffer's wider reading of Dickens's characters – fundamentally different from my own – in which they are not major or minor, but 'reconceptualize[d] [. . .] as egalitarian members of a [care] community' ('Disabling Marriage', p. 204).

190. Critics such as Martha Stoddard Holmes have treated Sloppy as intellectually disabled (*Fictions of Affliction*, p. 6, p. 59), but it seems to me a moot point whether Sloppy's eccentricities of speech and fixation on particular ideas and activities – such as turning Betty Higgins's mangle – actually exceed those of other non-disabled minor male characters who are supposed to be distinguished by their simplicity and fidelity, and are often married off to minor female characters who greatly exceed them in acuity, such as *David Copperfield*'s Mr Barkis, who expresses few ideas besides being willin', and marries Peggotty, or *Dombey and Son*'s Mr Toots, who marries Susan Nipps despite his comic vacuity.

191. Dickens had already amputated a character's legs for punitive and (cruelly) comic effect in *Barnaby Rudge*, in which Simon Tapertit, Gabriel Varden's over-reaching and treacherous apprentice, loses his legs in the Gordon Riots; his injury is depicted as poetically just rather than lamentable (*Barnaby Rudge*, p. 657). The totally different symbolism of the hero Joe Willet's lost arm illustrates how varied Dickens's use of disability could be, even within one novel. Joe's relation to Simon partially mirrors Jenny's relation to Silas, in that both Simon and Silas are punished for trying to get above their social (and narrative) place, while Jenny and Joe play assistive plot roles.

192. Dickens, *Mutual Friend*, p. 43.
193. Morgentaler, 'Dickens and the Scattered Identity of Silas Wegg', p. 92.
194. Dickens, *Mutual Friend*, p. 82.
195. Ibid.; O'Connor, *Raw Material*, p. 130.
196. *Our Mutual Friend* (BBC, 1998).
197. Gavin, 'Dickens, Wegg, and Wooden Legs'.
198. Dickens, *Mutual Friend*, p. 45.
199. Ibid. p. 52, p. 52, p. 58.
200. Ibid. p. 58.
201. Ibid. p. 789.
202. Ibid. p. 790.
203. Ibid. p. 582.
204. Ibid. p. 491, p. 309.
205. Schor, *Dickens and the Daughter of the House*, p. 201.
206. Mitchell and Snyder, *Narrative Prosthesis*, pp. 48–9.

Chapter 2

# At the Margins of Mystery: Sensational Difference in Wilkie Collins

'Mr Blake!' he said. 'Look at the man's face. It is a face disguised – and here's a proof of it!'

He traced with his finger a thin line of livid white, running backward from the dead man's forehead, between the swarthy complexion, and the slightly-disturbed black hair. 'Let's see what is under this,' said the Sergeant, suddenly seizing the black hair, with a firm grip of his hand.

My nerves were not strong enough to bear it. I turned away again from the bed. . . . 'He's pulling off his wig!' whispered Gooseberry, compassionating my position, as the only person in the room who could see nothing.

There was a pause – and then a cry of astonishment among the people round the bed.

'He's pulled off his beard!' cried Gooseberry.

There was another pause – Sergeant Cuff asked for something. The landlord went to the washhand-stand, and returned to the bed with a basin of water and a towel.

Gooseberry danced with excitement on the chair. 'Come up here, along with me, sir! He's washing off his complexion now!'

The Sergeant suddenly burst his way through the people about him, and came, with horror in his face, straight to the place where I was standing. . . .

'Open the sealed letter first –' . . . I read the name that he had written. It was – *Godfrey Ablewhite*.

'Now,' said the Sergeant, 'come with me, and look at the man on the bed.'

I went with him and looked at the man on the bed.
GODFREY ABLEWHITE![1]

In this scene, at the climax of Wilkie Collins's most famous detective novel, *The Moonstone* (1868), the disguise of the thief is literally washed away, so that beneath the face of the dark stranger, the face of the familiar villain emerges. As readers, we have been led to suspect the disabled servant Rosanna Spearman, the trio of Indians, and the transgressively strong-minded and uncooperative heroine Rachel Verinder, but the true culprit turns out to be a man who is, nominally and literally, able and white.

The dynamics of the scene are doubly sensational. On one hand, it enacts the narrative upending of the social order, in putting the character with the most social capital, as a white, handsome, able-bodied, charitable, respectable gentleman, in the position of the villain. Whereas melodrama frequently reveals the morally elevated but socially oppressed to be entitled, by birth, to a higher social station, and the corrupt but socially powerful to have usurped their position,[2] Collins effectively reverses this traditional mechanism for reconciling the novelistic and social orders. He reveals the thief to be not a foreign sailor in disguise as a gentleman, but a gentleman in disguise as a foreign sailor. At the same time, the scene is sensational in a somatic as well as a social sense, with the bodily appearance of the sailor revealed to be nothing but a red herring, as one of the most fundamental signs by which bodies are read and categorised in the novel – skin colour – is washed away. No wonder the narrator, Franklin Blake, turns away in horror, unable to watch, for the revelation of the culprit's identity involves a dismantling of the body that is liable to induce vertigo in any reader, even if we guiltily share Gooseberry's childishly unapologetic fascination.

The scene enacts and literalises the proposition that has underpinned the detective plot of the whole novel, which is that the body itself is an unreliable sign. Collins has encouraged us to place a high premium on the signs of the body, supplying detailed physical descriptions of every character, as though this will help us decipher their identity in relation to the mystery at hand. Who is beautiful, who is handsome, who is ugly, disabled, racially other – these are the signs we have been encouraged at every turn to look for and decipher, and yet here they are revealed to be totally unreliable. It is not simply that the villain turns out to have been handsome and innocent-looking; he also turns out to have been able to fake the signs of the body completely, until the hand of the detective deciphers them in death.

As my reading of this scene hopefully makes clear, the questions raised by characterisation and embodiment in Collins's work both build on those discussed in the last chapter and offer some new departures. Where Dickens has long been seen as the great creator of character, Collins's work, strongly associated as it is with the genre of sensationalism, has instead been read as primarily plot-driven. Whereas this used to be seen as the cause of Collins's inadequacies when it came to characterisation,[3] there has in recent years been a critical shift towards seeing Collins's plot-driven treatment of character as innovative and exciting; Ronald Thomas, for example, suggests that 'the most significant contribution to the history of the novel made by Collins and the other immensely popular sensation novelists is not in their construction of sensational plots, but in their conversion of character into plot'.[4] The image of character *becoming* plot neatly captures the way in which Collins's mysteries depend upon the unstable (because unknown) relation of characters to the plot at hand: is the character before us the thief, or the virtuous hero who will be rewarded by the marriage plot? Will this minor character assume importance in the plot that is to come, or is their presence merely a red herring?

The body is one of the main signs by which we can attempt to decipher characters' identities when all other signs can be faked; when, as in the quotation above, the signs of the body are themselves fraudulent, the instability of character in relation to the plot becomes truly dizzying. Peter Brooks observes that when we read any narrative, 'we read in a spirit of confidence, and also a state of dependence, that what remains to be read will re-structure the provisional meanings of the already read'.[5] In Collins's work, we are in fact forced to read in a breathless state of anticipation based on a *lack* of confidence in our own reading, as we await the plot twist that will pull the carpet from under our feet. It is because we do not know who characters are in relation to the plot that mystery is sustained and sensation generated by the final revelation. At the same time, we read knowing that such a final settlement *will* be made, and therefore that the instability of characters' identities is only temporary. Yet this solution is itself rendered problematic by Collins's approach to his characters' bodies; Thomas's assertion that in Collins's fiction 'identity can be ascertained with finality because it is grounded in the verifiable and material truth of the body'[6] underestimates the extent to which Collins undermines our faith in the availability of such a stable 'truth'.

By representing disabled characters who are objects of admiration and love, and able-bodied characters who see themselves as deformed because their love is rejected, beautiful women with masculine intellects and women with massively powerful bodies and exaggeratedly feminine minds, aggressive men who cross-dress and conventionally handsome men with entirely feminine behaviour, Collins destabilises the categories by which we read bodies.[7] Gender, class, race and, above all, disability are no longer fixed hierarchies that are written on the body for us to read. In an age of phrenology, when, as Pamela Gilbert points out, 'bodies were not merely developed or decorated according to a certain social class, but were biologically classed',[8] Collins's sustained assault on our ability to read the bodies of his characters sensationally undermines narrative and social order. When his contemporary, Henry Mansel, complained that characters in sensation fiction were mere representatives of 'classes', rather than truly convincing individuals,[9] he may have intended only to denigrate Collins's work (and work like it), but he also draws our attention to the way in which the hierarchically arranged categories by which characters are sorted in novels (and wider society) are highlighted by Collins's treatment of character. As Ann Cvetkovich puts it, Collins's fiction 'renders social structures not just tangible or concrete, but visible . . . produc[ing] the embodiment, in both the literal and the figurative senses, of social structures'.[10] The characters whose embodiment is so used are sufficiently complex to destabilise these very containing structures, and this includes the disabled characters who, as Kate Flint points out, are represented in such a way as 'to collapse boundaries between the able-bodied and the impaired'.[11]

While there is no doubt that Collins's representation of disabled characters is fascinating precisely for this reason, I am not suggesting that Collins should be retrospectively recruited for twenty-first-century liberal causes. Mark Mossman goes too far, I think, in claiming that in 'Collins's work the abnormal body becomes the disabled body, in our sense of the term; representations of the abnormal become critical potentialities and locations of transformation, moments of disability perspective'.[12] In his representation of characters such as Rosanna Spearman, Limping Lucy and Ezra Jennings, Collins does indeed invest sympathy and attention in characters whose stigmatised bodies hold them at a painful distance from the narrative centre, but he also makes exploitative use of the unusual body, displaying characters' physical difference for sensational effect – and sometimes, as in *The Law and the Lady*, he does both in his treatment of a single character. As D. A. Miller's seminal Foucauldian analysis of *The Woman in White* demonstrates, Collins's novel is somatically oriented not merely in highlighting his characters' bodies and bodily sensations, but in seeking to affect the reader's body through the shocks and thrills of the narrative.[13] While this may sometimes take the form of de-naturalising our own bodily sensations and senses – for example, in the representation of Lucilla Finch's blindness in *Poor Miss Finch* – and thus encourage more sympathetic identification with those whose bodies are constructed as aberrant,[14] it also takes the form of displaying bodily difference in order to make us start or shriek, where the same character's body *could* be represented in a much less dramatic (and much less dehumanising) way. When Miserrimus Dexter is described in his wheelchair as 'a fantastic and frightful apparition, man and machinery blended in one',[15] for example, it would be disingenuous to claim this as a moment of 'disability perspective' rather than simply (or at least simultaneously) an invitation to gawk.

Moreover, while Collins does indeed present us with plot-lines in which traditional hierarchies are overturned – so that women make the best detectives, gentleman philanthropists the worst villains, and vulnerable 'cripples' the best plotters – his conclusions almost always re-establish the order that has been so threatened. While it is true that our confidence in these restorative conclusions is tempered by the temporary unsettling of the categories by which the novel (and society) is ordered, and characters' uncertain relation to plot along the way has opened up disconcerting possibilities for mobility and flux, it is none the less the case that the final positioning of Collins's characters tends to be conventional.

This liminal positioning of disability in Collins's work actually mirrors Collins's own critical position rather well: he has not enjoyed the solid dominance of Dickens, but nor has he ever been cast into critical oblivion like Yonge and Craik. Tamar Heller has convincingly argued that Collins's fiction actually stages his own uncertain relationship to the literary canon, enacting the suppression of the feminine (specifically of feminine writing) in order to suppress sensationalism's inheritance from the female gothic, and establish the novels' claim to literary seriousness.[16] Mark Mossman and Sue Lonoff have both drawn attention to Collins's own unusual body and frail health, suggesting that his identity as an invalid inflected his portrayal of disabled characters and perhaps fuelled his interest.[17] Certainly, the sheer number of physically impaired characters in Collins's fiction is striking; whether this is connected to a humanitarian and socially radical spirit (as Mossman, Stoddard Holmes and Flint suggest), or to a more straightforward desire to shock (as D. A. Miller might have it), it surely contributed to the characterisation of sensation fiction as being *in itself* aberrant and unhealthy, acting on the body of its readers in a destructive and dangerous way.[18]

Before examining Collins's complex engagement with disability in his later works, *The Moonstone* (1868), *The Law and the Lady*

(1875) and *Poor Miss Finch* (1872), it will be helpful to turn first to the novel which established his reputation as a sensationalist, *The Woman in White* (1860). In Marian Halcombe and Count Fosco, Collins creates characters whose unusual bodies disrupt the flow of narrative attention to such an extent that he risks displacing the main characters completely; his containment of this risk, and the question of why he raises it in the first place, are the issues with which I begin.

## 'Sensations which I would rather not feel': Stealing the Show in *The Woman in White*

In the last chapter, I suggested that Dickens's minor characters are continually at risk of stealing the show from his 'straight' principals, the eccentricities and peculiarities that mark their minorness actually rendering them more interesting to the reader than their supposedly dominant counterparts. In *The Woman in White*, Collins pushes the Dickensian structure of the pattern hero and heroine, surrounded by vivid minor characters, to a sensational extreme, rendering his heroine *so* blank that she is literally exchanged for someone else, and his minor characters so vivid that they actually wrest control of the novel away from its narrator at certain points. While the novel does not prominently feature disabled characters (apart from the archetypally hypochondriac invalid, Mr Fairlie), sensation is generated by bodily difference, and our reaction to the spectacle of such difference is tested and teased in the depiction of Marian Halcombe and Count Fosco.

Both these characters ostensibly play an assistive role, Marian acting as confidante and foil to the novel's romantic leads, Laura and Walter, and Fosco as the side-kick to the novel's arch-villain, Sir Percival. However, both characters draw our attention away from the supposedly central characters and towards themselves, partly because of their unusual (and stigmatised) bodies. Acting as mirror-images to one another, each registering the other's attractiveness and calling our attention to the central role they *should* play, Fosco and Marian disrupt the plot that works to sideline them, demonstrating the sensational power of the unusual body.

Walter's first description of Marian, which records his astonishment at the juxtaposition of her conventionally feminine body and incongruously masculine, hirsute face, plays with the novelistic tradition of describing a character by itemising their salient (and synecdochal) bodily features, from which we can infer more about their interiority and their role in the novel to come. Here, bodily features are listed, only for the significance they had been accruing to be overturned, as Walter registers '(with a sense of surprise which words fail to express), The lady is ugly!'[19] Walter's close, even lascivious, attention to Marian's physical beauty while he admires her from behind, and his excitement at the prospect of seeing her close up, had led us to expect that we were to meet a conventionally attractive heroine, and to presume that she would be the romantic heroine of the story. We have been primed for such a meeting by the fact that Walter's preparation for his new life at Limmeridge consisted of 'wondering . . . what the Cumberland ladies would look like',[20] as though this would dictate the shape of the marriage plot to come. Now, however, reader and narrator find that our expectations have led us to miscast Marian, as the apparently beautiful heroine turns out to be a character whose body is rendered extraordinary by its incongruence with her face, thus surely relegating her to the status of a minor character and, in Walter's terms, ugliness.[21] His exaggerated protestations of surprise testify to the anger and shame he retrospectively feels at the erotic desire he felt for her before he saw her face, an experience that so disorientates him that it produces 'a sensation oddly akin to the helpless discomfort familiar to us all in sleep, when we recognise yet cannot reconcile the anomalies and contradictions of a dream'.[22] There is, however, nothing dreamlike about the description of Marian. Its vividness derives from its particularity and detail, qualities that are strikingly absent from the subsequent description of her sister Laura; indeed, Walter actually suggests that the reader substitute for such a description our own memory 'of the first woman who quickened the pulses within you'.[23] All beloved women, it seems, are interchangeable: it is the unmarriageable Marian who is one of a kind, and who commands our attention.

The recognition that Marian is far more vivid and attractive than her bland, passive sister Laura is offered within the text only by Count Fosco, who avows a preference for 'magnificent' Marian over 'poor pretty flimsy blonde' Laura.[24] Disconcerting as it is to find that, as readers, we are more in tune with the villain's perception of Marian and Laura than the hero's, we may find ourselves more disconcerted still by the possibility that Marian returns Fosco's admiration. Like Marian herself, Fosco combines incongruent bodily features, in the juxtaposition of his powerfully masculine presence – '[h]e looks like a man who could tame anything' – with his fondness for pets and his feminine palate, to which he draws attention: '"A taste for sweets,' he said in his softest tones and tenderest manner, 'is the innocent taste of women and children. I love to share it with them."'[25]

Marian attempts to forestall any possibility that she could find him physically attractive by casting his bodily excess as repulsive, noting primly that she has 'always especially disliked corpulent humanity'.[26] Yet, in his aberrance, he is far more vivid than Walter, as Marian herself admits: 'It absolutely startles me, now he is in my mind, to find how plainly I see him! – how much more plainly than I see Sir Percival, or Mr Fairlie, or Walter Hartright.'[27] She explicitly attests to the disruptive, disturbing effect his physicality has upon her, when she records that his eyes 'have at times a cold, clear, beautiful, irresistible glitter in them, which forces me to look at him, and yet causes me sensations, when I do look, which I would rather not feel'.[28]

When Fosco purloins and reads her diaries, he gloats over these descriptions: 'I feel how vivid an impression I must have produced to have been painted in such strong, such rich, such massive colours as these.'[29] Although, of course, we accept that, as the novel's villain, Fosco can never be a serious romantic prospect for its detective–heroine, yet his claim to have a disproportionately strong effect upon her is well founded. Fosco is only the henchman for the real villain, Percival Glyde, but Marian's feelings towards Percival are thrown into the shade by the murderous rage that Fosco's professions of admiration incite in her: '"Walter!" she said, "if ever those two men are at your mercy, and if you are obliged to spare one of them, don't let it be the Count."'[30] Just as Laura's blankness threatens her place as the novel's heroine, so Fosco's vividness enables him to usurp the position of master-villain. Through inserting his own commentary into Marian's diary, he even briefly usurps the editorial role of its controlling narrator, Walter.

However, if Marian and Fosco's energies sustain the novel, it seems that they must be quenched at its resolution. In Fosco's case, narrative justice demands such a defeat, and when we last see him, stretched out on a slab in the Paris morgue, 'unowned, unknown; exposed to the flippant curiosity of a French mob', we must be aware that it is poetically just that a villain who has so enjoyed his own powers of performance and narrative should meet the 'dreadful end' of becoming an inanimate spectacle.[31] Marian's silencing, while equally necessary for the restoration of social and narrative order, is far more painful and disappointing. After so much valiant detecting and counter-plotting in Walter's absence, once he returns, she is denied any part in his long-awaited confrontation with Fosco, and there is more than a trace of relish in the emphasis of Walter's remark that '[i]t was my turn to hold *her*'.[32] Although Walter claims to give her the last line of the narrative, assigning to her the role of the 'good angel' who should 'end our story', he does not risk returning the pen to her hands.[33]

The novel's conclusion is essentially restorative of the social order it had appeared to discredit. The wicked baronet, Sir Percival, is revealed to be illegitimate, and therefore a usurper of the social role he had misused; Laura is re-married to a more worthy husband and provides a male heir to inherit her property; Marian is safely contained in the role of maiden aunt. This conclusion also re-asserts the hierarchical arrangement of bodies that had been temporarily reversed by its sensational depiction of a sexually magnetic 'corpulent' man and an erotically appealing woman 'altogether wanting in those feminine attributes of gentleness and pliability', a state of affairs that is written on her face, in 'the dark down on her upper lip [which] was almost a moustache', and her 'large, firm, masculine mouth and jaw'.[34] However, their ultimate silencing and sidelining does not altogether undo the previous investment of attention and even erotic appeal in characters whose bodies are declared aberrant and inadequate, an investment that anticipates Collins's representation of disabled characters in his later work.

Moreover, the apparent interchangeability of Laura and her illegitimate, dispossessed and half-mad half-sister, Anne Catherick, throws into doubt the legitimacy of the marriage plot that ostensibly resolves some of the novel's more troubling questions. If Laura and Anne look so like one another that they can be put in one another's places by the novel's villains, then why does Walter fall in love at first sight with Laura, but not Anne? As Ann Cvetovich points out, Laura's first appearance is *preceded* by Anne's, and so we are forced to conclude that it is Laura's wealth and social status, as much as her beauty, that ensnare Walter, even while we are being asked to attribute his feelings wholly to the physicality that supposedly attests to her character.[35] If that physicality is capable of being read so differently by others, does it have any stable meaning at all – and can the marriage plot legitimately be based upon it? Collins was to return to these questions with greater urgency in *The Law and the Lady* and *Poor Miss Finch*, but they haunt *The Woman in White*, and are not wholly laid to rest by the conclusion, which, as Judith Sanders puts it, offers a 'fearful and angry view' of marriage as a narrative destiny for women,[36] and only partially works to reconcile us to Marian's sidelining in the narrative settlement. Clearly, these questions continued to trouble Collins, for in *The Moonstone*, the exclusion of the 'ugly' woman from the marriage plot plays a major role in the narrative.

## 'He ought to have known it': Reading the Signs of the Body in *The Moonstone*

When we first meet the disabled servant, Rosanna Spearman, she is marked as a minor character in every possible way. The narrator, Gabriel Betteredge, goes so far as to refuse to play his customary role and relate her back story, on the grounds that it cannot possibly be important, forestalling readerly curiosity with the blandishment, 'I don't like to be made wretched without any use, and no more do you.'[37] Of course, this unwillingness to narrate her sad history is couched in terms of his sympathy for her, and is based on the assumption that we too would be made 'wretched', were we to hear it. Still, our attention is being drawn to the fact that, while we *would* sympathise *if* we knew more, there is no necessity for us to do so: Rosanna does not merit that much space in the narrative. She offers a kind of commentary on her own narrative position when she describes to Gabriel the spot to which she is continually drawn, the shivering sands, as 'look[ing] as if it had hundreds of suffocating people under it – all struggling to get to the surface, and all sinking lower and lower in the dreadful deeps!'[38] Rosanna herself appears as a suffocated character with no way of getting to the surface of a narrative, which, whatever it will be about, is explicitly *not* about her.

Written off from the very beginning as a character in whom it would be 'of no use' to invest our attention, Rosanna is briefly revealed to have a criminal past, to have reformed and been taken on as a housemaid by Lady Verinder as an act of charity, and to be 'the plainest woman in the house, with the additional misfortune of having one shoulder bigger than the other'.[39] As this summary suggests, Rosanna is marginalised in almost every possible way: in social terms as a working-class disabled woman, and in narrative terms as a servant who is unlikely to generate the standard plot-line involving servant-girls – as inappropriate objects of desire for the hero or villain of the piece – because she is disabled and ugly. The only clue to her possible importance to the plot at hand – the criminal past that may direct our attention to her as a possible suspect as the moonstone's thief – turns out to be a red herring. Rosanna will matter as a romantic agent far more than as a suspect, and this is the identity that our first view of her body totally obscures.

Just as we can confidently identify Rosanna as a marginal character at first sight, so Franklin Blake is made to fit the mould of a romantic hero, as 'a bright-eyed young gentleman ... with a rose in his button-hole, and a smile on his face that might have set the

Shivering Sand itself smiling at him in return'.[40] Before we know anything specific about Franklin's character in the sense of his personality, we recognise the character in which he appears here, as the type of a romantic hero, in the melodramatic tradition. It should not therefore surprise us that Rosanna reacts to him *as* a type, falling in love with him on the instant, before she knows anything about him: 'Her complexion turned of a beautiful red, which I had never seen in it before; she brightened all over with a kind of speechless and breathless surprise.'[41] After all, women throughout the novel, from the heroine Rachel to Rosanna's fellow housemaid Penelope, react to Franklin's sexual allure and his narrative and social status as a handsome, able-bodied, upper-class gentleman. What *is* surprising is the importance with which Rosanna's desire comes to be invested. It turns out to be the source of the mystery to which much of the rest of the novel is devoted: her love for Franklin is the clue the other characters miss, and his failure to notice her has consequences not only tragic to herself, but of the utmost significance for Franklin and Rachel. It is because Rosanna loves Franklin that she acts to conceal what she knows to be his part in the theft (not realising, of course, that he was acting under the influence of opium and therefore without his own knowledge), and because she loves him that she tries to use her knowledge, and her concealment of it, to win his attention. It is because she despairs at his failure to notice her, even then, that she buries the evidence of the stained nightgown, leaves the letter that explains it all with her friend Lucy, and kills herself, taking her knowledge with her and impeding the solving of the crime for a large chunk of the novel. Both providing the ultimate explanation and motivating its concealment, Rosanna's love for Franklin literally holds up the mystery.

This is true not only in a structural sense – as her buried story, in the form of her letter, directs us to the buried clue that will unlock the mystery, the stained nightdress – but also in an emotional one. By the time Rosanna kills herself, she has become a powerfully sympathetic character, and Collins both acknowledges and heightens her centrality to our reading experience by giving her a lengthy narrative of her own, in the form of her letter, enabling her to describe her experience of love and perceived rejection in her own words. As Martha Stoddard Holmes puts it, Collins 'not only represents Rosanna as a desiring subject but structures the novel so that she herself articulates her desire and frustration, uttering a memorable critique of normative culture's view of all the marginal human categories she inhabits'.[42] In addition to stimulating sympathy for her, and perhaps even identification with her, Rosanna's letter also works to alienate us from the novel's hero, Franklin, because of his inadequate reaction to it. He refuses even to read the second half of her letter, and cannot understand what he does read, reacting to her very blunt opening statement, 'I love you', with blank incomprehension: 'What does it mean?' he asks Betteredge.[43] Betteredge, in turn, protects Franklin from the knowledge of his own part in Rosanna's suicide, claiming once again that it would be of no use for him to know.[44] Even after her structurally central place in the narrative has been established, Betteredge still sees her as a person whose story is of little utility, and Franklin simply refuses to engage with her attempt to force him to recognise her love. The way that the novel's plot works to reward its major characters, its chosen few, and to marginalise those whose role is fundamentally ancillary, is thrown into painful relief by Rosanna's letter, and by Franklin's reaction to it.

It has already been suggested that Rosanna's impossible love for Franklin had a dignity of its own, in the scene between Betteredge and his daughter Penelope, in which he laughed at the absurdity of 'a housemaid out of a reformatory, with a plain face and a deformed shoulder, falling in love, at first sight, with a gentleman', and she rebuked him for being 'cruel'.[45] Yet if the disparity between Rosanna and Franklin renders her love for him hopeless, Sergeant Cuff also suggests that, far from being 'mad', it is entirely predictable:

> 'Hadn't you better say she's mad enough to be an ugly girl and only a servant?' he asked. 'The falling in love with a gentleman of Mr Franklin Blake's manners and appearance doesn't seem to me to be the maddest part of her conduct by any means.'[46]

There is a sense in which Rosanna's attraction to Franklin – and his indifference to her – merely confirm our expectations of who will be considered desirable, coinciding exactly with the characters' relative social and narrative capital. Being asked to consider Rosanna's pain, and view the novel's events from her marginalised position, may force us into an unusual relationship with a minor character, but her love for Franklin does not cause us to question the basis of the narrative order.

Rosanna herself recognises its legitimacy, casting physical appearance as not incidentally but fundamentally important, not only to a person's desirability, but to their very identity. When she is trying to make herself realise the impossibility of her passion for Franklin, she does so not through reminding herself of her social station or criminal past, but by looking in the mirror, where she might 'take . . . warning'.⁴⁷ Rosanna's sense of the overriding importance of physical beauty leads her to dispute Rachel's right to Franklin's affections, not on the grounds of her moral character or less sincere feelings, but on the basis that she is not as physically beautiful as Franklin believes. Betteredge's insistence that Rachel Verinder's good looks 'were in her flesh and not in her clothes' is countered by Rosanna's claim that 'it does stir one up to hear Miss Rachel called pretty, when one knows all the time that it's her dress does it, and her confidence in herself'.⁴⁸ The same structure of feeling revealed by Betteredge's remarks about Rachel's body is present here: even a character who is considered ugly apparently considers physical beauty to be of such importance that it is wrong for clothing or confidence to conceal a lack of it, as though physically conforming to a pre-determined aesthetic standard were an inherent and even moral quality in a person. For both Rosanna and Gabriel, it matters that the social consensus that Rachel is beautiful is underpinned by the objective beauty of her body; both insist that in the attribution of 'prettiness', somatic authenticity is possible, as though the body were an objective sign that pre-exists or transcends the social, so that beauty and ugliness could be essential, rather than subjective or contingent, states.

Franklin's obtuseness regarding Rosanna Spearman's true feelings and motivations are therefore well grounded within the world of the novel, given the general consensus that beauty is a necessary attribute for a romantic heroine. However, Collins complicates matters for the reader by depicting Rosanna herself as an object of desire for her friend, Lucy Yolland. Lucy's disability is marked in the text even more strongly than Rosanna's by the fact that she is nearly always called by her nickname, 'Limping Lucy', and Betteredge tries to cast their relationship as sentimentally satisfactory, positing that 'the two deformed girls had . . . a kind of fellow-feeling for each other'.⁴⁹ However, it transpires that this is a rather spectacular understatement when Lucy confronts Betteredge after Rosanna's death:

> 'I loved her,' the girl said softly. 'She had lived a miserable life, Mr Betteredge – vile people had ill-treated her and led her wrong – and it hadn't spoiled her sweet temper. She was an angel. She might have been happy with me. I had a plan for our going to London together like sisters, and living by our needles. That man came here, and spoilt it all. He bewitched her. Don't tell me he didn't mean it, and didn't know it. He ought to have known it. He ought to have taken pity on her. "I can't live without him – and, oh, Lucy, he never even looks at me." That's what

she said. Cruel, cruel, cruel. . . . Mr Betteredge, the day is not far off when the poor will rise against the rich. I pray Heaven they may begin with *him*.[50]

Her words are particularly incendiary, given that Collins chose to set the novel in 1848, the year of revolution. In Lucy's view, Franklin's emotional denseness and his class position are interlinked, and Rosanna's invisibility in his eyes not an unfortunate mismatch of personal feelings, but a systematic wrong done to her, which only social revolution could right. Yet Lucy is not merely destructive in her vengeful revolutionary vision. She is also able to imagine a space in which her desire need not have been tragic; she articulates the possibility of female solidarity and lesbian desire. Above all, she is able, and enables us, to imagine a disabled woman as an agent *and* object of love. This matters so much because it makes it impossible to share Rosanna's confidence in the availability or even existence of the essential somatic reality that would confer legitimacy upon the novel's final settlement. By showing us that Rosanna *was* loveable, Lucy forces us either to recognise that there is no necessary connection between being thought beautiful and being found loveable, and that the bodily features that strike one onlooker as 'plain' might strike another as lovely.

Needless to say, Franklin does not understand. When Lucy later addresses a similar harangue directly to him, he reassures himself that 'the one interpretation I could put on her conduct has, no doubt, been anticipated by everybody. I could only suppose that she was mad.'[51] Apparently, it is simply incredible to Franklin that Lucy does not react to what he takes to be his universal sexual allure for women: 'Let me not be vain enough to say that no woman had ever looked at me in this manner before.'[52] He is shown here to have a strong sense of his own narrative role as romantic hero, which makes it impossible that he should be regarded with 'abhorrence' by anyone, nor that he should understand himself as having caused pain; he goes so far as to refuse to go on reading Rosanna's letter, lest he be forced to see himself in this light. Although he is both hero and, at this point, narrator, Franklin's obtuseness leads us to disassociate ourselves from his perspective, an alienation that is exaggerated by the fact that, soon afterwards, Franklin is placed in the position of the novel's villain, apparently convicted by the paint stains on his nightshirt. We are forced to distrust either his narration or the material evidence with which we are faced. Of course, we ultimately discover that Franklin's position was literally a false one, as Godfrey

Ablewhite was the true thief – and yet there is a sense in which his position was fitting. Franklin may not be a thief, nor a murderer, as Lucy claims, but some of kind of guilt insistently attaches itself to him, guilt that cannot be wholly dissipated by the novel's apparently restorative conclusion.

The idea that the signs of the body are fundamentally unstable is further developed by the introduction in the latter half of the novel of the character Ezra Jennings, another minor personage who is socially marginalised by the stigmatised body that enables him to play a pivotal role in the narrative. His narrative trajectory also troubles our confidence in the justice of the plot's final settlement: while a crucial difference between Rosanna and Ezra is that he willingly acts as an assistant to both the marriage plot and the detective process, where Rosanna had sought to impede both, his narrative fate is not dissimilar. Despite his heroic efforts to bring about a happy ending for our hero and heroine, and his success in so doing, he still dies alone.

If the moral of Ezra Jennings's characterisation – that we should not judge by appearances – is simple enough, yet it is significantly complicated by the representation of his body, which Collins imbues with symbolic significance. Gabriel Betteredge misreads Ezra's appearance through the lens of insular and, we suspect, racial prejudice, explaining that 'his appearance is against him'.[53] In coming to recognise Ezra's true worth as a loyal friend and talented scientific observer, we may feel that we rise above such a reading of his body – and yet it would be more true to say that we are shown how to read the signs of his body differently than that we are encouraged to see them as incidental or insignificant. His parti-coloured hair, for example, in which black and white are said to be mixed 'without the slightest gradation of grey to break the force of the extraordinary contrast', can retrospectively be read as a sign of the mixed-race heritage he later reveals to Franklin: 'I was born, and partly brought up, in one of our colonies. My father was an Englishman; but my mother – .'[54] His distinctively shaped nose, moreover, said to have 'presented the fine shape and modelling so often found among the ancient people of the East',[55] may not have been the sign of untrustworthiness or criminality, but it does turn out to correspond to his greater openness to the irrational and subconscious aspects of human psychology – which bluff Englishmen such as Mr Bruff and Gabriel Betteredge scorn and discount – and his (ultimately useful) connection with the 'eastern' drug, opium.

It is, of course, Ezra's wasting illness, his 'incurable internal complaint', which has led him to his dependence on opium, and disability is thus connected, subtly, with racial difference, as it is with femininity: Ezra has, he tells us, a 'female constitution'.[56] The modern critical tendency to align those social constructions and experiences that are marginalised by colonialist, heteronormative patriarchy – femaleness, queerness, blackness and disability – is, in fact, already present in Collins's novel, which draws together these conditions in its representation of Ezra and Rosanna. Between them, these characters capture all of these experiences, and express their interconnection as disqualifications for the kind of narrative authority, narrative sympathy and narrative space that Franklin Blake is able to claim. However, Collins also stages the reversal of this narrative economy, not only by positioning an understanding of Rosanna's story as essential to comprehending the mystery, but by making Ezra's experience and understanding of opium essential to its resolution.[57]

Although this is a resolution from which Ezra will be banished, and he is made to connive at his own narrative obliteration, Collins allows Ezra to disrupt the flow of narrative attention by drawing sympathy away from the couple whose union will complete the novel and resolve its marriage and detective plots. As narrator for a section of the story, Ezra commands our attention and sympathy, perhaps even more strongly than Rosanna did, in being allotted more space and, tainted with no impure motives or unworthy thoughts, emerging as a loyal and scrupulous character, unjustly mistrusted wherever he goes, and as a survivor of a tragically abortive love affair. While he echoes Gabriel Betteredge's verdict on Rosanna's history, in declaring his story not worth the telling – 'I decline to weary or distress you, sir, if I can help it'[58] – we are given access to his diary, so that we can gain greater exposure to his experience than he considers we will need. Indeed, his assurances as to his own insignificance act as a form of paralepsis: by telling us not to think about his past and not to regard his pain, he draws our attention to both.

This is especially true of the novel's conclusion, when Ezra disappears from the narrative immediately after his experiment has established Franklin's innocence and reunited the lovers. Although Ezra has instructed that his papers should be burnt and he should be buried in an unmarked grave, he is in fact memorialised by a death-bed scene, related in a letter from Mr Candy. This sentimental set piece – complete with the conventional crying out of the lost beloved's name, the kiss, the eyes raised to the light and the beatific peacefulness of the last moments – effectively undoes Ezra's final effort at self-erasure, distracting us from Rachel and Franklin's happiness, to which Mr Candy makes a (perhaps pointedly) bald reference at the end of his moving account of Ezra's death.[59] The plight of those characters who are shut out of the marriage plot is highlighted here in such a way that the conclusion of the novel, while it restores the disrupted narrative order, cannot restore our complacency about it. In fact, at the very moment when the heroine and hero are reunited – when Rachel kisses Franklin, immediately after his innocence has been demonstrated to her by Ezra's opium-based experiment – we are actually asked to imagine Ezra in her place: 'She was just touching his forehead with her lips. . . . She looked back at me with a bright smile, and a charming colour in her face. "You would have done it," she whispered, "in my place."'[60] This has, naturally, given rise to queer readings of the relationship between Ezra and Franklin,[61] but it also requires us to consider the difference between Rachel and Ezra as characters, in particular their differing relation to the marriage plot, which gives one a central place in the novel and her heart's desire, and condemns the other to narrative oblivion.

Ezra is not the only disabled character in the novel who shares a particular bond with its heroine. Alexander Welsh suggests that Rosanna has to be expelled from the narrative because she 'reduplicates the frank sexuality of the novel's heroine and is punished for it, so that in the poetic justice of the thing the heroine need not be punished'.[62] Seeing Rosanna as a scapegoat for Rachel draws our attention to the likeness between the two women, already suggested by their alliterative names: not only do both love Franklin, but both women are characterised as being damaged, Rosanna by her physical defect (her 'deformed' shoulder) and Rachel by what Gabriel calls her 'one defect . . . that she had ideas of her own, and . . . judged for herself, as few women twice her age judge for themselves in general'.[63] Lillian Nayder suggests that this links her to Limping Lucy, rather than Rosanna, as Lucy 'is characterized by a deformity that embodies her class injury . . . [and] recalls the "one defect" that Betteredge perceives in her social superior, Rachel Verinder: the desire for female autonomy'.[64] We can, in fact, read Rosanna and Lucy as two different avatars for Rachel, the one embodying her unswerving, even fanatical devotion to Franklin, the other voicing the resentment against him that she suppresses for much of the novel. Andrew Mangham has suggested that, in her stigmatised body and criminalised past, Rosanna 'personifies the delinquent proclivities and somatic incapacities that were central to mid-Victorian definitions of femininity';[65] it might be truer to say that, between them, Rachel, Rosanna and Lucy offer a hydra-headed personification of femininity, giving voice to one another's frustrations and mirroring each other's desires. Rachel's praiseworthy devotion to Franklin has its dark shadow in Rosanna's destructive, even deranged, passion for him, her silence on his behalf distortedly mirrored in Rosanna's willingness to pervert the course of justice in his interests, while both women's experience of rejection or betrayal at his hands is given voice in Lucy's resentful outbursts and accusations. Moreover, all three women recall the three Indians in different ways: Rachel in her darkness, Lucy in her revolutionary ambitions, and Rosanna in being unjustly suspected of theft, but, like them, acting outside the law. Ezra, of course, has an even closer connection to the Indians, with his 'Eastern' appearance and presumably Indian mother.[66]

The likeness of the novel's disabled characters to its heroine and to the trio of Indians matters because it draws together the injustices and difficulties of the marriage plot, and the parallel complexities of the detective plot. This is particularly pertinent when we consider that the conclusion of the mystery includes the solving of the crime, but not the restoration of the moonstone to its legal possessor (Rachel), concluding instead with its return to India. We witness this restoration in a final snippet of narration from Mr Murthwaite, the character who has always had the most sympathy with the Indians, considering the moonstone to be their rightful property. While it is beyond the scope of this chapter to analyse the novel's ambivalent and complex view of Empire, it is clear that the ambivalence over who rightfully owns the moonstone complicates our sense of where true villainy lies in the novel, just as the pain of those characters who are excluded from the marriage plot leads us to doubt the justice of its resolution. This instability is developed in Collins's next detective novel, *The Law and the Lady*, in which the mystery turns out to hinge on suicide, rather than murder, and in which the marginalised and disabled Miserrimus contests the place of the novel's unprepossessing hero, with sensational results.

## 'Please pity me!': Miserrimus Dexter and the Politics of Affect in *The Law and the Lady*

Published seven years later and after a number of intervening novels, *The Law and the Lady* marks Collins's return to the themes of *The Moonstone*. For one thing, Miserrimus Dexter and his beloved Sara Macallan mirror Lucy Yolland and Rosanna Spearman. Both Miserrimus and Lucy are disabled figures, considered eccentric and even mad by their communities; they love women who are judged plain and, rather than returning their passionate devotion, are unrequitedly in love with the romantic hero. Both of their love objects kill themselves as a result of the hero's rejection, and it is out of resentment against the hero that both withhold the information that is the key to the mystery. However, between the publication of *The Moonstone* and *The Law and the Lady*, Collins had written explicitly about the politics of the body, and specifically about disability, in *Man and Wife* (1870) and *Poor Miss Finch* (1872) – to which I will return in the next section – and the influence of this work can be seen in the differences between the representations of Lucy and Rosanna, and Miserrimus and Sara.

For one thing, whereas disability is one facet of Rosanna's unsuitability as a romantic heroine, and sits alongside her class identity, criminal past and lack of conventional beauty as traits that disqualify her from the marriage plot, Miserrimus is a wealthy, talented, handsome gentleman. His disability therefore constitutes, rather than contributes to, his exclusion from the marriage plot. Sara, on the other hand, is 'just' plain. By untangling ugliness and disability, and apportioning them to two separate characters, both romantically rejected, Collins is able to explore the categories of ability and beauty separately, and, conversely, can thereby explore their interconnectedness more effectively than he could when one character bore the stigma of both ugliness and disability.

Moreover, whereas Rosanna's suicide was an incident along the way to the revelation of the true mystery of *The Moonstone*, and her love for Franklin essentially an engaging subplot, Sara's suicide *is* the mystery of *The Law and the Lady*, and Eustace's rejection the source of the criminality that follows (if we understand suicide as a criminal offence, as it then was, and Miserrimus's perjury as a crime arising from it). It was relatively easy to see Lucy's love for Rosanna as pure-hearted and noble, drawing Rosanna away from criminality and illicit passion, and towards a life of sisterly industry; there is no suggestion that Lucy bears any responsibility for her suicide, nor does her outburst of resentment against Franklin significantly disrupt the plot. However unwillingly, she still hands over the revelatory letter, effectively assenting to her assistive role, even while she rails against it. Miserrimus, on the other hand, is a far more troubling figure, whose adulterous passion for Sara leads him to show Eustace's diary to her, knowing that it will reveal indifference and even aversion, and hoping that this will induce her to run away with him. Instead, it drives her to suicide; Miserrimus's decision to conceal Sara's suicide letter then sets the plot in motion by generating the mystery. As a minor character in the detective plot that temporally succeeds and narratively precedes this act of deception, Miserrimus strains against his allotted place in the novel, not only trying to muscle his way into the marriage plot, but drawing Valeria into his toils through his irresistible élan as a storyteller and performer. Right up to the point when he loses his mind, Miserrimus tries to exert control over the narrative, and he succeeds, I think, in providing an alternative view of events, a kind of counter-narrative in which his devotion was noble, Sara's rejection tragic and Eustace's behaviour culpable. His success prevents either Valeria or the reader from fully assenting to the narrative order restored by the novel's conclusion. Miserrimus's interrogation of what it means to be a 'cripple' speaks not just to the politics of disability, but to the politics of plotting: by the end of the novel, we are no longer confident that we understand who is beautiful, who is loveable, who has the right to play detective or romantic lead, or who must be consigned to narrative oblivion.

Valeria's investigations into her husband's trial for his first wife's murder, and her attempt to overturn the 'not guilty' (rather than 'innocent') verdict that he feels makes it impossible for them to live together, lead to her first encounter with Miserrimus in the trial report. She is inspired by the report of his behaviour – which she has woefully misinterpreted – to visit him at his home, which turns out to be an 'ancient' manor house marooned in a suburban wasteland. We are explicitly told that Miserrimus has purchased, rather than inherited, this gothic pile;[67] we are to understand, then, that he has deliberately supplied himself with a quintessentially sensational setting, as though self-consciously making himself into a character from sensation fiction before his practically minded family's horrified eyes. He has then filled it with gothic props, 'plaster casts . . . of the heads of famous murderers', a skeleton, the tanned skin of a French marquis, and his own paintings, which defy 'Nature' in favour of 'Horrors' and 'the supernatural'.[68] After the domestic scenes that have preceded Valeria's decision to turn detective, Miserrimus appears as a wilful throwback to the gothic, determinedly anachronistic and self-dramatising.

He is, in fact, engaged in a kind of private theatrical performance when Valeria arrives. Ignoring his request not to be disturbed, Valeria succumbs to her curiosity, opening the door to his rooms and secretly watching him 'propell[ing] the chair at its utmost rate of speed' as he imagines himself to be 'Napoleon, at the sunrise of Austerlitz! . . . Nelson . . . Shakespere!'[69] In an image that both dehumanises and aggrandises him, he is described by Valeria as a 'fantastic and frightful apparition . . . the new Centaur, half man, half chair', envisioned as terrifyingly hybrid rather than physically vulnerable or inadequate. This impression is heightened by the mischievous pleasure he takes in the idea that he might have 'run them over' or 'ground them to powder for presuming to intrude'.[70] Using a wheelchair seems less pitiable than menacing in this scene, and Miserrimus is depicted as equally physically powerful when he is out of his chair, moving with 'prodigious speed' across the room 'as lightly as a monkey, on his hands'.[71]

This scene – in which Mrs Macallan 'irritably' observes that 'he has made a good show of himself'[72] – introduces us to the idea of Miserrimus as a performer, an impression that is developed in his next meeting with Valeria. This time, however, knowing himself to have an audience and prepared for her visit, Miserrimus does not assume the identity of others, but performs his own, in ways which are far more discomfiting for both Valeria and the reader. While Valeria apparently felt comforted, rather than otherwise, at the thought of the 'allowance' that must be made for him because of his (implicitly) pitiable disability, she is mortified when he *asks* her for this reaction, calling himself a 'poor solitary creature cursed with a frightful deformity' who 'languish[es] for pity'.[73] Valeria attempts to re-assert her control over the situation by laughing at him, but when he fails to be 'offended' by her laughter, as she expects, and instead 'laid his head luxuriously on the back of his chair, with the expression of a man who was listening critically to a performance of some sort', she is immediately made 'serious' and declares herself 'ashamed'.[74] Miserrimus's apparent indifference to her mockery seems to make her more uncomfortable than his embarrassment would have done; clearly, Miserrimus ought to be ashamed that he is pitiable and ashamed that he is amusing, rather than pre-empting and demanding these responses.

Moreover, in looking back at Valeria, Miserrimus troubles the proper direction of scrutiny, in which, as the able-bodied, normal viewer of his deviance, and in addition acting in the role of detective, *she* can scrutinise *him*, but *he* cannot look back at *her*. In modern critical terms, Valeria treats Miserrimus as 'stareable', to quote Rosemarie Garland-Thomson, but she does not want to be caught staring (or, in this case, laughing) or have her staring commented upon.[75] Garland-Thomson suggests that 'staring as stigma assignment doubly shames starees – both for their supposed flaws and for exposing their starers';[76] applying this paradigm here, Valeria claims such shame but is discomfited by Miserrimus's lack of it, when the shame should be doubly shared by him. In the terms of the novel, he is including Valeria in the 'show' Mrs Macallan says he makes of himself, this time playing the role of spectator rather than actor. If Mrs Macallan felt there was something shameful in even witnessing such a show (as her eagerness to leave suggested), it is perhaps unsurprising that Valeria is ashamed to be co-opted into it completely.

Miserrimus's costume is another aspect of his performance that troubles Valeria, who notes the 'inveterate oddity of his dress', in appearing in a pink silk jacket and 'massive bracelets of gold'.[77] As has already been discussed, disability was frequently characterised as feminising in fiction of the period, and so we might hypothesise that this costume is a comment upon an aspect of Miserrimus's 'crippled' identity, were it not for the fact that he then insists there *is* nothing inherently feminine in such an outfit, since, '[a] hundred years ago, a man in pink silk was a gentleman properly dressed'.[78] Valeria already exists in a complicated relation to conventional gender codes: having married a man described by his strong-minded mother as 'one of the weakest of living mortals',[79] she has disobeyed his express instructions and taken up the detective enquiries he is too feeble to pursue himself. The novel opens with the lines from the marriage service that outline a woman's duty of obedience to her husband;[80] Valeria has already found herself totally unable to live up to this obligation, and the reader has been forced to question the soundness of its premise by her obvious superiority to her husband in courage, loyalty and resourcefulness (something that is explicitly commented upon by her mother-in-law, much to Valeria's irritation). Miserrimus's suggestion that the signs of gender identity are historically specific, and therefore unstable, occurs in a context that renders it particularly charged; when he proceeds to show her his embroidery and demonstrate his gourmet cookery – something that he suggests is a naturally male preserve[81] – he effectively holds up a mirror to Valeria's normative expectations about gender identity, in which it is *her* views that appear distorted.

This extends to his challenge to her confidence in the beauty codes that assure her of her own attractiveness and the first Mrs Macallan's ugliness. Contrary to the claims of the other witnesses at the trial, Miserrimus insists that Sara Macallan was a beauty, and, more disconcertingly still, that Valeria resembles her.[82] Having heard testimonies during the trial that presented Sara as an unloved and unlovely woman, whose shamefully unreciprocated passion for Eustace led to their marriage, and whose lack of beauty then repelled him, we are now confronted with Miserrimus's perception of her as a 'martyred angel' to whom Valeria cannot quite be compared: 'A far more charming face . . . . But no – not a more beautiful figure . . . . Something – but not all – of her enchanting grace.'[83] To learn that Sara was beloved is one thing, but to be asked to imagine her as more physically attractive than Valeria is completely disconcerting, when her ugliness has been so important to the novel's plot.

The question of whether Sara Macallan could be said to have been an attractive woman is one on which much of the novel's plotting turns, with her anxiety about her physical appearance turning out to be at the heart of the mystery. We eventually learn that Sara had the arsenic by which she eventually committed suicide – leading to the suspicion that she was murdered – in her possession because she was using it as a cosmetic to improve her complexion; whether she was physically unattractive enough to require such a cosmetic, and thought her appearance sufficiently important to have used it, are therefore key questions at the trial. Moreover, it is never firmly distinguished from the questions of whether she had a pleasant temperament, whether she and Eustace were happily married, and whether he harboured a secret passion for Mrs Beauly that might have driven him to murder his wife: these questions are all collapsed together in the retrospective analysis of Sara's body. Lest we miss the importance of beauty as an identity category, rather than an incidental descriptive detail, Valeria draws our attention to the issue as she reads the trial report. She is 'disagreeably' exercised by the question of what Eustace's erstwhile lover, Mrs Beauly, looked like, and whether she and Mrs Beauly are 'the least in the world like one another', as she is by the question of whether Eustace is still in love with Mrs Beauly.[84] Indeed, she strings the questions together, as though the answers are necessarily connected.

In this context, Miserrimus's claim that Sara was not merely loveable, but actually beautiful, is one with tremendous disruptive power, forcing us to question the reality of the categories by which the novel is organised. Miserrimus himself poses a challenge to those categories in combining deformity and handsomeness; as Valeria puts it, 'a young girl, ignorant of what the Oriental robe hid from view, would have said to herself the instant she looked at him, "Here is the hero of my dreams!"'[85] She quickly clarifies that she is 'speaking of him, of course, from a woman's, not a physiognomist's, point of view', but no such physiognomist is available to offer an alternative reading. Given his subsequent behaviour, we hardly need a physiognomist to tell us that the 'gentleness' and 'quietness' that Valeria praises in her husband's countenance might be signs of what his mother calls his 'weak and wayward' character, and yet, despite her apparent confidence that Miserrimus's disability is pitiable, Valeria goes so far as to doubt that her husband's limp constitutes even a 'little drawback'.[86] Dexter may have been mad, in the lawyer Mr Playmore's eyes, to propose 'seriously' to the woman he loved, but Valeria considers that her husband's 'slight limp when he walks has (perhaps to my partial eyes) a certain quaint grace of its own, which is pleasanter than the unrestrained activity of other men'.[87] Disability can, apparently, be an added attraction in the eyes of the some beholders.

Valeria's confidence that whether or not Sara was beautiful, and what Mrs Beauly looked like, will solve the mystery of whether and to what extent either was beloved, therefore appears utterly misplaced in the context even of her *own* readings of the bodies around her. In fact, greater force is carried by Miserrimus's observation that love is fundamentally illogical: 'There are some men whom the women all like; and there are other men whom the women never care for. Without the least reason for it in either case.'[88] Such a statement fundamentally undermines the logic of the marriage plot, by which some characters are fitted to play the leading roles and others have to be discarded, thereby encouraging the reader to re-consider Miserrimus's own relation to it.

He is an equally disruptive figure when it comes to the detective plot: despite being the subject of study, he repeatedly turns his gaze back on to the investigator herself, and tries to thwart her enquiries by laying a trail of false clues, constructing a narrative in which, confusingly, there is an element of the truth that Valeria herself wishes to suppress. Miserrimus's challenges to both marriage and detective plots are brought together in the scene when he attempts to mislead Valeria about his own actions, and take up the role of master-plotter, leading to the erotic climax that so offended *The Graphic*'s editor.[89] Here, we see both the apogee and the total collapse of Miserrimus's performative attempts to control his own narrative role and to manipulate his effect upon others. We see him first through the eyes of the housekeeper as less than human, 'a Thing ... which curdled my blood'.[90] Watching him sleep, the usually pitying Valeria also sees him as hideous, alien and, once again, not quite human, acknowledging that she can 'hardly wonder that the poor old housekeeper trembled from head to foot when she spoke of him!'[91] Once Miserrimus is awake, however, he manipulates his onlookers into the pity they do not initially feel, appealing to Benjamin as 'a poor deformed wretch with a warm heart', deserving of pity.[92] He then spins Valeria a story about the events surrounding

Sara's death, attempting to cast suspicion on Mrs Beauly, obscuring his own actions and dwelling on his grief; whether because she is moved by this performance of vulnerability, or because she is ashamed to think of how she saw him when he was asleep, Valeria 'pitied Miserrimus Dexter, at that moment, as I had never pitied him yet', and 'put my hand, without knowing what I was about, on the poor wretch's shoulder', assuring him of her pity.[93]

Pity is, of course, an inadequate response to what we can retrospectively recognise as the complex and culpable nature of Miserrimus's performance of naive amateur detection. A far more sophisticated planter of clues than Valeria is a follower of them, he has only been pretending to project himself into the position of Mrs Beauly and imagine what she would do – knowing full well, in point of fact, that she could not have murdered Sara Macallan because he knows that she killed herself, and why. His remembrance of Sara is indeed passionate, but it is rather less straightforwardly pitiable than Valeria imagines: he not only loved her, but also drove her to suicide in a fruitless attempt to turn her against her husband. Yet even upon re-reading, with the knowledge of his guilt in our minds, Miserrimus voices his feelings for Sara in terms so compelling that we cannot easily dismiss them as simply or only culpably and irresponsibly lustful. He draws on the tropes of blameless, hopeless love in the period, revealing that, as he cried over her corpse, 'I stole one little lock of her hair. I have worn it ever since; I have kissed it night and day.'[94]

If this gestures recalls Smike's pure and hopeless love for Kate Nickleby, also symbolised by the lock of hair worn round his neck, at the next moment Miserrimus's actions rather recall Quilp's guilty passion for Little Nell, as he catches Valeria's hand 'and devoured it with kisses', his lips 'like fire' and his arm around her waist.[95] When Benjamin arrives to rescue her, Valeria reasserts his disabled identity, in such a way as to disarm the threat he has momentarily posed: 'I held him at the door with all my strength. "You can't lay your hand on a cripple," I said.'[96] Miserrimus's temporarily self-assertive (indeed, aggressive) persona immediately collapses; having been shown, definitively, that he is no Smike, we are now reminded that he is also no Quilp, for he suddenly, and finally, really does seem pitiable – not self-consciously and deliberately so, but involuntarily, and to his own shame:

> Miserrimus Dexter had sunk down in the chair. The rough man lifted his master with a gentleness that surprised me. 'Hide my face,' I heard Dexter say to him, in broken tones. He opened his coarse pilot jacket,

and hid his master's head under it, and so went silently out – with the deformed creature held to his bosom, like a woman sheltering her child.[97]

Valeria's previous attempts to read Miserrimus as childlike were doomed to failure but here he does appear vulnerable, as Valeria's sexual rejection is compounded by her reminder that he is not to be treated like any other inappropriately aggressive man but is beyond the pale of masculine retribution, just as he is, in Valeria's eyes, beyond the pale of sexual desire. Rather than setting the issue to rest, however, this re-assertion of Miserrimus's crippled identity only compounds our complex feelings about his place in the narrative.

The mystery begins to unravel after Miserrimus's admission that he stole into Sara's room to kiss her corpse; his love for Sara turns out to be at the heart of the mystery, as we then learn that it was his attempt to persuade her to leave her husband, by showing her his diary, which led her to kill herself. Conversely, it is when he is revealed as the novel's villain that Miserrimus appears at his most pitiable; as Mr Playmore exclaims,

> 'what he must have suffered, villain as he was, when he first read the wife's confession. He had calculated on undermining her affection for her husband – and whither had his calculations led him? He had driven the woman whom he loved to the last dreadful refuge of death by suicide!'[98]

Moreover, Sara's letter reveals the similarity between her own experience and Miserrimus's, a likeness that might have drawn them together but, in fact, only drove them apart. The man with the beautiful face and incomplete body, and the woman with the beautiful body and the marred face, might have been seen as the perfect match for one another, but although Miserrimus's experience of being treated as less than fully human was exactly mirrored in her own experience of rejection, this did not lead Sara to have any pity for Miserrimus's 'guilty and horrible love'.[99] Instead, she was disgusted by his desire – just as her husband was disgusted by hers. To underscore this parallel, Sara makes the link between herself and Miserrimus explicit, writing that she had 'for deformed persons . . . almost a fellow-feeling . . . being that next worst thing myself to a deformity – a plain woman'.[100] The line between the disabled and the 'normal' is broken down here, with a lack of conventional beauty being seen to disable a woman in a romantic plot-line, and both characters denied full personhood by the object of their desires. What truly disables characters within the novel seems to be not the degree of their physical difference from the 'normal', but the refusal of others to recognise them as fully human, captured in Eustace's failure to 'look' at Sara 'at all', which convinces her that she should kill herself, and the repeated descriptions of Miserrimus as an animal, 'a maundering mad monster who ought to be kept in a cage'.[101]

Miserrimus himself is guilty of exactly the same denial of human subjectivity in his treatment of his cousin and servant, Ariel. She is a physically strong but developmentally disabled woman, described by Mrs Macallan as 'an idiot' and by Miserrimus as 'a mere vegetable'.[102] Although he tells Valeria that there is 'latent intelligence, affection, pride, fidelity' in her, 'half-developed' as she is,[103] he merely enjoys the power that her adoration gives him, and has no qualms about exploiting her unwavering devotion to play cruel games with her. In a sense, Ariel is a stand-in for every character in the novel – including Valeria herself – who is in love. Aviva Briefel points out that 'Valeria' contains an anagram of 'Ariel', and argues that there is 'an important resemblance between the two women'.[104] Startling as the juxtaposition of abused Ariel and assertive Valeria initially appears, there are disturbing similarities in their attitudes to their beloved men: Ariel's request, when Valeria is angry with Miserrimus, that she should '[t]ake it out on Me . . . . Beat me . . . . Don't vex *him*' is really only a simplified and more extreme version of Valeria's closing plea to the reader, 'Abuse *me* as much as you please. But pray think kindly of Eustace, for my sake.'[105] If Valeria can overlook Eustace's abandonment, deception and repeated acts of ingratitude, then she seems to think that we should be able to overlook them too, exactly as Ariel expects Valeria to treat Miserrimus with the same exaggerated respect that she does. Of the trio of excessively devoted women, Sara goes the furthest, killing herself in the belief that this action will free Eustace to marry the other woman she had discovered he loved.[106] To be in love, in this novel, is to be treated badly, and to accept bad treatment: Ariel loves Miserrimus, who ignores her in his adoration for Sara, who rejects him and loves Eustace, who in turn overlooks her in his passion for Mrs Beauly and, now, Valeria (whom he also abandons, although she manages to effect a reunion with him in spite of himself).

This pattern of cruelly overlooked desire recalls that of *The Moonstone* but is twisted a notch tighter, since Eustace, who stands at the top of this tragic chain, seems singularly unfitted for his place there, and is actually put on trial to determine whether he is the novel's villain. The verdict of 'not proven', which it was Valeria's purpose to overturn, is surely upheld by the novel's final revelation that it was Eustace's diary entries – admittedly never intended for her eyes – that drove Sara to suicide and despair. Her answering letter, intended both to avert any mystery from accruing to her death and, perhaps, to win her husband's love or at least gratitude, remains tragically private. Having played the detective throughout the novel, on a quest to uncover the truth, Valeria finally takes Miserrimus's place as its obfuscator, persuading her husband not to read Sara's letter. Ultimately, she believes her marital happiness to rest on Eustace's ignorance of his own true relation to the mystery – and this happiness seems precarious enough, as Valeria cries in his arms, thinking of 'those other wives . . . whose husbands . . . would have spoken hard words to them'.[107] She does not speak Sara's name, but then she hardly needs to: the first Mrs Macallan haunts the novel's conclusion, as does her doomed lover, Miserrimus, and his fatally faithful Ariel. The novel's first illustrator clearly recognised this displacement of sympathy and attention away from the marriage plot that is the novel's ostensible culmination: the final illustration depicts not the happy, reunited couple, but Miserrimus's grave, upon which the loyal Ariel has died.[108]

Miserrimus has lost his mind while trying to tell an alternative story, in which he was not guilty of prompting Sara's death and in which she never killed herself, but was murdered. In his imaginative powers, Miserrimus might be seen to have much in common with Jenny Wren, another disabled storyteller, but where her creative energies were directed towards the furtherance of the marriage plot and the upholding of the narrative order, Miserrimus has tried to subvert it. In boasting of his ability to vary his style in order to sustain his audience's interest,[109] Miserrimus could be read as a parody of Collins himself, and the breathlessly impatient Valeria, who only wants to get to the *point* of the story (the plot), as a stereotyped sensation reader. However, in trying to usurp narrative control in order to undermine the narrative order, using his storytelling powers to re-cast himself as a romantic hero instead of a villain, Miserrimus goes too far: his powers are stripped from him and he falls 'mute', his once-animated face 'vacant'.[110] Valeria calls this 'the foretold doom', in reference to the doctor's prediction that he would one day lose his mind, but it is also 'foretold' in being the only narrative fate possible for Miserrimus: he has to be deprived of his plotting abilities for the plot to be properly resolved.[111] It was his dexterity as a plotter that set the mystery in motion, but in order for it to be fully unravelled, his plotting has to end, and in order for the marriage plot to come to its proper conclusion, he has to be removed as an obstacle.

Collins thereby upholds the narrative order, but at such high cost that it is impossible for us to be set at rest by the conclusion. Where guilt was clearly personified in *The Woman in White*, and could therefore be purged, Miserrimus's death gives us no such satisfaction. As Valeria herself says, 'I knew him to be cruel; I believed him to be false. And yet, I pitied him!'[112] From Ariel's perspective, it is Valeria who is to be blamed for Miserrimus's death – '"You have done this!" she shouted to me'[113] – while the reader is likely to feel distinctly ambivalent towards Eustace, whose cause Valeria is still pleading in the novel's last line. Even the scapegoating of Godfrey Ablewhite, which gave outlet to our uneasy sense that the able, white men of the novel bore unrecognised responsibility for its crimes, gave us a greater sense of relief than Collins grants us here. By investing Miserrimus not only with power and knowledge, but also with all the animation, distinctiveness and eccentricity that Eustace lacks, and with a strength of feeling that allies him with the novel's heroine, Collins draws our sympathies out to the periphery, forcing us to question the role Miserrimus has been allotted by virtue of his unusual embodiment and his identity as a 'cripple'.[114] Our surge of sympathy for and interest in Miserrimus destabilises the narrative economy by which he is marginalised; in making us question the basis for the novel's economy of space and sympathy, Collins claims a greater share of both for Miserrimus Dexter, putting sensationalism to affective work.

## Blindness and Blueness in *Poor Miss Finch*

In his Dedication to *Poor Miss Finch*, Collins makes a bold claim for both the originality and the realism of his portrayal of disability. Where previous writers have 'always exhibited [blindness], more or less exclusively, from the ideal and the sentimental point of view', he says, he intends 'to appeal to an interest of another kind, by exhibiting blindness as it really is'.[115] This claim may seem bizarrely ill founded when we find ourselves confronted by a truly baroque plot, in which the blind heroine's irrational aversion to dark colours presents unforeseen difficulties when her lover is (coincidentally) turned dark blue by the nitrate of silver he takes to cure his epilepsy, and his attempted concealment of this calamity enables his previously devoted twin brother, who has been maddened by love for Lucilla, to impersonate him when her sight is temporarily restored, almost leading her to marry the wrong brother. If, however, we take Collins's prefatory statements about this unusual and generically hybrid novel seriously, they offer a key to understanding its radical depiction of disability, particularly in terms of its plotting.

In all the texts I have so far discussed, disability is to be found at the margins of the novel, frequently exerting tremendous inward pressure and sometimes wrenching its affective trajectory out of shape, but never situated securely at its centre. In *Poor Miss Finch*, however, the blind Lucilla is the romantic heroine of the novel, which is structured around her achievement of marriage and motherhood. More strikingly still, the marriage plot is not derailed by her blindness, but by its cure. Her return to sightlessness marks the novel's swerve away from sensationalism and its return to its well-worn course and matrimonial conclusion.[116] Perhaps most surprisingly of all, Lucilla does not achieve this (for a disabled character) exceptional narrative fate through being exceptionally virtuous or winning the love of an exceptional man, but rather through her total ordinariness as a romantic heroine. She is beautiful, independently wealthy and lacking in sound parental guidance, making her the ideal subject for a romantic plot-line; in terms of her personality, she is depicted by Collins as quintessentially and sympathetically feminine, in being wilful but soft-hearted, romantic and sensual but not problematically transgressive sexually. Neither as self-effacing as Laura and Nora, nor as wilful and wild as Marian and Magdalene,[117] she is a heroine who stands out from Collins's other heroines (and anti-heroines) mainly because of the moderation of her characterisation. Our narrator, Madame Pratalungo, is convinced by 'a sudden inspiration' that she will love Lucilla because of her pitiable situation as a woman who is '[y]oung – lonely – blind', but in fact comes to like her for her own endearing qualities, as a self-possessed, high-spirited young woman who cheerfully confesses herself both vain and greedy, but also shows herself to be a loyal friend, a charitable neighbour and a hopeless romantic.[118]

Within days of moving in with her, Madame Pratalungo is already putting the villagers' 'compassionate' appellation 'Poor Miss Finch' into ironic quotation marks, having discovered Lucilla to be anything but 'poor'. The plot of the novel continues to ironise the title, not only by highlighting Lucilla's total lack of self-pity, but also by turning on an (ultimately) happy love story, in which Lucilla is the most appreciative – and active – of romantic heroines. Madame Pratalungo marks the contrast between Lucilla's sense of herself and the villagers' ideas about her, when she leaves Lucilla to think about her lover in bed:

> 'Do you think he is getting fond of me?' she asked, the last thing at night . . . . 'Go away with your candle,' she said. 'The darkness makes no difference to me. I can see him in my thoughts.' She nestled her cheek comfortably on the pillows, and tapped me saucily on the cheek, as I bent over her. 'Own the advantage I have over you now,' she said. '*You* can't see at night without your candle. *I* could go all over the house, at this moment, without making a false step anywhere.' When I left her that night, I sincerely believe 'poor Miss Finch' was the happiest woman in England.[119]

Scenes such as this, in which Lucilla asserts the compensations of her blindness – and Collins subtly draws our attention to the senses Lucilla *does* have, and the pleasure she takes in them, by pointing out how she 'nestles' against her pillows – bear out Collins's claim in the Preface that his novel will illustrate his belief that 'the conditions of human happiness are independent of bodily affliction, and that it is even possible for bodily affliction itself to take its place among the ingredients of happiness'.[120]

This avowed intention leads Collins to portray Lucilla's blindness in a strikingly realistic way, recalling his claim to 'examin[e] blindness as it really is', by treating it, not as a symbol or stimulus to moral elevation, but as an incidental physical impairment.[121] As such, it is shown to have affected Lucilla's character and to shape her life, but is also subject to negotiation by Lucilla herself in practical ways that minimise its inconvenience. Lucilla's own view of blindness is carefully established as distinct from the sighted narrator's view, and it is both more and less dramatic: very occasionally, and in specific ways, she is extremely frustrated by her inability to see, and she catches at the opportunity to restore her vision with an impetuousness that worries some of her sighted advisors. However, she also insists that her blindness has significant compensations and advantages, joking that 'she sincerely pitied the poor useless people who could only see!',[122] and finally choosing not to hazard another operation to restore her sight. The plot is shaped so as to bring out both the perils and the benefits of Lucilla's blindness, ultimately – as we would expect, since she is the heroine and must have a happy ending – concluding in such a way that her blindness is conducive, rather than obstructive, to her marital happiness.[123] Despite the sensational plotting that precedes it, the tone of the novel's conclusion is deliberately prosaic and measured: 'the one thing essential was the thing she possessed. Her life was a happy one. Bear this in mind – and don't forget that your conditions of happiness need not necessarily be her conditions also.'[124]

Given that disability is represented as an insuperable bar to matrimony in most of Collins's other novels, we might ask why he departs so radically from his usual practice in this particular novel. I would suggest that the clue lies in the contemporary critical reaction to the novel as a new departure for Collins in generic terms: the reviewer for the *Athenaeum* protested that '[t]he sanctifying influence of *Cassell's Magazine* ... is feebly apparent in every chapter', concluding that this was 'a sensation novel for Sunday reading'.[125] If we take this complaint seriously and acknowledge that *Poor Miss Finch* is different from the sensation novels Collins wrote both before and after it, in its exclusively domestic setting and sustained emphasis upon the marriage plot rather than upon criminality, then its radical departure in terms of its depiction of disability becomes explicable.

As the novels discussed in the next chapter illustrate, domestic realist fiction of the 1850s, 1860s and 1870s routinely depicted disability as a part of familial and social life, and not infrequently formed marriage plots around disability. In parallel with sensation fiction, bodily difference and bodily suffering were being treated in very different ways and put to very different uses in domestic fiction written by female authors for largely female audiences – and it is with this tradition that *Poor Miss Finch* is engaged. The realistic, detailed depiction of physical disability in the novels of Charlotte M. Yonge, both as a medical phenomenon subject to practical intervention and management, and as an unremarkable part of family life – for example, the treatment of Charles Edmonstone's tubercular hip in *The Heir of Redclyffe* (1853) or Geraldine Underwood's arthritis in *The Pillars of the House* (1873) – is mirrored in Collins's treatment of Lucilla's blindness.[126] The affective work to which disability is put in the fiction of Dinah Mulock Craik – such as *Olive* (1850) or *A Noble Life* (1866) – is recalled in this novel, which is concerned with disrupting and challenging sentimental portrayals of disability. Like Craik, Collins allows a disabled woman to be a romantic heroine, but on terms very different from those imposed on Craik's Olive: not only does Lucilla fail to be made saintly by her experience of blindness, which has clearly rendered her no more or less morally inspiring than any other likeable but fallible romantic heroine, but she signally fails to exert a particularly purifying influence on those around her. (Falling in love with her might bring out some of Oscar's best features but it has a disastrous effect on his twin, Nugent, who is driven to deception and duplicity by his frustrated passion.) These connections make *Poor Miss Finch* a crucial novel in bridging the gap between sensational and domestic fiction of the period, illustrating one of the important differences between the novels I have previously dealt with and those addressed in the next chapter. By giving the novel a firmly domestic setting and a strongly female perspective and emphasis, Collins is able to situate his disabled heroine in a very different relation to the novel's plot from that of any of the disabled characters discussed hitherto.

Lucilla's blindness is only one facet of the novel's treatment of disability, however: we also have to contend with a blue romantic hero. Oscar's epilepsy is depicted in fairly realistic terms – for example, in the description of his first fit[127] – but Collins's treatment of the discoloration of his skin, a side-effect of the nitrate of silver cure, could hardly stand in starker contrast. Critics have tended to dismiss the novel's 'blue' plot-line as a bizarre, sensational twist, but I wish to suggest that it can be taken seriously as the complement to the blindness plot-line, with both together forming a holistic view of disability as a social and novelistic phenomenon.

Lucilla's disability – blindness – is treated as pure impairment. Its consequences are practical, its frustrations and compensations literal and direct, concerned with actions she can and cannot perform, sensations she can and cannot experience. Beside the pity of the villagers – which we never see directly – the social aspect of her disability is not depicted at all: no one suggests, in the entire novel, that Lucilla should not marry because she is blind, nor that her restored sight increases her attractiveness, and she is blind when she eventually marries. Oscar's blueness, on the other hand, is *purely* a socially constructed disability, having no aspect of physical impairment to it at all. This is highlighted by the fact that he takes the nitrate of silver in order to cure himself of a genuinely distressing and inconvenient physical condition, and yet is considered rash and foolish for doing so. When Madame Pratalungo upbraids him for being 'deliberately bent on making yourself an object of horror to everybody who sees you', Oscar asks her to 'consider the prospect that is before me! Day after day, week after week, month after month, always in danger, wherever I go, of falling down in a fit – is that a miserable position? or is it not?'[128] Yet even this consideration barely reconciles Madame Pratalungo to his change of appearance, and when she first sees him with Lucilla, she reacts to his darkened skin with horror:

> I saw her fair cheek laid innocently against the livid blackish blue of *his* discoloured skin. Heavens, how cruelly that first embrace marked the contrast between what he had been when I left him, and what he had changed to when I saw him now! His eyes turned from her face to mine in silent appeal.... 'You, who love her, say – can we ever be cruel enough to tell her of *this*?'[129]

Lucilla's blindness might seem to render Oscar's blueness doubly unimportant, since not only is it a purely aesthetic change, but she cannot experience it for herself, and to her senses of hearing and touch, Oscar is as attractive as he ever was. However, her aversion to dark colours renders it ominously significant, leading Oscar to take refuge in secrecy from the possibility of her rejection, and thus setting in motion all the confusion that follows. However, Lucilla's attitude to his blueness is only an exaggeration of Madame Pratalungo's own horror; Madame Pratalungo speaks of Nugent's making the 'sacrifice' of being *thought* blue for Oscar's sake, and despite the general consensus that Lucilla's fear of dark colours is 'ridiculous', Madame Pratalungo describes the other blue person she meets (before Oscar's treatment has begun) by saying that he is 'hideously distinguished' by 'a horrible colour'.[130]

It is, of course, possible to argue that Collins was exploring a physical condition as part of his avowedly realist project, since discoloration of the skin was a consequence of a contemporary treatment for epilepsy.[131] However, in light of the deliberately melodramatic ways in which Oscar's change in skin tone is described, and the exaggerated part it plays in the novel's plot, I think Samuel Lyndon Gladden is right to argue that, even in the (now remote) context in which readers might have encountered such a phenomenon, blueness 'functions as an empty signifier'.[132] Readers are not expected to have any particular or definite preconceptions about what it 'means' to be blue, and yet it is made very meaningful indeed in terms of putting Oscar beyond the pale, exiling him from the social community.[133] Oscar himself, at his most hopeful, presumes to think that Lucilla will still marry him only because she cannot see his colouring, while '[a]s for other persons, I shall not force myself on the view of the world',[134] and this attitude soon enables him to be ousted from his position in the novel. In this way, blueness is made a metaphor for disability in its social aspect: everyone, including Oscar himself, accepts that blueness will problematise and even prevent his marriage, and yet blueness has no practical or somatic significance in and of itself, but has to be read by others to become meaningful. Thus, when Lucilla is blind once again, she is happily reconciled with Oscar, not (as she explicitly says) because she has come to realise that blueness does not matter, but because she is blissfully unaware of his blueness: 'My life lives in my love. And my love lives in my blindness', she explains to Madame Pratalungo.[135]

Oscar's blueness, and the identity mystery to which it gives rise when he is impersonated by his brother, also enables Collins to probe in new ways the question that preoccupied his fiction in this period: who is fit to play what part in a novel, and how do we decide?[136] Collins explores these issues in *Poor Miss Finch* through the device of having physically identical twins both fall in love with the same, blind heroine. Lucilla can distinguish between them through her sense of touch – when she touches Oscar, she explains to Madame Pratalungo she feels 'a delicious tingle' that is absent when she touches Nugent – and is unswervingly adamant that she has chosen the right twin, angrily refusing to countenance Madame Pratalungo's suggestion that, had she met Nugent first instead of Oscar, 'Nugent might have been the man.'[137] Lucilla insists that they are not interchangeable: they may look the same and their voices may sound the same, but to her, Oscar is irreplaceable. Madame Pratalungo finds this particularly difficult to accept because Nugent is, in her eyes, superior in every way to his timid, sensitive twin Oscar: 'An irresistible man. So utterly different in his manner from Oscar . . . and yet so like Oscar in other respects, I can only describe him as his brother completed.'[138]

Lucilla's judgement is vindicated by the plot-line that follows. Oscar proves himself worthy to be the hero of the novel, in truly Dickensian fashion, by giving up his claim to the role. He leaves Dimchurch when Lucilla regains her sight and momentarily recoils from his blue face (believing him, of course, to be Nugent) so that his brother can have a chance to woo her, apparently never considering that Nugent might allow Lucilla to continue in her mistake by acquiescing to her assumption that he is Oscar. In a letter that echoes – perhaps parodically – Sidney Carton's final vision in Dickens's *A Tale of Two Cities* (1859), he declares:

> 'I have left Browndown for ever. . . . Perhaps, when years have passed, and when their children are growing up around them, I may see Lucilla again, and may take as the hand of my sister, the hand of the beloved

woman who might once have been my wife. . . . Forgive me and forget me; and keep, as I keep, that first and noblest of all mortal hopes – the hope of the life to come.'[139]

The problem with this saintly self-sacrifice, in the terms of this novel, is that it clears the way for Nugent to be overwhelmed by base temptation, so that there seems some justice in Nugent's complaint that Oscar 'tempted me to stay when he ought to have encouraged me to go'.[140] Moreover, it almost allows Lucilla to be cheated out of the marriage she has so explicitly desired and strenuously brought about.

Oscar's actions set in motion the plot-line of deception, detection and final revelation that occupies the rest of the novel, until it is brought to its reassuring matrimonial conclusion and domestic tranquillity is restored, with 'a dull wedding' that ultimately results in 'the married pair [being] as tranquil and as happy in their union as a man and woman could be'.[141] Retrospectively, we can see that it is Oscar who brought sensation into the novel, arriving with a tarnished character and an association with crime, and soon acquiring a disability that was treated in sensational fashion, while Lucilla's disability has repeatedly been associated with domestic realism. In the heightened sensitivity of her sense of touch, she is the one who can distinguish correctly which is the twin she should marry, and she chooses Oscar, the sentimental 'man of feeling', not his dashing brother Nugent.[142] Collins carefully obscures the question of whether Lucilla could still have reacted to Oscar's touch in the same way after her sight was restored, by having her touch only Nugent during the period in which she is sighted, and then refuse to attempt to restore her sight again after she is reunited with Oscar. However, the point is clearly made that Lucilla's perceptions as to who is truly fit to be her husband are clearer than those of her sighted companions – including the brothers themselves – and it is because she cannot see Oscar's blueness that she sees clearly.

If we take blueness as a metaphor for disability, then the didactic point is clear. This conclusion also marks a clear prioritising of Lucilla's perspective over Oscar's, and of domestic realist paradigms over sensational ones. When Collins returned to the detective sensational form in *The Law and the Lady*, as we have seen, disability was once again a marginalised, if transgressive, source of narrative energy and affect; here, it is rendered a source of stability and made central to the happy family scene with which the novel closes. The sensational uncertainty surrounding identity in Collins's sensation fiction is stripped away by Lucilla's unfailing sensory perceptiveness; she is confused only when she is made to mistrust her sense of touch. Here, a kind of somatic authenticity *is* shown to be possible, as Lucilla is able to tell who her true love is, through touching him. Crucially, however, she can access this somatic truth only when she cannot see the signs of the body that would mislead her: blueness turns out to be a red herring that only blindness can see through.

## Notes

1. Collins, *Moonstone*, p. 444.
2. The impoverished hero/ine's inherited (but hitherto unrecognised) entitlement to riches or gentility is a trope that occurs frequently in both novelistic and stage melodrama: for example, in Dickens's *Oliver Twist* (1839), Dion Boucicault's *The Poor of New York* (1857) and D'Ennery and Cormon's *Les Deux Orphelines* (1874).
3. A hostile review of *The Woman in White* in the *Dublin University Magazine*, for example, stated: 'Take [the plot] away, and there is nothing left to examine. There is not one lifelike character ... in the whole book' (*Wilkie Collins: The Critical Heritage*, p. 105.) Even in more sympathetic accounts of Collins's work, similar judgements persist; his admirer Lewis Melville acknowledged in 1903 that Collins 'always made his characters subordinate to his plot' ('Wilkie Collins', p. 361). In Henry Mansel's famous essay on sensation fiction, he claimed that it was inherently deficient in the portrayal of character because of its reliance on the thrills of plot, calling its characters 'but so many lay-figures on which to exhibit a drapery of incident' ('Art. Vii.', p. 486), an argument echoed by Walter M. Kendrick well over a century later when he suggested that character has a 'vehicular function' in sensation fiction ('The Sensationalism of *The Woman in White*', p. 71).
4. Thomas, *Detective Fiction*, p. 63.
5. Brooks, *Reading for the Plot*, p. 23.
6. Thomas, *Detective Fiction*, p. 63, p. 60.
7. These descriptions refer to Rosanna Spearman (*The Moonstone*), Sara Macallan (*The Law and the Lady*), Marian Halcombe (*The Woman in White*), Matilda Wragge (*No Name*), Miserrimus Dexter (*The Law and the Lady*) and Oscar Dubourg (*Poor Miss Finch*), respectively.
8. Gilbert, *Disease, Desire, and the Body*, p. 67.
9. Mansel, 'Art. Vii.', p. 486.
10. Cvetkovich, *Mixed Feelings*, p. 24.
11. Flint, 'Disability and Difference', p. 154. Similarly, Tamara S. Wagner suggests that Collins's 'increasingly intricate plots of detection trade on prevailing stereotypes [of disability] at the time in order to turn them into false clues, that both startle the reader, and warn of the dangers of

relying on conventional cultural categories' ('Ominous Signs or False Clues?', p. 47).
12. Mossman, 'Representations of the Abnormal Body', p. 487.
13. Miller, *The Novel and the Police*, p. 163.
14. For a detailed discussion of such de-naturalising of able-bodied readers' sensory experiences and ways of knowing – what she calls 'somatic epistemology' – in other sensation novels, see Ferguson, 'Sensational Dependence'.
15. Collins, *The Law*, p. 206.
16. Heller, *Dead Secrets*, pp. 6–8 and *passim*.
17. Mossman, 'Representations of the Abnormal Body in *The Moonstone*', p. 497; Lonoff, *Wilkie Collins and His Victorian Readers*, p. 158.
18. Mansel, 'Art. Vii', p. 512.
19. Collins, *Woman in White*, p. 31.
20. Ibid. p. 20.
21. Indeed, Lillian Craton and Rebecca Stern have suggested that Marian's characterisation is indebted to the freak-show performer Julia Pastrana, the 'bear woman' (Craton, *The Victorian Freak Show*, pp. 126–7; Stern, 'Our Bear Women, Ourselves', pp. 226–8).
22. Collins, *Woman in White*, p. 32.
23. Ibid. p. 50.
24. Ibid. p. 331.
25. Ibid. p. 220, p. 294.
26. Ibid. p. 220.
27. Ibid.
28. Ibid. p. 221.
29. Ibid. p. 343.
30. Ibid. p. 458.
31. Ibid. p. 640.
32. Ibid. p. 598.
33. Ibid. p. 643.
34. Ibid. p. 220, p. 32.
35. Cvetkovich, *Mixed Feelings*, p. 76.
36. Sanders, 'A Shock to the System', p. 77.
37. Collins, *Moonstone*, p. 21.
38. Ibid. p. 25.
39. Ibid. p. 22.
40. Ibid. p. 26.
41. Ibid.
42. Stoddard Holmes, 'Bolder with her Lover in the Dark', p. 72.
43. Collins, *Moonstone*, p. 309.
44. As Anthea Trodd points out, Franklin's refusal (or failure) to read all of Rosanna's letter also thwarts that the possibility of full understanding between employers and servants, 'and the household conditions which produced the mystery survive its solution' (*Domestic Crime in the Victorian Novel*, p. 85.)

45. Collins, *Moonstone*, p. 46.
46. Ibid. p. 113.
47. Ibid. p. 311.
48. Ibid. p. 52, p. 311.
49. Ibid. p. 124.
50. Ibid. pp. 183–4, emphasis original.
51. Ibid. p. 302.
52. Ibid. p. 301.
53. Ibid. p. 320.
54. Ibid. p. 319, p. 367.
55. Ibid. p. 319.
56. Ibid. p. 375, p. 369.
57. As Vicki Corkran Willey argues, 'Jennings's insight emerges from his Otherness . . . suggest[ing] that a synthesis [of Eastern and European experiences] is stronger than either of the two halves separately' ('Wilkie Collins's "Secret Dictate"', p. 231).
58. Collins, *Moonstone*, p. 375.
59. Ibid. p. 457.
60. Ibid. p. 426.
61. See Free, 'Freaks that Matter', pp. 273–6.
62. Welsh, *Strong Representations*, p. 233.
63. Collins, *Moonstone*, p. 52.
64. Nayder, *Unequal Partners*, p. 181.
65. Mangham, *Violent Women and Sensation Fiction*, p. 83.
66. Collins, *Moonstone*, p. 319, p. 367.
67. Collins, *Law*, p. 203.
68. Ibid. p. 247, pp. 229–30.
69. Ibid. p. 206.
70. Ibid. p. 206, p. 207.
71. Ibid. p. 207.
72. Ibid. p. 218.
73. Ibid. p. 222, p. 232.
74. Ibid. p. 233.
75. Garland-Thomson, *Staring*, p. 19.
76. Ibid.
77. Collins, *Law*, p. 232.
78. Ibid.
79. Ibid. p. 196.
80. Ibid. p. 7.
81. Ibid. p. 247.
82. Ibid. p. 216.
83. Ibid. pp. 215–16.
84. Ibid. p. 183.
85. Ibid. p. 214.
86. Ibid. p. 11, p. 312, p. 12.

87. Ibid. p. 278, p. 12.
88. Ibid. p. 238.
89. The editor of *The Graphic* magazine, in which the novel was first serialised, tried to censor this scene. Collins refused, leading to an acrimonious exchange of letters in the press (reproduced in an Appendix to the edition cited here, pp. 413–17). The scene may have contributed to the exceptionally hostile critical reaction to the novel in general and to the character of Miserrimus in particular (for representative examples, 'The Law and the Lady', *Athenaeum* and 'The Law and the Lady', *Saturday Review*), which continued well into the twentieth century, as Sue Lonoff illustrates in her summary of the novel's critical reception (*Wilkie Collins and His Victorian Readers*, p. 163). Stoddard Holmes offers a cogent explanation for why this scene has met with such critical hostility: 'The scene dramatizes the breaking of a particularly Victorian (and later) compact in which disabled people can be objects of sympathy and financial support as long as they refrain from disrupting a cultural frame that denies them agency and sexuality' ('Queering the Marriage Plot', p. 249).
90. Collins, *Law*, p. 292.
91. Ibid.
92. Ibid. p. 293.
93. Ibid. p. 294, p. 299.
94. Ibid. p. 298.
95. Ibid. p. 300.
96. Ibid.
97. Ibid.
98. Ibid. pp. 402–3.
99. Ibid. p. 387.
100. Ibid.
101. Ibid. p. 393, p. 324.
102. Ibid. p. 203, p. 211.
103. Ibid. p. 211.
104. Briefel, 'Cosmetic Tragedies', p. 475.
105. Collins, *Law*, p. 312, p. 413.
106. Ibid. p. 391.
107. Ibid. p. 399.
108. Hall, untitled illustration, *The Graphic*, p. 249.
109. Collins, *Law*, p. 255.
110. Ibid. p. 346.
111. Ibid.
112. Ibid. p. 329.
113. Ibid. p. 346.
114. For an alternative reading that argues that Miserrimus functions 'as Eustace's double', see Wagner, 'Overpowering Vitality', p. 491.
115. Collins, 'Dedication', *Poor Miss Finch*, pp. xxxix–xl (p. xil).

116. Collins had already experimented with writing a domestic–sensational novel with a disabled heroine some twenty years earlier in *Hide and Seek* (1854), which centres on an identity mystery surrounding the deaf Madonna Blyth. Martha Stoddard Holmes has argued convincingly that the incest plot-line in that novel, which thwarts Madonna's growing attachment to Zack and derails their marriage plot by revealing them to be siblings, functions as a safety-valve in displacing the question of whether a deaf woman can or should marry (Stoddard Holmes, *Fictions of Affliction*, p. 83). Collins hints at the cultural resistance to the idea of disabled women becoming wives and mothers by depicting Madonna's adoptive mother as an invalid and describing how, although her marriage to the painter Valentine Blyth has been happy and productive, it was opposed by Valentine's family, who 'all objected strongly to this match' on account of the bride's uncertain future health (*Hide and Seek*, p. 35). If critical censure was, as Stoddard Holmes suggests, at the heart of Collins's nervousness around depicting a disabled woman as an object of desire (rather than as a victim of one-sided passion), then his concerns were well founded; in reaction to *Poor Miss Finch*, a critic for *The Saturday Review* complained that it was distasteful to imagine a blind heroine as a love interest because 'it seems to us that an infirmity like blindness should chill the passions' ('Poor Miss Finch', *Saturday Review*, p. 283). The reviewer goes on to compare Lucilla unfavourably with Edward Bulwer-Lytton's Nydia, a blind character in *The Last Days of Pompeii* (1834), who suffers unrequited love and commits suicide, apparently a more fitting end for a blind heroine than a happy marriage.
117. Nora and Magdalene Vanstone are the sisters whose disinheritance is at the heart of the plot of *No Name* (1862); like the earlier Laura, the fairer sister Nora is passive, resigned and virtuous, while Magdalene resembles Marian in being dark, passionate and determinedly enterprising.
118. Collins, *Poor Miss Finch*, p. 4, p. 16.
119. Ibid. p. 65, emphases original.
120. Collins, 'Dedication', *Poor Miss Finch*, p. xl.
121. Similarly, in *Hide and Seek*, Collins treats Madonna's deafness as a specific, negotiable impairment rather than a metaphor, realistically portraying her use of sign language, something Jennifer Esmail persuasively argues his critics have missed when they read her lack of spoken language as symbolic of disenfranchisement (*Reading Victorian Deafness*, p. 87).
122. Collins, *Poor Miss Finch*, p. 89.
123. For two helpful but contrasting readings of the novel's marriage plot, see Tilley, *Blindness and Writing*, Ch. 7, and Stoddard Holmes, *Fictions of Affliction*, Ch. 3.
124. Collins, *Poor Miss Finch*, p. 424.

125. 'Poor Miss Finch', *Athenaeum*, p. 302.
126. Charlotte Yonge's family sagas are also satirically invoked, I think, by the comic representation of Mrs Finch's excessive fecundity, and Yonge's idealised representation of very large and religiously earnest families parodically reproduced in the pompous windbag Reverend Finch, his ludicrously 'damp' and perpetually nursing wife, and their fourteen children.
127. Collins, *Poor Miss Finch*, p. 93.
128. Ibid. pp. 110–11.
129. Ibid. p. 121.
130. Ibid. p. 171, p. 118, p. 105.
131. As Samuel Lyndon Gladden points out, the novel was composed at around the time when Collins's friend Dickens was being treated with nitrate of silver, and had suffered discoloration of the skin ('Spectacular Deceptions', p. 473). He goes on to construct a queer reading of the novel in which blueness stands in for Oscar's unspeakable homosexuality.
132. Ibid. p. 474.
133. Jessica Durgan has argued that blueness functions in the novel as a metaphor for racial difference, highlighting the discussion of the Indian officer's complexion (Collins, *Poor Miss Finch*, p. 340) as a moment of potential confusion between blueness arising from nitrate of silver treatment and natural, hereditary darkness of skin tone ('Wilkie Collins's Blue Period', p. 778). While I am not convinced that her reading of this particular scene holds water – since it involves discounting the likely possibility that the 'retired Indian officer' is an ethnically Caucasian Englishman who has served in India, rather than being ethnically Indian – her overall argument is productive and interesting.
134. Collins, *Poor Miss Finch*, p. 113.
135. Ibid. p. 418.
136. In *Man and Wife* (1870), the point that physical fitness is no qualification for heroism was didactically made through the contrast between the immoral but handsome and athletic Geoffrey Delomayn and the club-footed gentleman, Patrick Lundie.
137. Collins, *Poor Miss Finch*, p. 148, p. 172.
138. Ibid. p. 135.
139. Ibid. p. 272.
140. Ibid. p. 290.
141. Ibid. p. 423.
142. Wagner argues that Collins consistently depicts sentimental heroes, 'men of feeling', as superior to the more industrious, confident and athletic 'modern men' who were taking their place ('Overpowering Vitality', pp. 471–2); I agree, and see Oscar's characterisation as one of the clearest instances of this dynamic.

Chapter 3

# (De)Forming Families: Disability and the Marriage Plot in Dinah Mulock Craik and Charlotte M. Yonge

Miss Muloch [sic] has lately written a book which is not the less welcome because it is an anachronism. In it she unfolds the virtues of a crippled Earl, who nobly devotes his life to securing the happiness of all around him. This he does in so admirable, and at the same time so feminine, a manner, as to remind one of a type of character that has latterly dropped out of fiction. An angelic being with a weak spine, who, from her sofa, directed with mild wisdom the affairs of the family or the parish, was a favourite creation of our lady-novelists of the pre-Braddonian period. And it was no mere supernumerary or chance complement of the group which they depicted. It had a deeper meaning, and expressed two of the most creditable feminine instincts – the instinct to improve the world by means of those moral teachings which may be conveniently conveyed through some such mouthpiece, and the instinct to admire moral, as distinct from material, power. The perfecting of strength out of weakness, in the person of a disabled aunt or invalid sister, was a fascinating theme to such writers as Miss Yonge or Miss Sewell. They were fond of exhibiting moral influence in combination with infirmity, which gave a piquancy to their domestic hero-worship. It is quite natural that women of talent and refinement should feel a pleasure in propounding a view which tends in some degree to redress the balance of power between the sexes, and to remind their readers that, in spite of the vaunted superiority of man, there are heights of moral elevation, and even influence, which woman may claim as peculiarly her own.[1]

In this anonymous review of *A Noble Life* (1866), Dinah Mulock Craik's decision to depict her protagonist as disabled is read as a sign of her generic, religious and political affiliations. She is drawn together with Elizabeth Sewell and Charlotte M. Yonge to suggest that there is a school of female writers – already going out of fashion in 1866 – whose work is distinguished by its concern with disability. This concern is explicitly gendered female: it is not merely that Craik's (male) disabled protagonist is 'feminine', but that the decision to create him at all expresses 'the most creditable feminine instincts'. Implicitly, this reviewer draws together femaleness and disability as experiences and identities, suggesting that to depict morally powerful disabled characters 'tends in some degree to redress the balance of power between the sexes'. Later in the review, novelists who use disabled characters in this way are contrasted not only with sensation writers such as Mary Elizabeth Braddon, who have now usurped their place in the market, but also with those (now ascendant) women who do not understand that a woman's 'highest purpose' is fulfilled 'not by practising in law courts and lecturing on platforms'.[2] Craik and Yonge's treatment of disability is taken here as symptomatic both of the genre of their work, in setting them apart from sensation writers, and of what would now be called their gender politics.

As the preceding chapters have illustrated, disabled characters populate novels across the spectrum of Victorian fiction, but for this reviewer, disability appears as a hallmark of a particular kind of 'feminine' writing. This yoking together of Craik and Yonge is striking because they came from totally different religious and social backgrounds, and their work is as stylistically and thematically divergent as might therefore be expected. Dinah Mulock Craik was the daughter of a nonconformist minister who supported herself and her family through her writing, living independently in London as an unmarried woman, expressing a buoyant confidence in the potential of self-made men and women, and propagating an expansively Broad Church version of Christianity through her sentimental, tear-jerking novels. She would surely have felt herself to have little in common with Charlotte Yonge, the arch-conservative Tractarian, living in rural retirement and giving the proceeds of her novels away to charitable causes. Yonge's distrust of sentimentality, her aversion to the kinds of social change Craik embraces, and what Susan Colón has perceptively called the 'Tractarian aesthetics'[3] of her minutely detailed, cluttered realist novels, make her work utterly different from Craik's, and lumping them together as religious women writers does both a disservice.

Yet when Craik and Yonge's novels are compared with those I have discussed so far, there *is* something highly distinctive about their treatment of disabled characters, in terms not so much of their characterisation, but of their structural position. Disabled characters are accorded 'moral power' in many of the texts previously explored, but they tend to be found at the margins of the novels: they sometimes exert inward pressure, destabilising or disrupting the plot-lines that sideline or exclude them, and they frequently distract our attention from the ostensible centre of narrative attention, but we do not encounter them as protagonists. In contrast, two of Dinah Craik's novels have disabled protagonists, while another has a disabled narrator; almost every Charlotte Yonge novel prominently features a permanently disabled character, and most of her characters have to experience disability at some point. In this chapter, I wish to examine how the plot structures of their novels enable this investment of power and attention in conventionally marginalised characters and experiences. In particular, I will explore how their treatment of the marriage plot and the forms of their families allow disabled characters to take centre-stage, and foreground disability as a central, rather than a marginal, human experience.

I have singled Yonge and Craik out for attention because their fiction so prominently features disabled characters, but also because their treatment of disability has dominated their critical reception. It is my contention that their critical marginalisation is not coincidentally related to the central place they accord the socially and culturally marginalised experience of disability, but that their critical standing has closely reflected shifting attitudes towards the representation of disability and the idea of 'feminine' writing. In focusing on their treatment of disability and its gendered implications, the *Saturday Review* critic sets out the terms on which these writers have been judged ever since, his suggestion that their depiction of disabled characters is both 'admirable' and 'feminine' encapsulating the simultaneously laudatory and patronising attitude that rendered Craik and Yonge so popular in their own day, and so vulnerable to posthumous critical erasure.

Henry James's review of the same novel echoes the *Saturday Review* piece, in characterising Craik as a writer who embodies the feminine virtues, who is 'so transparently a woman' that her defects are 'charming and even sacred', and in linking these qualities (and their related flaws) to her depiction of disability, which becomes a symptom of both:

> We might cite several examples to illustrate that lively predilection for cripples and invalids by which she has always been distinguished; but we defer to this generous idiosyncrasy. It is no more than right that the sickly half of humanity should have its chronicler . . . .[4]

Although James praises such subject-matter as 'admirable', there can be no doubt that Craik is being damned with faint praise (certainly not by the time she has been called 'kindly, somewhat dull, pious, and very sentimental'), and that her 'generous idiosyncrasy' in writing about disability exemplified, for James, both her moral strengths and her literary limitations.[5] By the time of her death, critical opinion appears to have coalesced around the idea that Craik was as morally praiseworthy as she was canonically marginal;[6] her work was to suffer a yet steeper decline in critical terms after her death. When attempts were made to rehabilitate her reputation and rediscover her work in the 1970s and 1980s, both Elaine Showalter and Sally Mitchell felt the need to explain away or apologise for her recurrent treatment of disability.[7] Mitchell's admission that *A Noble Life* is 'embarrassing to read [because] . . . [w]e feel uncomfortable in the presence of deformity and pain; we feel sensitive about staring so openly at a cripple' makes explicit the connection between ostensible distaste for Craik's aesthetics and actual distaste for her subject-matter; it is not until disability has been translated into gender that Mitchell feels able to defend Craik's sentimental style.[8]

While the upsurge of interest in the work of forgotten women writers in the 1970s and 1980s undoubtedly contributed to Craik's re-discovery, and inspired Showalter and Mitchell's pioneering studies, it was not until disability became a subject of considerable academic interest that her work began to enjoy what might be called a revival. It is telling that the novel singled out for re-publication in the Oxford Popular Fiction series in 2000 was *Olive*, which has a disabled protagonist, rather than the far *more* popular *John Halifax, Gentleman*; as if to underscore the logic behind the choice, the edition bore on the front cover the slogan, 'The Story of a Girl's Triumph Over Prejudice'.[9] As Karen Bourrier points out in her introduction to the first special journal issue devoted to Craik's work, 'the majority of scholars at this critical moment are coming to Craik's work through a disability studies perspective'.[10]

Yonge's reputation has followed a very similar trajectory, with her fiction being praised as wholesome in the nineteenth and early twentieth centuries, while her depiction of disability was still seen as morally praiseworthy – actually described as 'medicine' for the soul in one review[11] – but condemned as distasteful and even morally culpable as cultural attitudes to disability hardened. Although Q. D. Leavis's hatchet job in the pages of *Scrutiny* was ostensibly concerned with Charlotte Yonge's literary shortcomings ('We are not concerned with her qualifications as a Christian but as a novelist,'

Leavis insisted), she returns again and again to the central place accorded to disabled characters in Yonge's fiction in order to convict her of being 'morbid'.[12] Ultimately, Leavis draws on the contemporary lexicon of disability to formulate her final condemnation: 'The limitations that produced moral triteness are paralleled by her worldly ignorance that cripples her fiction.'[13]

This could perhaps be dismissed as an idiosyncrasy of Leavis's, were it not for the fact that the much more sympathetic biography Leavis is reviewing, Georgina Battiscombe's *An Uneventful Life*, also offers a kind of apology for many of the disabled characters in Yonge's fiction. Battiscombe describes Margaret May as a 'sad bore' and Ermine Williams as 'obstinately unsympathetic', while she calls Yonge's lifelong friend Marianne Dyson, who was an invalid, 'one of the worst influences of her life'.[14] Mia Chen suggests that Battiscombe's hostile reaction to real and fictional disability is 'phobic', and it does indeed seem to rest upon the premise that Yonge must be rescued from her association with disability, in both her life and her fiction.[15] Yonge's attitude to her disabled characters – particularly those whose parents can, in eugenic terms, be in some way blamed for their disabilities – is singled out for criticism, not just by Battiscombe, but by other contributors to the volume of generally hagiographic essays on Yonge published in 1965.[16] The increasing difficulty that Yonge's depictions of disability caused for critics who wanted to uphold her reputation as morally inspiring clearly aggravated the fall from grace that would, in any case, have befallen the author in an era when literary didacticism was firmly out of fashion. Meanwhile, the interest in Yonge's work, which was already gathering momentum as a result of the wider rediscovery of the work of popular women writers, has been greatly accelerated as part of the growing interest in disability studies: disability is a prominent theme in the first journal special issue devoted to Yonge and in a recent collection of essays featuring her work, and it is her treatment of disability that leads to her prominent inclusion in two recent monographs on the mid-Victorian novel.[17]

As this brief survey illustrates, the critical trajectory of both authors has been shaped by readers' attitudes to their representations of disability, which has been as central to their reception as it is to the novels themselves. In their different ways, both authors can help us recover a way of writing disability that fell (or was pushed) out of the literary canon. The differences between their way of writing disability and that of the male authors I have examined so far, and also the differences between these writers themselves, are extremely suggestive, in terms of both the insight they give into these particular writers' work, and what they reveal about patterns of novelistic plotting in this period more generally.

For both authors, disabled characters proved useful as a means to explore alternatives to the marriage plot and to probe its merits and disadvantages. By shutting them out of the marriage plot, disability provided the need (and, in some cases, the pretext) for female characters to pursue independent careers. Conversely, by feminising male characters, excluding them from public life and financially rewarding work, disability also enabled both authors to interrogate the value of a life wholly confined to the domestic sphere. Yonge and Craik were writing at a time when the subject of 'redundant women' was everywhere, and both were themselves pursuing careers as single women, whilst presenting themselves as champions of traditional femininity in tracts such as Craik's *A Woman's Thoughts About Women* (1858) and Yonge's *Womankind* (1876).[18] Their fiction was therefore inevitably concerned with the subjects of whether, and how, women should support themselves independently, and the value of dependence and domesticity. Disabled characters enabled them to explore these themes without compromising their reputation for exemplary femininity and its associated political cautiousness.

For Yonge, disabled characters play a vital role in displacing marriage from the centre of her familial fictions, which tend to be shaped around characters excluded from the marriage plot. The formal structure of her multi-focused and capacious family sagas allows Yonge to depict alternatives to the marriage plot without writing it out completely, while her typological plotting and distinctively Anglo-Catholic imagery allot a central place to the image of the suffering body, which enables disability to signify as a meaningful and salutary life experience. The 'feminine' nature of this experience – highlighted by the *Saturday Review* critic – does not marginalise it in Yonge's work at all, but instead forms part of her attempt to universalise those values and activities culturally gendered female. By no means all of Yonge's disabled characters conform to the image of the 'angelic being with a weak spine' with which we began, but they are all made central to the families and novels in which they appear.

By contrast, in Craik's more compact and sentimentally structured works, disabled characters' inability to play the leading role in their own marriage plot is a source of tremendous narrative difficulty, frustration and pain. In *Olive* (1850), Craik manages to stage the integration of the disabled heroine into the marriage plot only through belatedly re-forming her hitherto stigmatised body, in a manœuvre that speaks to Craik's Muscular Christian association of physical and spiritual wholeness, and her equation of health and heterosexuality. The disabled character's exclusion from the marriage plot in *John Halifax, Gentleman* (1856) and *A Noble Life* (1866) is a major plot point, and Craik struggles – with partial success, in both cases – to form the family around the excluded disabled figure. In Craik's fiction, marriage remains the ultimate narrative reward and goal, and this undoubtedly causes structural problems in all three of the novels I will be examining. It does not, however, prevent her disabled characters from playing a central role.

The sentimental style of all three novels means that close attention is paid to the protagonist's affective responses, with emotional development being prized above all else. The association both in the novels and in the wider culture between disability and affective experience renders disabled characters ideal sentimental subjects, and necessary adjuncts to the affective development of able-bodied characters.[19] Moreover, these three novels demonstrate Craik's developing approach to writing a 'life' and, taken together, stage an interrogation of domesticity and its alternatives. *Olive* is a fairly conventional *Bildungsroman* (albeit with a heroine rather than a hero), beginning at the protagonist's birth, and concluding with her happy marriage and the promise of parenthood. However, her disability enables the heroine to forge an artistic career and thus expands the scope of the novel, even if it is ultimately contracted by her marriage. In *John Halifax, Gentleman*, Craik narrates a life such as might form the basis of a 'great man' biography, recording her hero's meteoric rise in the world and his public, political and commercial career, but does so from the perspective of a disabled bystander, whose experiences shape the novel in which he is structurally sidelined. In *A Noble Life*, Craik goes further, attempting to write a 'biography'[20] that is not merely inflected by but wholly focused on her subject's affective development and affective influence on those around him. His disability is treated as a hopeless bar to a public career in such a way that the experience of domesticity, and the values of the sentimental novel, are subjected to the closest scrutiny.

## 'Excluded from a woman's natural destiny': Disability as Possibility in *Olive*

*Olive* stands out from most of the novels I have discussed so far in being squarely centred on a disabled protagonist. Olive Rothesay is described at her birth as being 'deformed – born so – and [she] will remain so for life', and yet there is never any doubt that she is the heroine of the story.²¹ In fact, Craik puts disability to vital narrative work in this novel by using it to expand the possibilities of the female *Bildungsroman*. Olive's belief in her own exclusion from 'a woman's natural destiny' – meaning marriage – frees her to pursue an artistic career and to develop an independent life, leading Sally Mitchell to suggest that 'the defect that prevents Olive from being "a woman" allows her to be a person'.²² I would argue that Olive's disability actually allows her to *remain* a woman whilst being granted more opportunities and greater power than her gendered position would usually allow: it is Olive's disability that enables Craik to reconcile femininity with experience, independence and maturity.

Charlotte Brontë had created in *Jane Eyre* (1847) a female protagonist who launches herself into the world on her own initiative by deciding to 'advertise'.²³ Through her ability to earn her own living by practising her profession, Jane is able to make herself a novelistic heroine capable of sustaining her very own *Bildungsroman*. She was also widely condemned as totally unfeminine,²⁴ and it is here that the comparison with Olive becomes useful. There are clear echoes of *Jane Eyre* in *Olive* at the level of plot, and Sally Mitchell sees Craik's deformed heroine as having 'the emotional power . . . of *Jane Eyre* twisted one degree tighter'.²⁵ As Cora Kaplan points out, however, in her gentleness, resignation and docility Olive is the antithesis of the rebellious Jane, and Olive can therefore be read rather as a 'counter-text' to *Jane Eyre* than an imitation.²⁶ I see this conservative transformation of Brontë's heroine as being effected through disability, which acts as a safety valve, preserving Olive's femininity as she ventures to the very limits of the female sphere, saving her from the false forms of femininity that might otherwise tempt her, and enabling Craik to expand the narrative possibilities of the 'feminine' novel without jettisoning the very femininity she seeks to vindicate.

Characterising Craik as a typically feminine novelist in her superior grasp of character and inferior ability to construct a plot, R. H. Hutton complained that, in *Olive*, 'a small number of successive plots are threaded together in place of a single comprehensive plot'.²⁷ *Olive* does indeed have a tripartite plot structure, closely corresponding to its original three-volume form, in which the heroine appears in three different roles: as a daughter, as an artist and finally as a wife. It is in Olive's ability to move between these roles that her success as a heroine lies, and it is in enabling this flexibility that her disability performs such crucial narrative work.²⁸

Olive's disability initially leads to her rejection as a daughter, with her vain young mother, who 'had learned since her birth to consider beauty as the greatest good', feeling 'complete indifference' towards her, and her supposedly more serious-minded father 'putting his hands before his eyes, as if to shut out the sight' when he first sees her, five years later.[29] Although by this time it is clear that the prediction that she would be a 'poor cripple' was incorrect, as her curvature of the spine turns out to make no difference (at least none that is ever mentioned) to her mobility, it remains an aesthetic blemish in others' eyes – 'an elevation of the shoulders, shortening the neck, and giving the appearance of a perpetual stoop' – and her parents continue to regard her as a disappointment.[30] As a result, she experiences a childhood in which 'neither neglected nor ill-used, ... she never knew that fullness of love, on which one looks back in after-life'.[31]

At this point, however, the narrator pauses to tell us that, in spite of her parents' negligence, Olive's moral, artistic and spiritual development has already begun. She is depicted as a Romantic child of nature, who is able to discover for herself what others have to be taught, her intuitive religious faith and artistic sensibility compensating for her lack of nurture.[32] Far from suggesting that Olive is, for this reason, cut off from her inadequate parents, Craik depicts her as an exemplary daughter, who eventually wins their love and respect through her extraordinary tact, sympathy and perceptiveness. Ultimately, her father realises that she has 'the strong will and decision of a man, united to the tenderness of a woman', while, more fulsomely, her mother Sybilla finally declares her 'the most duteous daughter that ever mother had'.[33] Having learned nothing from them but having everything to teach them, Olive is able to take up a powerful, even monitory relationship to both her parents: she is, in an important sense, a self-made woman. While Olive is very far from being the only heroine of the period who is possessed of an apparently inexhaustible supply of patience for her unsatisfactory parent-figures,[34] her disability both externalises and heightens our sense that she is different from her parents, and has to be self-authored in her character.

Craik softens our view of Sybilla's failings as a mother by suggesting that she has been warped in her character by the over-valuation of beauty as a marker of female worth. After offering a rapturous description of her physical loveliness, the narrator accusingly asks the reader, 'But was there a soul in this exquisite form? You never asked – you hardly cared! You took the thing for granted.'[35]

Sybilla's apparently heartless treatment of her baby daughter is partially explained by the fact that 'she had been brought up like a plant in a hot-bed, with all natural impulses either warped and suppressed, or forced into undue luxuriance'.[36] Olive's neglected upbringing has to be contrasted, then, with what Craik clearly sees as the distorting effects of a falsely 'feminine' education, which serves Sybilla so poorly as a wife and mother. Our attention is drawn, for example, to the fact that Sybilla tries to win back her husband's lost affection 'not with a woman's sweet and placid dignity of love' but with 'the only arts she knew ... the whole armoury of girlish coquetry'; at just fifteen, Olive, by contrast, has 'learned a woman's wisdom', and can soothe her father as her mother cannot.[37] This opposition between the 'girlish' and the 'womanly' seems to me an attempt to distinguish between false and true forms of femininity, and it is the latter that disability is shown to promote. The admiration that turned Sybilla's head as a girl – and is shown to have an equally damaging effect on Olive's friend Sara, whose vanity leads her into flirting and faithlessness – is wholly absent from Olive's experience. Instead, she undergoes a crash-course in the virtues of self-forgetfulness, patience and humility, which are depicted as the mainstays of her success, not just as a daughter, but subsequently as an independent woman of the world.

Above all, Olive's experience of parental rejection, and her need to teach herself what her parents neglect to teach her, are shown to foster her religious life. Tellingly, it is immediately after her disastrous first ball, at which she is first explicitly made aware of her 'deformity', and finally understands 'why papa said I should never marry', that she experiences the religious vision in which 'God's immeasurable Infinite rose before her in glorious serenity'.[38] Olive's reliance upon God is prompted by her despairing sense that she is 'shut out forever' from 'the love which is the religion of a woman's heart'.[39]

In fact, this opposition between Olive's piety and 'the religion of a woman's heart' is ultimately shown to be a false one, for the experiences that have led Olive to this lonely place are distinctively feminine, and the religious life she achieves as a result is shown to be uniquely capable of resolving masculine doubts and thereby bringing about the domestic bliss Olive desires. Believing herself cut off from the possibility of marriage, Olive in fact develops the very qualities that fit her to be a wife, as her mother and friend do not: incapable of embodying the false femininity of Sybilla and Sara, Olive does not thereby become androgynous, but rather embodies the true femininity that is depicted as the complement of her future husband Harold's ideal masculinity. In the mean time, her piety leads her to the meekness that enables her to bear with both her parents. She embodies a femininity that is completely distinct from Jane Eyre's rebellious demand for justice, its power deriving from its inexhaustible patience and stoicism, based not on a sense of self-worth, but on religious faith.

Olive's ideal daughterliness does not consist solely of domestic virtues, however. By killing off her father, and bankrupting him for good measure, Craik creates the need for Olive to earn a living, and once again, it is her disability that enables her to do so without compromising her femininity. Her motives are shown to be thoroughly daughterly – Olive initially wants to become an artist in order to repay her father's debts[40] – but her decision is further justified by the fact that she considers herself to be unmarriageable. Her desire to devote herself to art does not therefore represent a rejection of marriage, and Craik is able to represent Olive's happiness in her artistic success without undermining her claim that 'there scarcely ever lived the woman who would not rather sit meekly by her own hearth, with her husband at her side, and her children at her knee, than be crowned Corinne of the Capitol'.[41] Craik's desire to find a compromise between the claim that it may be both necessary and desirable for a woman to pursue a remunerative career (as she did herself), and the acknowledgement that her true calling must be domestic, entailed contortions in her non-fictional writing, but here, Olive's disability allows Craik to square the circle, as 'that sense of personal imperfection which she deemed excluded her from a woman's natural destiny, gave her freedom in her own'.[42]

In her career as an artist, Olive's disability is depicted as cutting her off from other women and therefore putting her beyond the pale of comparison, or indeed emulation. In this respect, Olive's identity as deformed seems to overwrite her identity as female:

> Olive could do many things with an independence that would have been impossible to a beautiful and unguarded youth. Oftentimes Mrs. Rothesay trembled and murmured at the days of solitary study in the British Museum .... But Olive always answered with a pensive smile, 'Nay, mother, I am quite safe everywhere. Remember, I am not like other girls. Who would notice *me*?'[43]

As Dennis Denisoff points out, Olive's 'inability to attract the male gaze obviates her being categorized as a woman', and whereas this exclusion from femaleness had once been principally a source of pain, it now also liberates her for the career she loves.[44] Yet even as Craik allows us to see deformity as a potentially enabling condition, it also neutralises the challenge Olive's career would otherwise offer to a conventional conception of a woman's role, by reassuring the reader that it is conditional upon her exceptionality – that she *would* marry instead, if only she could.

Craik comes very close to suggesting that Olive is actually happier as a single woman artist than she would have been as a married woman, pointing out 'how ineffably beneath her own ideal' are the men Olive meets, as she sees 'her companions wedded to men who from herself would never have won a single thought',[45] and showing the oppressed life that Michael Vanbrugh's sister Meliora leads as his unregarded, unappreciated domestic slave, in comparison with the status Olive acquires as his pupil. However, the radicalism of this volume of the novel is significantly mitigated not only by Craik's repeated assurances that Olive is shut out from marriage, rather than freely choosing to avoid it, but by the fact that Olive's extreme unassertiveness and lack of self-esteem are proof against all success. Her painful experiences in the first volume of the novel seem to have rendered her utterly unable to develop confidence in herself, let alone display aggression when attacked. When Michael Vanbrugh reacts furiously to her refusal of his proposal of marriage, she does not respond to his misogyny – 'I thought were a great-souled, kindred genius – I find you a mere *woman*' – with any assertion of her own talent or rebuke to his egotism, but rather with a meek reminder of her own inadequacy: '"Look upon me!" said Olive, with a mournful meaning in her tone; "is such an one as I likely to marry?"'[46] Olive is never at risk of developing the kind of unfeminine self-assurance or self-esteem that would free her from the need for male approval because her experience of disability has imbued her with a sense of inadequacy that cannot be assuaged by worldly success, nor even, apparently, by the religion that is supposed to bring her comfort.

It is this total absence of self-assertiveness that enables Olive to become Harold Gwynne's wife in the third volume. Their relationship is predicated on the fact that while Olive is his superior in her religious faith, and is in fact able to lead the doubting clergyman back to Christianity, she treats him with unwavering deference, apparently happy to submit herself to him in everything besides religion: 'in his presence she unconsciously measured her words and guarded her looks, as if meeting the eye of a master'.[47] Indeed, Harold is marked out as Olive's future husband by the very fact of his ability to intimidate her; whereas with her younger admirer, Lyle Derwent, she feels confident in her greater worldly experience and the 'calm reality of her six-and-twenty years', in contrast, 'her spirit fell beneath the stern manhood of Harold Gwynne, and she grew once more a feeble, trembling, timid girl'.[48] The power dynamics of their relationship are reversed only when it comes to religion, and Olive's superior power of belief is explicitly gendered feminine, described by Harold as possessing 'the great beauty of a woman's religion'.[49] Olive never disputes his intellectual superiority, merely pointing out that religious faith does not depend upon it,[50] and once Harold has recovered his faith, with her help, he is able to take up the dominant role in their partnership. The last paragraph of the novel sees them standing together, Harold 'tossing back his head, and shaking his wavy hair, something lion-like', feeling himself 'strong and bold . . . stern to resist, daring to achieve, as a man should feel', while 'Olive, with her clinging sweetness, her upward gaze, was a type of true woman.'[51] Critics have attempted to read egalitarianism into this relationship,[52] but in fact Olive's marriage explicitly requires her to give up the emotional and financial independence she had developed in the novel's second volume. Once she has fallen in love with Harold, she is forced to recognise that art is no longer 'as once before the chief enjoyment and interest of her life', and once she is married, it is said to be 'a natural and a womanly thing that in her husband's fame Olive should almost forget her own'.[53]

Yet if this marriage represents something of a contraction of the field of Olive's endeavours as an independent woman, it is also an expansion of the field of possibility for Olive as a disabled character. Disability is ultimately made conducive to the very familial and romantic bonds it first appeared to threaten. As Martha Stoddard Holmes has pointed out, it is in her blindness that Sybilla truly comes to appreciate Olive's daughterly care and to see her clearly, their 'fulfilling intimacy predicated on interdependence'.[54] Although Harold Gwynne does not have to be blinded like Brontë's Rochester in order to recover his faith and win his place as the heroine's husband, he is injured in the fire from which he rescues Olive, and it is his temporary disability that enables her finally to express her long-repressed desire. Olive is liberated by his physical frailty both to nurse him – 'Every feeling of womanly shame vanish[ing] before the threatening shadow of death' – and to take up a more dominant position in their relationship than she can enjoy once he is recovered, replying to his admission of weakness by declaring herself 'strong' as she puts 'her arm under his head, and made him lean on her shoulder'.⁵⁵

If this was where the novel ended, then Craik's integration of her disabled heroine into the marriage plot would be fairly straightforward. However, there is a twist in the wish-fulfilment scene in which Olive finally brings herself to acknowledge to Harold her 'shame for that imperfection with which Nature had marked her from her birth'. His response complicates our sense that Olive's physical difference has been recognised and accepted:

> dispelling all doubts, healing all wounds, fell the words of betrothed husband – tender, though grave: 'Olive, if you love me, and believe that I love you, never grieve me by such thoughts again. To me you are all beautiful – in heart and mind, in form and soul.'
>
> Then, as if silently to count up her beauties, he kissed her little hands, her soft smiling mouth, her long gold curls. And Olive hid her face in his breast, murmuring,
>
> 'I am content, since I am fair in your sight, my Harold – my only love!'⁵⁶

Harold bears out his contention that Olive is 'all beautiful' by referring to a list of conventionally attractive attributes. He does not assure her that physical beauty is not in fact important, or that he sees her curved spine and sees no ugliness in it – he simply appears not to see it at all. Olive's body is re-formed before our eyes into that of a conventionally attractive heroine, her physical difference written out at the crucial moment.

It could, of course, be argued that Olive's disability has been shown to be a matter of perception, and therefore that she is quite literally un-disabled by the love of the novel's hero. If it was because she was deformed that she was unloveable, we might reason, then if she *is* loveable, she cannot be deformed. The fact that Olive never thinks of herself as deformed until she has been exposed to the cruel words of her false friend Sara and her drunken father could be used to shore up a reading of the novel by which Olive's deformity was only ever a matter of false perception, and to argue that Craik anticipates what would later be theorised as the social model of disability by showing how physical difference becomes 'deformity' only when it is read as such by others.⁵⁷

Yet while the nature of Olive's stigmatised physical difference – which constitutes no functional impairment – might draw out the social aspect of disability, and generate an exciting instability about the nature and meaning of 'deformity', it also enables Craik to write it out at the crucial moment, having sketched it in so lightly to begin with. As Elaine Showalter points out, the inconsistencies in Craik's representation of Olive's body throughout the text lead Craik into self-contradiction, repeatedly claiming Olive's physical difference as slight enough to be concealed by her hair or by a shawl, and yet significant enough to lead everyone to notice it as soon as she appears in public.[58] Moreover, there are considerable variations between earlier and later versions of the novel: in revising the novel for republication, Craik appears to have returned obsessively to those moments in the text when Olive's difference is defined.

At Olive's first ball, for example, after she has overheard Sara's unkind remarks about her undesirability as a dance partner, Olive asks her mother in the 1850 text, 'am I then so painful to look upon?'[59] In the 1875 revised text, she asks instead, 'am I really deformed?'[60] In a novel that is centrally concerned with the true meaning of Olive's physical difference, the slight alteration is highly significant: it matters whether Olive wants to know whether her deformity pains others, or whether she is 'really deformed'. Is she questioning the reactions of others to her difference, or the basis of that difference in itself? It is fitting that the very question that might be supposed to encapsulate the whole complex problem is itself destabilised through Craik's revisions, which represent not so much clarifications as thickenings of the complexity that characterise these moments. Having apparently wished to soften the doctor's initial declaration that Olive is 'deformed', Craik qualified the adjective in revision with 'slightly so – very slightly I hope',[61] and also removed Olive's reference to her 'sense of personal deformity' as a motivating factor in her decision to become an artist.[62] These revisions seem designed to weaken our sense of Olive's 'deformity', yet there are other examples in which her revisions serve rather to strengthen it: for instance, when she amends the opening of a later sentence from 'That sense of personal imperfection . . .' to the less equivocal 'That personal deformity . . .'.[63] These revisions are too inconsistent to have an over-arching effect; they seem rather to indicate Craik's uncertainty about how to define and describe Olive's physical difference, an uncertainty that comes to a forefront at the novel's conclusion.

In order for Olive to become Harold's wife, she has to become a 'type of a true woman',[64] and her physical difference has to be pushed to one side. In giving up the stature she had achieved as a daughter and artist, Olive is also able finally to put down the burden of her stigmatised difference, except in one important respect. We see her in the penultimate scene, 'by a child's bed – little Ailie's', stepmother rather than biological mother.⁶⁵ The dash in the sentence opens up a momentary pause in which we might wonder whether Olive *could* become a biological mother – but the gap is immediately closed.⁶⁶ Biological parenthood is typically the next stage in the marriage plot, represented in the final scenes of such prototypical *Bildungsromane* as *Jane Eyre* and *David Copperfield*, and Craik stops short of allowing Olive this final boon. However, up until this point, Craik has provided her heroine with an array of fictional rewards that might be favourably compared to David and Jane's. Disability has opened up, rather than closed down, Olive's potentiality as a heroine – surely begging the question why, in Craik's next novel, her disabled narrator is so thoroughly sidelined.

### 'The secondary character': The Role of the Disabled Narrator in *John Halifax, Gentleman*

*John Halifax, Gentleman* (1856) was by far Craik's most commercially and critically successful novel.⁶⁷ It is surely no coincidence that it is also, as J. Russell Perkin points out, her 'least typical', in its masculine narrative voice and, more importantly, its masculine structure and focus.⁶⁸ Accordingly, the disabled narrator, Phineas Fletcher, is positioned in a far more conventional way. He effectively stands on the sidelines of the novel, which takes the form of a biography of John Halifax, its plot driven by his inexorable rise to bourgeois prosperity and apparently corresponding success as a husband and father. Phineas is disbarred from both plot-lines, excluded from the public life in which John excels, and from the marriage plot which counter-balances it, explicitly as a result of the feminised character and identity that arise from his disability.

As Mary Klages has pointed out, Phineas's main role in the opening part of the novel is as 'the object that can demonstrate and strengthen Halifax's compassionate capabilities'.⁶⁹ Karen Bourrier's account of the two men's friendship emphasises the positive impact that his relationship with Phineas has upon John, treating their mutually helpful bond as 'the paradigmatic example' of how friendships between strong, silent men and their voluble, sensitive, physically frail counterparts were celebrated by the mid-Victorian novel.⁷⁰ Phineas does indeed have an essential role to play in preparing the eponymous hero for his leading role: John Halifax shows himself fit to be the hero of a sentimental novel through the exemplary 'compassion' of his response to Phineas's impairment, his strength established both in opposition to Phineas's weakness – 'Everything in him seemed to indicate that which I had not' – and as a response to it.[71] John's nurturing capabilities are represented as an aspect of his idealised masculinity: Phineas says that

> it was the first time in my life I ever knew the meaning of that rare thing – tenderness ... a quality which can exist only in strong, deep, and undemonstrative natures, and therefore in its perfection is oftenest found in men.[72]

Phineas, conversely, is feminised by this relationship, feeling himself to be in the position of 'the woman that [John] loved', and while this relationship is never pathologised – and is indeed tolerated within the novel to such an extent that Holly Furneaux can convincingly describe it as the source of 'queer creativity', and Talia Schaffer calls it 'a quasi-marital partnership' – it places Phineas in a kind of narrative limbo in which no plot-lines are available to him.[73] Where Furneaux and Schaffer both emphasise the pleasures of Phineas's relationship with John, I think it is important to recognise too the pain that Craik allows to seep into his narrative. Our attention is subtly drawn to the fact that as John blossoms into adulthood and moves ever closer to the centre of the narrative community, Phineas is increasingly diminished and sidelined.

On his twentieth birthday, for example, Phineas explicitly tells the reader that he woke 'to the consciousness that I was twenty years old, and that John Halifax was – a man; the difference between us being precisely as I have expressed it'.[74] He seems to reach this conclusion as a result of his recognition that he can never take over his father's tanning business nor marry, judging his character to be 'too feeble and womanish to be likely to win any woman's reverence or love. Even had this been possible, one sickly as I was, stricken with hereditary disease, ought never to seek to perpetuate it by marriage.'[75] Being a 'man' in the world of *John Halifax, Gentleman* means being a husband, a father and an economic provider: a man who cannot marry or work is therefore in a real sense no 'man' at all. Phineas's disability may enable him to perform vital narrative work as a narrator but it totally sidelines him in terms of plot: where Olive's disability ideally fitted her to certain feminine roles, Phineas's feminisation marginalises him from the narrative, for there is no analogous role for him to take up. Craik's gender politics should not be caricatured as trenchantly essentialist, bearing in mind her statement in *A Woman's Thoughts About Women* that

> each sex is composed of individuals, differing in character almost as much from one another as from the opposite sex ... and some of the finest types of character we have known among both sexes, are they not often those who combine the qualities of both?[76]

In *A Noble Life*, she was to develop the implications of this idea, casting a feminised disabled man as her hero – but here, Phineas's gender-bending puts him beyond the pale of normative plot structures, and Craik fails to create any new ones that could include him.

Although Phineas comes to be accommodated in the family John forms with his wife Ursula, his exclusion from the marriage plot is depicted in stark terms when he looks in at John and Ursula in their garden together and feels 'the fine line of division which was thus for evermore drawn between him and me'. As Phineas understands it, marriage is by definition the relationship that excludes, 'which, however kindly and fondly it may look on friends and kindred outside, has no absolute need of any, but is complete in and sufficient to itself'.[77] Even before John is married, Phineas declares himself to be 'considerably amused, and not ill-pleased, to see how naturally it fell out that when John appeared on the scene, I, Phineas, subsided into the secondary character of John's "friend"',[78] thus making explicit what we already suspect: that John's centrality is possible only at the price of Phineas's marginalisation. This is literally true in that John is able to succeed Abel Fletcher in his tanning business only because Phineas cannot do so, Phineas's inadequacy as a son providing the impetus for John's semi-adoption, which Phineas promotes. Phineas continues to play the role of John's assistant when he intercedes on his behalf during his courtship with Ursula, but once again, his intervention further sidelines him, since after John's marriage, Phineas is forced to accept yet another 'secondary' role. He appears not to play any active part in the life of the Halifax family, but to exist only as their biographer, observing the novel's action without participating.

Yet if Phineas is cut out of the novel's plot and serves primarily as a foil to John, it would be inaccurate to suggest that he commands no readerly attention, for he is not solely a sentimental object during the early part of the novel, but also a sentimental subject, whom we feel with, as well as for. While there are several representations in novels of this period of a relationship between an able-bodied and a disabled man, characterised by adoring dependence on one side and nurturing protectiveness on the other,[79] this one is unusual in being related from the perspective of the dependent. Whereas it is Nicholas's perceptions of Smike that dominate *Nicholas Nickleby*, so that we look *at* Smike *with* Nicholas and feel *for* him, here it is Phineas's eyes through which we see, and therefore it is his love for John that the text conveys most strongly. When John falls in love and marries, Phineas's exclusion from their relationship, and his sense of loss, intrude themselves upon the text, even as Phineas, as narrator, attempts to subordinate them to John's own feelings:

> 'Oh David – David!'
> 'Phineas, is that you? You have come out this bitter night – why did you?'
> His tenderness over me, even then, made me break down. I forgot my manhood, or else it slipped from me unawares. In the old Bible language, 'I fell on his neck and wept.'
> Afterwards I was not sorry for this, because I think my weakness gave him strength. I think, amidst the whirl of passion that racked him, it was good for him to feel that the one crowning cup of life is not inevitably life's sole sustenance; that it was something to have a friend and brother who loved him with a love – like Jonathan's – 'passing the love of women'.[80]

Phineas tries to justify his outburst by claiming it as 'good for' John, and attempts to re-direct our attention towards John's 'whirl of passion', which is the ostensible narrative focus of the courtship plot that is unfolding before us. Yet it is Phineas's pain that is made vivid for us, where John's feelings are merely the subject of hypothesis. Moreover, Phineas stakes a claim for the worth of his relationship with John by invoking the biblical model of David and Jonathan, even at the very point that it is being superseded by the courtship plot.[81] Similarly, when Phineas acknowledges his irrevocable exclusion from the marriage plot, we are drawn into his feelings, 'the hard struggle [that] was the only secret that [he] kept from John'.[82] In sharing his experience and learning the secrets he keeps from John, we are drawn towards Phineas as a sentimental subject. Arguably, it is John who recedes from us as the *object* of feeling (admiration, principally), while we share Phineas's experiences and perspective.

Moreover, Phineas's experience of domestic seclusion, his exclusion from the field of commerce and competition, and his adoring observation of his 'brother', unmatched by his capacity for practical aid, is one that a female reader is likely to share. Mitchell suggests that this is what makes Phineas an ideal narrator because he 'bridges the separate spheres of woman and man; he has a feminine viewpoint yet he can share a man's life and thoughts'.[83] This seems to me highly persuasive, and we do not have to translate disability into gender to observe the continuities and analogues between the experience and construction of femininity and disability in this novel, and therefore to recognise that by narrating John's successes from Phineas's perspective, Craik keeps faith with what the *Saturday Review* critic called her 'feminine' approach and identification. Commercial success and social recognition are narrated from the perspective of one who cannot share them, and we are drawn into this experience of exclusion even as John's triumphs are ostensibly celebrated.

Perhaps in an attempt to rescue the novel from this potentially destabilising identification, Craik chooses to replace Phineas as the sentimental centre of the narrative, about halfway through, with John and Ursula's blind daughter, Muriel. She is a far less complex sentimental object than Phineas because, unlike him, she has hardly a shadow of subjectivity: no interiority of hers intrudes itself upon the narrative, her own feelings about her disability are asserted to be wholly in keeping with onlookers' feelings (so she can both stimulate and instruct readers' responses), and the theodicy of the representation is made very clear. Muriel does unmitigated good to those around her, lifting their eyes heavenwards, and is temperamentally wholly suited to her condition, and entirely reconciled to it.[84]

If Muriel embodies the idea of the disabled child as a sentimental object in its purest form, her narrative fate fully reconciling what is religiously right with what is socially expedient, Phineas's presence in the narrative prevents so straightforward a view of disability from wholly dominating the novel. His disability is not so easily explained, nor so painless; his frustration and loneliness challenge us to find the 'meaning' of his suffering, and encode resistance, however slight, to his narrative fate. Phineas is not only a sentimental object, but has glimmers of subjectivity; he is at the very margin of the novel's plot, yet his is the voice we hear directly. In plot terms, the text thwarts Phineas's desire for John, but it obtrudes itself upon the reader's attention, none the less; one of Craik's most perceptive contemporary critics, R. H. Hutton, claimed he could hardly 'suppress a fear that Phineas Fletcher will fall hopelessly in love with John Halifax',[85] and it is this suppression – of desire, of pain, of full experience – that Phineas's narration registers. Perhaps because he is not allotted any conclusive narrative fate – he is not killed off or married off, or even integrated into a new family – but is left standing at the end of the novel, a witness and a biographer to a life he could not share, Phineas remains a troubling character, despite his repeatedly asserted identification with John's successes.

These contradictions and complexities continue to swirl about the disabled male protagonist in Craik's later novel, *A Noble Life* (1866), a text in which suppression is a motif continually invoked by the third-person narrator. The Earl embodies both Muriel's idealised response to disability and her uplifting effect on those around her, but because he does not die as a child and because he is a male 'angel', he is also imbued with some of Phineas's complexity, the exact nature of his 'nobility' remaining unsettlingly ambiguous.

### Paralepsis and Paralysis: The Impossibility of Plot in *A Noble Life*

> *A Noble Life* is embarrassing to read. There is almost no action. Scene after scene is constructed to show how much the Earl is to be pitied and to let other characters discuss him tenderly. We feel uncomfortable in the presence of deformity and pain; we feel sensitive about staring so openly at a cripple.[86]

I begin with Sally Mitchell's verdict upon *A Noble Life* because it points to an important truth about the novel: not only is the protagonist disabled, but disability is the novel's subject, and it is impossible to read *A Noble Life* without confronting one's own attitude to disability as a phenomenon in the real world. Moreover, the embarrassment that Mitchell acknowledges in the face of this subject-matter is a reaction that the text anticipates and even mirrors. Rather than facing its subject head on, this is a novel that circles anxiously about a centre from which we are frequently distanced, a character whose thoughts are explicitly withheld from us, a condition we are assured we cannot imagine, and a relationship that is never quite named.

Craik announces her subject in her opening sentences, as though afraid that it might be missed or misread; there is a defensiveness in her admission that the reader 'will not find [the Earl's] name in "Lodge's Peerage"', and in her insistence, as though in the face of contradiction, that

> I think among what we call 'heroic' lives – lives the story of which touches us with something higher than pity, and deeper than love – there never was any of his race who left behind a history more truly heroic than he.[87]

By citing the Earl's erasure from other narratives, and asserting his right to the title she has given him in the face of anticipated objection, Craik seems to pre-empt Mitchell's criticism, claiming that a response 'higher than pity' is due to her subject. By stating that the novel is 'more like a biography than a tale',[88] Craik also draws attention to its structure, which is also highlighted in the title: she offers us not a *Bildungsroman*, which follows its subject from birth to marriage or (usually 'and') maturity, but a 'life', which takes us from birth to death. Yet this is a 'life' that lacks the structuring features of *John Halifax, Gentleman*, and indeed of contemporary biographies of great men, for the Earl's life is defined primarily in the negative: he does *not* have a career, he does *not* marry, he does *not* have a son. Where Olive's disability expanded her potentiality as the subject of a *Bildungsroman*, and Phineas's disqualified him as a biographical subject, fitting him instead to be a biographer, Craik draws attention here to her attempt to write a 'life' of a man whose disability feminises him – as Phineas's did – and yet whose disqualification from masculine achievements does not disqualify him from narrative centrality. Writing of the challenges facing working-class autobiographers, Regenia Gagnier suggests that 'perhaps what is most fundamentally "missing," . . . in much working-class autobiography is the structuring effect, apparent in any middle-class "plot", of gender dimorphism';[89] Craik faces a similar challenge in attempting to write a fictional 'life' of a disabled man. She meets it by substituting affective development and influence for the events that make up a conventional 'life' like John Halifax's, writing a sentimental 'life' in which nobility is a matter of feeling rather than action. Yet this affective plotting is in turn made impossible by her positioning of her protagonist at arm's length from the reader. The attempt to render the Earl's affective experiences sufficiently central to the narrative to replace the professional, artistic, interpersonal or familial experiences that would usually take centre-stage is thwarted by Craik's unwillingness to represent his emotional life, a hesitation that ultimately disables the novel itself, leading to paralysis at the level of plot.

Craik clearly sets out the terms on which the Earl's outwardly uneventful life can be read as 'noble', instructing her reader in how to read his disability in the opening scene in which the doctor and the minister are first confronted with the orphaned baby Earl. The minister's rejection of the doctor's suggestion that it would be better if the baby died, by asserting his belief that 'God can work out His wonderful will, if He chooses, through the meanest means – through the saddest tragedies and direst misfortunes',[90] amounts to a manifesto as to the purpose of disability, in the world and in the novel. Craik does not equivocate over the Earl's disability by representing it as a minor physical difference that does not constitute impairment – like Olive's – or as a generalised weakness like Phineas's, but draws attention in this first scene to the Earl's unusual body, 'thin, elfin, distorted, every joint and limb being twisted in some way or other'.[91] Over the course of the novel, she repeatedly acknowledges his physical impairments, pointing out that he cannot walk, struggles to hold a pen and suffers significant physical pain.[92] In this sense, then, Craik engages uncompromisingly with her subject. However, whereas Olive's experience of coming to see herself as 'deformed' and her developing emotional and religious life were vividly depicted, so that the reader saw from her perspective, sharing her experience of disability – as, despite his marginalised plot role, we share Phineas's – we see the Earl only from outside. Thoughts are imputed to him, his feelings are inferred: we cannot feel *with* the Earl because we so often do not know what he is feeling. The Earl's worthiness, his claim to 'something higher than pity', is made contingent upon his recognition that his experience cannot be shared with others, that 'the awful individuality of suffering' must be respected, and yet this disables him almost completely as a sentimental subject.[93]

At certain points in the novel, Craik appears to insist that the Earl is temperamentally fitted to his somatic condition, as Olive was to hers, that he has been spiritually compensated for his disability, and is therefore hiding nothing from the reader when he declares himself to be content:

> he never once said, what Helen . . . was always expecting he would say, Why had God given these soulless creatures legs to run and wings to fly, strength, health, and activity to enjoy existence, and denied all those things to him? . . . that bitter doubt, which so often came into Helen's heart, never fell from the child's lips at all . . . when she watched his inexpressibly sweet face, which had the look you sometimes see in blind faces, of absolutely untroubled peace, Helen was forced to believe this – God, who had taken away from him so much, had given him something still more – a spiritual insight so deep and clear that he was happy in spite of his heavy misfortune.[94]

Here, the Earl's resignation to the constraints of his impairments seems to be not the result of effort or even familiarity, but a spiritual gift, comparable to that of Muriel's 'peace' (invoked here by the reference to 'blind faces'). The reader's feelings about the Earl, and his fitness to play the didactic role that he has been assigned in justifying 'the ways of God to men', as Craik (quoting Milton) puts it elsewhere,[95] seem perfectly in harmony in passages such as this.

Yet the passage draws our attention to the fact that we see this harmony through Helen's eyes: she is 'forced to believe' it, we are told, a phrase that emphasises the fact that this is something she *believes*, not something she knows. We are reminded a little later that the Earl 'was exceedingly self-contained from his childhood. He seemed to feel by instinct that to him had been allotted a special solitude of existence, into which . . . none could ever fully penetrate and with which none could wholly sympathise'.[96] A sentimental object with whom 'none could wholly sympathise' is in fact no sentimental object at all: the Earl's contradictory position as the centre of an affective community from which he must yet keep himself apart is here highlighted, and its implications are disruptive for our reading of the novel as a straightforwardly sentimental text.

More explicitly still, when the Earl is nineteen and the medical attempt to alleviate his condition is made, and fails, he meets Helen's assurance that she knows how hard it has been with qualified assent: 'Yes – at least as much as you can know.' Helen is said to recognise at this 'the awful individuality of suffering', and the reader is allowed to glimpse – but only to glimpse – the experiences that are hidden from Helen: 'What was the minute history of the experiments he had tried, how much bodily pain they had cost him, and through how much mental pain he had struggled before he attained that "content", he did not explain even to Helen.'[97] When the narrative pauses in this way, our attention is drawn to what is being left out of this 'life', and the equivocation in phrases such as '[p]erhaps it was one of those merciful compensations that what he could not have he was made strong enough to do without' further leads us to doubt the completeness of the picture we are being offered.[98]

It is by no means obvious why we are not allowed to see more of the Earl's 'mental pain'. Sentimental texts thrive on the portrayal of anguished cries to Heaven and tearful crises; if we could enter into the Earl's frustration and then witness his spiritual triumph over it, surely we would be moved even more effectively, and sentimental communion would flourish? Clearly, there is something in the Earl's particular condition that renders it unrepresentable, something in his pain that is unspeakable, and this is what disrupts the sentimental paradigm that Craik has set up. We are given some indication of what it might be when the narrator depicts the Earl's successful entry into Edinburgh society. At this point, we are told that 'he never put forward his affliction so as to make it painful to those around him'.[99] The Earl can become the centre of 'a knot of real friends', he can even 'go out a little into society', overcoming 'the practical [difficulty] of locomotion . . . by a good deal of ingenious contrivance' – but all this must be done in a way that does not 'put forward' his affliction.[100] The Earl's disability is shown to be no bar to respect, to friendship, even to parenthood, provided he does not speak of it: his own acceptance 'by instinct that to him had been allotted a special solitude of existence' appears to be the condition of his acceptance by others.[101] We do not have to insist upon the Earl's difference because he insists upon it himself; we can open our hearts to him because he does not 'put forward' his claim to be there. At one and the same time, the Earl is allowed to take up a central place in the narrative, his physical difference represented as something to which his friends can become accustomed, a chiefly practical inconvenience that can be overcome through 'ingenious contrivance' – and yet this physical difference is represented throughout as an experience so absolutely 'other' that it is one with which no one can sympathise. Mitchell's embarrassment in the face of 'deformity and pain' is therefore pre-empted by Craik. The Earl can take up a place at the centre of the novel and at the centre of his community, but the price is his own recognition of his difference, and total abstention from any attempt to cross the distance this puts between him and those around him. Where Olive's sense of herself as deformed could be erased by 'the words of betrothed husband', 'dispelling all doubts, healing all wounds',[102] and subsequently her physical difference itself could be erased from the text, no such re-formation is possible for the Earl, whose relation to the marriage plot is complex and ambivalent.

As with Phineas Fletcher, there is never any question that the Earl will marry: 'I am the last Earl of Cairnforth,' he says, 'as if merely stating a fact beyond which there is no appeal.'[103] Yet whereas Phineas's primary love relationship is with John – and therefore, in the terms of the novel, firmly outside the scope of the marriage plot – the Earl's central relationship is with the minister's daughter, Helen Cardross, with whom he co-parents a child and ultimately lives in near-matrimony. The possibility of a conventional heterosexual relationship is therefore repeatedly invoked, even though it is never fully realised. We are quite explicitly told that after Helen kisses the Earl as a child, 'from that minute he loved . . . and never ceased loving her to the end of his days', while she feels for him 'a deep tenderness . . . not pity – something far deeper . . . actual reverence'.[104] Her feelings are not dealt with so explicitly once they reach adulthood, but the passion of her ambiguous relationship with the Earl is captured in the letter she writes to him upon her (uncharacteristically hasty, off-stage) marriage to his wicked cousin. Her letter, 'blurred as if large drops had fallen on the paper while she wrote', expresses guilt and loss far more forcefully than anything else, her claim 'nobody I love will lose me at all' undermined by its grief-stricken tone,[105] and still more by the Earl's reaction:

> And she had married him, and gone away with him – left, for his sake, father, brothers, friends – her one special friend, who was now nothing to her – nothing! Whatever emotions the earl felt – and it would be almost sacrilegious to intrude upon them, or to venture on any idle speculation concerning them – one thing was clear; in losing Helen, the light of his eyes, the delight of his life, was gone.[106]

Craik's insistence that it would be 'sacrilegious' to 'intrude' or 'speculate' upon the Earl's feelings represents a form of paralepsis, for these feelings are invoked by the very statement that they will not be shown, made present by their announced absence from the text.

The Earl sinks into a deep depression and is unable to leave his bed, even before he has discovered that Helen was duped into this (ultimately unhappy) marriage, indicating to the reader that it is the fact that she has married *at all* that prostrates him. The ambiguity of the Earl's status as Helen's 'one special friend' is highlighted by the fact that Helen did not, in fact, marry without reference to his wishes: her father assures the Earl that Helen agreed to marry the Captain chiefly because he 'spoke so warmly of you, expressed such gratitude towards you, such admiration of you', and even then only after he had (as she believed) consulted the Earl and obtained his consent.[107] The marriage that divides the Earl and Helen is therefore brought about only by the Captain's devious plotting, and is represented as a dire mistake.

Moreover, when Helen sends for the Earl because her husband is dying and her baby has just been born, the possibility that this mistake can be righted, and the Earl's devotion rewarded with marriage, is once again raised. He reacts to her summons

> as if an almost miraculous amount of endurance and energy had been given to that frail body for this hour of need ... as the strong, manly soul, counteracting all physical infirmities, rose up for the protection of the one creature in all the world who to him had been most dear.[108]

Yet Craik raises the possibility that they can now marry only to thwart it once again: we are soon assured that Helen will never remarry, and although she agrees to his proposal to adopt her son, she refuses his invitation to live at the castle with him. While the second volume of the novel principally concerns the Earl's developing relationship with Helen's son, Boy, and his success as a surrogate father, Craik highlights the persistent ambiguity in the relationship between Helen and the Earl by drawing attention to the diamond ring Helen wears on her ring finger, as a 'sort of guard' to her wedding ring, a gift from the Earl that she 'had accepted . . . as a pledge of amity, and had worn . . . ever since – by his earnest request', after her refusal of his other offers of assistance 'had almost produced a breach between them – at least the nearest approach to a quarrel they had ever known'.[109] Is this ring a 'guard' to her wedding ring because it ensures that she will never marry again, and that her relationship with the Earl is instead of a marriage? Or are we supposed to follow the more obvious inference, that she wears his ring because their relationship is *like* a marriage, or an engagement to be consummated in the next life? Craik draws us into such speculation and yet refuses to reveal more about either the Earl's feelings or Helen's. The Earl reacts to Helen's decision not to allow her son to take solely the Earl's surname, but to retain his father's as well, only by remaining 'long silent',[110] and this is a silence that the narrator refuses to break.

Helen's continuing desire to remain loyal to her husband, even though their relationship was utterly unsatisfactory, is inexplicable unless we place Craik's treatment of marriage in the context of Muscular Christianity and the views of its most influential literary proponent, Charles Kingsley. Laura Fasick suggests that Kingsley's view of marriage as utterly central to a healthy spiritual life – what Charles Barker calls his 'eroticized Christianity' – was underpinned by gender essentialism, since he believed that men and woman 'could only achieve this mutually beneficial union . . . by retaining the distinctive features of their respective sexes'.[111] When viewed from within this structure of feeling, Olive's ability to marry, when Phineas cannot, is wholly logical, and it becomes clear why the exemplary Earl is denied what Craik treats as the ultimate narrative reward. The otherwise virtuous Helen's susceptibility to the Earl's wicked cousin – despite his total inadequacy as a romantic figure, as an adventurer with an expression of 'weakness and indecision', 'uncandid' and 'rather sinister'[112] – is explicable only if we accept that it is natural for a woman to desire the only man available to her. Commenting on Kingsley's essay, 'Nausicaa in London', Fasick points out that, in Kingsley's terms, 'Homer's heroine is the superior of modern women both because of her greater physical grace and because of her willingness to admire and wish for a strong man as a husband.'[113] Despite Helen's affection and admiration for the Earl, the 'sexless, companionate love' that Mitchell sees as idealised in the novel is repeatedly shown to fall short of Helen's needs.[114] Just as Olive took pleasure in professional success and financial independence, but finally finds her greatest satisfaction in 'clinging sweetness', 'nestled' up to a man who is 'the very quintessence of pride',[115] so Helen appears to desire something that is missing from her relationship with the Earl, and although Captain Bruce is so unimpressive a specimen, still his identity as an able-bodied man (suffering from illness but not 'deformed') enables him to win the love that the Earl is, painfully, denied.

The compromise that Craik reaches through the thwarted marriage plot opens up a space for the disabled protagonist to be in a relationship and at the centre of a family in which he and his beloved are 'not unhappy',[116] but the negative terms of this formulation reveals how unsatisfactory this relationship is at the level of plot. The couple cannot move forward: the plot of the novel stalls when Helen returns to Cairnforth and yet refuses the Earl's invitation to live with him at the castle, limping towards a conclusion that is reached only in the Earl's death. We are assured that '[i]n spite of its outward incompleteness, it had been a noble life – an almost perfect life', but it is the incompleteness that leaves the strongest impression.[117] Craik's final unwillingness to redefine the marriage plot, evident also in *Olive* and *John Halifax, Gentleman*, means that this compromise must be shown to be unsatisfactory, a poor substitute for a 'real' marriage, which finally appears to depend upon a totalising kind of heterosexuality, made possible only by both partners' ability to embody and perform their 'true' gender identity. Disability, which in all three novels at least potentially unsettles gender identity, disrupts this paradigm: that it proves surmountable in *Olive* seems finally to rest upon the equivocal nature of Olive's 'deformity', and the final alignment of her disability and her gender identity. It is at this point of impasse that I wish to turn to Charlotte Yonge and her very different treatment of the marriage plot, which enables her disabled characters to take up a correspondingly different position.

### 'Of wonderful use to everyone': An Invalid's Place in *The Heir of Redclyffe*

*The Heir of Redclyffe* (1853) was Charlotte Yonge's first bestseller, the novel that established her popular (and subsequently critical) success.[118] Although it is significantly different in its style and plotting from the family chronicles that followed it, and for which Yonge has been best known, *The Heir of Redclyffe* anticipates many of their distinguishing features, particularly in its treatment of disability. Charles Edmonstone's place at the centre of the Edmonstone family, his invalidism rendering him their 'undisputed sovereign',[119] establishes the structural role played by disabled characters in Yonge's depiction of family life. Although Charles's disability appears to disqualify him as a romantic agent, and the idea that he might marry is never raised, the marriage plots of the novel are essentially shaped around his exclusion. The idealised romantic relationship between Charles's younger sister Amy and the hero, Guy Morville, redefines marriage as *primarily* familial, rather than incidentally so, and Charles's inclusion in their relationship becomes a measure of its worth. By contrast, his sister Laura and his priggish cousin Philip attempt to forge an exclusive and private romantic relationship, an attempt that is condemned as misguided and leads to an unsatisfactory marriage. Ultimately, even the novel's ostensibly exemplary marriage plot is sidelined, as Guy's early death returns Amy to her natal family unit; it is her relationship with Charles that is celebrated by the novel's conclusion, and that forms the basis of her lasting happiness. The novel opens and closes with scenes that feature Charles centrally, and although he is, to some extent, marginalised by the marriage plots that intervene, the reader largely perceives and judges them from Charles's perspective.

As Karen Bourrier persuasively argues in a fascinating essay on disability in *The Heir of Redclyffe*, Charles effectively acts as the reader's substitute within the novel, with its 'affective trajectory from the opening's ennui through the upheavals of emotion to the ending's quiet restraint . . . best represented by Charles, who is both a stand-in for and the most accurate reader of the novel's plot'.[120] Although Charles very rarely leaves the sofa to which he is bound by his painful tubercular hip joint, this does not prevent him from playing a crucial role in the novel's plot, which turns on the re-emergence of the ancient feud between the two branches of the Morville family, represented by Guy and Philip, and the progress of their parallel love stories with the two Edmonstone sisters. On the contrary, as Bourrier points out, Charles's immobility is essential for the progression of these plots. It generates the frustration and boredom that cause Charles to attempt to stir up Guy's temper and re-kindle the family feud; it gives Guy the opportunity to display and develop his virtue, and Philip to show his profound self-righteousness, through their contrasting attitudes to Charles and very different offers of assistance; and it allows Charles the leisure to observe and comment upon Philip's unjust treatment of Guy, while generally preventing him from actively intervening to prevent it.[121] (He can, for example attest to the injustice of Guy's banishment, but simultaneously be too ill to gather the proof to exonerate him.)

Not only is Charles's disability essential to his role in the plot, but I would argue that Yonge's treatment of it leads us to rely on Charles as a guide, because it marks him out as a firmly realist character, who, after Guy's arrival at Hollywell, finds himself navigating an unfamiliar world of gothic romance and struggling to adjust – exactly like the novel's readers. As several critics have pointed out, *The Heir of Redclyffe* is a generically hybrid novel,[122] and while its potent blending of gothic and romantic traditions with the current trend for domestic realism may account for some of its enormous contemporary popularity, it also poses problems for its readers. We are constantly at risk of feeling as though the joke is on us, when the plot of the novel we are reading, and in which we are likely to have become profoundly invested, is satirised by Yonge's own characters, who mock novelistic – and especially gothic – conventions, and tease each other for expecting novelistic plots to materialise, only for exactly those plots to emerge. It is in this context that Charles's struggle to understand how to 'read' Guy becomes so important, as it exactly mirrors the struggle that readers expecting to encounter domestic realism may find in reconciling the different generic strands of the novel before them.

Initially, Charles is unable to accept that Guy's behaviour is within 'the bounds of probability', but through exposure to Guy's extraordinary goodness, he comes to modify his sense of the probable, until he becomes Guy's greatest champion against Philip's maliciously motivated attempts to smear his character, insisting, 'he had only been so much better than other people that nobody could believe it', which does indeed turn out to be the case.[123] Because Charles is characterised in a firmly realistic mode, and belongs in a realistic domestic novel, we know exactly how to read him, and we are repeatedly drawn in to identify with his emotional experiences. We can therefore read the other characters and the plot-lines in which they are involved *through* him, and thus come to understand how Guy's other-worldly goodness, represented through romantic and gothic tropes, might inflect the 'real'.

Charles's status as a realistic character in a novel with an increasingly archetypally gothic plot-line is partially established through the self-consciousness of his reaction to his disability. George Levine has suggested that realism is distinguished by its attempt 'to make literature appear to be describing directly not some other language but reality itself' through 'self-contradictorily dismiss[ing] previous conventions of representation'.[124] Charles explicitly invokes his own awareness of such 'previous conventions' by referring to the role he 'should' play as an invalid, thus bringing to mind the reader's experience of other fictional invalids, only to highlight his own deviation from such a stereotype. After a bout of serious illness, which overlaps with Guy's banishment from Hollywell, Charles jokes about the 'grand opportunity' he has wasted:

> 'If I could but have got up ever so small an alarm, I would have conjured my father to send for Guy, entreated pathetically that the reconciliation might be effected, and have drawn my last breath clasping their hands, thus! The curtain falls!' He made a feint of joining their hands, put his head back, and shut his eyes . . . .[125]

Charles is, of course, incapable of playing the role of saintly reconciliatory invalid, having spent his illness desperately trying to intervene in the quarrel, railing against Philip and upbraiding Amy for her patience, having 'said much more than was right or judicious, so that his advocacy only injured the cause'.[126] When he imagines himself as the actor in a death-bed scene, then, we are encouraged to laugh at such 'conventions of representation', in Levine's words, having come to know Charles as a flawed young man, capable of great courage and stoicism, but also of considerable spite and bad temper – an imperfect but sympathetic character, in short, with whom readers are likely to identify themselves.

Such identification is developed by his reaction to other characters, especially in the first half of the novel. While the rest of the Edmonstone family, and, above all, Guy himself, seem to take officious Philip at his own estimation and insist upon his virtues, the reader is certain to be irritated by his self-righteous, priggish attitude, and by his attempts to thwart loveable Guy's engagement to Amy. This is exactly the perspective that Charles voices: for example, when he rolls his eyes at Guy's expression of contrition for having finally lost his temper with Philip – '[Charles] thought all this a great fuss about nothing, indeed he was glad to find there was any one who had no patience with Philip.' He even attempts to stir up Guy's resentment further because he is 'ready to do anything for the sake of opposition to Philip', a state of affairs with which the reader will almost certainly sympathise.[127] Although some critics have objected to what they see as Yonge's exaggerated dedication to filial obedience, and consequent failure to realise that her readers would naturally want Amy to be true to Guy, even if it means defying her parents (when they are misled by Philip into forbidding the couple to correspond), in fact Yonge anticipates and reflects exactly this reaction through Charles, who calls Amy's behaviour 'absurd'.[128] By voicing this commonsense perspective – which he attributes to 'every one' except unswervingly high-minded Amy and Guy – Charles essentially mediates between their romantic outlook and the realist context in which they are situated. With Charles, we can be frustrated by the otherworldly goodness of the romantic hero and his true love, but we can also see how it might affect more ordinary mortals (like ourselves): how the romantic might inflect the real, and how ideal standards might work upon the imperfect, striving subject. With Charles, we can rail against the plot of the novel, and, having identified with his viewpoint, ultimately accept its moral fitness as he does.

Moreover, Charles plays a crucial role in modifying and illuminating the marriage plots of the novel, as the extent of his inclusion is made a measure of the worth of romantic relationships. In an essay focusing on the re-configuration of marriage in *The Clever Woman of the Family* (to which I shall be returning), Talia Schaffer draws attention to the fact that Guy's proposal to Amy takes place literally across the body of Mrs Edmonstone, asking what it would mean 'to find romantic speech liberated, not constrained, by the presence of the mother?'[129] I would suggest that the answer to this question also solves the puzzle that has so exercised critics, as to why Laura's secret understanding with Philip – involving as it does no secret correspondence, let alone any improper physical intimacy – should attract such extreme narrative punishment.[130]

Laura's real fault is not that she technically disobeys her parents – which, as she heatedly points out to Amy, is hardly the case[131] – but rather that she conceives of her relationship with Philip as exclusively theirs, involving no one else. Her love for him therefore draws her away from her natal family, so that, at Amy's wedding, Laura feels 'as if she was acting a play, sustaining the character of Miss. Edmonstone, the bridesmaid at her sister's happy wedding; while the true Laura, Philip's Laura, was lonely, dejected, wretched'.[132] Laura has come to feel that 'the true Laura' is 'Philip's Laura', rather than Amy's Laura, or, indeed, Charles's: he has no part to play in this relationship.

Amy and Guy's relationship, on the other hand, is always understood to involve the entire family, including Charles. There are three people involved in their first real love scene, and this patterning is extended to the depiction of their wedding morning, on which 'the first sight' of the wedding guests is 'Guy's light agile figure, assisting Charles up the step ... Amy, her deep blushes and downcast eyes almost hidden by her glossy curls, stood just behind, carrying her brother's crutch.'[133] In reference to this scene, Karen Bourrier suggests that 'the interests of male friendship supersede the marriage plot';[134] while I agree with her suggestion that Guy's relationship with Charles is so close that his love for Amy can be read as a kind of transference, this seems to me to reflect not so much Yonge's emphasis on male friendship, but rather Guy's passionate attachment to the entire Edmonstone family. It is said to be 'a special delight to Amy that Hollywell and her family were as precious to him for their own sake as for hers', and while there is particular emphasis on Guy's relationship with Mrs Edmonstone and Charles, it is Charlotte's feelings that are brought out in the scene immediately following Guy and Amy's wedding, as she alights from the carriage 'holding his hand, and felt that she could never forget the moment when her new brother first kissed her brow'.[135] As another member of the family who intends not to marry,[136] Charlotte is, like Charles, heavily invested in Guy and Amy's relationship. Whereas such investment is shown to be one-sided, even tragic, in *John Halifax, Gentleman*, in which Phineas's agony in coming second in John's affections is never shown to be reciprocated by John, Amy has 'silent crying-fits' at the thought of leaving her family, and Guy is 'tremulous' at parting from Charles.[137] Moreover, in the preceding chapter, Guy's only specific instructions concerning the refurbishment of Redclyffe have consisted of 'prints for the walls, a piano, a bookcase, and a couch for Charles'.[138] Clearly, Yonge assumes as a matter of course that Charles will be a regular visitor, if not a resident, in Amy and Guy's future home.

This is a perfect example of what Talia Schaffer has called the 'familiar' approach to marriage that characterises Yonge's fiction, in which romantic love is far less important than the couple's commitment to their wider social and familial community.[139] However, I would argue that *The Heir of Redclyffe* goes further than offering a familiar approach to marriage: it anticipates Yonge's later family chronicles in sidelining the marriage plot altogether, and in securing the reader's support for this narrative manœuvre by enlisting our sympathy so firmly with the disabled character who most benefits by it. It is not enough for Yonge that Charles be made welcome in Amy and Guy's marital home: instead, she almost immediately returns Amy to the bosom of her natal family, and specifically to Charles's companionship, by killing off Guy just three months after their marriage. Speaking from his death bed, Guy himself sees this as the silver lining of Amy's widowhood: '"And Charlie – I shall not rob him any longer. I only borrowed you for a little while," he added, smiling.'[140] Our last view of Amy is beside Charles in a carriage on Laura's wedding day, happily planning her permanent residence in her natal family home, and her contentment as a widow is held up in clear contrast to Laura's 'harassed, anxious life' with Philip.[141] While Amy's relationship with the angelic Guy is utterly idealised, it seems to be at its very best *after* his death, when her devotion to his memory can co-exist unproblematically with her family ties, and particularly with her relationship with Charles.

Charles's situation, then, is never represented in the same way as Philip Wakem's or Phineas Fletcher's. His own inability to marry is never discussed within the novel: his frustration at his inability to act as he would wish, because of his physical impairment, is dwelt upon at some length and with great sympathy, but it is nowhere implied that the tragedy of his life is that he cannot marry. Within the emotional structure of the novel, this would indeed seem odd, for he is already at the centre of the family that Guy so strongly wishes to join. The novel's doomed relationship is the one between Philip and Laura, which had denied the centrality of the familial relationships Laura finally struggles to rebuild.

Moreover, there is a deeper sense in which Charles's disability can be understood as a blessing within the terms of the text. Philip and Laura's great unhappiness is most comprehensible when it is read in the light of the novel's ultimately revealed moral world-view, which shows worldly prosperity and concern for social, material and economic advancement as directly and inversely proportional to spiritual security. This is captured in the title: Guy's real identity turns out to be as 'heir' to the Christian soul's inheritance, heir to sin (through being fallen) but also heir to redemption (as Christ's 'heir' through his religious faith), and so ultimately 'heir' to the heavenly kingdom. Though coming into his *worldly* inheritance, as 'Heir of Redclyffe', Philip must suffer 'all that man is heir to' in the sense of sin, repentance and temptation, whereas Guy, in giving up his worldly inheritance, wins his struggle to his spiritual inheritance: his salvation. Philip has covertly longed to be the heir of Redclyffe, but such an inheritance turns out to be tainted: it is because he has inherited Redclyffe that Philip is enabled to enter parliament and become 'a distinguished man', and as a result, he and his wife have 'little space for domestic pleasure'.[142] Amy's joy at bearing a posthumous daughter rather than a son, so absolutely incomprehensible to Philip himself, is entirely logical when understood in this way: her daughter Mary Verena is shut out by the entail from inheriting Guy's earthly property, but this only makes her more surely the heir to Guy's best legacy, the revelation that true victory lies in defeat and true inheritance is won through renunciation. In being the heir to *this* legacy, rather than to his cursed property, Mary Verena is clearly blessed.

This understanding implicitly re-conditions our view of Charles's disability. Earlier in the novel, he expressed his frustration that invalidism excluded him from the place in the public sphere to which his class and gender would otherwise have entitled him, preventing him from joining Guy at Oxford, where he predicts that Guy will 'take [his] place among the men of [their] day'.[143] Guy was sympathetic in this scene, but also gently suggested how Charles might make better use of his 'talents' through pursuing a domestic course of study with Amy, not for any worldly reward, but for its own sake. From these seeds, Charles gradually comes to be a better brother, perceiving the value of his work at home; we see him at last with Amy in the carriage, on the way home from Laura's gloomy wedding, and hear their plans to bring Mary Verena up together. On the very next page, the narrator's summary of Philip's life as a member of parliament shows that the 'place' Charles once coveted is in fact far less happy than the one he now occupies, and thus there is an underlying truth to Charles's final claim to be 'better off than if [he] had as many legs as other people'.[144]

His wryly humorous expression at this point is not merely convincingly characteristic, but also represents a subtle acknowledgement on Yonge's part of the apparent perversity of a truly Christian world-view from a realist perspective: we have to accept what appears counter-intuitive to receive profound truth, and, like Charles, we may struggle to find expression for these truths in daily discourse. Charles's gradually changing attitude towards his own disability is a crucial bridge between Guy's ideal, and therefore remote, trajectory as a Christian, and the cynical realism with which Charles (and the novel reader) initially approaches the narrative, but which comes to be modified through experiencing Guy's goodness.

Finally, we see Charles in the place of an unmarried daughter rather than son, exercising his talents domestically, influencing Philip's political career from within the family and advising his sister on his niece's education. What is striking is that this place has come to seem enviable, his disinheritance from man's estate a blessing rather than a loss. This is the structure of feeling that I will now pursue into Yonge's squarely domestic novel, *The Daisy Chain*, in which the invalid takes up an exemplary place within the community that is central to the novel: that of the family.

### 'It is best for me as it is': Invalidism and Exemplary Celibacy in *The Daisy Chain*

In her Preface to *The Daisy Chain* (1856), Charlotte Yonge called the novel 'a Family Chronicle – a domestic record of home events, large and small, during those years of early life when the character is chiefly formed'.[145] So successful was this self-styling that the edition I have used here (the twelfth) uses the phrase 'A Family Chronicle' as a subtitle; by the following decade, Yonge was being described in reviews as 'the best of our family chroniclers' and even 'our Household Laureate'.[146] Although she continued to write many other kinds of fiction, this was the genre for which she became most famous, and the idea that her readership was exclusively female, and her principal subject 'home events', can be traced to this emphasis.[147] When the *Saturday Review* critic with whom I began this chapter complained that the heroine of 'this class of fiction . . . spent [her life] in the solution of a series of small parochial and domestic problems', he was clearly thinking of Yonge's family chronicles rather than her historical novels or *The Heir of Redclyffe*.[148] Similarly, his description of 'the angelic being with a weak spine, who, from her sofa, directed with mild wisdom the affairs of the family or the parish'[149] unmistakeably refers to Margaret May, who became the prototype for so many other saintly invalids in later novels aimed at young women and girls.[150]

Yonge's positioning of invalids in her family chronicles became one of their defining features, to such an extent that novels featuring disabled characters prominently tended to be read as domestically inflected – and, conversely, family chronicles inspired by Yonge's feature disabled characters almost as a hallmark of generic affiliation.

For example, at the end of *The Trial* (1864), the sequel to *The Daisy Chain*, we recognise that the sensational plot of the novel has been resolved and we are safely back in the realm of domestic realism when an invalid is once more placed at the centre of the May family; the now-disabled Averil Ward is brought into the May household as Tom's wife, and we are told that '[h]er sofa is almost a renewal of the family centre that once Margaret's was'.[151] Margaret is the 'centre' not only of the May family, as this formula suggests, but also of the novel in which she appears and the genre that novel came to define. She is the personification of the gradually revealed, typological plot of *The Daisy Chain* – which is also the essential plot of all Yonge's family chronicles – her experience of disability treated as both metaphoric and metonymic of all Christian experience. The centrality of this experience, which is inextricably bound up with the embrace of celibacy, works to displace the marriage plot from the centre of the narrative, a displacement that, I will argue, comes to define Yonge's version of the family chronicle.

Margaret's place in the plotting of *The Daisy Chain* also points to a crucial feature of Yonge's family chronicles, which is that their structure enables them to position disability very differently from domestic novels by, for example, Craik. Yonge's reference to *The Daisy Chain* in the Preface as 'an overgrown book of a nondescript class' is not empty self-deprecation, but points to the structural features that were to define her family chronicles: their capaciousness in length, their structural looseness, and their marginalisation of the conventional plot structures of the *Bildungsroman*. These features all allow disabled characters like Margaret to occupy pivotal positions in their novels, not in spite but because of the immobility and celibacy that we might expect to frustrate the novelistic plot.

*The Daisy Chain* follows the fortunes of the eleven May siblings, after a disastrous carriage accident that kills their mother and permanently disables the eldest sister, Margaret, at the opening of the novel. Its meandering structure frequently obscures its narrative trajectory, which is underpinned by Ethel's ultimately fulfilled desire to build a school and church at the impoverished and neglected nearby village, Cocksmoor. The novel's narrative arc is, in fact, tightly constructed. Ethel's resolution to see the church built is made at the very beginning of the novel, before the sudden bereavement that throws the family into confusion. As they gradually begin to adjust to life without their mother, their collective moral progress – and especially Ethel's – is marked by the stages of the progress towards the building of the church; and the novel finally concludes when the church has been consecrated and Ethel re-affirms her lifelong dedication to its service. Along the way, however, this overall design can be difficult to see, and in wading through the sometimes amusing, sometimes tedious conversations, mishaps and interruptions of daily life in the May family, we share Ethel's education in patience and perseverance. The novel's stylistic features correspond closely to Yonge's theological commitments: as Susan Colón has pointed out, such 'cluttered' realism 'requires readers to sift through common life in search of typological significance . . . train[ing] the reader to look for potential reserved truths in the midst of entirely unsacramental activity and details'.[152] Critics who suggest that there is a fundamental contradiction between realism and didacticism misunderstand Yonge's view of reality, as Gavin Budge explains: 'If reality itself is providentially motivated, then Yonge's "Church views" would be best served by the attempt to represent reality, even if it did not fall neatly into cut and dried patterns.'[153] There is thus no risk, from Yonge's perspective, that depicting reality, in all its complexity and confusion, will undermine her religious ideology, and from a Tractarian perspective, it is most desirable that religious truth should reveal itself gradually in its immanence, rather than immediately and dramatically.

Margaret May's characterisation perfectly exemplifies these key features of Yonge's domestic realism. The *Saturday Review* critic's reference to Yonge's invalids as 'angelic' is misleading, in that it might encourage us to read Margaret as a purely static character who, like Agnes Wickfield or Little Dorrit, has no need to develop, being already fully formed in her idealised femininity. In fact, Margaret gradually grows in character and in religious understanding over the course of the novel, as her siblings do, and while her disability is ultimately revealed to have been of the utmost spiritual utility, along the way it is not always easy to see the purpose that it serves. It is only retrospectively that we perceive Margaret's disability to have been the lynch-pin of the novel's typological plot and Margaret herself as its symbolic centre.[154]

She is not introduced as an exemplary or exceptional character, but as 'a fine, tall, blooming girl of eighteen', with a yet-incomplete resemblance to her mother, and with the same inclination to resent the strictures of feminine propriety that we have already seen in Ethel: 'there was a little sigh of disappointment; and when she was out of hearing, she whispered, "Oh! lucky baby, to have so many years to come before you are plagued with troublesome propriety!"'[155] In the last scene in which we see Mrs May alive, she cautions Margaret against the temptation of 'seeking to be the first', but Margaret is resistant to her warning, her 'colour deepening' (presumably as she thinks of her sweetheart Alan) as she insists that 'there is always some person with whom one is first'.[156]

Through her experience of disability, Margaret moves gradually towards accepting her mother's perspective, and, once she has done so, follows her in death. The process is accelerated by her disability, but like her siblings' comparable moral development, takes place gradually. Increasingly prevented from taking the active part in the household she so desires, Margaret learns to resign herself to patience and passivity, and incrementally comes to recognise the truth of her mother's caution. At first, she takes too much upon herself as the manager of the household, deciding not to refer the matter of her younger brother Tom's tendency to cheat to their father, '[forgetting] that he was the real authority' and failing to detect 'her own satisfaction at being first with every one in the family'.[157] When this mistake leads Dr May to send Tom to school with his brothers and to his being drawn there into graver acts of dishonesty, Margaret recognises that she has been guilty of '[s]elf-sufficiency' – perhaps the most common source of error in Yonge's novels – and accepts that this 'is a good lesson against [her] love of being first'.[158]

This understanding enables Margaret to see her experience of degenerative disability in a monitory light, as she is increasingly made dependent upon those around her by her worsening health and prevented from managing the family in practical ways. Recognising that she will not recover her physical strength, she tells Richard that her disability has saved her from the temptations that have (for the time being) overwhelmed their worldly sister Flora, and that she is glad to be 'set aside from it all, good for nothing but for all you dear ones to be kind to'.[159] In this formulation, being forced to give up one's 'aspirations' (the novel's subtitle) is a blessing; when she knows she is dying, Margaret reflects that 'the temptation of her character had been to be the ruler and manager of everything, and she saw it had been well for her to have been thus assigned the part of Mary, rather than of Martha'.[160]

Although Margaret never draws us into her experience of disability by expressing frustration or anger as, for example, Charles Edmonstone does,[161] these episodes show that she is supposed to be a character who has flaws to overcome, and in this, her experience is directly analogous to that of all her siblings. Disability does not so much set her apart, as give her a head start on the trajectory that they *all* follow in their spiritual development. The comparison with her sister Flora is revealing: Flora, too, comes to better self-understanding and true humility, but only after she has entered into an unsatisfactory marriage, lost her first child through unintentional neglect, and suffered agonies of guilt. Margaret's disability is truly 'best' (as she claims), if it has spared her the sufferings Flora has to undergo on her journey towards greater self-knowledge and religious faith.

Margaret herself is initially resistant to abnegating her 'aspirations' in some respects, particularly her aspiration to marry. She and Alan Ernescliffe become engaged at a time when medical opinion is in favour of her full recovery, and there is a general consensus that they cannot marry unless she recovers her ability to walk. (Only the worldly Flora suggests that they could marry anyway, which implicitly discredits the suggestion.) When she realises that she will not recover, Margaret intends to write to Alan breaking off their engagement, unable to see the point of a betrothal that cannot end in marriage. However, she gradually comes to understand that their unconsummated relationship has transcendent worth, and this is confirmed at the level of plot: it is because of the uncertainty of their future together that they first turn to their hopes for the church at Cocksmoor, and thus, in the terms of the novel, they exchange temporary happiness for permanent bliss.[162] Although they are physically separated, Yonge underscores the abiding nature of the couple's union by having Alan go to sea on a ship called the *Alcestis* (after the figure from Greek mythology famous for her death-defying loyalty to her husband Admetus), and having Margaret greet the news of his death – which fittingly takes place in the Loyalty Isles – with the declaration: 'It is unbroken!'[163] Mrs May's caution against 'fix[ing] our mind on any affection on earth' is more than borne out, as the couple's spiritualised relationship allows Margaret to greet Alan's death as a blessing, rather than a tragedy, and results in their final, perfect union in death:

> Now, what was mortal of him lay beneath the palm tree, beneath the glowing summer sky, while the first snow flakes hung like pearls on her pall. But, as they laid her by her mother's side, who could doubt that they were together?[164]

Moreover, the thwarting of Margaret's marriage plot is made essential to the completion of the wider plot of the novel. It because they cannot marry that Alan goes to sea, because he loves Margaret that he endows the church, and because he dies at sea that the church can be built. The idea that the church-building plot is literally built on the failure of the marriage plot is underscored when Margaret's engagement ring is set into the stem of the chalice in the church her lover endowed for her sake, the consecration of the church rendered a direct substitute for their wedding.

It is Margaret's disability that makes such sublimation of sexual passion necessary, but the trajectory of her life represents in microcosm that which her non-disabled sister Ethel has decided to embark upon by the end of the narrative, a decision that the reader is implicitly encouraged to admire. Margaret essentially sets the example of ideal womanhood that Ethel follows, and celibacy is represented as one of its crucial aspects. The terms in which Ethel envisages her life at the novel's conclusion closely recall Margaret's words to Richard when she spoke of how she had been saved from ambition, and weaned from wishing to be 'first' by her disability: Ethel sees a life in which she will 'cease in turn to be first with any', 'becoming comparatively solitary in the course of years', with the supreme comfort of her 'treasure above'.[165]

This resonance merely serves to emphasise the influence Margaret has exerted over her younger sister throughout the course of the entire novel. It is Margaret who persuades Ethel to renounce her Classical studies, and through encouraging her to aspire, above all else, to be 'a useful, steady daughter and sister at home ... The sort of woman that dear mamma wished to make you, and a comfort to papa', indirectly inspires her vow of celibacy, which is explicitly figured as an act of devotion to her father and her family.[166] It is Margaret who first encourages Ethel's ambitions for Cocksmoor, and by pointing out the cumulative significance of the 'little isolated individual things' that Ethel can accomplish (but which initially frustrate her), shows her how to go about accomplishing her grand plans.[167] As Ethel develops the qualities of patience and forbearance that Margaret herself embodies, combining them with the intellectual prowess that makes her a perfect companion for her clever father, Margaret fades into the background, reappearing to offer advice whenever Ethel wavers. Caring for Margaret is repeatedly shown to develop Ethel's feminine qualities and capacities, and is it Margaret's withdrawal from actively managing the household that enables Ethel to step into her place. Margaret's disability is thus doubly necessary to Ethel's development, both in enabling Margaret to set an example for her, and in making space for her. Indeed, I would argue that it is a measure of Margaret's power as a character that Yonge has to kill her off so that Ethel can take up her place at the centre of the family: invalidism has traditionally been associated with feminine powerlessness, but Margaret's invalidism makes her so powerful that she has to die before Ethel can truly come into her own as a heroine.[168]

At first, Ethel's decision to renounce both her Classical studies and the possibility of marriage might seem emblematic of purely feminine experiences and ideals, since her brother Norman has to renounce neither. There is certainly an element of truth in the idea that what Margaret is modelling for Ethel is essentially a survival strategy for women in a patriarchal world: as June Sturrock has pointed out, Ethel's attempts to keep up with Norman's studies would surely have ended in frustration in any case, since she would be excluded from higher education on account of her gender, something to which Margaret herself draws Ethel's attention.[169] However, the May brothers' trajectories suggest that Margaret's model of Christian virtue is *universally* desirable in the world of the family chronicle. As Claudia Nelson indicates, 'Yonge consistently uses the circumscribed feminine lot to chastise the egotistical and to teach the earnest of both sexes,' and in fact, the brother Ethel envies undergoes a disciplinary process more severe than her own.[170] Norman's academic career leads him to religious doubt, incipient mental breakdown and, upon recovering his faith, the complete abandonment of academic life for missionary work in New Zealand. The pride in his academic prowess that led him to despise Ethel's work at Cocksmoor is thoroughly humbled, and in becoming a missionary he eventually embraces a more extreme version of exactly that work, as he leaves behind 'this world of argument and discussion . . . and go[es] to the simplest and hardest work'.[171]

The claim that Yonge ultimately treats prowess in traditionally masculine fields as spiritually dangerous may seem incompatible with her stated 'full belief in the inferiority of woman'.[172] In fact, however, it is quite consistent when read within a religious framework in which such 'inferiority' is valuable in itself. For Ethel to submit to her father's authority is to prepare herself to submit to Church authority and thus to God's; for Margaret, to be disbarred from worldly action is to be forced to focus on the other-worldly. To be a woman is, in Yonge's world, to be conscious of one's own inferiority, and such consciousness induces the humility that is so desirable in a Christian, the contrition requisite for salvation. In a scheme in which the first shall be last and the last first, mortification and restriction are spiritually desirable, as better preparing the Christian for salvation. Margaret's extreme form of femininity ultimately seems to be powerful precisely because hers are the virtues that all her fellow-characters, including the male ones, must learn to emulate.[173]

It seems highly telling that, of all the May brothers, Norman is the one who marries, and that he does so immediately before leaving the novel for foreign shores. His eldest brother Richard, on the other hand, a clergyman whose profound goodness is overlooked by Dr May because of his lack of 'masculine' cleverness (but whose worth Margaret always recognises), remains celibate. While Melissa Schaub sees this 'puzzling femininity' in Richard as a sign of the commitment to realism that, in her view, undermines Yonge's didactic purpose in *The Daisy Chain*, I would argue that it is fully consistent with Yonge's general elevation of values conventionally coded 'feminine' in the novel, and with her depiction of celibacy as a state fundamentally superior to matrimony.[174] Yonge's preference for celibacy in the clergy was shared by many of her fellows Tractarians – most famously by Newman, who championed clerical celibacy long before his conversion to Roman Catholicism[175] – but it is notable that her happily celibate clergymen are typically depicted as being already in possession of the feminine skills that other men must marry to acquire. Richard, for example, is already master of the maternal virtues that his father develops over the course of the novel, able to soothe his younger siblings 'with gentleness and fondling care, like his mother', and to teach Ethel 'to thread a needle, tie a bow, and stick in a pin'.[176] It is a recurrent pattern in Yonge's fiction that those male characters who already possess the feminine skills necessary to flourish in the family and the parish do not need to marry, and while Norman May's spiritual recovery is made equally to depend upon his abandonment of academia and his marriage, the suspicion remains that, if he had never fallen into doubt, he would not now need to fall into matrimony.

If marriage acts as a safeguard for those male characters who are tempted by the world, and is unnecessary for men who already possess feminine virtues, for female characters in the family chronicle it appears mainly as a temptation away from home duties. Ethel is enabled to resist the momentarily attractive possibility of a romance with her cousin Norman Ogilvie when she thinks of 'her father oppressed and lonely, Margaret ill and pining . . . the children running wild', in sharp contrast to Flora, whose eagerness to marry is explicitly said to betray insufficient regard for her natal family.[177] She is duly unhappy in her worldly marriage, but even Norman's ostensibly desirable marriage is shown to leave a painful gap in the family.[178] *The Daisy Chain* sets the pattern for Yonge's family chronicles, in which the most virtuous and serious-minded siblings remain celibate, while the family's flightier members rush to marry – a pattern that enables the celibate invalid to act as the exemplar, rather than the exception.[179]

In *The Daisy Chain*, the connection between celibacy and disability, and between celibacy and spiritual growth, is made absolutely explicit in the portrayal of Margaret May's disabled friend, Cherry Elwood.[180] She explains to Margaret that her fiancé broke their engagement when she suffered permanent spinal injury, but now: 'I do see how some, as are married, seem to get to think more of this world; and now and then I fancy I can see how it is best for me as it is.'[181] The idea that disability might enable a Christian to think less of 'this world' and more of the next is common to Christians across the sectarian spectrum in this period, but Yonge's tendency to think of disabled characters not just as exemplary but as typical Christians is, like her preference for celibacy in clergymen, traceable to her distinctively Anglo-Catholic sensibilities. Where a Broad Church writer like Craik emphasises the Christian's hope of future physical wholeness – with the Earl dreaming happily of 'find[ing] one's self strong, active' in heaven[182] – Yonge emphasises the value of bodily suffering in *this* world, not only to increase the believer's need for spiritual consolation, but to aid them in their quest to imitate Christ.[183] In his sermon 'On the Value and Sacredness of Suffering', the leading Tractarian clergyman E. B. Pusey describes the condition of 'the halt, [and] the maimed' as 'our ordinary lot', before suggesting that suffering 'is allotted most to those whom He loves most' because it is 'a purifying for Heaven'.[184] Yonge draws on exactly these ideas when she describes Margaret's death agonies as 'her full share of the Cross'.[185] Although belief in the spiritual efficacy of suffering was by no means restricted to Anglo-Catholics in this period, Yonge's positioning of disability can be seen to reflect what Esther T. Hu describes as the 'central' place accorded to suffering in Tractarian theology,[186] something we can see in the Anglo-Catholic predilection for images that depict the physically broken Christ hanging on the cross, in the form of the crucifix, rather than the empty cross – reminder of the resurrection of Christ rather than his suffering before it – favoured by those of a Low and Broad Church persuasion.

It is not only Yonge's particular religious commitments that enable her to position disabled characters differently in her plots, but the form of the family chronicle. The desirability of celibacy and the prioritising of sibling attachments must co-exist with the marriage plot if the families at the heart of these texts are to be reproduced – and it is in this respect that the form of the family chronicle particularly suits Yonge's purposes. Margaret May does not have to carry the plot of *The Daisy Chain* by herself, any more than does Ethel, for the family chronicle is characterised by its multiply focused narrative. The novel follows their male siblings to school and their sister Flora to London, and can include marriage plots without Margaret or Ethel falling from celibacy. The unusual aspect of these novels is that, whereas the marriage plot structures most Victorian novels, and particularly the *Bildungsroman*, with a happy marriage symbolising personal fulfilment and the completion of both the character's development and the novel itself, in Yonge's family chronicles the marriage plot is just one among many plot-lines. Disabled characters' exclusion does not therefore marginalise them in plot terms; on the contrary, it renders them particularly useful to able-bodied siblings, who can find in them life-partners and dependants without having to leave the natal family unit.[187] Yonge's family chronicles are fundamentally concerned with the preservation of the natal family that, in a typical *Bildungsroman*, the hero or heroine would have to leave in order to form a new family. The disabled sibling who cannot leave this first family therefore becomes a powerful figure, a magnet for straying family members, and the sign of its continuing necessity and usefulness.

### Ermine Williams and the Necessity of Marriage in *The Clever Woman of the Family*

I would like to end this chapter by offering a counter-example drawn from another domestic realist novel by Yonge – although, crucially, not a family chronicle – which seems to me to be the exception that proves the rule. In *The Clever Woman of the Family* (1865), we are faced with a Yonge novel that defies June Sturrock's otherwise persuasive case that 'none of [Yonge's] novels could be described as marriage novels'.[188] Not only does our wayward heroine Rachel Curtis, having abandoned her misguided (and ultimately disastrous) career as a feminist philanthropist, finally marry a kindly army officer, but so, too, does the novel's saintly invalid, the true 'clever woman', Ermine Williams. We might well ask why Yonge depicts disability as no bar to matrimony here, when in the family chronicles it consistently represents an insuperable impediment.[189]

The answer is that the most idealised character in this novel has to marry because Yonge commits herself so wholeheartedly to marriage as the solution to what Anthony Trollope had formulated the year before as the question: 'What should a woman do with her life?' The answer that his narrator offers to the 'flock of learned ladies asking that question', which was to '[f]all in love, marry the man, have two children and live happy ever afterwards',[190] might seem wholly alien to Yonge, a writer whose novels, as we have seen, so rarely fall into such cut-and-dried patterns, yet this is exactly the fate to which Rachel is ultimately consigned (even down to the number of children). Her role-model, then, cannot be allowed to remain a single woman, living in an all-female household and supporting herself through her writing, without offering a competing model of what a woman might 'do with her life', and this is a novel in which – unusually for Yonge – no such competition is tolerated.[191] Having supported herself and her sister through her writing but maintained a cloak of anonymity, Ermine potentially offers an attractive model of how a 'clever woman' might support herself and live both independently and modestly, in irreproachably feminine virtue, and Yonge seems determined to represent this state as a preparation for, rather than an alternative to, married life.

This drastic turn to the marriage plot is a mark of how serious a threat to familial and social harmony Yonge perceived secular feminism to be in the mid-1860s. Rachel's disastrous attempt to set up a feminist organisation originally called the FULE (hastily changed to the FUEE) clearly echoes the founding of the SPEW by the Langham Place feminist group, while the journal to which she intends to send her article, *The Englishwoman's Hobby Horse*, seems a pointed reference to *The English Woman's Journal*, edited by Bessie Raynor Parkes and closely associated with the SPEW.[192] Rachel's abandonment of celibacy in favour of marriage seems a desperate narrative solution to the untrammelled energy of the single woman, which appears in this novel as uncharacteristically threatening. Although Rachel is in so many ways a successor to Ethel May – intellectually curious, earnest, well intentioned – she is quite unlike her in the nature and scale of the challenge she poses to male authority. Where Ethel embodies the truth of her father's dictum 'the higher the mind, the readier the submission' in her willingness to follow Margaret's guidance, and in her distrust of her own ambitions,[193] Rachel will not heed advice from the men around her and is disrespectful towards the (admittedly unimpressive) local curate. Retrospectively, she sees both her crisis of religious faith and her absolute failure of judgement as symptomatic of the lack of male authority figures in her life: 'I should have been much better if I had had either father or brother to keep me in order,' she says, while Ermine suggests that Rachel is 'just what [she] should have been without papa and Edward to keep me down'.[194] The need for the individual to submit themselves to the guidance of those in authority runs through the family chronicles but it is rarely so definitely gendered; as Elisabeth Juckett argues in relation to *The Pillars of the House*, the family chronicles are '[d]ogmatically driven more than gender prescriptive'.[195] The sense that Rachel embodies a threat to domestic peace that only the drastic imposition of male authority can contain throws Yonge's flexible conception of family life off balance, and leads her to represent marriage as the only possible solution to the crisis she precipitates.

In another sense, however, Ermine's relation to the marriage plot is consistent with Charles Edmonstone's and Margaret May's. If Ermine did not marry, the novel's overall plotting would be much more clearly punitive; as it is, although Rachel feels at one point that her acceptance of Alick's proposal of marriage is 'an additional humiliation', that she is 'falling, if not fallen, from the supreme contempt of love and marriage',[196] Ermine's marriage enables us to read her narrative fate more optimistically. As Martha Stoddard Holmes and Talia Schaffer have so convincingly argued, Ermine's idealised relationship with Colin Keith encourages us to see marriage as a relationship that is more about mutual care-giving and tenderness than anything else; as they point out, both Colin and Alick have themselves experienced disability, and it is their expertise as nurses that marks them as exemplary husbands.[197] Kim Wheatley astutely suggests that both men demonstrate a 'feminized capacity to nurture', and it seems to me that it is this that enables them to exert authority in an unthreatening and fundamentally feminine way, and that makes Rachel's marriage – for all that it involves her submission to Alick's authority – register above all as a return to the comfortable realm of feminine domesticity, and an escape from the nightmarish, sensational world of fraud and disgrace into which her foray into the public sphere had plunged her.[198]

Rachel's marriage, then, is encoded as a return to female values, rather than a capitulation to male ones, and not only does her own temporary experience of disability (in the form of severe illness) provide the starting-point for Alick's courtship and their eventual marriage, but it is Ermine Williams's decision to marry that points the way. Essentially, marriage as a narrative fate is made palatable to the reader only in so far as it is mediated through disability, with Ermine's marriage providing a blueprint for Rachel's. While the marriage plot functions very differently here from the way it does in the family chronicles, acting as a recuperative rather than disrupting force, the invalid's relation to the marriage plot remains exemplary. As in *The Heir of Redclyffe* and the family chronicles, it is the disabled character who sets the terms on which marriage relates to the formation of the family.

## Notes

1. 'Novels, Past and Present', pp. 438–9.
2. Ibid. p. 439.
3. Colón, 'Realism and Reserve', p. 222.
4. James, 'A Noble Life', p. 846.
5. Ibid. pp. 848–9.
6. For examples of this trend, see W.S., 'Obituary. Mrs. G. L. Craik', and Oliphant, 'Mrs Craik'.
7. Showalter, 'Dinah Mulock Craik and the Tactics of Sentiment', p. 16; Mitchell, *Dinah Mulock Craik*, p. 112.
8. Mitchell, *Dinah Mulock Craik*, p. 64.
9. Craik, *Olive; The Half-Caste*, ed. Cora Kaplan.
10. Bourrier, 'Introduction: Rereading Dinah Mulock Craik', p. 2.
11. Cooper, 'Charlotte Mary Yonge', p. 857.
12. Q. D. Leavis, 'Charlotte Yonge and "Christian Discrimination"', pp. 153–4.
13. Ibid. p. 155.
14. Battiscombe, *Charlotte Mary Yonge*, p. 94, p. 64, p. 63.
15. Chen, 'And There Was No Helping It', para. 16.
16. See Battiscombe, *Charlotte Mary Yonge*, p. 165, and Gillie, 'Serious and Fatal Illness', p. 104.
17. See *Women's Writing*, 17.2 (August 2010); Juckett's and Schaffer's essays in Wagner (ed.), *Antifeminism and the Victorian Novel*; Bourrier, *The Measure of Manliness*; Schaffer, *Romance's Rival*. Yonge's work is also strikingly prominent in the special editions focused on disability of both *Nineteenth-Century Gender Studies*, 4.2 (Summer 2008) and *Victorian Review*, 35.2 (Fall 2009).
18. The longstanding question of what unmarried women ought to do with their lives was given new urgency by the revelation in the 1851 census that women considerably outnumbered men in the population and many would therefore be unable to marry, a debate that was further stoked by William R. Greg's provocative 1862 article 'Why are Women Redundant?' (subsequently expanded into a book). In the 1850s and early 1860s, the idea that unmarried women were 'redundant' would have been highly personal for both of these writers: Yonge never married, while Craik did not marry until 1864, and was therefore single when she wrote *Olive*, *John Halifax, Gentleman* and *A Woman's Thoughts About Women*. (It should be noted that, before her marriage, she wrote as Miss Mulock, and after it as Mrs Craik; I have referred to her throughout as Dinah Mulock Craik, as this is how she is generally now published, but this was never how she styled herself.)
19. For a detailed discussion of the association between physical disability and affective experience, see Stoddard Holmes, *Fictions of Affliction*, pp. 1–4 and *passim*.

20. Craik, *Noble Life*, vol. 1, p. 4.
21. Craik, *Olive*, vol. 1, pp. 10–11. Further references are to this three-volume Chapman and Hall edition (1850) unless otherwise stated; the one-volume 1875 edition contains significant textual variants, which will be discussed.
22. Ibid. p. 58; Mitchell, *Dinah Mulock Craik*, pp. 30–1.
23. Brontë, *Jane Eyre*, p. 86.
24. In a scathing review, Elizabeth Rigby (subsequently Eastlake) famously called Jane Eyre 'the personification of an unregenerate and undisciplined spirit ... a heathen mind ... proud, and ... ungrateful' ('*Vanity Fair*', p. 173).
25. Mitchell, *Dinah Mulock Craik*, p. 30. To give just a few examples of the novels' similarities in terms of plotting: both include a problematically passionate female character from the Caribbean; both feature a fire; both have a romantic hero with a ward/daughter in need of care; both heroines have to bring the doubting or irreligious hero back to the Christian faith; both heroines suffer rejection as children.
26. Kaplan, 'Introduction', *Olive; The Half-Caste*, p. x. Robyn Chandler similarly suggests that we should read Olive as 'Jane rechristianized [and] refeminized' ('Dinah Mulock Craik: Sacrifice and the Fairy-Order', p. 179).
27. Hutton, 'Novels by the Authoress of "John Halifax, Gentleman"', pp. 471–2.
28. Tabitha Sparks has similarly argued that 'Olive's deformity allows her to shape-shift into a number of conventionally exclusive destinies' ('Dinah Mulock Craik's *Olive*', p. 3). However, whereas Sparks stresses the androgynous qualities that Olive develops as a result of her disability, I read Olive's disability as promoting and preserving those feminine qualities that would otherwise be threatened by her independence and experience.
29. Craik, *Olive*, vol. 1, pp. 34–5; vol. 1, p. 58.
30. Ibid. p. 34; vol. 1, p. 57.
31. Ibid. p. 96.
32. Ibid. pp. 97–8.
33. Ibid. p. 137; vol. 2, p. 313.
34. In Dickens's work alone, Madeline Bray, Little Nell, Agnes Wickfield and Little Dorrit come immediately to mind.
35. Craik, *Olive*, vol. 1, p. 17.
36. Ibid. p. 39.
37. Ibid. p. 119, p. 121.
38. Ibid. p. 182, p. 140, p. 191.
39. Ibid. pp. 192–3.
40. Ibid., vol. 2, p. 32.
41. Ibid. p. 55.
42. Craik, *A Woman's Thoughts*, pp. 89–90 and *passim* in Ch. 3; Craik, *Olive*, vol. 2, p. 58.

43. Craik, *Olive*, vol. 2, pp. 58–9.
44. Denisoff, 'Lady in green with novel', p. 165. Similarly, Antonia Losano argues that it is because Olive is not an aesthetic object that she is able to become an artist (*The Woman Painter in Victorian Literature*, pp. 182–3).
45. Craik, *Olive*, vol. 2, pp. 123–4.
46. Ibid. pp. 158–9.
47. Ibid. pp. 268–9.
48. Ibid. p. 264.
49. Ibid. p. 179.
50. Ibid. pp. 179–80.
51. Ibid., vol. 3, p. 375.
52. Losano, for example, suggests that Olive's marriage 'reunites her with the economic fruits of her labor' (*The Woman Painter in Victorian Literature*, p. 65). While this is partially true in a literal sense – in that Olive had been giving Harold some of the proceeds from her painting in order to repay her father's debt to him – it is surely more significant that she ceases to earn money of her own once they are married, and that even if she did, her earnings would legally belong to him rather than to her.
53. Craik, *Olive*, vol. 3, p. 69; vol. 3, pp. 356–7.
54. Stoddard Holmes, 'Victorian Fictions of Interdependency', p. 4.
55. Craik, *Olive*, vol. 3, p. 307, pp. 320–1.
56. Ibid. pp. 349–50.
57. Ibid., vol. 1, p. 182, p. 211.
58. Showalter, 'Dinah Mulock Craik and the Tactics of Sentiment', p. 15.
59. Ibid. p. 187.
60. Craik, *Olive* (1875), p. 88.
61. Craik, *Olive*, vol. 1, p. 10; *Olive* (1875), p. 5.
62. Craik, *Olive*, vol. 2, p. 15; *Olive* (1875), p. 146.
63. Craik, *Olive*, vol. 2, p. 58; *Olive* (1875), p. 165.
64. Craik, *Olive*, vol. 3, p. 375.
65. Ibid. p. 357.
66. It is possible to read this differently, as an instance of poetic justice that marks Olive's final victory over her false friend Sara Derwent, who once ridiculed the idea 'of Olive's stealing any girl's lover' (ibid., vol. 1, p. 180), since it is Sara's child whom Olive now mothers and her widower whom Olive has married. As Stoddard Holmes points out, Olive is thereby rewarded with 'the literal place – complete with husband and child – of the non-disabled heroine' (*Fictions of Affliction*, p. 48).
67. Mitchell points out that Hurst and Blackett had worn out four sets of plates resetting the type by 1858, that there were copies from eleven separate English publishers before 1898 and that American pirates produced at least forty-five different editions by 1900 (*Dinah Mulock Craik*, p. 47). The novel's popularity was such that a retrospective essay

on Craik's career in *The Bookman* suggested that she 'is remembered as the writer of one book' (Ellis, 'Dinah Maria Mulock', p. 1).
68. Perkin, 'Narrative Voice and the "Feminine" Novelist', p. 32.
69. Klages, *Woeful Afflictions*, p. 67.
70. Bourrier, *The Measure of Manliness*, p. 2.
71. Craik, *Halifax*, p. 65.
72. Ibid. p. 29.
73. Ibid. p. 65; Furneaux, 'Negotiating the Gentle-Man', p. 117; Schaffer, *Romance's Rival*, p. 171.
74. Craik, *Halifax*, p. 52.
75. Ibid. p. 55, p. 53.
76. Craik, *A Woman's Thoughts*, p. 73.
77. Craik, *Halifax*, pp. 204–5.
78. Ibid. p. 128.
79. For an extended discussion of such relationships, see Bourrier, *The Measure of Manliness*, particularly her discussion of Phineas and John's relationship in Ch. 2, pp. 52–75.
80. Ibid. p. 142.
81. Kiran Mascarenhas has suggested that the invocation of David and Jonathan carries sinister undertones, since David's friendship does such harm to Jonathan in the biblical story ('*John Halifax, Gentleman*: A Counter Story', pp. 261–2). However, since Craik uses this bible story to illustrate the ideal of male friendship in *A Woman's Thoughts* (p. 136), this reading does not seem to me persuasive. Allusions to David and Jonathan had strong contemporary resonance when used in this way: Charles Kingsley, for example, wrote to his wife that if she had been male, 'we should have been like David and Jonathan' (Chitty, *The Beast and the Monk*, p. 52).
82. Craik, *Halifax*, p. 53.
83. Mitchell, *Dinah Mulock Craik*, p. 47.
84. Craik, *Halifax*, pp. 221–2. For an extended and helpful discussion of Muriel's characterisation, see Klages, *Woeful Afflictions*, pp. 67–74.
85. Hutton, 'Novels by the Authoress of "John Halifax, Gentleman"', p. 475.
86. Mitchell, *Dinah Mulock Craik*, p. 64.
87. Craik, *Noble Life*, vol. 1, pp. 3–4.
88. Ibid., vol. 1, p. 4.
89. Gagnier, *Subjectivities*, p. 44.
90. Craik, *Noble Life*, vol. 1, p. 28.
91. Ibid., vol. 1, p. 24.
92. Ibid. p. 64, p. 154, p. 181.
93. Ibid. p. 4, p. 180.
94. Ibid. pp. 126–8.
95. Craik, 'To Novelists', p. 441.
96. Craik, *Noble Life*, vol. 1, pp. 156–7.

97. Ibid. pp. 180–2.
98. Ibid. p. 157, emphasis added.
99. Ibid., vol. 2, p. 10.
100. Ibid. pp. 7–8.
101. Ibid., vol. 1, pp. 156–7.
102. Craik, *Olive*, vol. 3, p. 349.
103. Craik, *Noble Life*, vol. 1, p. 238.
104. Ibid., vol. 1, pp. 89–90, pp. 96–7.
105. Ibid., vol. 2, pp. 51–2.
106. Ibid. pp. 27–8.
107. Ibid. pp. 36–7.
108. Ibid. pp. 100–1.
109. Ibid. pp. 215–16.
110. Ibid. p. 236.
111. Fasick, 'Charles Kingsley's Scientific Treatment of Gender', p. 93; Barker, 'Erotic Martyrdom', p. 466.
112. Craik, *Noble Life*, vol. 2, p. 265.
113. Ibid. p. 98.
114. Mitchell, *Dinah Mulock Craik*, p. 65.
115. Craik, *Olive*, vol. 3, pp. 375–6.
116. Craik, *Noble Life*, vol. 2, p. 207.
117. Ibid. p. 299.
118. Thompson, *Reviewing Sex*, p. 101.
119. Yonge, *Heir*, p. 10.
120. Bourrier, 'The Spirit of a Man', p. 120. In her subsequent monograph, *The Measure of Manliness*, Bourrier develops this reading and argues that 'Yonge makes an implicit connection between invalidism and authorship in the character of Charles Edmonstone' (p. 46).
121. Bourrier, 'The Spirit of a Man', p. 123, pp. 126–7.
122. For example, J. Russell Perkin calls it a 'theological romance' (*Theology and the Victorian Novel*, p. 78), while Tamara S. Wagner argues that the novel 'contributed centrally to a domestication of the Gothic' ('Stretching "The Sensational Sixties"', pp. 216–17).
123. Yonge, *Heir*, p. 15, p. 260.
124. Levine, *The Realistic Imagination*, p. 8. Although Gavin Budge has convincingly demonstrated that George Levine's definitions of realism are problematic in their wider relation to Yonge's work ('Realism and Typology', pp. 194–6), I think Levine's definition is very helpful in this instance.
125. Yonge, *Heir*, pp. 265–6.
126. Ibid. p. 185.
127. Ibid. p. 38, p. 39.
128. Brownell, 'The Two Worlds of Charlotte Yonge', p. 172; Yonge, *Heir*, p. 187.
129. Schaffer, 'Maiden Pairs', p. 95.

168  Plotting Disability in the Nineteenth-Century Novel

130. For a sampling of the widely varying explanations that critics have offered, see Brownell, 'The Two Worlds of Charlotte Yonge', p. 172; Budge, *Charlotte M. Yonge*, pp. 176–8; Thompson, *Reviewing Sex*, p. 103; and Wolff, *Gains and Losses*, p. 135.
131. Yonge, *Heir*, p. 431.
132. Ibid. p. 301.
133. Ibid. pp. 292–3.
134. Bourrier, 'The Spirit of a Man', p. 122.
135. Yonge, *Heir*, p. 290, p. 300.
136. Ibid. p. 299.
137. Ibid. pp. 291–2.
138. Ibid. p. 287.
139. See Schaffer, *Romance's Rival*, especially pp. 142–8 and pp. 181–90.
140. Yonge, *Heir*, p. 363.
141. Ibid. p. 463.
142. Ibid. p. 363.
143. Ibid. p. 71.
144. Ibid. p. 462.
145. Yonge, *Daisy Chain*, p. v.
146. 'New Novels', *John Bull*, p. 446; 'Cheap Edition of the Novels and Tales of Charlotte M. Yonge', *The Country Gentleman*, p. 1403. Tellingly, critics wishing to praise Yonge for her 'masculine' rather than 'feminine' virtues were inclined to praise her historical novels and denigrate her family chronicles. For example, having praised *The Heir of Redclyffe* for 'delight[ing] in all that is manly and high-spirited', a *Quarterly Review* critic suggested that '[a]dmirable as her "family chronicles" . . . are . . . it cannot be denied they are not every man's affair' ('Charlotte Mary Yonge', *The Quarterly Review*, p. 535), while in *The Independent* Graham R. Tomson (complaining along the way of the prevalence of illness, which 'is a characteristic of the school to which Miss Yonge belongs') commented upon 'the vast superiority of her historical over her domestic novels' ('Women Authors of To-Day', p. 8).
147. For an extended discussion of the many reviews in which Yonge's work was read as quintessentially feminine, see Thompson, *Reviewing Sex*, pp. 89–107. This trend is neatly illustrated by Edith Sichel's claim that '[i]t is impossible to imagine many men reading Miss Yonge . . . . It would be as if we dreamed of them taking high tea *in perpetuo*' ('Charlotte Yonge as a Chronicler', quoted in Thompson, *Reviewing Sex*, pp. 92–3).
148. 'Novels, Past and Present', p. 439.
149. Ibid. p. 438.
150. Margaret was re-incarnated as the saintly Beth March in Louisa May Alcott's bestselling *Little Women* (1868–9) – a novel that specifically references *The Heir of Redclyffe* (p. 25) – and even more clearly as

Cousin Helen in Susan Coolidge's perennially popular novel *What Katy Did* (1872). For a further discussion of the parallels between Yonge and Coolidge's work, see Foster and Simons, *What Katy Read*, pp. 76–7, and Hale, 'Disability and the Individual Talent'.
151. Yonge, *The Trial*, p. 439.
152. Colón, 'Realism and Reserve', p. 228.
153. See, for instance, Sandbach-Dahlström, *Be Good Sweet Maid*, p. 7, and Schaub, 'Worthy Ambition', pp. 65–6, p. 81; Budge, *Charlotte M. Yonge*, p. 66.
154. Much symbolic play is made with the significance of Margaret's name – inherited from her mother – and its derivation from the French 'marguerite', meaning 'daisy', connecting her with the 'daisy chain' of Dr May's dream; when she dies, he calls her 'the first link of his Daisy Chain drawn up out of sight' (Yonge, *Daisy Chain*, pp. 61–2, p. 647). For further discussion of the significance of flower imagery in the novel, see Schaffer, 'Taming the Tropics', pp. 206–7.
155. Yonge, *Daisy Chain*, p. 3, p. 12, p. 5.
156. Ibid. p. 18.
157. Ibid. p. 160.
158. Ibid. pp. 196–7.
159. Ibid. p. 411.
160. Ibid. p. 633.
161. For further discussion of this issue, see Chen, 'And There Was No Helping It', para. 16.
162. Yonge, *Daisy Chain*, p. 307.
163. Ibid. p. 498.
164. Ibid. p. 19, p. 648.
165. Ibid. p. 667.
166. Ibid. p. 181, p. 393.
167. Ibid. p. 59.
168. Scholars of invalidism, including Diane Prince Herndl and Maria Frawley, have argued that, for some Victorian women, assuming the mantle of invalidism was a way of wielding power in their families and communities, that it was potentially 'a strategy of subversion' (Herndl, *Invalid Women*, p. 3 and *passim*, and Frawley, *Invalidism and Identity*, p. 199 and *passim*).
169. Sturrock, 'Heaven and Home', p. 36; Yonge, *Daisy Chain*, p. 181.
170. Nelson, *Boys Will Be Girls*, p. 20.
171. Yonge, *Daisy Chain*, p. 210, pp. 518–19.
172. Yonge, *Womankind*, p. 1.
173. This valorisation of apparently passive feminine values resonates with Philippa Levine's claim that, for mid-Victorian feminists, 'the most effective weapon was not the total rejection of [gender] ideology but rather a manipulation of its fundamental values' (*Victorian Feminism*, p. 13). Gavin Budge points out that this would have been

doubly familiar to Yonge, since not only did conservative feminists claim 'simply to pursue the implications of gender opposition even more consistently than the dominant culture', but this was a strategy employed by the arch-conservative Tractarians themselves (*Charlotte M. Yonge*, pp. 287–8).

174. Schaub, 'Worthy Ambition', p. 73.
175. Newman stated in his *Apologia* that he became convinced at an early age 'that it would be the will of God that I should lead a single life', while in a letter of 1840 he had written, 'I have a repugnance to a clergyman's marrying. I do not say that it is not lawful – I cannot deny the right – but whether a prejudice or not, it shocks me' (*Apologia*, p. 34; 'My Illness in Sicily', p. 137). Kingsley's suspicion of such views clearly informed his public attack on Newman,'What, Then, Does Dr. Newman Mean?', in which Newman's remarks about celibacy are singled out for criticism. For further discussion of this issue, see Buckton, 'An Unnatural State'. For a discussion of how the Tractarian tolerance for, and even encouragement of, female celibacy was considered subversive, see Engelhardt, 'The Paradigmatic Angel in the House'.
176. Yonge, *Daisy Chain*, p. 37, p. 57.
177. Ibid. pp. 433–4, p. 407.
178. Ibid. p. 651.
179. To give just three of many examples: in *The Daisy Chain*, Richard, Margaret and Ethel stay single, while vain Flora and arrogant Norman marry; in *The Young Stepmother* (1861), awkward but loveable Sophy stays celibate while her shallow sister Lucy makes a disastrous marriage; while in *The Pillars of the House* (1873), heroic Felix, sympathetic Geraldine and worthy Clement intend not to marry, while selfish Alda and rash Edgar both marry young (and unhappily).
180. It is interesting to note that her name closely resembles that of Geraldine (nicknamed 'Cherry') Underwood, the 'lame' artist of *The Pillars of the House*, who receives far greater narrative attention: perhaps Yonge's mind continued to run on the undeveloped psychological and narrative possibilities of Cherry as a character.
181. Yonge, *Daisy Chain*, p. 311.
182. Craik, *Noble Life*, vol. 2, pp. 290–1.
183. Similarly, in *The Pillars of the House*, the dying Reverend Underwood tells his eldest son Felix, who is on the point of becoming head of the family, that their family motto 'Under Wood, Under Rode' (the novel's subtitle) offers a key to the Christian life: 'Bear thy cross, and thy cross will bear thee, like little Geraldine's cross potent – Rod and Rood, Cross and Crutch – all the same etymologically and veritably' (vol. 1, p. 35). This image draws together Cross and Crutch in such a way that Felix's disabled sister Geraldine, who needs a crutch to walk, is constructed not as an aberrant but as a typical Christian, an idea that is strengthened when she later calls her arthritic ankle her 'Cross'

(vol. 1, p. 357). Disability is thereby figured as central – rather than exceptional or peripheral – to Christian experience, as it is in *The Heir of Redclyffe* and *The Daisy Chain*.
184. Pusey, 'The Value and Sacredness of Suffering', p. 131.
185. As Michael Wheeler points out, belief in the existence of purgatory was not narrowly restricted to Roman Catholics in the nineteenth century, although it was strongly associated with a High Church, rather than Evangelical, position (*Heaven, Hell, and the Victorians*, pp. 74–7).
186. Hu, 'Christina Rossetti', p. 156.
187. In *The Pillars of the House*, for example, Geraldine becomes indispensible to Felix precisely because she seems to him 'set apart from marriage'; after Felix's death, she becomes the life-partner of another brother, Clement, a gentle, celibate clergyman who was teased as a child for his effeminacy but as an adult becomes an exemplary priest and one of the novel's titular 'pillars' (Yonge, *Pillars*, vol. 2, p. 130; p. 517). Together, they bring up their orphaned nephew, very much as Amy and Charles form a partnership to bring up the fatherless Mary Verena. For a discussion of Yonge's idealisation of brother–sister pairings – usually in explicit preference to matrimony – see Sanders, *The Brother–Sister Culture*, pp. 97–9.
188. Sturrock, 'Heaven and Home', p. 16.
189. To give just a few examples: it is generally agreed in *The Daisy Chain* that Margaret cannot marry unless she recovers her ability to walk; in the sequel *The Trial*, the invalid Averil Ward only marries Tom May because she believes that she will very soon die; in *The Pillars of the House*, it is widely assumed that Geraldine will never marry (although she does receive a proposal, which she refuses).
190. Trollope, *Can You Forgive Her?*, p. 110. (This novel was first published as a book in 1865, the same year as *The Clever Woman*, but serial publication began in 1864, and thus his narrator first posed this question in print in 1864.)
191. It is telling that Rachel's cousin, Fanny Temple, who is allowed to remain unmarried, not only has shown herself willing to submit to male authority on every occasion, characterised as having 'an air of dependence almost beseeching protection', but ultimately sets up a partnership with her children's governess, Ermine's sister Alison, which is explicitly figured as a marriage (Yonge, *Clever Woman*, p. 8, p. 358). This neatly enables Alison – another potentially independent single woman – to be absorbed into a large family, replete with male members to whom she will eventually be able to defer.
192. Ibid. p. 145, p. 89. Rachel explains that FULE stands for the Female Union for Lacemaker's Employment, while FUEE is an acronym for Female Union for Englishwoman's Employment, both of which clearly recall the Lambeth Place group's Society for the Promotion of

the Employment of Women (abbreviated to SPEW). For more information on the Langham Place group, the SPEW and *The English Woman's Journal*, see Levine, *Victorian Feminism*, pp. 86–90.
193. Yonge, *Daisy Chain*, p. 183.
194. Yonge, *Clever Woman*, p. 95, p. 367.
195. Juckett, 'Cross-Gendering the Underwoods', p. 131.
196. Ibid. p. 274.
197. Stoddard Holmes, 'Victorian Fictions of Interdependency', pp. 32–3; Schaffer, *Romance's Rivals*, pp. 186–7.
198. Wheatley, 'Death and Domestication', p. 902.

# Chapter 4

# Terminal Decline: Physical Frailty and Moral Inheritance in George Eliot and Henry James

In a stultifying provincial setting, a promising young girl named Maggie struggles to thrive. She is undervalued by her unimaginative mother, and unappreciated by her adored brother, whose education is consistently prioritised over hers. Just when we fear that there is no one to offer a helping hand to our intelligent and sweet-natured heroine, however, she meets her first real friend, an invalid who is able to offer her wise counsel and real sympathy. Inspired and encouraged by this friendship, Maggie grows into a morally serious young woman, and finds herself able to make the ultimate sacrifice for her brother's sake when the moment of choice comes. The reward for her selfless devotion is immediately forthcoming: saved from the engulfing waters in which her inconvenient brother drowns, Maggie makes a happy marriage and lives to bless the memory of her departed disabled mentor.

As the reader will by now have guessed, I am not in fact describing the plot of George Eliot's *The Mill on the Floss* (1860), but rather that of Elizabeth Gaskell's novella *The Moorland Cottage*, published ten years earlier. Although the relative obscurity of Gaskell's text means that few readers today are likely to be struck, as Swinburne was, by Eliot's 'palpable ... obligation' to Gaskell, the structural similarities between the two texts are unmissable when they are considered side by side.[1] What makes the comparison illuminating, however, is the differences that these similarities throw into relief: whether by coincidence or influence, Eliot works with the same basic plot structure as Gaskell, and in her hands, the sentimental is transformed into the tragic.

It is a transformation that is captured in microcosm by Eliot's treatment of Gaskell's disability plot. In both novels, the heroine makes a friend whose disability sets them apart from their narrative community, and forces them to remain on the sidelines of the novel's action. In both cases, this enforced passivity is shown to have developed the disabled character's emotional and intellectual capacities, enabling them to sympathise with the heroine as no other character can, and endowing them with moral insight that they share with her while she is still struggling to see her way forward. In Gaskell's text, however, the invalid Mrs Buxton fully embraces this narrative role, and plays it to perfection. She brings out the best in Maggie simply through her 'ready understanding and sympathy', and through the example of a life that, 'in its uneventful hours and days, spoke many homilies'.[2] Although Mrs Buxton does not intervene directly in Maggie's story and dies less than halfway through the narrative, she leaves a moral legacy behind her and is shown to exert a shaping influence on the future. Not only has she moulded Maggie's character, but she essentially makes Maggie's marriage plot from beyond the grave: in death, she brings her son Frank and Maggie together when they are united by their shared grief for her, and acts as their intercessor, when thinking of her prompts her husband to relent towards Maggie and reconsider his objection to the match.[3] As though concerned that the reader might have missed these heavy hints about Mrs Buxton's influence, Gaskell concludes the story with a sentence that underlines the ongoing power and presence of this apparently passive, literally absent character:

> Over both old and young the memory of one who is dead broods like a dove, – of one who could do little during her lifetime; who was doomed only to 'stand and wait,' who was meekly content to be gentle, holy, patient, and undefiled, – the memory of the invalid Mrs. Buxton.[4]

This final sentence perfectly sums up what we might call the redemptive disability plot, in which the physical suffering and social isolation occasioned by disability are compensated by moral growth in the disabled subject, which in turn enables them to exert a beneficial moral influence on others in life, and leave a moral legacy behind them in death.[5]

George Eliot employs the same basic plot structure but twists it into a very different shape. Philip Wakem, too, must stand to the side of the action – but, unlike Mrs Buxton, he chafes against this inactivity, and attempts to thrust himself into Maggie's marriage plot as her suitor rather than merely her confidant. He achieves real moral insight as a result of his sufferings, and makes a valiant attempt to communicate his 'strong sympathy' to Maggie – but she goes to her death uncomforted, still tormented by the thought of the pain she has caused.[6] Most radically of all, Eliot reverses the pattern of influence and survival: rather than having an able-bodied heroine inspired by the virtues of a disabled exemplar, Eliot has her disabled character inspired by the life of the able-bodied woman he has loved, and it is he, rather than his beloved, who lives on into the future beyond the last page of the novel, bearing witness to her life. Our expectations about how moral and biological inheritance interact in the novel are upended by the fact that it is the 'always solitary' Philip who survives, while Maggie – 'so young, so healthy'– dies.[7] The basic shape of the redemptive disability plot remains evident, as disability is still treated as an experience enabling moral growth and endowing the disabled character with a moral legacy that they need to pass on. In Eliot's hands, however, this plot-line takes a tortuous form, tangled up with anxiety about heredity and futurity.

I do not contrast Gaskell and Eliot's treatment of the disability plot in order to convict Gaskell of sentimentality and praise Eliot for hard-headedness, but rather to illustrate their contrasting sense of how novelistic plot can best represent reality and, accordingly, how disability should be plotted in fiction. It is this divergence between Eliot's sense of reality and Gaskell's – fundamentally similar to that of the authors discussed in the last chapter – that explains Craik's bewildered and indignant response to *The Mill on the Floss*. It is not that she could not appreciate Eliot's aesthetic achievement, nor that she cast aspersions on the author's personal morality;[8] what pained her was the novel's plotting, which she saw as morally wrong because it misled the reader about the nature of reality. Craik does not deny that some lives may seem to be as fruitless as Maggie's. What she disputes is that they are really so:

> it may be urged that fiction has its counterpart, and worse, in daily truth . . . . All this is most true, so far as we see. But we never can see, not even the wisest and greatest of us, anything like the whole of even the meanest and briefest human life.[9]

The risk, then, of writing as well as George Eliot, but plotting so ruthlessly, is that the reader may mistake the limits of the author's vision for the limits of God's care, and take the confusion of the fictional narrative for confusion in the design of reality itself.

Craik has, I think, put her finger on the real difference between Eliot and herself.[10] While Eliot shared Craik's belief in the moral responsibilities of the author – it is not, I think, difficult to imagine Eliot saying, as Craik does in this essay, that 'the modern novel is one of the most important moral agents of the community'[11] – she did not share Craik's belief that reality is providentially shaped. Instead of setting out 'to justify the ways of God to men', as Craik (echoing Milton) demands,[12] Eliot's fiction bears at times almost *un*bearable witness to the difficulty of living in the world she described to Frederick Myers, when, 'taking as her text . . . the words *God, Immortality, Duty*, – [she] pronounced, with terrible earnestness, how inconceivable the *first*, how unbelievable the *second*, and yet how peremptory and absolute the *third*'.[13] In a world in which God is inconceivable, immortality unbelievable but duty peremptory and absolute, Maggie's dilemma is both tragic *and* realistic, as for Craik or Gaskell it could never be.

The sentimental mode in which Gaskell writes in 'The Moorland Cottage' has become in such a world untruthful, even as its central questions – how can young women find their way in patriarchal communities? How should we balance the claims of the family and the daughter, the community and the individual? – continue to be relevant, and its basic plot structure persists. As we shall see, the redemptive disability plot was one to which George Eliot and her successor Henry James continually returned, and which they re-shaped in ways that reflected their diminishing readiness to offer narrative solutions to social and moral problems through the neat resolution of plot. Tracing these authors' use of the redemptive disability plot, we can see that its slow decline occurred in tandem with late Victorian realists' increasing scepticism about the possibility of creating plots that were both morally satisfying and, in any meaningful sense, realistic. Staging the tottering or even the failure of the redemptive disability plot offered a way of exploring the tension between the desire for an ethically motivated plot with a morally restorative conclusion – what we might call a Victorian plot – and the desire to reflect a reality seen to be shaped by other forces entirely. The redemptive disability plot was also a vehicle for the expression of these authors' proto-modernist anxieties about heredity and futurity.

In *The Mill on the Floss*, Eliot draws on the conventional association between disability and moral inheritance, making use of the plot structures familiar from *The Moorland Cottage* and many of the texts discussed in the last chapter, and re-working them in the service of a new kind of realism. Where Mrs Buxton – like Margaret May, or the Earl of Cairnforth, or any of Dickens's frail angels – is happy to be of use to someone else, and to get out of the way when her narrative work is done, Eliot draws out the moral ambiguities involved in making use of someone else's life, even for benevolent purposes. Philip Wakem's moral investment in Maggie's life is depicted as a potential source of moral redemption, but it is also shown to be fraught with danger and difficulty. In *Daniel Deronda*, Eliot explores the same concerns in her depiction of the consumptive visionary Mordecai; while he embraces his role as a conduit for a moral and intellectual inheritance, rather than pining to be the protagonist of his own story, Eliot plots the novel in such a way that his decision to live *through* Daniel appears increasingly troubling. In James's early masterpiece, *The Portrait of a Lady* (1881), he engages with similar anxieties through his depiction of the protagonist's consumptive benefactor. Heir to both Philip Wakem and Mordecai Cohen, Ralph Touchett invests in Isabel's life in a literal sense, an investment shown to have ambiguous motives and disastrous consequences – and yet he remains the bearer of the only hope the conclusion allows. Through the failure of the marriage plot and the shipwreck of Ralph's ill-fated attempt to live through Isabel, James yet allows the reader some hope for the possibility of new plots, built on the catastrophic failure of the old, in a redemptive death-bed scene. Returning to similar materials some twenty years later in *The Wings of the Dove* (1902), James allows the reader no such relief; the missing death-bed scene, I will argue, is totemic for the final failure of the redemptive disability plot in this novel. Milly Theale's material inheritance becomes a source of fatal temptation to our hero and heroine, while her moral inheritance cannot be received by a pair of plotters whose mutual recrimination and regret make for a bleak conclusion, one that I read as the nadir of the long decline of the redemptive disability plot.

Before we can appreciate the full significance of Milly's missing death-bed scene and her tragically unread letter, however, we need first to understand why Eliot chose to confront the reader with Maggie Tulliver's all too vivid death by drowning, and why Philip's letter of forgiveness fails to prevent it.

## 'This gift of transferred life': Learning to Love Maggie in *The Mill on the Floss*

Maggie fell on her knees against the table, and buried her sorrow-stricken face. Her soul went out to the Unseen Pity that would be with her to the end. Surely there was something taught her by this experience of great need; and she must be learning a secret of human tenderness and

> long-suffering, that the less erring could hardly know? 'O God, if my life is to be long, let me live to bless and comfort –'
>
> At that moment Maggie felt a startling sensation of sudden cold about her knees and feet: it was water flowing under her. . . . She was not bewildered for an instant – she knew it was the flood![14]

Maggie might not be 'bewildered for an instant' by the sudden arrival of the flood waters at the end of *The Mill on the Floss*, but it is a reaction that few readers can have shared. Rushing in under Maggie's door, and bearing her onward to heroism and death, the flood appears as if in immediate answer to her prayer for help, but is a hideous parody of the narrative solution we had trusted Maggie's author to provide. It dissolves her seemingly insoluble problems and definitively answers the question of what she should do with her life, but it does so at the expense of violating the implicit contract between novelist and novel reader. When Maggie prays that 'there was something taught her by this experience', she is only making explicit the belief that we have been carrying through hundreds of pages – for what are we reading, after all, but Maggie's *Bildungsroman*? Yet it turns out that Maggie's story is leading her not onwards, but back to where she started. Just a few pages after throwing herself on the mercy of the 'Unseen Pity', she drowns in her brother Tom's arms, the conditions of their conflict washed away as they are returned to a pre-lapsarian state of perfect unity, 'living through again in one supreme moment the days when they had clasped their little hands in love, and roamed the daisied fields together'.[15]

As generations of critics have forcefully pointed out, it is a solution that cannot satisfy us, for the novel in which we have invested so much emotional and intellectual energy has been up to now an explicitly and insistently *realist* novel. Almost exactly at its midpoint, as if anticipating our complaints about the restrictive nature of its plot, the narrator appeals to us to put aside our resentment at being 'stifled for want of an outlet towards something beautiful, great, or noble', and to commit ourselves to her quasi-scientific 'observation of human life'.[16] If we have kept faith with this realist manifesto when the narrator called upon it to justify Maggie's many disappointments and failures, then we can hardly help demanding that Maggie's moment of triumph also be consistent with it, and take place in the same world, on the same terms, as her long drawn-out struggles did. As Barbara Hardy trenchantly argues, 'such struggles are not settled by floods'.[17] Or rather, they are so settled only in our fantasies: there is no denying the element of wish-fulfilment in the arrival of a flood that enables Maggie to die heroically so soon after she has thought despairingly of the 'trials to come' in the life before her. As George Levine says, it is a moment of 'psychological triumph' for Maggie; the problem is that it is 'inimical to the realist's enterprise'.[18] Nor is it entirely satisfying as a fairy-tale conclusion, providing, as it does, an evasion rather than a solution to the problem of how Maggie can live down her social disgrace and find her way out of the desperately difficult position in which her author has placed her. Alien as Craik's view of the novelist's responsibilities to her characters now seems, it is near impossible not to share her basic assessment (expressed in the review discussed earlier) that it is '*not* right to paint *Maggie* only as she is in her strong, unsatisfied, erring youth – and leave her there'.[19]

Maggie is not, however, the only 'unsatisfied, erring youth' in *The Mill on the Floss*. The description could equally well be applied to Philip Wakem, the young man who has loved Maggie from childhood, but whose curvature of the spine, which marks him as 'deformed' in the eyes of his fellow characters, has disabled him as a romantic hero. Growing up in an intolerant, narrowly conformist community in which Tom Tulliver's 'superstitious repugnance to everything exceptional' is shown to be typical, Philip has, like Maggie, struggled with loneliness, frustration and thwarted desire.[20] Unlike Maggie, however, his struggles do not end in disaster. Instead, his experience of loving Maggie, and of finally bringing himself to accept that she cannot return his love, leads him to a moment of moral epiphany. At what seems the nadir of his painful career, when he knows that Maggie has eloped with his handsome, able-bodied rival, Stephen Guest, and will never return his romantic feelings, he writes a letter that, I would argue, marks the moral fulcrum of the text. For Philip does something more than offer Maggie his sympathy or forgiveness. He testifies to the transformative experience of loving her, assuring her that:

> no anguish I have had to bear on your account has been too heavy a price to pay for the new life into which I have entered in loving you. ... The new life I have found in caring for your joy and sorrow more than for what is directly my own, has transformed the spirit of rebellious murmuring into that willing endurance which is the birth of strong sympathy. I think nothing but such complete and intense love could have initiated me into that enlarged life which grows and grows by appropriating the life of others; for before, I was always dragged back

from it by ever-present painful self-consciousness. I even think sometimes that this gift of transferred life which has come to me in loving you, may be a new power to me.[21]

What Eliot allows Philip to articulate here is nothing less than a fully developed moral manifesto for living, and indeed for reading. Although Maggie herself fails to see it, Philip's letter is not, finally, a cry of pain, but an extended account of what loving her has done for him, and, by implication, what loving her might do for the reader. Maggie can read only the record of suffering, but as readers we surely hear the note of triumph, and sense Philip's joy in having transcended 'painful self-consciousness' and achieved 'enlarged life'. Pain is a part of the story Philip tells, but in his account it is ultimately lost in the experience of genuinely unselfish love, which turns out to be sustaining, even life-giving, 'suffic[ing] to withhold [him] from suicide'.[22]

It is tempting to return to the imagery of flooding when speaking of Philip's overwhelming, self-dissolving sympathy for Maggie, but the comparison would be a false one, for what Philip achieves here is not the drowning of his former passion in a new tide of sympathy, but rather, a new synthesis of duty and desire.[23] Love does not have to be renounced for unselfishness because love has *become* unselfishness: Philip's desire for Maggie has turned into a 'devotion that excludes [selfish] wishes' – has become, in other words, the desire for her good. Having learned to love Maggie like this, he nurses a hope that he will have a 'new power' to relate to others in the same way. This 'birth of strong sympathy' is the ultimate ethical achievement in an Eliot novel, staged again and again in scenes of moral awakening, most famously in *Middlemarch* (1872) when, having resolved to 'clutch [her] own pain and compel it to silence', Dorothea looks out of her window at sunrise and recognises her shared humanity with the strangers she sees on the road.[24]

The crucial difference here is that, while Philip's letter may be comparable to Dorothea's epiphany both in its contents and in its emotional charge, it is not given comparable weight by the novel's plotting. Not only is the letter positioned in the narrative in such a way that we are all too likely to hurry past it, and then to forget it in the drama of the flood, but its lack of any tangible result is bound to undermine our sense of its significance. Dorothea's inspiring generosity of spirit finds its outlet in action that has a substantive effect on those around her, and paves the way for a happy conclusion to her own marriage plot, leading her to a life of 'incalculably diffusive' influence.[25] Philip's declaration of unselfish love for Maggie, on the other hand, has no discernible effect on Maggie's emotional state. She receives the letter as coals of fire upon her head, and totally fails to heed either Philip's appeal that she free herself from guilt on his account, or his astute assessment of Stephen's shortcomings, which we might have hoped would lessen her sense of loss. Far from moving on, freed from regret and comforted by Philip's assurance that her good intentions have not been in vain, Maggie remains mired in the grief and guilt from which only death frees her.

For himself, Philip's moral triumph over jealousy and selfishness has to be its own reward, for he is offered no other. After Maggie's death, we are starkly told that, while Stephen visits Maggie's grave 'with a sweet face beside him', Philip is 'always solitary'.[26] How much comfort we take from the fact that he finds 'great companionship . . . among the trees of the Red Deeps, where the buried joy seemed still to hover – like a revisiting spirit' depends on how far we can accept that the 'gift of transferred life' is still a gift when the life in question has been cut short.[27] If we believe that 'caring for [Maggie's] joy and sorrow more than for what is directly [his] own' will enable Philip to invest similarly in the lives of others, then we can perhaps share Barbara Guth's optimistic assessment that he will 'go on to a full life'.[28] If we take his words more literally, and understand his happiness to be built on hers, then the flood that puts an end to the possibility that Maggie will one day realise her potential for happiness becomes doubly tragic. An observer deprived of the beloved he lives to observe, Philip is, in this reading, reduced to a ghostly figure, haunting the novel's final paragraphs.

In a sense, then, Philip's narrative trajectory and final plight conform closely to the expectations established by many of the novels we have examined so far: as a disabled man, his desire to participate in the marriage plot is doomed, and he has to learn to accept a marginal role in the heroine's story, as nothing more than an observer. Viewed from another angle, however, Eliot allows us to see this familiar disability plot in a new light, for Philip does not conveniently die at the end of the novel like Smike or Ezra Jennings, getting out of the heroine's way so that she can live a full life without him. Nor is he made a tool in her moral development, a cog in the machine of her story. Instead, he is the survivor left standing after the flood; *he* is the one who has discovered what Maggie calls the 'secret of human tenderness and long-suffering'.[29] Seen in this light, Maggie becomes an actor in the story of Philip's development, rather than vice versa, and the monitory experience of disability central to the novel's real *Bildung*, which is not Maggie's, but Philip's.

This account of *The Mill on the Floss* is bound to ring hollow to some extent, however, for it involves reading past the passage with which I began, past the ending that elicits such powerful resentment on the part of readers, and leaves us with such an overwhelming sense of fruitlessness. Any account of the novel that demands that we treat Philip's moral epiphany as compensation for Maggie's misery belies its tragic force; a satisfactory account of the novel surely has to address not just what Philip learns through loving Maggie, but why he is prevented from helping her – why, as Guth puts it, Eliot 'provided Maggie with a rescuer, but prevented the rescue'.[30] Philip's disability is absolutely central to this question, which goes to the heart of Eliot's conception of realism. Ultimately, the novel asks us to accept both that it would be unrealistic for Maggie to remain faithful to her disabled lover when faced with an able-bodied one, and that this reality is both 'natural' and (morally) unbearable. The conflict between the two realities – one scientific, one moral – cannot be resolved by the realist author because it is a condition of life in secular modernity. Eliot's re-writing of the disability plot is a vital part of this re-definition of realism, and it depends upon Philip's inability to act as Maggie's rescuer.

Eliot goes to some lengths in the early part of the novel to lead the reader to hope that Philip and Maggie's relationship need not be tragic, casting Philip as the character who is singularly fitted to bring happiness to our heroine, and to find it himself in doing so. When we are introduced to Philip in the second book, the likeness is all too apparent between sweet-natured but sadly unappreciated Maggie and this similarly talented, similarly sensitive schoolboy, who, like her, is misunderstood by those around him, and most especially by Tom. His needs correspond exactly to Maggie's gifts, and hers to his. Their interactions soon take on a romantic aspect; looking into Maggie's eyes, Philip wonders what 'made Maggie's dark eyes remind him of the stories about princesses being turned into animals? . . . . I think it was that her eyes were full of unsatisfied intelligence, and unsatisfied, beseeching affection.'[31] Enabled by 'her own keen sensitiveness and experience under family criticism' to respond more sensitively to his disability than anyone else, Maggie is soon offering to kiss him, and promising, 'I shall always remember you, and kiss you when I see you again, if it's ever so long.'[32] The family feud that divides these childhood sweethearts seems the perfect plot device first to complicate, and then to be resolved by, their romantic relationship. A young man who has suffered from being 'excepted from what was a matter of course with others'[33] is bound to strike us as an ideal suitor for our exceptional heroine, an idea made explicit by Maggie's kind-hearted cousin Lucy, when she says:

> 'It is very beautiful that you should love Philip ... I can't help being hopeful about it. There is something romantic in it – out of the common way – just what everything that happens to you ought to be. And Philip will adore you like a husband in a fairy tale. ... Wouldn't that be a pretty ending to all my poor, poor Maggie's troubles?'[34]

By the time Lucy paints this optimistic picture of Maggie and Philip's future marriage, however, it is impossible for an attentive reader to share her 'hopeful' attitude, and not only because the narrator has emphasised so often that we are not reading 'a fairy tale'. It has become clear by this point that, as Dorothea Barrett bluntly puts it, 'no matter how intellectually and spiritually appropriate Philip might be for Maggie, Maggie also has sexual needs that cannot be fulfilled by Philip'.[35] The deformity that 'awaken[s] the old pity'[36] in Maggie makes him incapable of awakening her desire as an adult woman, which is instead evoked by the emphatically able-bodied masculinity of Stephen Guest. Inferior as he is to Philip as a companion, Maggie finds the offer of Stephen Guest's 'firm arm' to lean on 'strangely winning'; male strength, the narrator suggests, 'meets a continual want of the imagination' in 'most women'.[37]

Retrospectively, we can see that even Philip's original attempt to cast the child Maggie as a fairy-tale princess hinted at the trouble to come: she reminded him not simply of stories about princesses, but 'of the stories about princesses *being turned into animals*'.[38] The 'animal' side of the adult Maggie is in fatal tension with the 'tranquil, tender affection for Philip', which has so strong a hold on what we might call the romantic side of her nature.[39] When Lucy observes 'the physical incongruity' between Maggie and Philip, her mistake is in supposing that it would affect only 'a prosaic person like cousin Tom, who didn't like poetry and fairy tales'.[40] In fact, it strongly affects Maggie herself, and Eliot goes out of her way to make sure that it affects the reader, too; Dorothea Barrett points out that there is a 'very unusual' awkwardness in Eliot's description of the pair when they kiss, produced by 'the strain in George Eliot's urgency to foreground [the] inappropriateness' of a sexual relationship between them.[41]

As Talia Schaffer has pointed out, it is not only in 'a fairy tale' that we can imagine Maggie being essentially right that 'there is nothing but what [she loves Philip] for'.[42] In a different kind of novel, there *would* be no other factors worthy of serious consideration: in novels that celebrate what she calls familiar marriage, based on affection, friendship, shared interests and mutual respect rather than on sexual desire, Philip and Maggie would have been ideally suited. Maggie's dilemma therefore becomes, in Schaffer's telling, the expression of a struggle between two models of disability and two models of marriage, with familiar marriage and a fundamentally social model of disability, in which dependence produces desirable networks of community and care, competing with romantic marriage and a medical model of disability that casts physical frailty as personal inadequacy. Maggie's tragedy, in Schaffer's view, is that she is caught between Victorian and modern paradigms, at a historical moment when 'the choices are so finely balanced as to be impossible'.[43]

Schaffer's reading is a powerful one but understates, I think, the continuity that exists between Eliot's way of representing disability and, for example, Dinah Mulock Craik's. She, too, shows her disabled men as unmarriageable: as we have seen, Phineas Fletcher explicitly casts his disability as excluding him from matrimony on the grounds that it feminises him, and constitutes a potentially hereditary taint, while the Earl of Cairnforth – despite being wealthy, clever and charming – accepts that he will never marry, and has to suffer the pain of his beloved Helen marrying the first (relatively) non-disabled man she meets.[44] In both cases, however, Craik provides a plot in which the disabled man's particular gifts come to the fore, and in which his exclusion from the marriage plot serves a providential purpose, which gradually emerges. The crucial difference between Eliot's plotting and Craik's is not Eliot's casting of Philip's disability as an insuperable barrier to his being found sexual attractive, but in her refusal to make Philip's exclusion from the marriage plot appear as part of a providential scheme.[45] Instead, it is depicted simultaneously as natural, and as bitterly unfair, a source of tragedy to all involved.

Eliot ensures that the reader will resent Philip's exclusion from the marriage plot by having the most forceful expression of the idea that a woman's desire for strength in a lover is natural, and that any exception to this pattern would be a perversion, come from the consistently unsympathetic Tom Tulliver. Moreover, the narrator goes out of her way to ensure that we see in his disgust at Philip and Maggie's relationship the workings 'of an old boyish repulsion and of mere personal pride and animosity', and the sheer cruelty of his threats – 'I'll thrash you – and I'll hold you up to public scorn' – ensures that we are as unlikely to side with him as Maggie, who is stung into one of her rare expressions of contempt for Tom and his small-minded self-righteousness.⁴⁶ At the level of plot, however, Eliot shows that there is a grain of unpalatable truth in Tom's characterisation of Philip and Maggie's relationship as unnatural. After all, their engagement cannot survive Maggie's first contact with a handsome, able-bodied man, for all that he is, as so many critics have pointed out, a strikingly inadequate match for her. Rather than concluding, as did Leslie Stephen, that 'George Eliot herself did not understand what a mere hair-dresser's block she was describing',⁴⁷ we can see Stephen Guest's mediocrity as a device that emphasises how deeply unsatisfying Maggie finds her relationship with Philip, which in turn suggests that the popular prejudice Tom describes against a man like Philip 'turning lover to a fine girl' is rooted in reality.

As is made clear by her decision to put these words into Tom's mouth, however, this is not a reality that Eliot is in any way inclined to celebrate. Instead, she confronts the reader with a world in which the 'natural' has a highly tenuous connection to the moral, and the two are sometimes in direct opposition. While we may rejoice in the success of Philip's attempt to persuade Maggie not to give up all intellectual pleasures, on the grounds that 'no one has strength given to do what is unnatural', it is not so easy to wish Stephen success when he claims that it would be 'unnatural' for either of them to honour their former promises in the light of their feelings for each other, urging her that they 'can't help the pain it will give. It is come upon us without our seeking – it is natural.'⁴⁸ When he insists again that to fulfil their promises would be 'unnatural', Maggie counters: 'Love is natural; but surely pity and faithfulness and memory are natural too.'⁴⁹

The difference between these usages of the word 'natural', which strain away from one another, reflects the increasing difficulty of claiming that something must be right if natural (and vice versa), as natural science moved away from morally and religiously structured ways of seeing reality. Evolutionary theory offered a natural world that was not a mirror of the divine, but a dynamic, self-authoring and, above all, morally neutral system in which, in Gillian Beer's words, 'there was no need to invoke a source of authority outside the natural order: in which instead of foreknown design, there was inherent purposiveness'.⁵⁰ If we consider the plotting of *The Mill on the Floss* in the light of Darwin's theory of evolution by means of natural selection – and we know that Eliot read *On the Origin of Species* while writing the novel – then, as Gordon Haight says, it is hard not to see Maggie's 'entirely instinctive' attraction for Stephen as a reflection of the fact that in 'simple biological terms Stephen is a better mate for her than the sickly Philip', and her rejection of Stephen's 'natural' appeal as demonstrating Eliot's sceptical attitude to 'the optimistic assumption that the course of evolution was always towards the best'.[51]

This is an assumption that, as Gillian Beer demonstrates, is all too tempting for the reader of Darwin, as 'intentionalist language keeps creeping into accounts of evolution'.[52] The very subtitle of *On the Origin of Species*, *The Preservation of Favoured Races in the Struggle for Life*, carries the suggestion of both intention and value judgement: to describe something as 'favoured' is, inevitably, to say something more than that it is better adapted for survival in particular conditions. Although at the time Eliot was writing *The Mill on the Floss*, the idea that human evolution could be expedited through eugenics – that natural selection was not efficient enough, and deliberate selection should be employed to ensure that the race developed in the right direction – had not yet emerged into the mainstream, Eliot was clearly troubled by the possibility that Darwin's theories might lead to the elision of the 'natural' and the 'right', of evolution and improvement. (Indeed, it was her close friend Herbert Spencer who first coined the phrase 'survival of the fittest', which went on to be so important to eugenicist arguments and thinking.)

Heredity is a major theme of *The Mill on the Floss*, but its workings are hard to fathom, and consistently resistant to human manipulation. Early on in the novel, Mr Tulliver laments the fact that he deliberately chose a wife who was good-looking rather than clever – in his formulation, not 'o'er-'cute' – only to have a son who took after her, in being blond but slow, and a dark, clever daughter who took after himself, despite the fact that 'an over-'cute woman's no better nor a long-tailed sheep'.[53] He claims that this is the problem 'wi' the crossing o' breeds: you can never justly calkilate what'll come on't . . . it's like as if the world was turned topsy-turvy. It's an uncommon puzzlin' thing.'[54] In a sense, we are offered a clue to this 'puzzle', with our ''cute' narrator on hand to explain how the children's physiognomies reflect their characters.[55] Moreover, we are clearly supposed to understand that Mr Tulliver's simplistic and utilitarian world-view, in which women are essentially breeding stock to be compared to sheep, is seriously inadequate. But we are not, finally, given access to a world in which Maggie's intelligence *would* be 'good' for anything, and while her superior moral intelligence might be taken as a fulfilment of the narrator's promise that the young Tullivers' story will illustrate 'the onward tendency of human things [to] have risen above the mental level of the generation before them',[56] that promise is surely at the bottom of the Floss by the novel's end.

We can see the 'onward tendency of human things' as ongoing only if we take Philip to be Maggie's moral heir, perhaps understanding his 'accidental'[57] – rather than congenital – deformity as the variation that enables him to take the next step in moral evolution, his disability the chance mutation that enables him to embody the forgiving, selfless love that this community sorely needs. But what does it say for this 'onward tendency' that Maggie's moral inheritor is a character who will have no biological heir – who is explicitly said to be 'always solitary'?[58] The plot of moral evolution seems diametrically opposed to the Darwinian plot of evolution through natural selection – and the novel's *overall* plotting suggests that reality is shaped by the latter, not the former. Disability acts as a potent symbol for the injustice of a world in which those who are morally fitted to further 'the onward tendency of human things' may be biologically unfit to do so, and in which 'the gift of transferred life' can be an unbearable burden.

In *The Mill on the Floss*, the ethics of this 'gift', at least, seem reasonably clear. Philip is morally enriched by his investment in Maggie's life: it might not ultimately lead to his happiness, but we are not, I think, encouraged to think that his attempt to live through her might be wrong in itself. In *Daniel Deronda*, however, Eliot takes up the idea of 'transferred life' and makes it figure both more centrally and more problematically in a novel that revolves around questions of futurity and inheritance. Far removed as the quasi-murderous Gwendolen Harleth might seem from sweet Maggie Tulliver, and distant as provincial St Oggs and Mudport are from multicultural London, fashionable Leubronn and the mysterious East, *Daniel Deronda* revisits many of the pressing questions of *The Mill on the Floss*, and offers still fewer reassuring answers.

### 'This yearning for transmission': Plotting the Future in *Daniel Deronda*

We meet the consumptive Mordecai almost exactly halfway through *Daniel Deronda* (1876), although his appearance in the novel appears to mark not the turning point of our hero's plot, but its beginning. Until Mordecai's arrival, we have been grappling not so much (*pace* Thackeray) with a novel without a hero, as with a hero without a plot. Daniel possesses every requisite feature for a novelistic hero, ideally suited to play his part in the marriage plot, being handsome, healthy, wealthy and good, and equally well qualified to star in an identity mystery, never having known his mother and living in uncertainty as to his parentage. Yet he has so far signally failed either to intervene effectively in the marriage plot (our heroine Gwendolen having just married someone else), or to make any investigation into his own origins. Daniel finds it so easy, in fact, to identify with the stories of others that he seems to have no chance of finding a story of his own, as though he is already at the end of the familiar Eliotian plot and has stalled there, with nowhere further to go. He seems to have gone on developing in the direction of 'strong sympathy' (to quote Philip Wakem) and arrived at the point where his 'many-sided sympathy' and 'innate balance' have become not life-giving, but petrifying.[59] As the narrator explains, his 'too reflective and diffusive sympathy was in danger of paralysing him', so that he longs for 'some external event, or some inward light, that would urge him into a definite line of action, and compress his wandering energy.... But how and whence was the needed event to come?'[60]

It is to come, we soon discover, from the encounter that promptly follows with Mordecai, the terminally ill character who believes he has the definitive answer to the question of what Daniel should do with his life, and indeed to the questions posed by both marriage and identity plots: who Daniel should marry, and who his parents really are. Mordecai supplies Daniel with the 'make-believe of a beginning' without which, as the epigram to the first chapter assured us, 'men can do nothing'.[61] The teasing tone of that epigram – itself a bit of 'make-believe', a play on our unmet expectation that it will be a quotation from a pre-existing source text – prepares us to be sceptical about Mordecai's belief that the facts regarding Daniel's past will align with his desires regarding Daniel's future. Yet it is a belief that the novel's plotting fully justifies. From the moment Mordecai appears on the scene, the redemptive disability plot erupts into *Daniel Deronda* and rescues its protagonist from the compromised world of mixed motives, imperfect knowledge, illicit desires and sordid need in which he has so far struggled to find a place. Our expectation (or fear) that Eliot's realistic plotting will refuse Daniel the 'external event' he desires, and force him to come to terms with a reality inimical to his wishes – as it refuses and forces Gwendolen – is overturned by the disability plot in which Mordecai stars.

Tellingly, Daniel's moral superiority to those around him has already been indicated through an image that connects him, at one remove, to physical disability. His belief in his own illegitimacy, the narrator tells us, 'might be compared in some ways with Byron's susceptibility about his deformed foot'.⁶² This is integrated into his moral trajectory, as the narrator explains that the sense of 'entailed disadvantage – the deformed foot doubtfully hidden by the shoe' – is an 'inexorable sorrow' that 'in the rarer sort . . . takes the form of fellowship and makes the imagination tender'.⁶³ It is a sign of how singularly favoured a hero Daniel is, however, that Eliot enables him to have the morally improving benefits of 'entailed disadvantage' without its narrative penalties; he is not, in fact, excluded by his supposed illegitimacy from playing the leading role in the epic national story in which Mordecai casts him, because he turns out to be the legitimate son of Jewish parents. The benefits of the redemptive disability plot accrue entirely to Daniel, while its burdens are borne entirely by Mordecai.

Unlike Philip Wakem, however, Mordecai embraces his allotted plot role without the slightest sign of resentment or the inkling of a caveat. Endowed with the diligence and persistence to study his people's history, with the intellectual gifts needed to understand it, and with a strong desire to bring about the future he foresees for them, Mordecai has been prevented from carrying out what he believes is his Zionist mission to lead the Jewish people back to their homeland by the onset of tuberculosis. Rather than despairing at his ever-worsening physical frailty and the prospect of early death, however, he has accepted that his role is not to act upon his vision, but to transmit it to another. To this end, he has sought a spiritual heir to carry out his work for him, whom he has apparently imagined as a melodramatic hero straight from central casting: 'a man who would have all the elements necessary for sympathy with him, but in an embodiment unlike his own . . . beautiful and strong'.⁶⁴ When Mordecai finds this 'more beautiful, . . . stronger, . . . more-executive self' in Daniel, he takes nothing but pleasure in having discovered his heir, despite the fact that he believes Daniel's destiny to be dependent upon his own death, when his 'long-wandering soul [will be] liberated from this weary body, it will join yours, and its work will be perfected'.⁶⁵

As this formulation reveals, Daniel's place in the epic plot Mordecai foresees is entirely contingent upon Mordecai's unfitness to fill it. In fact, Eliot makes explicit the idea that Mordecai has been disabled by the novel's plot. Although he offers a medically plausible explanation to Daniel of how he contracted tuberculosis, he adds that it was when he was forced (by the eruption of the subplot involving his family break-up – the distant source of Daniel's marriage plot) to turn back from his Zionist mission to Palestine that his 'life was broken' – a 'breaking' that seems to have immediately manifested itself in the breaking-down of his hitherto healthy physical body.[66] As with Daniel's origins (to which I will return), Mordecai's illness is depicted as the *result* of narrative events as much as it is their cause, an effect of the plot to which it ostensibly gives rise. This way of reading his disability marks Mordecai's separation from the realist world to which Daniel has hitherto been confined. It makes sense that 'slow death' should follow the moment when his 'life was broken', not in a realist world of medical diagnosis and scientific remedy, but in the parallel world of epic that Mordecai inhabits, and that represents an escape, both temporal and spatial, from the prosaic reality of modernity.[67] As he explains to Daniel, he believes that his vision of the Jewish people's future, and his desire to make it a reality, arose from 'the soul fully born within [him]', inherited from his forebears and bringing 'its own world – a mediæval world'.[68] Although this world exists in the temporal past, Mordecai brings it into the present in his own person – Daniel's first impression of Mordecai is that his 'physiognomy' is one 'that might possibly have been seen in a prophet of the Exile, or in some New Hebrew poet of the mediæval time'[69] – and believes that it provides the key to the glorious future that will be realised in 'the East'. This alternative space is defined almost entirely in the negative, as somewhere free from the obstacles Mordecai encounters in London, which closely reflect the things Daniel himself most longs to be free from: sordid family drama, petty concerns about money, employment and respectability, the demand for clear political programmes of action. Confined to a world in which these things predominate, the prosaic world of Gwendolen and Grandcourt, and even the kindly Cohens (whose genial vulgarity so disgusts Daniel), Mordecai sickens and dies. The realist world cannot support him, any more than can the realist novel; ultimately, he leads Daniel beyond the scope of the realist, and into a future that the novel cannot represent.

Up until this point, however, we are forced to encounter Mordecai's characterisation, his pronouncements and his plot-line in the light of the characters, pronouncements and plot-lines that surround him – and in this light, they take on an altogether more troubling dimension. Mordecai himself may be the purest embodiment of the archetypal disabled angel with a legacy – his desires entirely unselfish, his motives unalloyed and his power to shape the future apparently absolute – but he is surrounded by characters who hold up a realist mirror to his beliefs, actions and experiences. We do not, for example, read his disquisition on the redemptive power of 'the surpassing love, that loses self in the object of love' in isolation, but in dialogue with his listener's response: 'No, Ezra, no.'[70] Mirah's alternative way of reading the Midrash story does not cancel out Mordecai's, but it forces us to see the obverse side of it, just as Gwendolen's relationship with Daniel holds up a distorted mirror to Daniel's dealings with Mordecai, and the Princess's passionate protest against being made use of offers a disturbing parallel to Mordecai's joyful acceptance of his ancillary plot role. At every turn, Mordecai's way of being and seeing is tested against the experience of the other characters, who inhabit the realist world from which he alone stands apart. The reason why F. R. Leavis was so misguided in his attempt to bifurcate the novel into two halves and then discard the non-realist half is not, I would argue, because Eliot succeeded in aesthetically harmonising the two, but rather because the dissonance between their motifs is at the heart of her design.[71]

In reading the novel in this way, I seek to build on critical work in recent years that discusses the interdependency and interpenetration of the novel's two halves, often referred to as the 'English' half (revolving around the marriage plot, Gwendolen and Grandcourt) and the 'Jewish half' (revolving around the identity plot, Mirah and Mordecai).[72] Here, however, I want to consider the novel as being split, not along Jewish and non-Jewish lines, but into realist and non-realist halves, with the latter structured by the redemptive disability plot, and the former seething with problems that that plot cannot solve. All the novel's characters apart from Mordecai, Gentile and Jewish, inhabit this intractably realist world, until Daniel is enabled by his relationship with Mordecai to join him on the other side of realism and become the heir to his epic future. It is a chain of inheritance from which the reader is peculiarly excluded: we are able to share in Philip's moral epiphany, to learn to love Maggie as he does, to apply our experience of loving her to our dealings with others, but we are not able to share Daniel's journey to the Promised Land. Instead, like Mordecai, we can only dream of the East; we never see it. Abandoned on the shores of England, along with the novel's other characters, we are left with the intractable problems of this realist world, which the redemptive disability plot has failed to solve, even as it has triumphantly liberated Daniel from its constraints.

Take, for example, the problems of narrative justice and compensation, those ongoing questions of Eliot's realist fiction. Mordecai refuses to read his own life story as an illustration of the basic injustice of a godless world, although it would certainly be open to such a reading. He was prevented from making the journey he dreamt of by the actions of his reprehensible father, his noble purpose frustrated by petty obstacles, which in turn caused his own fatal illness. As any saintly invalid should, however, Mordecai instructs us in how to read his story typologically, as a narrative that makes manifest the justice of divinely ordered reality: 'Mine was the lot of Israel. For the sin of the father my soul must go into exile. For the sin of the father the work was broken, and the day of fulfilment delayed.'[73] It makes perfect sense, according to Mordecai's world-view that, just as the soul itself is an inheritance, so too are suffering and punishment, and that we can therefore find a just cause for his suffering if we seek it in the actions of his forebears. Our sense of justice will not, therefore, be outraged when we set his life into a wider narrative, within which it makes sense.

When Daniel applies this logic to Gwendolen Harleth's plot-line, however, it does not convince. Daniel encourages Gwendolen to read her own story as a moral fable in which misery is the result of wicked actions; in their conversations, her moral culpability is synecdochally represented by her gambling, which he witnesses in the novel's opening scene and subsequently convinces her was morally wrong. She seizes on this explanation of her plight, seeing her marital misery as a punishment for having taken Lydia Glasher's rightful place as Grandcourt's wife: 'I wanted to make my gain out of another's loss – you remember? – it was like roulette.'[74] Yet reading Gwendolen's story in this way requires that we read past certain salient facts. For one thing, as Ellen B. Rosenman points out, Daniel's statement about gambling – that it is wrong because 'our gain is another's loss' – simply does not make sense when applied to roulette, 'in which any numbers of players can win'.[75] What makes roulette fearful is not its ruthless logic, but its terrifying senselessness; likening marriage to roulette, then, necessarily suggests not the workings of moral cause and effect, but the powerlessness of the players and the randomness of chance. The parallel encourages us to recognise the fact that, much as Daniel encourages her to think otherwise, it is illogical to see Gwendolen's marriage as injurious to anyone other than herself: Gwendolen has *not* truly injured Lydia Glasher because there is absolutely no reason to think that Grandcourt would have married her if he had not married Gwendolen. He has already refused to do so, and on what possible basis can we attribute subsequent soft-heartedness and relenting to the implacable Grandcourt? Certainly, the miserably powerless Lydia blames Gwendolen, but it is Grandcourt himself who is the architect of her misery (and who would surely have made her still more miserable had she succeeded in marrying him), not

Gwendolen, who in any case marries Grandcourt only when she has completely run out of other ideas for financially supporting herself and her family. Her gambling is nothing more than a 'make-believe of a beginning' for the suffering that follows – just as her belief that she has 'sinned herself away' from a life with Daniel overlooks the fact that, as a Gentile, she was disqualified from becoming his future wife before she started.[76] There is little to suggest that, had Gwendolen heeded the grim advice of the novel's epigraph and let her 'chief terror be of [her] own soul', she would have been able to save her family from penury, or find a bearable future for herself. As Margueritte Murphy suggests, 'Eliot's insistence on [Gwendolen's] guilt seems almost a screen for her powerlessness.'[77]

The flimsiness of this 'screen' is revealed, I think, when Grandcourt drowns, and Gwendolen believes herself guilty of his death because she desired it. Although Daniel encourages her remorse as 'the precious sign of a recoverable nature' – her guilt a just punishment for wicked wishing – he is 'almost certain that her murderous thought had had no outward effect'.[78] In the world Gwendolen inhabits, reality is inimical to her desires; she cannot effect change by wishing. Yet her words, 'I saw my wish outside me',[79] powerfully resonate with the scenes earlier in the novel (and those yet to come) in which Mordecai *does* see his wish outside himself, his power throwing her powerlessness into starker relief. When Mordecai imagines the coming of his spiritual heir, we are told that he imagines someone who looks exactly like Daniel rowing towards him on Blackfriars Bridge on sunset– and we then see this happening, exactly as he foresaw it.[80] Unlike Gwendolen, whose fantasies of power are a masochistic compensation for her powerlessness, Mordecai's 'yearnings [and] conceptions' really do take 'the form of images which have a foreshadowing power'.[81] His wishes 'appear outside' himself not only in the unfolding of future events but in those that lie firmly in the past. As Daniel anxiously points out, he cannot make himself Jewish by wishing to be so – 'What my birth was does not lie in my will' –but Eliot plots the novel in such a way that Daniel's past comes to seem not only, in Cynthia Chase's words, 'an effect of narrative requirements', but even an effect of Mordecai's declaration of his belief in Daniel's Jewish identity, which has the 'performative quality . . . of a conversion . . . a speech act that changes the identity of the person who is the object of the ritual'.[82]

The idea that terminal illness is accompanied by spiritual insight is a staple of the invalid narrative, but Eliot pushes the connection between physical frailty, imaginative power and moral legacy to new extremes in her depiction of Mordecai's apparently limitless claim to Daniel's life, and his power to make his wishes a reality. At first, she locates his powers on a spectrum with those of other consumptives, linking his prophetic visions with 'the hopefulness which is often the beneficent illusion of consumptive patients'; in Mordecai, this is 'wholly diverted from the prospect of bodily recovery and carried into the current of this yearning for transmission'.[83] We soon see, however, that the sympathetic capacities of the saintly invalid become in Mordecai a capacity for breaking down of the boundaries of self. For Mordecai wants to do something rather more than find a sympathetic soul whom he can inspire with high ideals, like Gaskell's Mrs Buxton or Eliot's earlier consumptive, Mr Tryan,[84] and he is not content with the 'gift of transferred life' in the same sense as Philip Wakem. Where Philip has been figuratively 'initiated ... into that enlarged life which grows and grows by appropriating the life of others',[85] Mordecai seeks literally to appropriate Daniel's life. When Daniel assures him of practical assistance and – in a phrase that echoes Philip's claim to 'strong sympathy' – tells him, 'I feel strongly with you,' Mordecai responds: 'That is not enough . . . . You must be not only a hand to me, but a soul . . . seeing the vision I point to – beholding a glory where I behold it!'[86] In other words, Mordecai does not guide Daniel by sympathising with him and then enabling him to see his own way forward, as we expect the saintly invalid to do. Instead, he demands that Daniel become his second self – 'something more ample than the second soul bestowed, according to the notion of the Cabbalists, to help out the insufficient first' – seeking to appropriate his 'blooming human life' as a vessel for 'all that [is] worthiest' in himself'.[87] He claims Daniel's life as a way to defeat death, explaining to Daniel that he will live on through him: 'You will be my life.'[88] At the very end of the novel, Mordecai's death is figured as the consummation of what Mordecai calls the 'marriage of [their] souls'; Daniel's marriage to Mordecai's sister Mirah, which occurs in the penultimate scene, takes secondary place as a merely biological mirroring of the absolute spiritual union that Mordecai and Daniel achieve.[89] In this extraordinary realisation of the 'transmission' Mordecai yearned for, he succeeds not simply in influencing Daniel, but entering into him, as Daniel becomes both the heir to Mordecai's ideas and the heir to Mordecai's soul. This is a role that Daniel, of course, is all too willing to accept. Ideally suited by character and life experience to take on someone else's life mission and make it his own, already looking for an 'external event' to 'compress his wandering energy',[90] and lacking any other outlet for his high ideals, he is only too happy to act as Mordecai's vessel, and to make of himself a hero in the process.

In isolation, this plot-line might seem to mark the high point of the redemptive disability plot-line that flourished in fiction over the thirty years before *Daniel Deronda* was published, and Mordecai's incantatory speeches the swansong of the disabled angel with a legacy. In context, however, Mordecai's realised desire to appropriate Daniel's life leaves a bitter taste in the reader's mouth. Throughout the rest of the novel, Eliot sows seeds of doubt about Daniel's ethic of self-giving, which finds its apogee in his decision to make his life over to Mordecai. Over and over again, female characters express reservations about the joys of a 'transferred life', and their doubts cannot but colour our view of the idealised relationship that Daniel and Mordecai enjoy.

For one thing, not all female characters are as ready as Gwendolen to accept that Daniel is right to think of selflessness as an absolute good. At the Meyricks' home, Mirah admiringly expresses her sense of Daniel's readiness to meet others' needs by sacrificing himself, as if anticipating the exchange with Mordecai that is soon to come:

> 'Mr Hans said yesterday that you thought so much of others you hardly wanted anything for yourself. He told us a wonderful story of Bouddha giving himself to the famished tigress to save her and her little ones from starving. And he said you were like Bouddha.'[91]

Amy and Mab Meyrick, however, do not share Mirah's rapturous response:

> 'But *was* it beautiful for Bouddha to let the tiger eat him?' said Amy, changing her ground. 'It would be a bad pattern.'
> 'The world would get full of fat tigers,' said Mab.[92]

What the prosaic Meyrick sisters bring out here are the dangers latent in Daniel's apparently harmless ethic of doing no harm to others, at whatever cost to one's self. His conviction that 'unlike the great Clive, [he] would rather be the calf than the butcher' carries the risk, in their account, that butcherly behaviour might actually be *encouraged* by too compliant a calf.[93] Such a line of thinking points us to the suspicion that Daniel's 'hatred of all injuries' might amount to an inability to judge the gravity of relative harms, or to see that there is no injury-free action in a competitive world.[94] How the

Meyrick sisters' words might apply to his own plot-line becomes clear as Daniel 'laughed, but defended the myth' on the grounds that it is 'an extreme image of what is happening every day – the transmutation of self'.[95] In this scene, we both see Daniel's perfect readiness to undergo such 'transmutation' at Mordecai's hands, and are alerted to the potential inapplicability of such 'transmutation' in the realist world occupied by other characters.

In this exchange, Mirah takes Daniel's side, but her perspective changes. By the time Mordecai is telling her the Midrash story of the selfless Jewish maiden who sacrificed herself for love of the king, her outlook is different. Having experienced the pain of love for Daniel and jealousy of Gwendolen, Mirah now sees, instead of a beautiful ideal realised in a parable, the easily misinterpreted and complex workings of individual need. It is, she tells Mordecai, more likely that the girl chose to die in place of the woman beloved by the king because she 'wanted the king when she was dead to know what she had done, and feel that she was better than the other. It was her strong self, wanting to conquer, that made her die.'[96] What Mirah offers here is the realist reading of the Midrash story: realist, not because it is uglier than Mordecai's reading – his world-view, after all, has plenty of space for suffering and punishment – but because it is rooted in individual psychology rather than the abstract workings of moral principles. Mirah's reading suggests that our motives are frequently obscure, even to ourselves, and that actions that seem derived from high ideals arise, in reality, from personal need. It is inevitable, I think, that we will connect her words to her brother's claim, immediately before he tells this story, to 'hold the joy of another's future within me: a future which these eyes will not see, and which my spirit may not then recognize as mine'.[97] We cannot help but ask whether Mordecai's desires are truly selfless, whether 'yearning for transmission' is not inspired by the 'strong self' that will not accept death, but yearns to live on. Mirah raises the possibility that Mordecai sees, not what is, but what he needs to see; as she says bleakly, when he offers his idealistic interpretation of what is happening in this tale of apparently selfless action: 'You can make the story so in your mind.'[98] If we read Mordecai's version of the redemptive disability plot in the light of Mirah's analysis of the Midrash story, it takes on an altogether darker colouring.

Moreover, Mordecai's attempt to neutralise Mirah's subversive words by telling her that she judges by fiction rather than 'by [her] own heart, which is like our mother's', has the opposite effect from the one he intends.[99] Rather than summoning the presence of this supposedly selfless paragon, whom we never meet, it is likely to remind the reader of the text's most memorable mother: the unforgettably self-assertive figure of Daniel's mother, Leonora, a one-woman refutation of Mordecai's claim that selflessness is natural to women. Unlike Mirah, Leonora does not remain silent in the face of assertions about women's true calling for renunciation. Instead, she holds the stage in a pair of extraordinary scenes in which she expresses her passionate unwillingness to renounce her own desires, and explains to Daniel her lifelong determination not to live for others, but 'to live out the life that was in me, and not to be hampered by other lives'.[100] More subversively still, Leonora insists that her decision to reject her father's religion and his plan for her life, and to follow instead her own desires and pursue her career as a singer, has not made her unhappy: 'I *was* happy,' she tells Daniel, as if defying him to contradict her.[101] The regret she expresses is not for having ignored her father's wishes or rejected her son, but for having given up her career on the stage for a brilliant second marriage, in the mistaken belief that her voice was failing her; only in that failure of nerve does she acknowledge that she 'miscalculated'.[102]

Fascinatingly, Leonora likens the temporary failure of her vocal powers to a 'fit of forgetfulness', as if she sees her sudden musical forgetfulness as a punishment for her attempt to forget her father's demand that she 'was to be what he called "the Jewish woman" under pain of his curse', her unwillingness to remember what she most wants to forget horribly avenged by an inability to remember what she values the most.[103] This punitive 'fit of forgetfulness' becomes in her telling 'a fit of illness',[104] as though physical disability alone could force her into the parts – regretful daughter, domesticated wife – that she had been determined not to play. If this temporary illness thwarted her desire to be on the stage, it is her present, terminal illness that has thwarted her resolution never to tell Daniel of his Jewish origins, as she explains to him: 'Do I seem now to be revoking everything? – Well, there are reasons ... shadows are rising round me. Sickness makes them.'[105] Once again, physical frailty and the power of memory are connected, but this time it is the *inability* to forget, brought on by disability, that has broken her will:

> 'It is illness, I don't doubt that it has been gathering illness, – my mind has gone back .... Then it is as if the life I have chosen to live, all thoughts, all will, forsook me and left me alone in spots of memory, and I can't get away: my pain seems to keep me there. My childhood – my girlhood – the day of my marriage – the day of my father's death – there

seems to be nothing since. Then a great horror comes over me . . . when my strength goes, some other right forces itself upon me like iron in an inexorable hand; and even when I am at ease, it is beginning to make ghosts upon the daylight.'[106]

Like Mordecai, Leonora has been forced by disability to play a transmitting role, but whereas for him this represents the ultimate compensation for bodily suffering and even death, for Leonora, it is a nightmarish defeat of her will to resist. Where Mordecai rejoices to find an old soul 'born again within [him]',[107] and wants above anything to transmit that soul to Daniel when he dies, she experiences the return of her father's spirit as an entirely unwelcome possession. In both cases, the body's frailty seems to dissolve its boundaries, making it porous to the spirit, but whereas this allows Mordecai and Daniel to achieve an ideal spiritual marriage, as Mordecai 'breathe[s]' his soul into Daniel, Leonora's experience seems more analogous to rape, as her father's spirit 'forces itself upon' her.[108] She finds herself unable to resist her father's desire that she pass on Daniel's spiritual inheritance to him, revealing his Jewish origins and giving him the chest containing her father's papers, but even as she does so, she insists: 'I don't consent. We only consent to what we love. I obey something tyrannic.'[109] Terminal illness forces both Leonora and Mordecai into an ancillary role in an epic national plot, and leads both to pass on a spiritual inheritance to Daniel, but whereas Mordecai embraces his role as a vessel, Leonora fights against it to the last.

In fact, although Leonora reads her relationship with Daniel entirely through the prism of her relationship with his grandfather, treating him as a pawn in their ongoing struggle, for the reader who has never known Daniel Charisi, the Jewish patriarch with whom she must struggle for control over Daniel's future would seem to be Mordecai. They both, effectively, want Daniel to act as an avatar for their own desires: he would make Daniel his 'more-executive self', while she claims, 'I chose for you what I would have chosen for myself.'[110] What they both most deeply desire for Daniel is that he act on their feelings about Judaism: Mordecai wants to Daniel to embrace and perpetuate the traditions that he loves, while Leonora wants him to cast off what she sees as the shackles of that same tradition, the 'teaching . . . that pressed on me like a frame that got tighter and tighter as I grew'.[111] Where Mordecai wants to see the past revived in the future, Leonora wants to break away from it completely: their competing visions for Daniel's future life arise from their competing versions of Jewish history. Both view this history as a line of patriarchal figures passing on to their sons an inheritance both biological and spiritual, but whereas for Mordecai this familial way of seeing past and future is comforting, it represents for Leonora the perpetuation of patriarchal tyranny, personified by her father, the man whom she insists 'never thought of his daughter except as an instrument'.[112] Where Mordecai rejoices in the idea that he is part of a great chain of inheritance, she revolts against being treated as a 'makeshift link',[113] valued for what she might transmit rather than for herself. In her defiant speeches about her father's abusiveness, she not only draws our attention to the patriarchal nature of the inheritance Mordecai is so keen to pass on – which passes through women, not to them – but voices a powerful protest against being used at all.

There can be no doubt that in the battle waged for Daniel's soul, Mordecai is the decisive victor. The novel's plotting works to thwart Leonora's designs; the 'stronger Something' that Daniel claims 'has determined that [he] shall be all the more the grandson... [she] wished to annihilate' is, at a literal level at least, the will of the author, who has plotted the text so as gratify Mordecai's desires and totally defeat Leonora's.[114] At the same time, however, the novel is plotted so as to give Leonora a power disproportionate to her brief appearance. For one thing, she is *the* pivotal figure in Daniel's marriage and identity plots: he can neither lead his people nor marry Mirah until he knows he has a Jewish mother. For another, her powerfully articulated story draws together threads that have been woven throughout the rest of the novel: Mirah's struggle with a tyrannical father who forced her on to the stage is reflected in her battle with the father who did not want her to sing; the second marriage she made in despair recalls Gwendolen's disastrous marriage, which also resulted from her belief that she could not support herself as a professional singer; her impotent fury reminds us of Lydia Glasher, whose attempt to secure her son's inheritance is a mirror image of the Princess's opposite struggle to keep her son from his patrimony. All these women struggle against the 'stronger Something' that would keep them in their subordinate place and silence their singing. Only sweetly diminutive Mirah gets her heart's desire (to be married to Daniel), and even then, the reader cannot help suspecting that it is as an avatar for Mordecai that she is truly valuable to him. As for Leonora, the humbled Princess, she is left mourning her father's triumph. As she sadly says, after Daniel has received his inheritance at her hands, 'I have after all been the instrument my father wanted.'[115]

In Leonora's resistance to being made an 'instrument', however, I think Eliot offers a powerful counter-narrative to Mordecai's ecstatic embrace of a life lived for, and even through, another. Her resistance to being made use of has been broken down by disability, but she both perceives and resents her schematic function. Moreover, her thwarted attempt to plot a different future colours our view of Mordecai's successful plotting. Once we have seen family life through Leonora's eyes, Mordecai's vision of the past and future as knitted together as families are – 'the past becomes my parent, and the future stretches towards me the appealing arms of children' – seems less than benign.[116] And although Mordecai's metaphor suggests ongoing development and change, we can hardly help but notice that he essentially imagines the future as a return to the past. It is not simply that he understands his people's future as a return to where they started from, but that it figures so powerfully in the novel as a flight from modernity, a going forward that is really a turning back. The fact that we are never shown *how* Daniel is going to bring about Mordecai's Zionist dream, the sheer vagueness of his mission, means that his journey to the East takes him beyond the boundaries of our knowledge, beyond even what we have been invited to imagine. For much of the novel, we have been encouraged to identify with Daniel, but in the end, as the narrative dies with Mordecai, Daniel becomes a figure we cannot follow. We see, in the end, only as far as Mordecai sees.

Far more definite and real for us than the promised future into which Daniel sails are those who are excluded from it. Gwendolen's despair upon realising that she is to be denied a happy second marriage plot, her 'smothered' cry as she realises that Daniel is not her reward for all her repentance and suffering – that there *is* no reward, that she is 'forsaken' – are far more vivid than the future good Daniel is apparently going to bring about.[117] She, too, is returned to her beginnings, to the company of her mother and sisters, but it is difficult to see this as a rebirth so much as an admission of defeat, a negative answer to the question that Gillian Beer suggests the novel poses, that of 'whether there can be new plots for stories about women'.[118] Beer sees something of 'the dangerous power of the uncharted future' in the indeterminacy of Gwendolen's ending, but we could just as easily see the unmarried, childless Gwendolen's exclusion from the inheritance plot as an exclusion from futurity altogether.[119] Shut out of the chain of transmission, Gwendolen is not one of the chosen people, and therefore has no pre-ordained future. To translate this into Darwinian language, she is not among the 'favoured races' Darwin mentions in the subtitle of *On the Origin of Species*.

Even within that 'favoured race', it seems that some are more favoured than others. Mordecai's death at the very point when

Daniel sets out to forge the future draws our attention to the fact that only the physically fit arrive in the Promised Land in Eliot's vision. As Oliver Lovesey points out, Daniel 'is recognized as Mordecai's executive self partly as he represents a eugenicist's ideal' of physical strength and beauty; he and Mirah are 'an exemplary couple . . . well adapted to the rigors of sexual selection'.[120] Although Eliot employs the disability plot in such a way that Mordecai is able to exert a shaping influence on the future, and is invested with a moral power that seems directly linked to his physical frailty and inability to survive, the fact that his illness is *terminal* – unlike Philip Wakem's physical disability, for example – suggests that it is the fit who will inherit the earth, however worthy the unfit may be in moral terms. For all the compensations he is offered, Mordecai cannot but draw our attention to the plight of the losers in the struggle for existence.

Significant in this regard is the fact that Mordecai's redemptive message is, as we have already seen, applicable only to the chosen people. Biology is destiny in this novel, not just in the sense that the physically unfit have no place in the future, but in that all those who are biologically excluded from Judaism have to stay in prosaic, degraded England, while only those of pure Jewish descent get to escape to the Holy Land. Turning to *Daniel Deronda* after *The Mill on the Floss*, it might seem that we have turned away from secular realism and towards religiously oriented epic – a world in which Mordecai is right to believe that reality is divinely shaped, and the chosen people are actors in a pre-ordained story – but it is a profoundly secular world for all non-Jewish characters. Put simply, Christianity is nowhere in *Daniel Deronda*. The question of whether Daniel was baptised never arises; the idea that he must cast off Christianity to embrace Judaism is never mentioned, apart from a passing, perfunctory reference to his (apparently unproblematic) 'Christian sympathies'.[121] Assuming a largely non-Jewish readership, Eliot only depicts the workings of a faith they are unlikely to share, and a great national destiny from which they must feel themselves excluded. Narrative solutions to the problems posed by the realist narrative are so few and far between, in fact, that it is no exaggeration to say that plot itself breaks down in the realist part of the novel: the marriage plot goes nowhere, the inheritance plot short-circuits. It is this breakdown of plot to which James was returned in *The Portrait of a Lady*, a novel in which he re-locates Eliot's disability plot in the realist world she had used it to escape.

## 'Putting wind in her sails': Enabling Failure in *The Portrait of a Lady*

Turning from *Daniel Deronda* to *The Portrait of a Lady* (1881) is an experience analogous to that of turning from *The Moorland Cottage* to *The Mill on the Floss*: the structural similarities in their plotting are glaringly obvious, but these familiar narrative building blocks are used to construct an entirely different fictional edifice. James's debt to Eliot is considerably greater than Eliot's to Gaskell, however, not only because *Deronda* provides a far richer source text than Gaskell's relatively slight novella, but because his transformation of *Deronda*'s plot rests largely on the incorporation of elements inherited from other Eliot novels. Isabel is, as F. R. Leavis argued, the heiress to Gwendolen Harleth – a headstrong beauty who makes a bad gamble by marrying a 'sterile dilettante' who sets out to break her spirit – but it would be equally true to say that she is a daughter of idealistic Dorothea Brooke, and of 'loving, large-souled Maggie'.[122] One way to describe Isabel's position at the end of the novel is that she is a heroine with Dorothea's moral scruples and forgiving spirit, trapped in a marriage like Gwendolen's, and facing a moral conundrum as apparently impossible as Maggie's. In a further twist, her disabled confidant Ralph Touchett is heir to both Philip Wakem and Mordecai Cohen, combining Philip's mixed motives and impossible love for the heroine with Mordecai's terminal illness and valuable legacy.

Like Mordecai, Ralph shapes the protagonist's future by making her his heir, and, like Mordecai, he is prompted to do so by his own enforced inaction. Unlike Mordecai, however, he is tragically incapable of foreseeing the consequences of his bequest, which turn out to be disastrous. By re-imagining Mordecai as a flawed, realistic character, endowed with a material as much as a moral legacy, James twists together the epic and domestic plot-lines of *Daniel Deronda*, eliding Gwendolen's miserable marriage plot and Daniel's heroic inheritance plot in Isabel Archer's agonising *Bildung*, in which the redemptive disability plot seems to work against itself. As we shall see, however, James does ultimately turn back to this plot-line as a way to evade the bleakness of his own conclusions, using Ralph's death-bed scene as a means to recover an Eliotian way out of Isabel's moral dilemma.

Like Mordecai's, Ralph's consumption is represented primarily as a disqualification from action, the condition that disables him from acting as the protagonist in his own story. Although he has been 'a young man of promise', his tuberculosis means that he is now 'restricted to mere spectatorship at the game of life', a way of living that is likened to 'reading a good book in a poor translation – a meagre entertainment for a young man who felt he might have been an excellent linguist'.[123] Unlike Mordecai, however, Ralph has no very clear idea of what he would have done had he not been incapacitated by the illness that strikes him down, not at the outset of a heroic journey to the Holy Land, but during his time working in his father's bank. In his contemporaries' opinion, he had already sacrificed the 'career' he might have had through his unwillingness to part from his father and return to his native America, so his illness seems rather the result of his failure to embrace a life of action than its cause.[124] As he reflects when trying to 'reconcile himself to sacrifice', 'there was really nothing he had wanted very much to do'.[125] Nor does Ralph immediately seize upon Isabel, as Mordecai seizes upon Daniel, as the 'second self' who might realise his thwarted ambitions. Although he sees her arrival in his house as an 'open-handed gift of fate', the 'compensation' he anticipates from her presence in his life is merely the pleasure of observing her: 'To think of Isabel could only be for him an idle pursuit, leading to nothing and profiting little to any one.'[126]

Where Mordecai is characterised by clarity of purpose and vision, then, Ralph is characterised by their lack. James encourages the reader from the very beginning to suspect that Ralph deceives himself about the extent and nature of his interest in Isabel, just as he deceives himself about the extent of his resignation in the face of inaction. The narrator explicitly introduces the possibility of Ralph's falling in love with Isabel in his opening character sketch, a hint that is bound to make us suspicious when Ralph asks himself 'whether he were harbouring "love" for this spontaneous young woman from Albany', and 'judged on the whole he was not', concluding that she is 'nothing more than an entertainment to him'.[127] We might take this as confirmation that Isabel is right to detect 'an odious want of seriousness' in Ralph, were it not for the fact that his stance is so transparently self-protective.[128] The real state of the case is made clear when his father demands whether or not he is in love with Isabel and he acknowledges that he 'should be if – if certain things were different', citing as insuperable barriers his beliefs 'that people, on the whole, had better not marry their whole cousins', and 'that people in an advanced state of pulmonary disorder had better not marry at all'.[129] Ralph excludes himself from Isabel's marriage plot, then, not out of disinclination to participate, but on the grounds that he is biologically unfit to do so. Unlike Philip Wakem, Ralph never struggles against his exclusion, but it casts a different light on his eagerness to free Isabel from the need to marry anyone else, and goes some way towards explaining her scepticism about his advice in that regard, since, as she correctly points out, he is 'not disinterested!'.[130]

It is in this context of painfully ambiguous feeling that Ralph, like Philip and Mordecai, finds a way to insert himself into the inheritance plot as a compensation for his exclusion from the marriage plot. Where Mordecai seeks a spiritual heir to whom he can leave his own soul, and Philip turns his impossible love into a moral investment in the heroine's life, Ralph finds a less exalted but more practical way to convert exclusion into participation. He turns his 'interest' in Isabel to her material profit by literally investing in her life: having explained to his father that he can never marry Isabel, he persuades him to leave her half his enormous fortune, the £60,000 that will enable her, in his words, to 'meet the requirements of [her] imagination'.[131] Although this bequest is the opposite of Mordecai's in being decidedly material – its exact financial value specified – and in its eventual results, its *intended* effects are strikingly similar. Ralph intends that this money will make Isabel the heroine she longs to be, and will enable her to make a voyage of discovery: 'I should like', he explains to his father, 'to put a little wind in her sails ... put it in her power to do some of the things she wants ... launch her upon the world.'[132] Such a bequest, he argues, 'will make her free'.[133] Ralph has always shown himself keenly aware of the connection between wealth and freedom of action, demanding early on in the novel, when his mother first describes Isabel as 'quite independent', whether the word is being 'used in a moral or in a financial sense'.[134] As he explicitly tells his father, the point of this financial bequest is to make her as independent in the latter sense as he now believes her to be in the former.

Viewed from one angle, then, Ralph's gift is a generous, even a selfless one. Not only does he diminish his own inheritance in order to make Isabel wealthy, but he insists that she should not be told that he is her benefactor, so that she is free of any sense of obligation, as well as of financial constraint. Although his bequest has disastrous consequences, it could be argued that his mistake is as 'generous' as he later claims Isabel's to be,[135] arising simply from his over-estimation of her good judgement. Such a view would be comforting, but would not, I think, do justice to the real complexity of either of their moral positions. Just as Isabel's mistake in regard to Osmond arises from a refusal to listen to those around her, which is essentially a refusal to acquire vitally important knowledge – a willed innocence that amounts to deliberate ignorance – so Ralph's misjudgement of Isabel's capacities arises from a refusal to take seriously the risks his father explicitly points out to him:

> 'Doesn't it occur to you that a young lady with sixty thousand pounds may fall victim to the fortune-hunters?' . . .
>
> 'That's a risk, and it has entered into my calculation. I think it's appreciable, but I think it's small, and I'm prepared to take it.'[136]

There is something chilling about Ralph's calmness in the face of Isabel's danger here. We might attribute it simply to his overriding faith in her good judgement, but I think there is also a lingering element of his earlier, fundamentally flippant attitude towards Isabel as 'nothing more than an entertainment to him'.[137] When Daniel suggests that he 'speak[s] as it were for [his] mere amusement', he readily accepts the charge: 'So it is, a good deal.'[138] Although we might wish to characterise this as mere self-deprecation, James repeatedly suggests that Ralph does not give proper weight to his momentous interference in Isabel's life precisely because he treats it as a show. Indeed, he offers a justification for doing so, telling Isabel – apparently only half-joking – that his own inability to act as he would wish *entitles* him to treat her life as entertainment:

> 'What's the use of adoring you without hope of reward if I can't have a few compensations? What's the use of being ill and disabled and restricted to mere spectatorship at the game of life if I really can't see the show when I've paid so much for my ticket?'[139]

Although James leaves us in no doubt as to the sincerity of Ralph's suffering on her account when she makes her disastrous choice of husband – there is nothing calm about his attitude when the crisis comes and he is 'shocked and humiliated', 'cold about the heart', 'sick', 'ashamed' – we can hardly help feeling that Isabel is more right than she knows when she charges him with exploiting her: 'You say you amused yourself with a project for my career – I don't understand that. Don't amuse yourself too much, or I shall think you're doing it at my expense.'[140]

At this point, when the seriousness of his intervention in her life is plain to see, when she stands on the precipice of a trap that would never have been set for her without Ralph's bequest, we can see that Ralph did amuse himself 'at her expense', simply by dint of trying to live through her. When her sister-in-law later confronts her with the idea that she is 'a woman who has been made use of', the description can be applied to her dealings with Ralph almost as much as to her dealings with Osmond and Madame Merle.[141] His material investment in her life is the sign of an emotional investment so complete that he has treated her as if she were an avatar for his own repressed desires, failing to see the extent of her danger because he failed to see her as an individual with needs and desires separate from his own. And despite the fundamental benevolence of his intentions, Ralph, too, has put her in a false position and concealed the true nature of their relationship, by denying her any knowledge of his part in her fortune. In his desire to make her free, he has actually denied her the chance to make a genuinely free choice about whether she wants him to make over half of his fortune to her – has embroiled her, in fact, in a plot of his own.

Although there is a wearingly chauvinist subtext to Ralph's misjudgement of Isabel's needs and capacities,[142] it carries more interesting implications if we consider Ralph as a kind of avatar for the author, and his disastrous intervention in her life a meta-fictional exploration of an author's responsibilities towards his characters. As Millicent Bell points out, Ralph is like his author in being 'a tolerant and affectionate, as well as richly perceiving, sponsor of [Isabel's] development', and yet, in the end, he 'is one of those who "plots" against her – and this suggests that James understands, too, that a plot is something he cannot help making'.[143] Why this particular plot? In a patriarchal society in which marriage gives men power over women, and all women are expected to marry if they can, it is almost impossible for Isabel to imagine a future for herself outside of the marriage plot: she does try, insisting to Ralph that a woman can do 'other things besides marry', but her ideas about *what* she might do are never made clear, and she has no rejoinder to Ralph's discouraging verdict, '[t]here's nothing she can do so well'.[144] Ultimately, the limits of her imagination are the limits of her freedom: convinced that Ralph was right all along – there is 'nothing she can do so well' as to marry – Isabel fails to imagine the cruelty her husband has in store for her, or the depths to which other women might, in their powerlessness, be forced to stoop. As Ralph laments, she is 'ground in the very mill of the conventional', enmeshed in a plot that is – for all its gothic elements – a grimly realistic one in what it reveals about the imaginative power of patriarchy, and in its revelation of the brutality that lies at the heart of unequal power relations.[145] The plot of the novel cruelly, but I think credibly, reveals Ralph's naivety in believing that, if Isabel were materially free, she would be so imaginatively, and that he himself could play the part of the saintly invalid – the angel with a legacy – without ambivalence, complication or self-interest. Essentially, James turns the redemptive disability plot against itself, so that it becomes the source of the novel's tragedy: the very plot that seemed to offer Isabel a way *out* of limited, realist narrative becomes the means by which she becomes irrevocably entrapped in it.

For James refuses to free Isabel from the trap of her marriage to Osmond by conveniently killing him off, as Eliot killed off Tito, Casaubon and Grandcourt, or even by sending a well-timed flood to put an end to her ordeal, as the waters of the Floss put an end to Maggie's. Knowing that Madame Merle 'made' her marriage to Osmond so that Isabel would leave money to their illegitimate daughter Pansy, knowing that she has been their 'tool', knowing too that her benefactor, 'the beneficent author of infinite woe', is in fact Ralph, the one who loves her best – knowing all this, Isabel must also face the fact that she can see no honourable way of freeing herself from her marriage, and that she has many years of life still before her: 'Deep in her soul – deeper than any appetite for renunciation – was the sense that life would be her business for a long time to come.'[146] It is at this truly desperate point in the novel that James turns back to the redemptive disability plot. Ralph's imminent death gives Isabel perhaps the only excuse that would be sufficient in her own eyes for leaving her marital home, and for telling someone the truth about her misery. This, in turn, is made a turning-point in the novel, as the dying Ralph is granted the power to bequeath Isabel a second legacy – not, this time, a monetary fortune, but a gift of understanding and love that is imbued with the power to 'put wind in her sails' as the first, failed legacy could not.

Estranged since their confrontation before her marriage, feeling deeply for one another but unable to express their mutual concern and knowledge – she believing that she can protect him by concealing her marital misery, he feeling that he must spare her the humiliation of telling her that he sees through her pretence – the extremity of the position in which Ralph and Isabel now find themselves finally frees them both to tell the truth: 'nothing mattered now but the only knowledge that was not pure anguish – the knowledge that they were looking at the truth together'.[147] As this formulation suggests, despite the painfulness of what they confess to one another, their exchange exemplifies what Miriam Bailin calls the 'therapeutic function' of the Victorian sick-room scene, as their mutual agony gives way to 'extraordinary gladness'.[148] Although Isabel understands her escape to Gardencourt as a merely temporary respite from her life in Rome, the moment she shares with Ralph here is depicted as not only joyous, but transformative:

> 'Here on my knees, with you dying in my arms, I'm happier than I have been for a long time. And I want you to be happy – not to think of anything sad; only to feel that I'm near you and I love you. Why should there be pain? In such hours as this what have we to do with pain? That's not the deepest thing; there's something deeper.'
>
> 'You said just now that pain's not the deepest thing. No – no. But it's very deep. If I could stay –'
>
> 'For me, you'll always be here,' she softly interrupted. It was easy to interrupt him.
>
> But he went on, after a moment: 'It passes, after all; it's passing now. But love remains. I don't know why we should suffer so much. Perhaps I shall find out. There are many things in life. You're very young.'
>
> 'I feel very old,' said Isabel.
>
> 'You'll grow young again. That's how I see you. I don't believe . . . I don't believe that such a generous mistake as yours can hurt you for more than a little.'
>
> 'Oh Ralph, I'm very happy now,' she cried through her tears.
>
> 'And remember this,' he continued, 'that if you have been hated you've also been loved. Ah but, Isabel – *adored*!' he just audibly and lingeringly breathed.
>
> 'Oh my brother!' she cried with a movement of still deeper prostration.[149]

This moment of sentimental communion draws much of its power, I think, from the fact that Ralph has assumed the authority of the dying. We believe him when he promises her that she will 'grow young again'; we have faith in his prediction that her 'generous mistake' cannot 'hurt [her] for more than a little'. Ralph has no practical solutions to her dilemma, but he offers the hope of a better future, and Isabel's 'prostration' before him encourages us to share her faith in the power of his conviction. Just as we wanted to believe with Maggie that 'something [was] taught her by this experience of great need',[150] so we want to believe with Isabel that this is a turning point in her story, not its end – that she can learn from her suffering and go on to better things, that while pain passes, 'love remains'. In this scene, James encourages that hope, irradiating the bleakness of the choice Isabel must make with the warm glow of appreciation: 'If you've been hated you've also been loved. Ah but, Isabel – *adored*!' Ralph offers Isabel the gift of unconditional love and absolute faith – and at last, he seems to share Mordecai's power to shape the future by force of will, to make Isabel 'young again' simply by 'see[ing]' her as such.

It is the scene Maggie and Philip do not get to have, and it gives Isabel the strength to carry on. Whereas the idea that 'life would be her business for a long time to come' had previously sounded like a threat, it now seems like a promise, with Ralph's prediction that she will 'grow young again' ringing in our ears.[151] Before Isabel returns to the realist world of constrained choices and lesser evils – 'She had not known where to turn; but she knew now. There was a very straight path'[152] – she is allowed to see the Gardencourt ghost. This 'vague, hovering figure' who offers Isabel a momentary glimpse into a world beyond the material, and beyond the scope of the realist novel is, of course, Ralph himself.[153] Just as his death-bed scene offers the emotional release that this relentlessly unsentimental novel has denied us, a scene in which the claims of the 'strong self' are wholly in abeyance, so in death he is allowed to flout its apparent limits as a supernatural apparition.

Isabel is powerless to change her situation, but James invests real dignity in the power she does possess to make a deliberate moral choice about how she will react to it. Unpalatable as the modern (or indeed any other) reader will probably find her decision to return to her abusive husband, it does mark her fulfilment of her overriding ambition throughout the novel, which has been 'to choose'.[154] Finally, and for the first time in the novel, Isabel is able to make a choice in full knowledge of the conditions in which she makes it. Material powerlessness does not, in the end, entail moral powerlessness, and Madame Merle is not able to rob Isabel of her capacity 'to choose'. Moreover, in the failure of the plotters to bring Isabel down to their level – for she has remained generous, capable to the last of pitying Madame Merle's suffering – and in her fidelity to her promise not to abandon her stepdaughter Pansy, we have grounds for hope that Isabel will yet bring good out of evil. It is a thoroughly Eliotian conclusion, in which 'strong sympathy' has the last word – and it is finally brought about only through recourse to the redemptive disability plot. In the end, it is Ralph who enables Isabel to face the failure of her marriage plot, and who launches her at last into a future in which we can still invest hope. For the invalid who had wanted to put 'wind in her sails' so that she 'could see the world', it might seem a small triumph to start her instead down a 'very straight path' – but he does, at least, get to do that much. It is not until James gives us a novel, some twenty years later, in which there is no opportunity for unrestrained speech and sentimental connection, in which his readers are denied both the death-bed scene and the comforting assurance that pain passes while love remains, that the redemptive disability plot is finally and fatally found wanting.

## 'The least bit brutal': Survival of the Fittest in *The Wings of the Dove*

*The Wings of the Dove* (1902) is a novel of failed plots long before Kate Croy and Merton Densher's scheme to inherit Milly Theale's fortune spins out of control and culminates in the recrimination, regret and despair of the final scene. Easy as it is to forget it by the time of that final crash, in the novel's opening chapter Kate Croy attempts to set in motion an alternative plot for her life, and make of herself a totally different kind of heroine from the cool-headed schemer we later admire so fearfully. Explaining to her disgraced and penniless father that her wealthy aunt has offered to sponsor her entry into society and make a great marriage for her, on the condition that she break off all contact with him, she offers to come and live with him instead, to give up her chance of social advancement for family loyalty, to make 'the fact that we're after all parent and child . . . count for us'.[155] Kate may have the poise of a Becky Sharp, but she attempts here to act the part of an Amelia Sedley; although she is clear-eyed about her amoral father's shortcomings as a mid-Victorian heroine could never be, she is as ready here to do her daughterly duty by an inadequate father as any Little Dorrit or Agnes Wickfield.

It is not to be. Our would-be heroine finds herself out of a part from the outset, as the family drama she attempts to put on is booed off stage by her family members themselves. Far from being touched, her father calls her a 'weak thing' for sharing her meagre income with her needy sister, and reacts to her proposal to come and live with him at first with disdain – 'you're of feebler intelligence than I should have ventured to suppose you' – and then with disgust: 'you make me sick!'[156] What she ought to do, as he patiently explains, is to 'work' her Aunt Maud by protesting loudly against the 'invidious treaty' she is being asked to sign; that way, he suggests, Aunt Maud may feel obliged to treat her even more handsomely, and she will 'get something *for* giving up' – the 'something' being the material gains of a great marriage, which he will be all too happy to share with her.[157] Neither he, nor her ostensibly respectable sister Marian – who declares it Kate's 'greatest duty' to marry for money[158] – sees anything laudable in Kate's desire to give up her prospects of worldly advancement. In fact, in a blackly comic twist, her father laments the *lack* of familial loyalty she shows in making the offer she does, claiming that 'family sentiment, in our vulgarised, brutalised life, has gone utterly to pot'.[159] It would take a heroine as dead to irony as Amelia Sedley herself not to laugh at this; intelligent Kate cannot fail to see the funny side. But there can be no doubt, I think, that she is entirely serious when she says that she 'came really hoping [he] might have found some way' to let her stay with him, nor when she later tells Densher that she made the offer 'to save [her]self – to escape'.[160]

In Kate's thwarted desire for a plot of self-sacrifice and daughterly devotion, we can see in microcosm the yearning for lost plots that runs through *The Wings of the Dove*. Trapped in a bleakly materialist world in which sentimental plots no longer work, the characters' longing after impossible plots spills over into disastrous attempts to write (or right) these plots for themselves. Kate's is by far the most sophisticated – and ultimately the most destructive – of the plots the characters hatch, but she is merely the most adept of the novel's many plotters, none of whom ultimately gets what they want. Kate is unsuccessful in her attempt to 'sacrifice nobody and nothing' in a bid to 'try for everything',[161] eventually finding that she cannot have the money *and* the man she wants, but neither does Susan Stringham succeed in her plot to keep Milly alive by making her believe herself beloved by Densher, nor Lord Mark in his plot to marry Milly and inherit her money, nor Aunt Maud in her plot to marry Milly to Densher, nor Densher in his plot to make Milly go on believing that he has been rejected by Kate without having to tell any direct lies. Even naive Milly fruitlessly attempts to plot, when she schemes to keep her illness a secret, and succeeds in deceiving no one at all. Not one of the novel's plots unfolds as any one of its plotters intends: the many marriage plots ultimately result in not a single marriage, and the beneficiary of the inheritance plot refuses the bequest that has been the object of so much scheming.

Behind these failed marriage and inheritance plots stands the most painful failure of all: the failure of the disability plot. In all of the novels examined in this chapter so far, this plot has brought an element of moral clarity into the increasingly compromised world of the realist novel, in which other plots have stalled. All too often, as we have seen, it seemed to be stretched too thin, or present only in a distorted form – Philip's moral epiphany apparently finding no effective outlet, Mordecai's moral vision reaching only his chosen (male) heir, and Ralph's bequest to the heroine being mixed in its motives and disastrous in its results – but it none the less provided a kind of ethical scaffolding to these formally challenging novels, enabling at least elements of the narrative to take on a clearly discernible moral shape. Philip's letter assures us that Maggie has changed one life, at least, for the better; Mordecai gives Daniel the mission he craves; on his death bed, Ralph gives Isabel both the understanding and the hope that she needs to face the future. The form the disability plot takes may be tortuous, and its mirroring in other plots darkly suggestive, but in all these cases, physical failure is bound inextricably to a morally redemptive legacy. When we learn, then, that our morally virtuous and materially wealthy American heroine Milly is terminally ill, we surely expect that she too will redeem our strong but struggling protagonists through the legacy she leaves them, that her physical decline will be paralleled and at least partly compensated by the moral elevation she achieves herself and confers on others. When Milly becomes Kate's friend, and we begin to suspect that she is in love with Merton Densher herself, the redemptive disability plot seems about to emerge in its purest form. The tragedy of Milly's early death, we foresee, will be redeemed by the value of her legacy, which will enable the beleaguered and sorely tempted lovers to marry without sacrificing Kate's loyalty to her family, to remain true to one another *and* rise above the moral corruption around them.[162] Milly's material legacy will be morally sanctified by the sacrifice she makes in enabling Kate to do what she cannot, her money transformed from a source of temptation and degradation into a force for romantic fulfilment and moral elevation. As the inheritance plot and the marriage plot are neatly brought together through the disability plot, the horror of untimely death will be transformed, too, into a sentimentally satisfying tableau of love and sacrifice, as Milly joins the hands of her friend and her beloved on her death bed, and bids them be happy.

This is, of course, precisely what does not happen. Instead of providing our protagonist with a means of escape from conflicting loyalties, Milly's terminally ill state proves a fatal temptation to Kate, who learns of it while she is on the lookout for some as yet undiscovered way of reconciling her secret engagement to Densher with her family's demand that she repair their ruined fortunes through an advantageous marriage. There is no way of squaring this circle without money – and money is precisely what Milly has. On her side, Kate has what she realises Milly wants above all else: the love of Merton Densher. If Kate gives Milly what she wants, Milly will inadvertently give Kate what *she* wants; the reason why Kate's plot is so diabolically attractive is that it seems to right the injustices of both their positions, to compensate both for what life has so cruelly denied them. If Milly is going to die very soon, why should she not die believing herself beloved? After all, Densher really does like her very much, and he really does want to be kind to her. If Milly is going to leave her fortune to someone, why should she not leave it to Densher? After all, she really does love him, and really does want to make his fortune.

The answer to both these questions is, of course, that Milly's wealth is hers, and she ought to have the chance to make a choice about what to do with what belongs to her. It is this opportunity to choose that Kate would deny her, by concealing the fact that Densher is already pledged to marry Kate, and will do so as soon as either one of them comes into money.[163] In his early sketches for the play that would become *The Wings of the Dove*, James imagined that his anti-heroine would have solid reasons for concealing this reality: 'She knows the girl dislikes her – say she has jilted the girl's brother, who has afterwards died. At any rate, there is a reason for the dislike . . . "if she knows the money is to help you to marry me, you *won't* have it, never in the world!"'[164] In the richly ambivalent situation he eventually created, however, no such antipathy exists between Milly and Kate; on the contrary, they genuinely like one another. As the melodramatic clarity of the early version gives way to an altogether messier and much more painful moral tangle, the unfolding of Kate's over-ingenious plot is the more distressing to witness, I think, not only because it is rooted in her better impulses as well as in her worst, testament to her benevolent intentions as well as her overweening ambition, but because we cannot help suspecting all the time that it is unnecessary. It seems never to occur to Kate that if she told Milly the whole truth about her circumstances, then Milly might freely choose to leave her money, or that, knowing Densher loved Kate, she might still choose to leave money to him. Again and again we are told that Milly is generous, benevolent, like a princess – but Kate never appeals to that generosity, never trusts Milly with full knowledge. By concealing her engagement to Densher, she effectively tries to deny Milly the opportunity to play her rightful role of the saintly invalid who (like Mrs Buxton in *The Moorland Cottage*) makes the heroine's marriage plot from beyond the grave. Kate's apparent inability to conceive of the possibility of such a plot-line effectively stymies it: she denies Milly the chance to give her freely what she needs, by not letting her know that she needs it.

Viewed from one angle, it seems to be Kate's 'brutality' that renders her unable to imagine that she could ask Milly to give her what she desires, rather than attempting to wrest it from her. Although the narrator assures us that her 'compassionate imagination [is] strong', there is another side to her attitude to Milly's illness, as she admits to Densher: 'I'm a brute about illness. I hate it. It's well for you, my dear . . . that you're as sound as a bell.'[165] If we take seriously Kate's claim to like and pity Milly, as I think we should, then we must also take this claim seriously, too. Milly herself has already noticed that Kate is

> with twenty other splendid qualities, the least bit brutal too, and didn't she suggest, as no one had yet ever done for her new friend, that there might be a wild beauty in that, and even a strange grace? Kate wasn't brutally brutal – which Milly had hitherto supposed the only way; she wasn't even aggressively so, but rather indifferently, defensively, and, as might be said, by the habit of anticipation. She simplified in advance, was beforehand with her doubts . . . .[166]

'The least bit brutal' is a strange and suggestive phrase, as if Milly thinks that Kate is as little brutal as possible, just barely as brutal as she needs to be to survive in an environment 'in which dangers abounded'.[167] Although she sees this much, Milly does not seem to have any sense that Kate's brutality might make her an unsafe confidante, nor that her own weakness might make her an easy prey for a huntress even 'the least bit brutal'. When, during an evening spent tête-à-tête with Kate, Milly does begin 'to be fairly frightened' at feeling herself 'alone with a creature who paced like a panther', she is disastrously ready to discount Kate's all too truthful warnings about her danger ('My honest advice to you would be . . . to drop us while you can') and happily accepts Kate's characterisation of her as 'a dove' without, apparently, giving any thought to the natural relationship between panthers and doves.[168]

If we think about Kate as a panther, her behaviour towards Milly does seem 'natural' in a baldly scientific sense. If we apply a crude kind of social Darwinism to the plot of *The Wings of the Dove*, transferring the idea that competition for survival is inevitable to interpersonal rather than simply biological relationships, and seeing what Herbert Spencer (and subsequently Darwin himself) memorably called 'the survival of the fittest' as desirable, then it might also seem 'natural' that wealth should go with health, that the beautiful heroine who is 'as strong as the sea' should have the means to marry her handsome young man.[169] If we follow the logic of this line of thinking to its eugenic conclusion, then it is clearly Kate – strong, clever, ruthless Kate, so brilliantly adapted to this environment – who has a right to the princess's throne, not its current occupant, the 'constantly pale, delicately haggard' Milly, who seems to have inherited whatever malady killed her parents and siblings.[170] In a suggestive phrase, Kate calls them her 'used-up relatives', and thinks of 'exquisite' Milly 'as the mere last broken link'; in the Preface, James describes her as 'the last fine flower . . . of an "old" New York stem'.[171] These descriptions all carry distinct echoes of a eugenically inflected view of heredity and value: they suggest that some branches of the human family are becoming exhausted ('used up'), that hereditary weakness is the result, even perhaps that it would be better for the health of the tree as a whole for these branches to be lopped off. Our sympathy for Milly works against such conclusions, of course, but thinking about her as a 'dove' works to some degree to naturalise her victimisation at the hands of Kate the 'panther', obscuring its moral dimension by making moral judgements seem irrelevant. Panthers cannot, after all, choose not to prey on doves.

Indeed, the moral dimension of Kate and Milly's relationship is one that *The Wings of the Dove* seems at times to deny altogether. There are moments when all that seems to matter to Kate, and even to Milly herself, is health and wealth. Milly has wealth and longs for health; Kate has health and longs for wealth. The missing third term here seems to be 'goodness', a quality repeatedly associated with Milly and from which Kate seems increasingly alienated. But does it matter if Milly is good? There is at least one point in the novel when she seems to feel that it does not. When she stands before the Bronzino portrait at Matcham with Lord Mark, who attempts flattery by likening her to its beautiful, jewel-laden subject, she weeps at the sight of

> a very great personage – only unaccompanied by a joy. And she was dead, dead, dead. Milly recognised her exactly in words that had nothing to do with her. 'I shall never be better than this.'
>
> He smiled at the portrait. 'Than she? You'd scarce need to be better, for surely that's well enough. But you are, one feels, as it happens, better; because splendid as she is, one doubts if she was good.'
>
> He hadn't understood.[172]

What has Lord Mark not understood here? That goodness does not matter? That Milly's goodness will do her no good at all because all that matters is whether she ends up 'dead, dead, dead'? Seeing only health and wealth, Milly seems to be saying, *is* really seeing; being 'good' does not actually make one person 'better' than another. The only 'better' that matters is 'getting better' in the sense her doctor, Luke Strett, might use the phrase, and neither Milly nor the lady in the portrait is 'well enough', in that sense.

Before coming back to this question of whether Milly's goodness matters, we need to consider the other thing that Lord Mark has not understood at this point (or, at least, that Milly thinks he has not understood). He does not understand that the portrait of a young woman who is now dead moves Milly particularly because she believes that she is very soon going to be dead herself. He does not understand that Milly is *only* 'well enough' in the sense of being wealthy enough to live however she likes, but is not 'well enough' in the physical sense to live at all. He does not understand this because Milly has chosen not to explain it. She chooses, in fact, not to explain it to anyone at all. Milly's attempt to deceive those around her about the reality of her illness is not a successful one: her lies are continually undermined by her physical appearance, which is so alarming as to prompt the question of whether she is 'as ill as she looks' and the answer that, if she were, she would already be dead.[173] It is made, however, with remarkable consistency. In consultation with her doctor, in intimate conversation with her companion, Susan Stringham, in private discussion with her friend Kate, and always and above all with her beloved Densher, Milly denies that she is dying.

Kate's scheme depends equally upon the reality of Milly's illness and upon Milly's denial of this reality. As she points out, before admitting that she is 'a brute about illness', it is not the case simply that she does not 'want knowledge' about Milly's illness, but that Milly 'herself doesn't want one to want it: she has, as to what may be preying on her, a kind of ferocious modesty, a kind of – I don't know what to call it – intensity of pride'.[174] The truth of Kate's statement is borne out by Milly's behaviour when she next sees Densher: 'it was the very possibility of his dealing with her as one of the afflicted that she had within the first minute conjured away. She was never, never – did he understand? – to be one of the afflicted for him.'[175] When they are in Venice and her illness has advanced considerably, she gives him 'an exquisite pale glare' even for asking whether it is 'safe' for her to leave the house, this acknowledgement of her physical frailty touching 'the supersensitive nerve of which she had warned him'.[176]

Still more remarkable than Milly's own determination to obscure the truth about her body is the extent to which the narrator colludes with her in doing so. Even when other characters – including her doctor – discuss her illness, we are never told exactly what it is. Mrs Stringham tells Maud after her consultation with the great surgeon that 'it isn't the case [Milly] herself supposed', and assents to the inference Maud draws that '[e]xamining her for what she supposed he [has found] something else', but she does not tell us what that 'something else' is: '"Ah," Mrs Stringham cried, "God keep me from knowing!"'[177] Kate claims to have an 'inkling of her complaint' but denies knowledge, telling Densher only that it is unlikely to be consumption because consumption is not incurable, that it 'may' be 'a case for surgery' and that she is under the care of Sir Luke Strett, at which Densher exclaims, 'Ah, fifty thousand knives! . . . One seems to guess.'[178] Exactly what he guesses, of course, we are not allowed to know.[179] In his Preface, James treats the desire for such knowledge as being in itself indecent, claiming that 'Milly's situation ceases at a given moment to be "renderable" . . . Heaven forbid, we say to ourselves during the whole Venetian climax, heaven forbid we should "know" anything more of our ravaged sister than what Densher darkly pieces together.'[180] This explanation for the decision not to 'render' Milly's physical experience of illness beyond the point that she is able to deny its reality to others is worded in ethical, even religious terms: James makes it sound as if we would be violating Milly by seeking to share her somatic experience.[181] Hiding Milly's body becomes a moral necessity, the only decent thing to do.

We are not so far away, here, from Densher's idea that telling Milly the truth would be 'brutal', as when he tells himself that there would be 'a peculiar brutality [in] shaking her off' by correcting her false beliefs about his relationship with Kate, and later, that he is doing the right thing by allowing Milly to think him her suitor because the 'law' in dealing with so vulnerable a person 'was not to be a brute'.[182] Not telling the truth *to* Milly and not telling the truth *about* Milly are effectively two sides of the same coin: Kate's plot depends as much on Milly's silence about her terminal illness as upon Densher's silence about the truth of their relationship. More than this, it is aided in its progress by Susan Stringham's silence about what she half-knows regarding Kate and Densher's relationship, on the grounds that a happy romance will somehow halt Milly's physical decline. Stated so baldly, Susan Stringham's delusion on this front seems incredible, but within the world of the novel, it appears all too reasonable. Even Milly's doctor treats her 'as if it were within her power to live', as if to tell her that it is not would be to condemn her to death, an idea that seems to have preoccupied James when he first sketched out the plot and saw his heroine being 'condemned to death ... by the voice of the physician'.[183] Almost everyone in the novel behaves as if speaking of Milly's illness would make it real, and must therefore be avoided at all costs. As Densher acknowledges to himself, at the point when Sir Luke has come to Venice to visit Milly and he knows she must be near death:

> He hadn't only never been near the facts of her condition – which counted so as a blessing for him; he hadn't only, with all the world, hovered outside an impenetrable ring fence, within which there reigned a kind of expensive vagueness made up of smiles and silences and beautiful fictions and priceless arrangements, all strained to breaking; but he had also, with every one else, as he now felt, actively fostered suppressions which were in the direct interest of every one's good manner, every one's pity, every one's really quite generous ideal. It was a conspiracy of silence, as the *cliché* went, to which no one had made an exception, the great smudge of mortality across the picture, the shadow of pain and horror, finding in no quarter a surface of spirit or of speech that consented to reflect it. 'The mere aesthetic instinct of mankind – ' our young man had more than once, in the connexion, said to himself; letting the proposition drop, but touching again just sufficiently on the outrage even to taste involved in one's having to *see*.[184]

Even at this point, Densher tells himself that the silence Milly and others have maintained has been the result of 'every one's really quite generous ideal'. He is willing to entertain the idea that it might be due to a 'mere aesthetic instinct', but this aesthetic revulsion from acknowledging 'physical suffering' and 'incurable pain' is never bluntly condemned as cowardly.[185] Indeed, James's Preface seems rather to prepare us to share in Kate's belief (to which Densher apparently assents) that Milly's 'beauty' lies in the fact that she has 'none of the effect ... of an invalid', will never 'smell, as it were, of drugs ... won't taste, as it were, of medicine', to see 'brutality' in the exposure, rather than the concealment, of the ailing body.[186]

One effect of this concealment is that some critics have found it impossible to believe that Milly's illness has any bodily basis at all. For Susanne Kappeler, for example, Milly's real malaise is psychosomatic, while for Jane Thrailkill, her death is literally the result of others wishing her dead.[187] Like Stephanie Byttebier, I am inclined to think that James's plotting ultimately works to expose as delusional this view of Milly's illness as a 'social effect' rather than a physical fact, albeit a delusion that is entertained by Milly herself, as well as encouraged and indulged by others for their own ends.[188] Along the way, however, James does obscure Milly's body to the point that critics can simply read through it or past it without flatly *mis*reading the text. A secondary effect of this concealment of Milly's body is that it eventually necessitates the concealment of Milly herself. At the point when she can no longer appear without smelling of drugs and tasting of medicine (as Kate puts it), she simply ceases to appear at all. The first time that she explicitly acknowledges her illness – when she tells Lord Mark, 'I'm very badly ill'[189] – is the last time we share her perspective; from this point onwards, she recedes from us until she vanishes completely.

This drawing back from Milly's perspective, which culminates in her being hidden from our view entirely in the ninth book and dead in the tenth, strengthens the impression already given by her relatively late arrival in the novel that Milly is more of an adjunct to the novel's real heroine, Kate, than she is a heroine in her own right. James defends himself from this charge in the Preface to the novel, insisting that Milly *is* his heroine, but that it was necessary to spend the first half of the novel developing the background against which she would shine. When explaining why the second half of the novel seems to him 'false and deformed', James vaguely claims that this is the result of 'foreshortening' so much material into so little space. Yet when he compares it to the 'long earlier reach of the book' in which there are 'no deformities', I think it is difficult to resist the implication that it is the need to conceal Milly's increasingly deformed body that deforms the text, that James's turning away from his ostensible heroine bends the novel out of shape.[190] Byttebier argues that it is in this very deformity 'that we are given a most provocative account of the emotional complications inherent in the spectatorship of suffering'.[191] The other side of this, however, is that the suffering itself recedes from our view to such an extent that it becomes difficult to care about it in the way we care about the plotters' pangs of conscience. It is highly telling, I think, that of the many competing critical accounts of the slippery but – for most readers – undeniable immorality of Kate's plot, some of the most compelling prioritise the wrong done to Kate and Densher *themselves*, rather to Milly.[192] The asymmetry of attention in these accounts between the cursory notice taken of Milly's suffering and the close attention paid to Kate and Densher's seems to me to reflect James's unwillingness to represent Milly's experience, which increases directly in proportion to her bodily decline, until she vanishes from our sight completely as her health collapses and she nears death. This absence makes it difficult to treat Milly as a person whose suffering matters in the same way as Kate's – encourages us, in fact, to share Kate's 'brutal' attitude. We do not witness her deathbed scene, and we do not read her last letter.

In her final bequest, however, Milly succeeds in wresting back some of what the plotters have attempted to take from her. She leaves Densher the legacy Kate has schemed for, in full knowledge that he is engaged to marry Kate; more than this, in the interview with Lord Mark in which he tells her of Densher and Kate's engagement, she convinces him that Densher really has been paying court to her, so that he will tell Aunt Maud, and Densher's way will be smoothed. In bequeathing her fortune to those who schemed to take it, she turns extorted gain to freely given gift. We cannot know for certain what she writes in her final letter to Densher, since Kate burns it unopened, but the fact that it is timed to arrive on Christmas Eve surely encourages us to infer that, like the Nativity, it represents the ultimate act of grace: unmerited and freely given forgiveness, a moral legacy to accompany and redeem the material (an idea surely strengthened by the revelation that her final – hidden – meeting with Densher leaves him feeling 'forgiven, dedicated, blessed'[193]). If we think of the letter in this way, then the repeated associations of Milly with the image of the dove take on a new significance: the dove is not only, as I have hitherto treated it, significant as an animal associated with beauty and vulnerability, but has significance in Christian iconography as the symbol of the Holy Ghost.[194] By leaving Densher (and, through him, Kate) money on which to marry, despite their perfidy, Milly attempts to act as just such a dove, bringing goodness out of treachery, turning betrayal and deceit into an opportunity for exceptional kindness and loyalty.

When she can no longer deny her failing body, when she is at the point of death and forced to recognise that she has no part in the marriage plot, Milly makes what I would call a heroic attempt to play the one part that is still left open to her: the part of the angelic invalid. The legacy she leaves should have the power to shape the future for the better, not only by allowing Kate and Densher to marry, but by testifying to the possibility of another kind of strength, another value system – the kind that Kate was trying to live by in the very beginning, in her spurned attempt to act the part of devoted daughter rather than scheming adventuress. Throughout the novel, we have wondered whether Milly is good because she can (literally) afford to be; whether she is 'better' than Kate only because, unlike Kate, she has everything she wants. What would Milly be, we wonder, if she really was 'a poor girl – with her rent to pay', as she at one point imagines herself?[195] This is the question that is answered by Milly's letter. When she has lost everything that mattered to her, dying and forsaken, Milly acts in a way that is generous, benevolent and forgiving. By leaving this redemptive legacy, she ensures that she will be something more than simply 'dead, dead, dead': she makes her goodness matter, by making it manifest itself beyond the limits of her life.

This is not, of course, a matter of certain knowledge, since Kate's burning of this letter denies the reader, as well as Densher, knowledge of its contents. In one sense, this does nothing to undermine its significance: to be denied knowledge of the contents of the letter is to be thrown back on faith, which seems entirely appropriate.[196] But for Kate and Densher, this refusal to read Milly's letter marks the beginning of their joint repudiation of Milly's legacy. Kate will not allow Densher to read the letter that surely bears Milly's forgiveness; Densher tells Kate that he intends to reject Milly's material legacy, and will not marry her unless she rejects it too. In the end, Milly cannot bring goodness out of evil because, between them, Kate and Densher will not let her. She cannot bring them together because mutual recrimination and guilt have already poisoned their relationship. Kate has already persuaded Densher to violate his own moral sense; he, in turn, has already perverted the one relationship that offered an escape from a transactional world (in which everybody 'works' and 'uses' everybody else) by extorting her sexual consent as the price of his co-operation in her scheme, effectively buying what she would not freely give. They have corrupted each other, and now each is the agent of the other's punishment, Kate in denying Densher knowledge of Milly's parting words, Densher in forcing Kate to make the choice between love and money that her whole plot was intended to avoid. It seems desperately sad, if fitting, that the final plot that this pair of miserable marplots derail is the plot of their own redemption. They cannot accept the gift that Milly offers them; they cannot use her money to marry and be happy together. The future beyond the last page of the novel is difficult to imagine: what will Kate do with the money, if she does accept it? What is left for Densher beyond regret and hack-writing? Like Madame Merle in the New York edition of *The Portrait of a Lady*, either one of them might 'vaguely wail', '[h]ave I been so vile all for nothing?'[197] One thing is certain: there can be no going back to 'the whole joy' that they first found together.[198] Kate is given the last line of the novel, and it states the possibilities of the future in purely negative terms: 'We shall never be again as we were!'[199]

In this novel of failed plots, however, perhaps this last failure is one that offers us a shred of hope. Milly's moral legacy is something that Densher, at least, is shown to yearn for. He keeps the thought of the letter that Kate burned

> back like a favourite pang; left it behind him, so to say, when he went out, but came home again the sooner for the certainty of finding it there. Then he took it out of its sacred corner and its soft wrappings; he undid them one by one, handling them, handling *it*, as a father, baffled and tender, might handle a maimed child. . . . he took to himself at such hours, in other words, that he should never, never know what had been in Milly's letter. The intention announced in it he should but too probably know; only that would have been, but for the depths of his spirit, the least part of it. The part of it missed for ever was the turn she would have given her act. This turn had possibilities that, somehow, by wondering about them, his imagination had extraordinarily filled out and refined. It had made them like a priceless pearl cast before his eyes – his pledge given not to save it – into the fathomless sea, or rather even it was like the sacrifice of something sentient and throbbing, something that, for the spiritual ear, might have been audible as a faint far wail. This was the sound he cherished when alone in the stillness of his rooms.[200]

The image of the father tenderly handling a 'maimed child' offers a powerful alternative to the revulsion from the failing body that has run so powerfully through the text, as Densher longs for the very proximity to disability that he had previously feared. Milly's voice, even if it has been reduced now to a 'faint far wail', is something he passionately desires to hear, and her forgiveness has for him the value of 'a priceless pearl'.[201] While Kate never expresses such regret, we can see in her burning of the letter an irrational act of self-harm that powerfully testifies to guilt. After all, if the only significant thing it could contain – as she claims to believe – is the news that Densher is being left a fortune, then there would be no reason to burn it. Her decision to do so proves that she knows it contains something other than this intimation of a material legacy, something she cannot bear to have spoken. Refusing to be forgiven might be a way of maintaining that you have done nothing wrong, but it might equally be a way of punishing yourself. In the end, Kate is not too 'brutal' to feel regret – only too brutal to accept forgiveness. If she were, as Milly put it, 'brutally brutal', she could surely have borne to read Milly's last letter; it is because she is not, in fact, a 'panther', but a woman capable of moral judgement, that she cannot bear to do so. In one of the cruellest twists in this desperately cruel novel, Kate's guilt – what Deronda might have called 'the precious sign of a recoverable nature'[202] – finds its only expression in the act that puts her beyond the reach of Milly's, and therefore Densher's, forgiveness.

Arguing that Milly 'brokers a saving shift in Merton Densher's consciousness', at least, Miriam Bailin suggests that she 'retains the Victorian sick person's odor of sanctity and power to redeem, though on a drastically reduced scale'.[203] The 'drastically reduced scale' of Milly's power when compared to, say, Ralph Touchett's, seems to me to be directly connected to James's drastically reduced willingness to write about the 'sickness' on which this power rests. In 1881, far from believing that 'the poet essentially can't be concerned with the act of dying', as he claimed in the Preface to *Wings*, he used Ralph's deathbed scene to stage a redemptive moment of sentimental connection and apparently prophetic sight, endowing Ralph with the power to bring about a better future for Isabel simply by seeing it and communicating that vision to her.[204] In the earlier novel, he also felt able to describe Ralph's ailing body in some detail, to give him realistic symptoms of tuberculosis, and – far from being unable to follow him into his sickroom – to show him on the point and even at the moment of death, in his appearance to Isabel as the Gardencourt Ghost. By 1902, when James turned once more to the disability plot to provide a way out of an even more grindingly materialist and utilitarian world, he found himself unable actually to represent the disabled body. Milly's illness is treated, throughout *Wings*, as something unspeakable and unwriteable, unbearable even to contemplate.

The novel does not – as I hope has become clear – in any way celebrate what it casts as the competitive, ruthless nature of the social world it depicts, and it is to that degree anti-eugenicist, a kind of lament for the values that social Darwinism would accord no place in the modern world, testifying to the ongoing need for the moral scrupulousness, charity and forgiveness that such a world-view largely discounts. James once mocked Dinah Mulock Craik's 'predilection for cripples and invalids', but he too turns to such a character to embody the values no longer prioritised in a 'brutal' modern world.[205] In his unwillingness to represent the body of that character, however, he tacitly accepts that disability is, in a literal sense, obscene: something that cannot be shown, must not be represented directly. He treats the disabled body as something unbearable in its ugliness, and his disabled heroine as heroic in her concealment of her disability. Yet out of that concealment comes disaster; at the level of plot, James clearly shows the distorting, damaging effects of 'the mere aesthetic instinct of mankind' when they involve a revulsion from 'physical suffering' and 'incurable pain' so complete that knowledge of these experiences is denied, and there is 'an outrage to taste involved in one's having to see'.[206] As Michael Wood acutely observes, *The Wings of the Dove* is a novel 'of willed and systematic blindness',[207] a novel about wanting not to know. I would argue that the central thing its characters want not to know about is disability, and that it is this desire that underpins their tragedy.

## Notes

1. Swinburne, 'A Note on Charlotte Brontë', p. 163. Eliot herself denied any knowledge of Gaskell's story; for further discussion of this issue, see Lumpkin, '(Re)Visions of Virtue'.
2. Gaskell, 'The Moorland Cottage', p. 18, p. 25.
3. Ibid. p. 78.
4. Ibid. p. 100.
5. A similarly schematic example of the redemptive disability plot can be found in another story by Gaskell written the same year, 'The Well of Pen-Morfa', in which a young woman embittered by a disabling accident recovers her moral balance through her relationship with an intellectually disabled girl, and then becomes an example to all around her.
6. Eliot, *Mill*, pp. 503–4.
7. Ibid. p. 522, p. 515.
8. Craik, 'To Novelists', p. 443.
9. Ibid. p. 447.
10. It seems only fair to note that Eliot herself would probably have resented any comparison being made between her work and Craik's, which in one letter she claimed was 'read only by novel readers, pure and simple' (*The George Eliot Letters*, vol. 3, p. 302).
11. Craik, 'To Novelists', p. 442.
12. Ibid. p. 442.
13. Myers, *Essays*, p. 269, emphasis original.
14. Eliot, *Mill*, p. 515.
15. Ibid. p. 521.
16. Ibid. pp. 272–3.
17. Hardy, 'The Mill on the Floss', p. 47.
18. Levine, *The Realistic Imagination*, p. 46. F. R. Leavis trenchantly argued that Eliot seriously weakened the novel by ending it with this 'dreamed-of perfect accident' (*The Great Tradition*, pp. 45–6); for a more sympathetic reading of this turn away from realism, see Beer, *George Eliot*, p. 98, and Fraiman, 'The Mill on the Floss, the Critics, and the Bildungsroman'.

19. Craik, 'To Novelists', p. 447, emphasis original.
20. Eliot, *Mill*, p. 340.
21. Ibid. p. 503.
22. Ibid.
23. Sara M. Putzell convincingly argues that Maggie too achieves this, in the 'one supreme moment' before her death, when for the first time her duty and her desire fully coalesce – but acknowledges that this synthesis is achieved in such a way that it is wholly dependent upon her death, and could not persist ('An Antagonism of Valid Claims', p. 241).
24. Eliot, *Middlemarch*, p. 741.
25. Ibid. p. 785.
26. Eliot, *Mill*, p. 522.
27. Ibid. p. 522, p. 503.
28. Guth, 'Philip: The Tragedy of "The Mill on the Floss"', p. 361.
29. Eliot, *Mill*, p. 515
30. Guth, 'Philip: The Tragedy of "The Mill on the Floss"', p. 371.
31. Eliot, *Mill*, p. 178. Ellipsis original.
32. Ibid. pp. 183–4.
33. Ibid. pp. 330–1.
34. Ibid. pp. 387–8.
35. Barrett, *Vocation and Desire*, p. 61.
36. Eliot, *Mill*, p. 297.
37. Ibid. p. 408.
38. Ibid. p. 178, emphasis added.
39. Ibid. p. 410.
40. Ibid. p. 411.
41. Ibid. p. 61.
42. Ibid. p. 334.
43. Schaffer, *Romance's Rival*, p. 194.
44. Craik, *Halifax*, p. 53; Craik, *Noble Life*, vol. 1, p. 238 and *passim*.
45. Interestingly, Craik does express indignation in her review of *The Mill on the Floss* that Eliot cruelly parts Maggie and Philip' ('To Novelists', p. 445), which seems somewhat quixotic, given the plotting of *A Noble Life* and *John Halifax, Gentleman*. Perhaps Craik was more willing to entertain the idea of disabled men as marriageable in other people's novels than in her own.
46. Eliot, *Mill*, pp. 346–7. For a detailed discussion of Philip and Tom's relationship, see Bourrier, *The Measure of Manliness*, pp. 77–97.
47. Stephen, *George Eliot*, p. 104.
48. Eliot, *Mill*, p. 329, p. 448.
49. Ibid. p. 449, p. 450.
50. Beer, *Darwin's Plots*, p. 12.
51. Haight, 'The Mill on the Floss', p. 344, p. 348.
52. Beer, *Darwin's Plots*, pp. 19–20.
53. Eliot, *Mill*, p. 12.

54. Ibid. pp. 19–20.
55. Ibid. p. 33.
56. Ibid. pp. 272–3.
57. Ibid. p. 161.
58. Ibid. p. 522.
59. Eliot, *Deronda*, p. 307.
60. Ibid. p. 308.
61. Ibid. p. 3.
62. Ibid. p. 147.
63. Ibid. pp. 148–9.
64. Ibid. p. 406.
65. Ibid. p. 406, p. 461.
66. Ibid. p. 461.
67. Ibid. p. 463, p. 461.
68. Ibid. p. 427.
69. Ibid. p. 326.
70. Ibid. p. 629.
71. Leavis, *The Great Tradition*, p. 80.
72. For three compelling but widely differing readings of the interaction between the two 'halves' of *Daniel Deronda*, see Ch. 8 of David Carroll's *George Eliot and the Conflict of Interpretations*, pp. 273–311; Sarah Gates, 'A Difference of Native Language', p. 718; and Ch. 1 of George Levine's *Realism, Ethics and Secularism*, pp. 25–50.
73. Eliot, *Deronda*, p. 463.
74. Ibid. p. 593.
75. Ibid. p. 284; Rosenman, 'Women's Speech', p. 240.
76. Eliot, *Deronda*, p. 3, p. 601.
77. Murphy, 'The Ethic of the Gift', p. 196.
78. Eliot, *Deronda*, p. 597.
79. Ibid. p. 596.
80. Ibid. p. 406, p. 422.
81. Ibid. p. 404.
82. Ibid. p. 430; Chase, 'The Decomposition of Elephants', p. 518, p. 522.
83. Eliot, *Deronda*, pp. 404–5.
84. The saintly minister in 'Janet's Repentance' in Eliot's *Scenes of Clerical Life* (1858).
85. Eliot, *Mill*, p. 503.
86. Eliot, *Deronda*, p. 428.
87. Ibid. p. 406.
88. Ibid. p. 461.
89. Ibid. p. 643, p. 695.
90. Ibid. p. 308.
91. Ibid. p. 399.
92. Ibid. p. 400.
93. Ibid. p. 151.

94. Ibid.
95. Ibid. p. 400.
96. Ibid. p. 629.
97. Ibid. p. 628.
98. Ibid. p. 629.
99. Ibid.
100. Ibid. pp. 536–7.
101. Ibid. p. 571, emphasis original.
102. Ibid.
103. Ibid. p. 547, p. 540.
104. Ibid. p. 549.
105. Ibid. p. 539.
106. Ibid. p. 545.
107. Ibid. p. 427.
108. Ibid. p. 695, p. 545.
109. Ibid. p. 541.
110. Ibid. p. 406, p. 538.
111. Ibid. p. 540.
112. Ibid. p. 567.
113. Ibid. p. 541.
114. Ibid. p. 568.
115. Ibid.
116. Ibid. p. 451.
117. Ibid. p. 690.
118. Beer, *Darwin's Plots*, p. 183.
119. Beer, *George Eliot*, p. 223.
120. Lovesey, 'The Other Woman', p. 509.
121. Eliot, *Deronda*, p. 566.
122. Leavis, *The Great Tradition*, p. 86; James, *Portrait*, p. 344; Eliot, *Mill*, p. 504.
123. James, *Portrait*, p. 51, p. 157, p. 53.
124. Indeed, there has been a critical tendency to read Ralph's invalidism as a symptom rather than a cause of his leisured lifestyle, and to see his illness as the somatic sign of his figurative commitment to consumption over production. See Bourrier, *The Measure of Manliness*, p. 103; Byrne, *Tuberculosis and the Victorian Literary Imagination*, pp. 151–2.
125. James, *Portrait*, p. 53.
126. Ibid. p. 73, p. 74, p. 149.
127. Ibid. p. 74.
128. Ibid. p. 72.
129. Ibid. p. 189.
130. Ibid. p. 344.
131. Ibid. p. 190.
132. Ibid.

133. Ibid. p. 159, p. 191
134. Ibid. p. 27.
135. Ibid. p. 596.
136. Ibid. p. 193.
137. Ibid. p. 74.
138. Ibid. p. 191.
139. Ibid. p. 157.
140. Ibid. p. 337, p. 346, p. 343.
141. Ibid. p. 540.
142. Alfred Habegger, for example, argues that James succumbs in this novel to his father's anti-feminism, finally punishing his heroine for her rebellious desires and making Ralph his 'scapegoat' (*Henry James and the 'Woman Business'*, p. 176).
143. Bell, *Meaning in Henry James*, p. 85, pp. 88–9.
144. James, *Portrait*, p. 159. For further discussion of how James's commitment to realism curtails Isabel's options in plot terms, see Fowler, *Henry James's American Girl*, p. 65.
145. James, *Portrait*, p. 568. As Roslyn Jolly notes, 'Ralph's use of the passive voice leaves the agent of punishment unspecified', and in fact Isabel is 'ground' not just by Osmond and Madame Merle, but also by the author of 'a narrative which defines its realism through the disillusionment of its characters' (*Henry James*, p. 52).
146. James, *Portrait*, p. 545, p. 423, p. 553.
147. Ibid. p. 567.
148. Bailin, *The Sickroom in Victorian Fiction*, p. 1; James, *Portrait*, p. 568.
149. James, *Portrait*, pp. 568–9.
150. Eliot, *Mill*, p. 515.
151. This scene has not always been read as redemptive; for example, see Pippin, *Henry James and Modern Moral Life*, p. 137.
152. James, *Portrait*, p. 581.
153. Ibid. p. 571.
154. Ibid. p. 79.
155. James, *Wings*, p. 10.
156. Ibid. p. 10, p. 15.
157. Ibid. p. 11.
158. Ibid. p. 30.
159. Ibid. p. 12.
160. Ibid. p. 14, p. 49.
161. Ibid. p. 52.
162. Ibid. p. 49.
163. In this, as Millicent Bell points out, Kate resembles a younger and more sympathetic Madame Merle (*Meaning in Henry James*, p. 300).
164. 'Appendix', in *Wings*, p. 515 (repr. from *The Notebooks of Henry James*, pp. 169–74).

## Physical Frailty and Moral Inheritance 229

165. James, *Wings*, p. 318, p. 255.
166. Ibid. p. 130.
167. Ibid.
168. Ibid. pp. 201–2.
169. Beer, 'Introduction', in Darwin, *On the Origin of Species*, p. xxii; James, *Wings*, p. 255.
170. James, *Wings*, p. 75.
171. Ibid. p. 124, 'Preface', in *Wings*, p. xxxiv.
172. James, *Wings*, p. 157.
173. Ibid. p. 252.
174. Ibid. p. 255.
175. Ibid. p. 269.
176. Ibid. p. 273, p. 393.
177. Ibid. p. 296.
178. Ibid. pp. 255–6.
179. The fact that Milly's illness is too fearful to be named but can be guessed by the name of her doctor leads Shizue Ebine to argue that Milly is supposed to have breast cancer, the illness that killed James's sister Alice just two years before he started planning the play that would eventually become *Wings* ('Did Milly Die of Tuberculosis?', pp. 52–3). Although Ebine builds a convincing case, I do not think that James's decision to obscure Milly's body so completely from the text can be attributed entirely to reticence about one particular disease; in his early notes, he is vague about the physical basis for his heroine's decline, describing it as '(consumption, heart-disease, or whatever)' ('Appendix', in *Wings*, p. 511), and the final version maintains this vagueness. The descriptions of her red hair and her paleness might, as Katherine Byrne notes, have encouraged contemporary readers to see her, not as having cancer, but as being consumptive (*Tuberculosis in the Victorian Novel*, p. 69). Talia Schaffer too calls her a 'paradigmatic Victorian consumptive invalid' ('The Silent Treatment', p. 234). That Milly Theale's name so closely resembles that of James's cousin Minny Temple, who died of consumption in her early twenties, surely strengthens the idea that she is supposed to have tuberculosis, but I would argue that James makes it impossible to be certain.
180. James, 'Preface', *Wings*, p. xliii.
181. James's use of sexually suggested language here ('know', 'ravaged') seems to pick up his suggestion in the same sketch that Milly and Densher's relationship must be physically unconsummated so as to avoid 'the ugliness . . . the nastiness . . . of the man's "having" a sick girl' ('Appendix', in *Wings*, p. 512).
182. James, *Wings*, p. 275, p. 349.
183. Ibid. p. 177; James, 'Appendix', in *Wings*, p. 511.
184. James, *Wings*, pp. 431–2.
185. Ibid. p. 432.

186. James, 'Preface', in *Wings*, p. xliii; James, *Wings*, pp. 254–5.
187. Kappeler, 'Fall in Love with Milly Theale', pp. 24–7; Thrailkill, *Affecting Fictions*, pp. 238–40.
188. Byttebier, 'None of the Effect of an Invalid', p. 166.
189. James, *Wings*, p. 329.
190. James, 'Preface', in *Wings*, p. xliv, p. xlv.
191. Byttebier, 'None of the Effect of an Invalid', p. 160.
192. Robert B. Pippin, for example, argues that Kate's moral mistake has 'something to do with the loss we suffer when others are so treated' (*Henry James and Modern Moral Life*, p. 177).
193. James, *Wings*, p. 463.
194. The dove is also powerfully symbolic in the Old Testament, particularly in the story of the Flood, when the dove brings an olive branch back to the Ark 'so Noah knew that the waters were abated from off the earth' (Genesis 8: 11) as a sign of God's forgiveness. The novel's title also recalls Psalm 55, in which the psalmist longs to have 'wings like a dove! For then would I fly away and be at rest' (Psalm 55: 6). The image of rising above one's enemies and flying away seems to me to strengthen our sense that Milly rises above the plot into which she has been drawn and achieves a kind of moral ascent in her final act.
195. James, *Wings*, p. 181.
196. Being put in a position where he must trust that Milly's letter offered forgiveness, but cannot know, potentially puts Densher in the position of the believer in John 20: 29: 'Blessed are those that have not seen, and yet have believed.' It also leaves the field open for a very wide range of plausible readings of Milly's bequest. These run the gamut from Peter Brooks's claim that, at the last, 'Milly has chosen the terms of her life and death in order for her sign to dominate the stage ... to produce finally the pure emblem of the dove' (*The Melodramatic Imagination*, p. 192), to Michael R. Martin's lively and cynical argument that Milly has simply succeeded in obfuscating the real source of her power – her wealth – by branding herself 'a dove', from which perspective 'Merton's behavior in the novel's last few pages looks less like ethical or spiritual redemption and more like the product of a distinct process of ideological mystification' ('Branding Milly Theale', p. 124).
197. James, *Portrait*, p. 518.
198. James, *Wings*, p. 68.
199. Ibid. p. 509.
200. Ibid. p. 502.
201. Although the reality of Densher's regret and longing are essential to my reading, I agree with Leo Bersani that any moral insight he achieves is at the price of appropriating Milly, 'mak[ing] her his own' in a way that fails to do justice to her fully independent personhood (*A Future for Astyanax*, p. 145), a failure that Kristin King suggests

relates to James's scepticism about his own methods of characterisation: 'Through Densher, James exposes the self-deception of the male writer who at first denies that he has discovered the American girl or has any "authority" (208) to speak about her, only to claim, finally, exclusive rights to her image' ('Ethereal Milly Theale', p. 9). More sympathetically, Athena Vrettos suggests that 'Densher's consciousness of his own moral failings and divisions of motivations, though not necessarily redeeming his character for the reader[,] . . . brings him closer to the complex perspective we have been invited to adopt', seeing his 'divided gaze' as 'an affirmation of James's hermeneutics' (*Somatic Fictions*, pp. 120–1).
202. Eliot, *Deronda*, p. 597.
203. Bailin, *The Sickroom in Victorian Fiction*, p. 139.
204. James, 'Preface', in *Wings*, p. xxii.
205. James, 'A Noble Life', p. 846.
206. James, *Wings*, pp. 431–2.
207. Wood, *Literature and the Taste of Knowledge*, p. 31.

# Coda

In its treatment of disability as unspeakable, the sick-room scene unwriteable and the invalid's parting words unreadable, *The Wings of the Dove* is proto-modernist. Whether we read Milly's terminal illness as a sign that she belongs in the past, or whether we accept that she belongs in the past because she is terminally ill, *The Wings of the Dove* associates disability with forms and values that are passing away from the modern world and cannot persist into the future. Other fin-de-siècle texts employ a similar strategy, with varying degrees of nostalgia for the Victorian values they invest in their disabled characters.

Lucas Malet's *The History of Sir Richard Calmady* (1901), for example, uses its protagonist's disability as a way of recovering mid-Victorian solutions to modern problems: in the end, Richard Calmady's disability enables him to embody a paternalist Christian socialism and to reject secular revolutionary ideology of class war, to achieve a companionate marriage that rescues his cousin from radical feminism and same-sex desire, and to come to terms with his paternal inheritance. Tellingly, Malet back-dates the novel by sixty years, staging her distinctively Victorian plot-line in a mid-nineteenth century setting. The idea that Richard's disability makes him a kind of throw-back, a relic of an earlier age, is literalised in the fact that his disability is an inheritance from his father and his forefathers, and more subtly suggested by the nature of the narrative settlement to which it gives rise: a domestic tableau in which religious doubt, political radicalism and disruptive extra-marital sexual energy are all contained and neutralised.

Writing in the same decade, E. M. Forster also created a protagonist whose disability is treated as a sign of his incongruence with the modern world – but in *The Longest Journey* (1907), Forster's disabled Richard, Rickie Elliot, has to die so that his ruggedly masculine, working-class half-brother can come into his inheritance. Rickie's club foot is, in turn, an inheritance from his degenerate, effete father, and although Rickie is a profoundly sympathetic character, it is made clear that the future does not belong to men like him. In a somewhat improbable accident, Forster cuts Rickie off at the knees, freeing him of his deformed foot at the cost of his life, and literalising the idea that disability needs to be cut out for the future to come to birth.

In his revulsion at Rickie's disability – the death of whose child, who would have walked with crutches had she lived, is, in a particularly grim moment, described as 'merciful'[1] – and his treatment of Stephen Wonham, the working-class half-brother against whom kindly but feeble Rickie is defined, Forster anticipates D. H. Lawrence's famous juxtaposition of the disabled and impotent aristocrat Clifford Chatterley and his virile gamekeeper, Mellors. In *Lady Chatterley's Lover* (1928), Clifford's physical disability is the result of his injuries in the war, from which he is said to have returned 'more or less in bits',[2] but despite this new context, Lawrence's treatment of disability in the novel strongly recalls Forster's Edwardian text, and indeed the plotting of his own earlier story, 'The Daughters of the Vicar' (1914). There, the schematic contrast between the fates of two sisters, one of whom chooses to marry a disabled, effeminate clergyman, and the other a physically powerful, handsome miner, is clear: Louisa, the sister who acts on her sexual desire for a virile, able-bodied man, has chosen the better part, while her sister Mary is inevitably frustrated by her union with Mr Massy, whose attentiveness as a parent does nothing to compensate for his basic inadequacy as a man. So repulsive – 'almost unthinkable' – is his body that Mary feels she has to get 'rid of her body' when she marries him, a denial of the physical that is treated as nightmarish, a kind of death-in-life.[3] By prioritising class position over physical wholeness, and respectability over passion, Lawrence shows us that Mary has made the hypocritical, the unsatisfying choice – in short, the Victorian choice. In her rugged miner, on the other hand, Louisa has embraced the future, just as Connie Chatterley later does in *Lady Chatterley's Lover*. Attitudes that James would undoubtedly have found 'brutal' are celebrated here as honest; the morally reprehensible thing is not to be revolted by physical disability, but to fail to turn away from it.

These very brief summaries do not do justice to the complexity of the texts they sketch, but I hope they serve to illustrate, however baldly, the association between disability and Victorianism in the modernist novel. As 'sentimental' and 'melodramatic' became terms of opprobrium, as new attitudes to sexuality made the matrimonial conclusions of the nineteenth-century novel seem moribund, and

Freudian analyses cast its plots as naive expressions of repressed and dimly understood desires, the turn away from the forms of the Victorian novel gave rise to a rejection of the narrative work performed by its disabled characters. Heaving the invalid off her couch was one way to mark a text's modernity; refusing to be touched by Tiny Tim's pitiful appeal or siding with Kate Croy over Milly Theale were ways *not* to be Victorian. The long shadow cast by the violence eventually committed in the cause of eugenics has made it difficult, I think, to acknowledge the revulsion from disability so often manifested in the writings of modernist authors, without seeming unjustly to hold them responsible for later and entirely non-fictional horrors.[4] Yet this revulsion is a crucial part of the history of the Victorian novel, its reception and its afterlife, as well as the history of disabled people as we have seen ourselves represented in fiction. It is beyond the scope of this book to tell that part of the story in the detail it deserves; I leave it to another critic to write the account that begins, rather than ends, with *The Wings of the Dove*.

The cast of characters we have dealt with here, however, did not simply down tools with the advent of modernism. As any avid reader will be aware, novelistic forms are never wholly obliterated and superseded by new ones; older trends persist in the backwaters and eddies of the literary marketplace, where outmoded plot structures and half-forgotten characters lurk, ripe for rediscovery and re-invention. Dickens, of course, never fell out of the popular imagination, however low an ebb his critical fortunes reached. Tiny Tim continued to hobble on to stages across the country in Christmas productions of *The Christmas Carol*, and as long as he did, and as long as Smike, Quilp, Esther Summerson and Little Dorrit were known to readers, melodramatic approaches to the disabled body continued to be available for imaginative use. Although Dickensian methods of characterisation fell out of favour with the realists who succeeded him – let alone with his modernist successors – they have never become truly unfamiliar or alien; they are too frequently resurrected in adaptations and imitations, or simply encountered through re-reading the perennially popular author himself.

Wilkie Collins has not enjoyed the same unfailing popularity with readers, but his influence on the detective novel, now inescapably associated with Arthur Conan Doyle and his celebrated super-sleuth Sherlock Holmes, can be seen in the genre's persistent use of the disabled body to destabilise the systems of knowledge by which the detective detects. In 'The Man With The Twisted Lip' (1891), for example, Conan Doyle has his master-detective temporarily fooled by a respectable gentleman's disguise as a facially disfigured hunchback; disability turns out not to be the sign of deviance so much as a sign that is faked in order for deviance (in this case, begging) to conceal itself. Compared with Collins, Conan Doyle's treatment of the disabled body seems positively tame – there are no gender-bending, sexually magnetic wheelchair-users in Sherlock Holmes stories that I have discovered – but he draws on the sensational tradition Collins had established in his treatment of the body as an untrustworthy sign of identity, open to almost endless manipulation. This is a tradition that lives on in contemporary detective films and television dramas in which perfectly convincing masks can be donned by enterprising criminals, and we are asked to believe that the great Sherlock Holmes cannot recognise his own sister when she hides in plain sight.[5]

Meanwhile, Charlotte M. Yonge and Dinah Mulock Craik may have fallen out of fashion and out of print, but their depiction of disability as a monitory and feminising experience remained alive and well in popular girls' school stories well into the twentieth century.[6] Lousia M. Alcott's Beth March and Susan Coolidge's Cousin Helen have kept the figure of the angel on the couch before young (especially young female) readers throughout the twentieth century, long after *The Heir of Redclyffe* and *The Wide, Wide World*, texts to which *Little Women* (1868–9) and *What Katy Did* (1872) make casual reference, had fallen into relative obscurity. Cousin Helen's self-sacrificing willingness after her disabling accident to see her fiancé marry her able-bodied best friend and set up house next door to her, and her view of immobility as an education in femininity ('the school of pain', as she calls it[7]), will mostly be encountered today by young readers who are unfamiliar with the genre of which they are, essentially, a hallmark – but for all such readers, the disability plot of *The Daisy Chain* or *Olive* will seem strangely familiar.

The disabled characters of the Victorian novel have gone on working, in other words, well into our own time, and I want to suggest that they still have something useful to offer us, not just as literary critics, but as readers who necessarily navigate our own culture's ideas about how bodies should work every day. In this book, I have explored just some of the work these characters performed in offering their authors ways to externalise emotional states and to manifest the injustices of a text's arrangement of characters and plot roles; in providing opportunities for sensational methods of characterisation to be put to affective work and disrupting the orderly conclusions of detective novels; in allowing their creators to explore the possibilities of lives lived outside masculine paradigms of success and to re-think the relationship between family formation and the marriage plot; and in enabling them to work through anxieties about heredity, modernity and futurity. The sheer variety of this narrative work, the sheer range of meanings that these bodies are made to bear, does not add up to one, 'Victorian' way of seeing disability. Instead, it testifies to the shifting nature of cultural constructions of disability, to the the mutability of our ideas about the body, the multiplicity of the purposes these ideas can be made to serve, and the possibility that always exists for re-invention. Stigmatised as their embodiment frequently is, ugly as they are sometimes declared, and excluded as they frequently are from the plot roles they long to fill, what these characters offer us, in the end, is hope: hope for further change, for new ways of imagining and organising bodies. Tracking disabled characters across the field of Victorian fiction, we cannot help but see that value judgements about bodies that are treated as self-evident in one genre would seem bizarre in another, that an attitude to illness treated as harmful but inevitable in 1902 would have seemed perverse only thirty years before. All too often in our own discourse, certain attitudes to bodily suffering, strength or appearance – attitudes that cause profound harm to people deemed disabled – are cast as 'natural', and therefore, however regrettably, beyond the pale of productive discussion or change. Recovering past ways of writing disability reveals that when it comes to our understanding of the body, there is simply no such thing.

## Notes

1. Forster, *Longest Journey*, p. 184.
2. Lawrence, *Lady Chatterley*, p. 5.
3. Lawrence, 'The Daughters of the Vicar', p. 59, p. 68.
4. For a discussion of the ubiquity of eugenic thinking in the early twentieth century, see Childs, *Modernism and Eugenics*, pp. 4–9, and Pick, *Faces of Degeneration*, pp. 5–11.
5. *Sherlock*, Series 4, TV, directed by Rachel Talalay, Nick Hurran and Benjamin Caron (UK: BBC, 2016–17).
6. Elinor M. Brent-Dyer's series of *Chalet School* novels, for example, feature several story-lines in which disability softens and feminises a problematically wilful girl (most prominently in *Eustacia Goes to the Chalet School* [1929]), while Enid Blyton's *Malory Towers* series

feature illness and impairment as improving experiences for tomboyish and unsympathetic girls, despite generally promoting a kind of latter-day Muscular Christianity in which playing sport develops moral character. (For particularly clear examples of disability plotlines, see *Upper Fourth at Malory Towers* (1949) and *Last Term at Malory Towers* [1951].)
7. Coolidge, *What Katy Did*, p. 140.

# Bibliography

## Primary Texts

Alcott, Louisa May, *Little Women* [1868–9] (Oxford: Oxford University Press, 2008).

Blyton, Enid, *Last Term at Malory Towers* [1951] (London: Egmont, 2014).

—, *Upper Fourth at Malory Towers* [1949] (London: Egmont, 2014).

Boucicault, Dion, *The Poor of New York* [1857] (London: John Dickens, 1884[?]).

Brontë, Charlotte, *Jane Eyre* [1847] (Oxford: Oxford University Press, 2008).

Brent-Dyer, Elinor M., *Eustacia Goes to the Chalet School* [1929] (London: Armada, 1985).

Collins, Wilkie, *Hide and Seek* [1854] (Oxford: Oxford University Press, 2009).

—, *Man and Wife* [1870] (Oxford: Oxford University Press, 2008).

—, *No Name* [1862] (Oxford: Oxford University Press, 2008).

—, *Poor Miss Finch* [1872] (Oxford: Oxford University Press, 2000).

—, *The Law and the Lady* [1875] (Oxford: Oxford University Press, 2008).

—, *The Moonstone* [1868] (Oxford: Oxford University Press, 2008).

—, *The Woman in White* [1860] (Oxford: Oxford University Press, 2008).

Coolidge, Susan, *What Katy Did* [1872] (Oxford: Oxford University Press, 2013).

Craik, Dinah Maria Mulock, *A Noble Life*, 2 vols (London: Hurst and Blackett, 1866).

—, *A Woman's Thoughts About Women* [1858], in Elaine Showalter (ed.), *Maude/A Woman's Thoughts About Women/On Sisterhoods* (London: Pickering & Chatto, 1993), pp. 59–216.

—, *John Halifax, Gentleman* [1856] (Stroud: Nonesuch, 2005).

—, *Olive*, 3 vols (London: Chapman and Hall, 1850).

—, *Olive* (London: Macmillan, 1875).

—, *Olive; The Half-Caste* (Oxford: Oxford University Press, 2000).

D'Ennery, Adophe Philippe, and Eugène Cormon, *Les Deux Orphelines* [1874], trans. N. Hart Jackson as *The Two Orphans* [1874], repr. in Dorothy Mackin (ed.), *Famous Melodramas: Six Plays and How to Stage Them* (New York: Sterling, 1982), pp. 121–74.

Dickens, Charles, 'A Christmas Carol' [1843], in *A Christmas Carol and Other Christmas Books* (Oxford: Oxford University Press, 2008).

—, *A Tale of Two Cities* [1859] (Oxford: Oxford University Press, 2008).

—, *Barnaby Rudge* [1841] (Oxford: Oxford University Press, 2008).

—, *Bleak House* [1853] (Oxford: Oxford University Press, 2008).

—, *David Copperfield* [1850] (Oxford: Oxford University Press, 2008).

—, *Dombey and Son* [1848] (Oxford: Oxford University Press, 2008).

—, *Great Expectations* [1860] (Oxford: Oxford University Press, 2008).

—, *Little Dorrit* [1857] (Oxford: Oxford University Press, 2012).

—, *Nicholas Nickleby* (London: Chapman and Hall, 1839).

—, *Nicholas Nickleby* [1839] (Oxford: Oxford University Press, 2008).

—, *Oliver Twist* [1839] (Oxford: Oxford University Press, 2008).

—, *Our Mutual Friend* [1865] (Oxford: Oxford University Press, 2008).

—, *The Letters of Charles Dickens*, ed. Madeleine House, Graham Storey and Kathleen Tillotson, Pilgrim edn, 12 vols (Oxford: Clarendon Press, 1965).

—, *The Old Curiosity Shop*, in *Master Humphrey's Clock*, 3 vols (London: Chapman and Hall, 1840–1).

—, *The Old Curiosity Shop* [1841] (London: Chapman and Hall, 1848).

—, *The Old Curiosity Shop* [1841] (Oxford: Oxford University Press, 2008).

Doyle, Arthur Conan, *The Adventures of Sherlock Holmes* [1892] (London: Penguin, 2008).

Eliot, George, *Adam Bede* [1859] (Oxford: Oxford University Press, 2008).

—, *Daniel Deronda* [1876] (Oxford: Oxford University Press, 2009).

—, *Middlemarch* [1872] (Oxford: Oxford University Press, 2008).

—, *Romola* [1863] (London: Penguin, 2005).

—, *Scenes of Clerical Life* [1858] (Oxford: Oxford University Press, 2009).

—, *The George Eliot Letters*, ed. George Sherman Haight, 9 vols (New Haven, CT: Yale University Press, 1954).

—, *The Mill on the Floss* [1860] (Oxford: Oxford University Press, 2008).

Forster, E. M., *The Longest Journey* [1907] (London: Penguin, 2006).

Gaskell, Elizabeth, 'The Moorland Cottage' [1850], in *The Moorland Cottage and Other Stories* (Oxford: Oxford University Press, 1995), pp. 3–100.

—, 'The Well of Pen-Morfa' [1850], in *The Moorland Cottage and Other Stories* (Oxford: Oxford University Press, 1995), pp. 123–43.

—, *Ruth* [1853] (Oxford: Oxford University Press, 2011).
James, Henry, *The Notebooks of Henry James*, ed. F. O. Matthiessen and Kenneth B. Murdoch (New York: Oxford University Press, 1947).
—, *The Portrait of a Lady* [1881] (Oxford: Oxford University Press, 2009).
—, *The Wings of the Dove* [1902] (Oxford: Oxford University Press, 2009).
Lawrence, D. H., *Lady Chatterley's Lover* [1928] (London: Penguin, 2006).
—, 'The Daughters of the Vicar', in *The Prussian Officer and Other Stories* [1914] (London: Penguin, 1976), pp. 50–102.
Malet, Lucas, *The History of Sir Richard Calmady* [1901] (Birmingham: University of Birmingham Press, 2003).
Thackeray, William Makepeace, *Vanity Fair* [1847] (Oxford: Oxford University Press, 2008).
—, *Can You Forgive Her?* [1865] (Oxford: Oxford University Press, 2008).
Yonge, Charlotte M., *The Clever Woman of the Family* [1865] (London: Macmillan, 1889).
—, *The Daisy Chain: Or, Aspirations: A Family Chronicle* [1856] (London: Macmillan, 1873).
—, *The Heir of Redclyffe* [1853] (London: Macmillan, 1888).
—, *The Pillars of the House: Or, Under Wode, Under Rode*, 2 vols [1873] (London: Macmillan, 1889).
—, *The Trial, Or, More Links of the Daisy Chain* [1864] (London: Macmillan, 1882).
—, *The Young Stepmother* [1861] (London: Macmillan, 1889).
—, *Womankind* (London: Mozley and Smith, 1876).

## Secondary Texts

Bailin, Miriam, *The Sickroom in Victorian Fiction: The Art of Being Ill* (Cambridge: Cambridge University Press, 1994).
Barker, Charles, 'Erotic Martyrdom: Kingsley's Sexuality beyond Sex', *Victorian Studies*, 44.3 (April 2002), 465–88.
Barrett, Dorothea, *Vocation and Desire: George Eliot's Heroines* (London: Routledge, 1989).
Battiscombe, Georgina, *Charlotte Mary Yonge: The Story of an Uneventful Life* (London: Constable, 1943).
Beer, Gillian, *Darwin's Plots: Evolutionary Narrative in Darwin, George Eliot and Nineteenth-Century Fiction* [1983], 3rd edn (Cambridge: Cambridge University Press, 2009).
—, *George Eliot* (Brighton: The Harvester Press, 1986).
—, 'Introduction', in Charles Darwin, *The Origin of Species* (Oxford: Oxford University Press, 1998), pp. vii–xxviii.

Bell, Millicent, *Meaning in Henry James* (Cambridge, MA: Harvard University Press, 1991).

Bersani, Leo, *A Future for Astyanax: Character and Desire in Literature* (London: Boyars, 1978).

Bolt, David, Julia Miele Rodas and Elizabeth J. Donaldson (eds), *The Madwoman and the Blindman:* Jane Eyre, *Discourse, Disability* (Columbus: Ohio State University Press, 2012).

Bourrier, Karen, 'Introduction: Rereading Dinah Mulock Craik', *Women's Writing*, 20.3 (June 2013), 1–6.

—, *The Measure of Manliness: Disability and Masculinity in the Mid-Victorian Novel* (Ann Arbor: University of Michigan Press, 2015).

—, '"The Spirit of a Man and the Limbs of a Cripple": Sentimentality, Disability and Masculinity in Charlotte Yonge's *The Heir of Redclyffe*', *Victorian Review*, 35.2 (Fall 2009), 117–31.

Bowen, John, *Other Dickens: Pickwick to Chuzzlewit* (Oxford: Oxford University Press, 2000).

Briefel, Aviva, 'Cosmetic Tragedies: Failed Masquerade in Wilkie Collins's *The Law and the Lady*', *Victorian Literature and Culture*, 37.2 (September 2009), 463–81.

Brooks, Peter, *Reading for the Plot: Design and Intention in Narrative* (Cambridge, MA: Harvard University Press, 1992).

—, *The Melodramatic Imagination: Balzac, Henry James, Melodrama, and the Mode of Excess* (New Haven, CT: Yale University Press, 1976).

Brownell, David, 'The Two Worlds of Charlotte Yonge', in Jerome H. Buckley (ed.), *The Two Worlds of Victorian Fiction* (Cambridge, MA: Harvard University Press, 1975), pp. 165–78.

Buckton, Oliver S., '"An Unnatural State": Gender, "Perversion," and Newman's "Apologia Pro Vita Sua"', *Victorian Studies*, 35.4 (Summer 1992), 359–83.

Budge, Gavin, *Charlotte M. Yonge: Religion, Feminism and Realism in the Victorian Novel* (Oxford: Peter Lang, 2007).

—, 'Realism and Typology in Charlotte M. Yonge's *The Heir of Redclyffe*', *Victorian Literature and Culture*, 31.1 (January 2003), 193–223.

Byler, Lauren, 'Dickens's Little Women; or, Cute as the Dickens', *Victorian Literature and Culture*, 41.2 (June 2013), 219–50.

Byrne, Katherine, *Tuberculosis and the Victorian Literary Imagination* (Cambridge: Cambridge University Press, 2011).

Byttebier, Stephanie, '"None of the Effect of an Invalid": The Trials of Empathy in Henry James's *The Wings of the Dove*', *The Henry James Review*, 35.2 (Summer 2014), 157–74.

Carey, John, *The Violent Effigy: A Study of Dickens' Imagination* (London: Faber and Faber, 1991).

Carroll, David, *George Eliot and the Conflict of Interpretations: A Reading of the Novels* (Cambridge: Cambridge University Press, 2006).

Chandler, Robyn, 'Dinah Mulock Craik: Sacrifice and the Fairy-Order', in Brenda Ayres (ed.), *Silent Voices: Forgotten Novels by Victorian Women Writers* (Westport, CT: Praeger, 2003), pp. 173–201.

'Charles Dickens', *Blackwood's Edinburgh Magazine*, 109.68 (June 1871), 673–95.

'Charlotte Mary Yonge', *The Quarterly Review*, 194.388 (October 1901), 520–38.

Chase, Cynthia, 'The Decomposition of the Elephants: Double-Reading *Daniel Deronda*', *PMLA*, 93.2 (March 1978), 215–27.

'Cheap Edition of the Novels and Tales of Charlotte M. Yonge', *The Country Gentleman*, 1431 (12 October 1889), 1403.

Chen, Mia, '"And There Was No Helping It": Disability and Social Reproduction in Charlotte Yonge's *The Daisy Chain*', *Nineteenth-Century Gender Studies*, 4.2 (Summer 2008), <http://www.ncgsjournal.com/issue42/chen.htm> (last accessed 21 May 2019).

Childs, Donald J., *Modernism and Eugenics: Woolf, Eliot, Yeats and the Culture of Degeneration* (Cambridge: Cambridge University Press, 2001).

Chitty, Susan, *The Beast and the Monk: A Life of Charles Kingsley* (New York: Mason/Charter, 1975).

Colón, Susan E., 'Realism and Reserve: Charlotte Yonge and Tractarian Aesthetics', *Women's Writing*, 17.2 (August 2010), 221–35.

Cooper, Edward H., 'Charlotte Mary Yonge', *Fortnightly Review*, 69.413 (May 1901), 852–8.

Craik, Dinah, 'To Novelists – and a Novelist', *Macmillan's Magazine*, 3.18 (April 1861), 441–8.

Craton, Lillian, *The Victorian Freak Show: The Significance of Disability and Physical Differences in Nineteenth-Century Fiction* (Amherst, NY: Cambria Press, 2009).

Cvetkovich, Ann, *Mixed Feelings: Feminism, Mass Culture, and Victorian Sensationalism* (New Brunswick, NJ: Rutgers University Press, 1992).

Darwin, Charles, *On the Origin of Species* [1859] (Oxford: Oxford University Press, 1998).

Davis, Lennard J., 'Dr. Johnson, Amelia, and the Discourse of Disability in the Eighteenth Century', in Helen Deutsch and Felicity Nussbaum (eds), *Defects: Engendering the Modern Body* (Ann Arbor: University of Michigan Press, 2000), pp. 54–74.

—, *Enforcing Normalcy: Disability, Deafness, and the Body* (London: Verso, 1995).

—, 'Foreword: Seeing the Object as in Itself it Really Is: Beyond the Metaphor of Disability', in David Bolt, Julia Miele Rodas and Elizabeth Donaldson (eds), *The Madwoman and the Blindman: Jane Eyre, Discourse, Disability* (Columbus: Ohio State University Press, 2012), pp. ix–xii.

Denisoff, Dennis, 'Lady in green with novel: The Gendered Economics of the Visual Arts and Mid-Victorian Women's Writing', in Nicola Diane Thompson (ed.), *Victorian Women Writers and the Woman Question* (Cambridge: Cambridge University Press, 1999), pp. 151–69.

'Disabled, Adj. and N.', *OED Online* (Oxford University Press), <http://libsta28.lib.cam.ac.uk:2123/view/Entry/53385> (last accessed 21 November 2018).

Durgan, Jessica, 'Wilkie Collins's Blue Period: Color, Aesthetics, and Race in *Poor Miss Finch*', *Victorian Literature and Culture*, 43.4 (December 2015), 765–83.

Easson, Angus, 'Emotion and Gesture in *Nicholas Nickleby*', *The Dickens Quarterly*, 5.3 (September 1988), 136–51.

Ebine, Shizue, 'Did Milly Die of Tuberculosis?: "The Physical" and "the Spiritual" in The Wings of the Dove', *Studies in English Literature* (May 1993), 51–63, <http://dl.ndl.go.jp/info:ndljp/pid/11074272/1> (last accessed 21 May 2019).

Ellis, S. M., 'Dinah Maria Mulock (Mrs. Craik)', *The Bookman*, 70.415 (April 1926), 1–5.

Engelhardt, Carol Marie, 'The Paradigmatic Angel in the House: The Virgin Mary and Victorian Anglicans', in Anne Hogan and Andrew Bradstock (eds), *Women of Faith in Victorian Culture: Reassessing the Angel in the House* (Basingstoke: Macmillan, 1998), pp. 159–71.

Esmail, Jennifer, *Reading Victorian Deafness: Signs and Sounds in Victorian Literature and Culture* (Athens: Ohio University Press, 2013).

— and Christopher Keep, 'Victorian Disability: Introduction', *Victorian Review*, 35.2 (Fall 2009), 45–51.

*Our Mutual Friend*, TV, directed by Julian Farino (UK: BBC, 1998).

Fasick, Laura, 'Charles Kingsley's Scientific Treatment of Gender', in Donald E. Hall (ed.), *Muscular Christianity: Embodying the Victorian Age* (Cambridge: Cambridge University Press, 1994), pp. 91–113.

Ferguson, Christine, 'Sensational Dependence: Prosthesis and Affect in Dickens and Braddon', *Lit: Literature Interpretation Theory*, 19.1 (March 2008), 1–25.

Flint, Kate, 'Disability and Difference', in Jenny Bourne Taylor (ed.), *The Cambridge Companion to Wilkie Collins* (Cambridge: Cambridge University Press, 2006), pp. 153–67.

Forster, E. M., 'Aspects of the Novel' [1927], in *Aspects of the Novel and Related Writings* (London: Edward Arnold, 1974).

Foster, Shirley, and Judy Simons, *What Katy Read: Feminist Re-Readings of 'Classic' Stories for Girls* (Basingstoke: Macmillan, 1995).

Foucault, Michel, *Discipline and Punish: The Birth of the Prison* [1975], trans. Alan Sheridan (London: Penguin, 1979).

Fowler, Virginia C., *Henry James's American Girl: The Embroidery on the Canvas* (Madison: University of Wisconsin Press, 1984).

Fraiman, Susan, '*The Mill on the Floss*, the Critics, and the Bildungsroman', *PMLA*, 108.1 (January 1993), 136–50.

Frawley, Maria H., *Invalidism and Identity in Nineteenth-Century Britain* (Chicago: University of Chicago Press, 2004).

Free, Melissa, 'Freaks That Matter: The Doll's Dressmaker, the Doctor's Assistant, and the Limits of Difference', in Marlene Tromp (ed.), *Victorian Freaks: The Social Context of Freakery in Britain* (Columbus: Ohio State University Press, 2008), pp. 259–82.

Furneaux, Holly, 'Negotiating the Gentle-Man: Male Nursing and Class Conflict in the "High" Victorian Period', in Dinah Birch and Mark Llewellyn (eds), *Conflict and Difference in Nineteenth-Century Literature* (Basingstoke: Palgrave Macmillan, 2010), pp. 109–25.

—, *Queer Dickens: Erotics, Families, Masculinities* (Oxford: Oxford University Press, 2009).

Gagnier, Regenia, *Subjectivities: A History of Self-Representation in Britain, 1832–1920* (New York: Oxford University Press, 1991).

Garland-Thomson, Rosemarie, *Extraordinary Bodies: Figuring Physical Disability in American Culture and Literature* (New York: Columbia University Press, 1997).

—, *Staring: How We Look* (Oxford: Oxford University Press, 2009).

Gates, Sarah, '"A Difference of Native Language": Gender, Genre, and Realism in "Daniel Deronda"', *ELH*, 68.3 (Fall 2001), 699–724.

Gavin, Adrienne E., 'Dickens, Wegg, and Wooden Legs', *Dickens Project: Our Mutual Friend: The Scholarly Pages* (1998), <https://omf.ucsc.edu/london-1865/victorian-city/wooden-legs.html> (last accessed 21 May 2019).

Gilbert, Pam, *Disease, Desire, and the Body in Victorian Women's Popular Novels* (Cambridge: Cambridge University Press, 1997).

Gillie, Annis, 'Serious and Fatal Illness in the Contemporary Novels', in Georgina Battiscombe and Marghanita Laski (eds), *A Chaplet for Charlotte Yonge* (London: Cresset Press, 1965), pp. 98–105.

Girard, René, *The Scapegoat*, trans. Yvonne Freccero (London: Athlone, 1986).

Gladden, Samuel Lyndon, 'Spectacular Deceptions: Closets, Secrets and Identity in Wilkie Collins's *Poor Miss Finch*', *Victorian Literature and Culture*, 33.2 (September 2005), 467–86.

Gordon, John, *Sensation and Sublimation in Charles Dickens* (Basingstoke: Palgrave Macmillan, 2011).

Greg, William Rathbone, *Why Are Women Redundant?* (London: N. Trübner, 1869).

Guth, Barbara, 'Philip: The Tragedy of "The Mill on the Floss"', *Studies in the Novel*, 15.4 (Winter 1983), 356–63.

Habegger, Alfred, *Henry James and the 'Woman Business'* (Cambridge: Cambridge University Press, 1989).

Haight, Gordon Sherman, '*The Mill on the Floss*', in Gordon Sherman Haight (ed.), *A Century of George Eliot Criticism* (London: Methuen, 1966), pp. 339–48.

Hale, Elizabeth, 'Disability and the Individual Talent: Adolescent Girlhood in *The Pillars of the House* and *What Katy Did*', *Women's Writing*, 17.2 (August 2010), 343–60.

Hall, Sydney P., untitled illustration, *The Graphic*, 276 (13 March 1875), 249.

Hardy, Barbara, '*The Mill on the Floss*', in Barbara Hardy (ed.), *Critical Essays on George Eliot* (London: Routledge & Kegan Paul, 1970), pp. 42–58.

Hayward, Sally, '"Those Who Cannot Work": An Exploration of Disabled Men and Masculinity in Henry Mayhew's London Labour and the London Poor', *Prose Studies*, 27.1–2 (2005), 53–71.

Heller, Tamar, *Dead Secrets: Wilkie Collins and the Female Gothic* (New Haven, CT: Yale University Press, 1992).

Herndl, Diane Price, *Invalid Women: Figuring Feminine Illness in American Fiction and Culture, 1840–1940* (Chapel Hill: University of North Carolina Press, 1993).

Heyns, Michiel, *Expulsion and the Nineteenth-Century Novel: The Scapegoat in English Realist Fiction* (Oxford: Clarendon Press, 1994).

Hu, Esther T., 'Christina Rossetti and the Poetics of Tractarian Suffering', in Holly Faith Nelson, Jens Zimmermann and Lynn Szabo (eds), *Through a Glass Darkly: Suffering, the Sacred and the Sublime in Literature and Theory* (Waterloo, ON: Wilfrid Laurier University Press, 2010), pp. 155–67.

Hutton, Richard Holt, 'Novels by the Authoress of "John Halifax, Gentleman"', *North British Review*, 29 (1858), 466–81.

Ingham, Patricia, 'Nobody's Fault: The Scope of the Negative in *Little Dorrit*', in John Schad (ed.), *Dickens Refigured: Bodies, Desires and Other Histories* (Manchester: Manchester University Press, 1996), pp. 98–116.

—, *The Language of Gender and Class: Transformation in the Victorian Novel* (London: Routledge, 1996).

James, Henry, '*A Noble Life*', *The Nation* (1 March 1866), repr. in Leon Edel (ed.), *Literary Criticism: Essays on Literature, American Writers, English Writers* (New York: The Library of America, 1984), pp. 845–8.

—, 'Our Mutual Friend', *The Nation* (21 December 1865), repr. in Leon Edel (ed.), *Literary Criticism: Essays on Literature, American Writers, English Writers* (New York: The Library of America, 1984), pp. 853–8.

John, Juliet, *Dickens's Villains: Melodrama, Character, Popular Culture* (Oxford: Oxford University Press, 2001).

Jolly, Roslyn, *Henry James: History, Narrative, Fiction* (Oxford: Clarendon Press, 1993).

Juckett, Elisabeth C., 'Cross-Gendering the Underwoods: Christian Subjection in Charlotte Yonge's *The Pillars of the House*', in Tamara S. Wagner (ed.), *Antifeminism and the Victorian Novel: Rereading Nineteenth-Century Women Writers* (Amherst, NY: Cambria Press, 2009), pp. 117–36.

Kaplan, Cora, 'Introduction', in *Olive; The Half-Caste* (Oxford: Oxford University Press, 2000), pp. ix–xxv.

Kaplan, Fred, *Sacred Tears: Sentimentality in Victorian Literature* (Princeton: Princeton University Press, 1987).

Kappeler, Susanne, 'Fall in Love with Milly Theale: Patriarchal Criticism and Henry James' "The Wings of the Dove"', *Feminist Review*, 13 (Spring 1983), 17–34.

Kendrick, Walter M., 'The Sensationalism of *The Woman in White*', *Nineteenth Century Literature*, 32.1 (June 1977), 18–35, repr. in Lyn Pykett (ed.), *Wilkie Collins* (Basingstoke: Macmillan, 1998), pp. 70–87.

King, Kristin, 'Ethereal Milly Theale in *The Wings of the Dove*: The Transparent Heart of James's Opaque Style', *The Henry James Review*, 21.1 (Winter 2000), 1–13.

Kingsley, Charles, '*What, Then, Does Dr Newman Mean?*': A Reply to a Pamphlet Lately Published by Dr. Newman* (London: Macmillan, 1864).

Klages, Mary, *Woeful Afflictions: Disability and Sentimentality in Victorian America* (Philadelphia: University of Pennsylvania Press, 1999).

Leavis, F. R., *The Great Tradition: George Eliot, Henry James, Joseph Conrad* (London: Chatto & Windus, 1960).

Leavis, Q. D., 'Charlotte Yonge and "Christian Discrimination"', *Scrutiny*, 12 (Spring 1944), 152–60.

Levine, George Lewis, *Realism, Ethics and Secularism: Essays on Victorian Literature and Science* (Cambridge: Cambridge University Press, 2011).

—, *The Realistic Imagination: English Fiction from Frankenstein to Lady Chatterley* (Chicago: University of Chicago Press, 1981).

Levine, Philippa, *Victorian Feminism 1850–1900* (London: Hutchinson, 1987).

Linton, Simi, *Claiming Disability: Knowledge and Identity* (New York: New York University Press, 1998).

Lonoff, Sue, *Wilkie Collins and His Victorian Readers: A Study in the Rhetoric of Authorship* (New York: AMS Press, 1982).

Losano, Antonia, *The Woman Painter in Victorian Literature* (Columbus: Ohio State University Press, 2008).

Lovesey, Oliver, 'The Other Woman in "Daniel Deronda"', *Studies in the Novel*, 30.4 (Winter 1998), 505–20.

Lumpkin, Ramona, '(Re)Visions of Virtue: Elizabeth Gaskell's "Moorland Cottage" and George Eliot's "The Mill on the Floss"', *Studies in the Novel*, 23.4 (Winter 1991), 432–42.

Mangham, Andrew, *Violent Women and Sensation Fiction: Crime, Medicine and Victorian Popular Culture* (Basingstoke: Palgrave Macmillan, 2007).

Mansel, Henry, 'Art. Vii.', *The Quarterly Review*, 113.226 (April 1863), 481–514.

Marchbanks, Paul, 'From Caricature to Character: The Intellectually Disabled in Dickens's Novels (Part One)', *Dickens Quarterly*, 23.1 (March 2006), 3–14.

Marcus, Steven, *Dickens: From Pickwick to Dombey* (London: Chatto & Windus, 1965).

Martin, Michael R., 'Branding Milly Theale: The Capital Case of *The Wings of the Dove*', *The Henry James Review*, 24.2 (Spring 2003), 103–32.

Mascarenhas, Kiran, '*John Halifax, Gentleman*: A Counter Story', in Tamara S. Wagner (ed.), *Antifeminism and the Victorian Novel: Rereading Nineteenth-Century Women Writers* (Amherst, NY: Cambria Press, 2009), pp. 255–70.

Mayhew, Henry, *London Labour and the London Poor* [1851–61], 4 vols (New York: Dover, 1968).

Melville, Lewis, 'Wilkie Collins', *Temple Bar*, 128.514 (September 1903), 360–8.

Michie, Helena, 'From Blood to Law: The Embarrassments of Family in Dickens', in John Bowen and Robert L. Patten (eds), *Palgrave Advances in Charles Dickens Studies*, (Basingstoke: Palgrave Macmillan, 2006).

—, *The Flesh Made Word: Female Figures and Women's Bodies* (New York: Oxford University Press, 1987).

—, '"Who Is This in Pain?": Scarring, Disfigurement, and Female Identity in "Bleak House" and "Our Mutual Friend"', *NOVEL: A Forum on Fiction*, 22.2 (January 1989), 199–212.

Miller, D. A., *The Novel and the Police* (Berkeley: University of California Press, 1988).

Mitchell, David T., and Sharon L. Snyder, *Narrative Prosthesis: Disability and the Dependencies of Discourse* (Ann Arbor: University of Michigan Press, 2000).

Mitchell, Sally, *Dinah Mulock Craik* (Boston: Twayne, 1983).

Morgentaler, Goldie, 'Dickens and the Scattered Identity of Silas Wegg', *Dickens Quarterly*, 22 (June 2005), 92–100.

Morris, Pam, *Dickens's Class Consciousness: A Marginal View* (Basingstoke: Macmillan, 1991).

Mossman, Mark, 'Representations of the Abnormal Body in *The Moonstone*', *Victorian Literature and Culture*, 37.2 (September 2009), 483–500.

Murphy, Margueritte, 'The Ethic of the Gift in George Eliot's "Daniel Deronda"', *Victorian Literature and Culture*, 34.1 (March 2006), 189–207.

Myers, Frederic William Henry, *Essays: Modern* (London: Macmillan, 1885).

Nayder, Lillian, *Unequal Partners: Charles Dickens, Wilkie Collins, and Victorian Authorship* (Ithaca, NY: Cornell University Press, 2002).

Nelson, Claudia, *Boys Will Be Girls: The Feminine Ethic and British Children's Fiction, 1857–1917* (New Brunswick, NJ: Rutgers University Press, 1991).

'New Novels', *John Bull*, 3425 (10 July 1886), 446.

Newman, John Henry, *Apologia Pro Vita Sua: A Reply to a Pamphlet Entitled 'What Then, Does Dr. Newman Mean?'* [1864] (London: J. M. Dent and Sons, 1912).

—, 'My Illness in Sicily' [1834–1840], repr. in *Autobiographical Writings* (New York: Sheed and Ward, 1957), pp. 137–8.

'Novels, Past and Present', *Saturday Review*, 21.546 (14 April 1866), 438–40.

O'Connor, Erin, *Raw Material: Producing Pathology in Victorian Culture* (Durham, NC: Duke University Press, 2001).

Oliphant, Margaret, 'Mrs Craik', *Macmillan's Magazine*, 57 (December 1887), 81–5.

Perkin, J. Russell, 'Narrative Voice and the "Feminine" Novelist: Dinah Mulock and George Eliot', *Victorian Review*, 18.1 (July 1992), 24–42.

—, *Theology and the Victorian Novel* (Montreal: McGill-Queen's University Press, 2009).

Phelan, James, *Reading People, Reading Plots: Character, Progression, and the Interpretation of Narrative* (Chicago: University of Chicago Press, 1989).

Pick, Daniel, *Faces of Degeneration: A European Disorder, c.1848–c.1918* (Cambridge: Cambridge University Press, 1989).

Pippin, Robert B., *Henry James and Modern Moral Life* (Cambridge: Cambridge University Press, 2000).

'Poor Miss Finch', *Saturday Review of Politics, Literature, Science and Art*, 33.853 (2 March 1872), 282–3.

'Poor Miss Finch: A Novel', *Athenaeum*, 2312 (17 February 1872), 202–3.

Price, Martin, *Forms of Life: Character and Moral Imagination in the Novel* (New Haven, CT: Yale University Press, 1983).

Pusey, E. B., 'The Value and Sacredness of Suffering' [1841], repr. in *Parochial Sermons*, 3 vols (London: Walter Smith, 1883), vol. 3, pp. 116–44.

Putzell, Sara M., '"An Antagonism of Valid Claims": The Dynamics of "The Mill on the Floss"', *Studies in the Novel*, 7.2 (Summer 1975), 227–44.

Rigby, Elizabeth, '*Vanity Fair; a Novel without a Hero*; *Jane Eyre; an Autobiography*', *Quarterly Review*, 84.167 (December 1848), 153–85.

Rodas, Julia Miele, 'Mainstreaming Disability Studies?', *Victorian Literature and Culture*, 34.1 (March 2006), 371–84.

—, 'Tiny Tim, Blind Bertha, and the Resistance of Miss Mowcher', *Dickens Studies Annual*, 34 (Summer 2004), 51–97.

Rorty, Amélie Oksenberg, 'A Literary Postscript: Characters, Persons, Selves, Individuals', in Amélie Oksenberg Rorty (ed.), *The Identities of Persons* (Berkeley: University of California Press, 1976), pp. 301–23.

Rosenberg, Brian, *Little Dorrit's Shadows: Character and Contradiction in Dickens* (Columbia: University of Missouri Press, 1996).

Rosenman, Ellen B., 'Women's Speech and the Roles of the Sexes in *Daniel Deronda*', *Texas Studies in Literature and Language*, 31.2 (Summer 1989), 237–56.

Sadrin, Anny, *Parentage and Inheritance in the Novels of Charles Dickens* (Cambridge: Cambridge University Press, 1994).

Sandbach-Dahlström, Catherine, *Be Good Sweet Maid: Charlotte Yonge's Domestic Fiction: A Study in Dogmatic Purpose and Fictional Form* (Stockholm: Almqvist & Wiksell International, 1984).

Sanders, Judith, 'A Shock to the System, A System to the Shocks: The Horrors of the "Happy Ending" in The Woman in White', in Marilyn Brock (ed.), *From Wollstonecraft to Stoker: Essays on Gothic and Victorian Sensation Fiction* (Jefferson, NC: McFarland, 2009), pp. 62–78.

Sanders, Valerie, *Eve's Renegades: Victorian Anti-Feminist Women Novelists* (Basingstoke: Macmillan, 1996).

—, *The Brother–Sister Culture in Nineteenth-Century Literature: From Austen to Woolf* (Basingstoke: Palgrave, 2002).

Schaffer, Talia, 'Disabling Marriage: Communities of Care in *Our Mutual Friend*', in Jill Galvan and Elsie Michie (eds), *Replotting Marriage in Nineteenth-Century British Literature* (Columbus: Ohio State University Press, 2018), pp. 92–219.

—, 'Maiden Pairs: The Sororal Romance of *The Clever Woman of the Family*', in Tamara S. Wagner (ed.), *Antifeminism and the Victorian Novel: Rereading Nineteenth-Century Women Writers* (Amherst, NY: Cambria Press, 2009), 98–115.

—, *Romance's Rival: Familiar Marriage in Victorian Fiction* (New York: Oxford University Press, 2016).

—, 'Taming the Tropics: Charlotte Yonge Takes on Melanesia', *Victorian Studies*, 47.2 (January 2005), 204–14.

—, 'The Silent Treatment of *The Wings of the Dove*: Ethics of Care and Late-James Style', *The Henry James Review*, 37.3 (November 2016), 233–45.

Schaub, Melissa, '"Worthy Ambition": Religion and Domesticity in *The Daisy Chain*', *Studies in the Novel*, 39.1 (Spring 2007), 65–83.

Schlicke, Paul, *Dickens and Popular Entertainment* (London: Allen & Unwin, 1985).

Schor, Hilary M., *Dickens and the Daughter of the House* (Cambridge: Cambridge University Press, 1999).

Schramm, Jan-Melissa, *Atonement and Self-Sacrifice in Nineteenth-Century Narrative* (New York: Cambridge University Press, 2012).

Shakespeare, Tom, 'The Social Model of Disability', in Lennard J. David (ed.), *The Disability Studies Reader* (New York: Routledge, 2013), pp. 215–21.

Showalter, Elaine, 'Dinah Mulock Craik and the Tactics of Sentiment: A Case Study in Victorian Female Authorship', *Feminist Studies*, 2.2/3 (January 1975), 5–23.

Sichel, Edith, 'Charlotte Yonge as a Chronicler', *The Living Age*, 229.2972 (22 June 1901), 783–87.

Siebers, Tobin, *Disability Theory* (Ann Arbor: University of Michigan Press, 2008).

Silver, Anna Krugovoy, *Victorian Literature and the Anorexic Body* (Cambridge: Cambridge University Press, 2002).

Sparks, Tabitha, 'Dinah Mulock Craik's *Olive*: Deformity, Gender and Female Destiny', *Women's Writing*, 20.3 (June 2013), 358–69.

Steig, Michael, *Dickens and Phiz* (Bloomington: Indiana University Press, 1978).

Stephen, Leslie, *George Eliot* [1902] (Cambridge: Cambridge University Press, 2010).

Stern, Rebecca, 'Our Bear Women, Ourselves: Affiliating with Julia Pastrana', in Marlene Tromp (ed.), *Victorian Freaks: The Social Context of Freakery in Britain* (Columbus: Ohio State University Press, 2008), pp. 200–33.

Stiker, Henri-Jacques, *A History of Disability* [1997], trans. William Sayers (Ann Arbor: University of Michigan Press, 1999).

Stirling, Edward, *Nicholas Nickleby: A Farce in Two Acts* (London: Webster, 1838).

—, *The Fortunes of Smike: Or a Sequel to Nicholas Nickleby; a Drama in Two Acts* (London: Sherwood, Gilbert and Piper, 1840).

Stoddard Holmes, Martha, '"Bolder with her Lover in the Dark": Collins and Disabled Women's Sexuality', in Maria K. Bachman and Don Richard Cox (eds), *Reality's Dark Light: The Sensational Wilkie Collins* (Knoxville: University of Tennessee Press, 2003), pp. 59–93.

—, *Fictions of Affliction: Physical Disability in Victorian Culture* (Ann Arbor: University of Michigan Press, 2004).

—, 'Queering the Marriage Plot: Wilkie Collins's *The Law and the Lady*', in Marlene Tromp (ed.), *Victorian Freaks: The Social Context of Freakery in Britain* (Columbus: Ohio State University Press, 2008), pp. 237–58.

—, 'Victorian Fictions of Interdependency: Gaskell, Craik, and Yonge', *Journal of Literary Disability*, 1.2 (January 2007), 29–41.

Sturrock, June, *'Heaven and Home': Charlotte M. Yonge's Domestic Fiction and the Victorian Debate Over Women* (Victoria: University of Victoria Press, 1995).

Swinburne, Algernon Charles, 'A Note on Charlotte Brontë' [1877], repr. in David Carroll (ed.), *George Eliot: The Critical Heritage* (London: Routledge & Kegan Paul, 1971), pp. 163–7.

'The Law and the Lady', *The Athenaeum*, 2469 (20 February 1875), 258–9.

'The Law and the Lady', *The Saturday Review*, 39.1011 (13 March 1875), 357–8.

'The Woman in White', *Dublin University Magazine*, 57 (February 1861), 200–3, repr. in Norman Page (ed.), *Wilkie Collins: The Critical Heritage* (London: Routledge & Kegan Paul, 1974), pp. 104–8.

Thomas, Ronald R., *Detective Fiction and the Rise of Forensic Science* (Cambridge: Cambridge University Press, 1999).

Thompson, Nicola Diane, *Reviewing Sex: Gender and the Reception of Victorian Novels* (Basingstoke: Macmillan, 1996).

Thrailkill, Jane F., *Affecting Fictions: Mind, Body, and Emotion in American Literary Realism* (Cambridge, MA: Harvard University Press, 2007).

Tilley, Heather, *Blindness and Writing: From Wordsworth to Gissing* (Cambridge: Cambridge University Press, 2017).

Tomalin, Claire, *Charles Dickens: A Life* (London: Viking, 2011).

Tomson, Graham R., 'Women Authors of To-Day: Charlotte M. Yonge', *The Independent* (27 November 1890), 8.

Trodd, Anthea, *Domestic Crime in the Victorian Novel* (Basingstoke: Macmillan, 1989).

Vrettos, Athena, *Somatic Fictions: Imagining Illness in Victorian Culture* (Stanford: Stanford University Press, 1995).

Wagner, Tamara S., 'Ominous Signs or False Clues? Difference and Deformity in Wilkie Collins's Sensation Novels', in Ruth Bienstock Anolik (ed.), *Demons of the Body and Mind: Essays on Disability in Gothic Literature* (Jefferson, NC: McFarland, 2010), pp. 47–60.

—, '"Overpowering Vitality": Nostalgia and Men of Sensibility in the Fiction of Wilkie Collins', *MLQ: Modern Language Quarterly*, 63.4 (December 2002), 471–500.

—, 'Stretching "The Sensational Sixties": Genre and Sensationalism in Domestic Fiction by Victorian Women Writers', *Victorian Review*, 35.1 (April 2009), 211–28.

Welsh, Alexander, *Strong Representations: Narrative and Circumstantial Evidence in England* (Baltimore: Johns Hopkins University Press, 1992).

Wendell, Susan, *The Rejected Body: Feminist Philosophical Reflections on Disability* (New York: Routledge, 1996).

Wheatley, Kim, 'Death and Domestication in Charlotte M. Yonge's "The Clever Woman of the Family"', *Studies in English Literature 1500–1900*, 36.4 (Autumn 1996), 895–915.

Wheeler, Michael, *Heaven, Hell, and the Victorians* (Cambridge: Cambridge University Press, 1994).

Willey, Vicki Corkran, 'Wilkie Collins's "Secret Dictate": *The Moonstone* as a Response to Imperialist Panic', in Kimberly Harrison and Richard Fantina (eds), *Victorian Sensations: Essays on a Scandalous Genre* (Columbus: Ohio State University Press), pp. 225–33.

Wolf, Sherri, 'The Enormous Power of No Body: *Little Dorrit* and the Logic of Expansion', *Texas Studies in Literature and Language*, 42.3 (October 2000), 223–54.

Wolff, Robert Lee, *Gains and Losses: Novels of Faith and Doubt in Victorian England* (New York: Garland, 1977).

Woloch, Alex, *The One Vs. the Many: Minor Characters and the Space of the Protagonist in the Novel* (Princeton: Princeton University Press, 2003).

Wood, Michael, *Literature and the Taste of Knowledge* (Cambridge: Cambridge University Press, 2005).

W.S., 'Obituary. Mrs. G. L. Craik (Miss D. M. Mulock)', *The Academy*, 807 (22 October 1887), 269–70.

# Index

References to notes are indicated by n.

abuse, 32, 43, 45, 55, 58–9
*Adam Bede* (Eliot), 10
Alcott, Louisa May, *Little Women*, 168n150, 235
anti-realism, 21–2, 25, 191–2
Archer, Isabel (character: *The Portrait of a Lady*), 17, 177, 202, 203–9
Ariel (character: *The Law and the Lady*), 100
attractiveness, 48–9, 60–1, 85–6, 95–6, 124–5, 129

Bailin, Miriam, 49, 207, 223
*Barnaby Rudge* (Dickens), 52, 73n191
Barrett, Dorothea, 183
Battiscombe, Georgina, *An Uneventful Life*, 120
beauty *see* attractiveness
Beer, Gillian, 185, 186, 200
Bell, Millicent, 206
*Bildungsroman*, 122, 123, 131
Blake, Franklin (character: *The Moonstone*), 83–8, 90–1
*Bleak House* (Dickens), 15, 25, 37, 45, 46–50, 53
blindness, 102–3, 104, 105–6, 107–8, 109
blueness, 106–8, 109
Blyton, Enid, *Malory Towers* series, 236n6
bodies, 2–3, 7–8, 24, 25–6, 75, 76–8
and *Bleak House*, 47–8
and *Little Dorrit*, 54–5, 57
and minor status, 22

and *The Moonstone*, 86, 88
and *Nicholas Nickleby*, 33, 34, 35–6
and *The Old Curiosity Shop*, 37–8, 39, 42
and politics, 92
and *The Wings of the Dove*, 218–19
and *The Woman in White*, 79–81, 82
Boffin (character: *Our Mutual Friend*), 64, 65
Bourrier, Karen, 119, 131, 144–5, 148
Braddon, Mary Elizabeth, 117
Brent-Dyer, Elinor M., *Chalet School* series, 236n6
Briefel, Aviva, 100
Brontë, Charlotte, *Jane Eyre*, 123
Brooks, Peter, 3, 10–11, 16, 76
Browne, Hablôt K., 27–8, 42–5
Budge, Gavin, 153
Byler, Lauren, 38, 42, 53, 54
Byttebier, Stephanie, 218, 219

Cairnforth, Earl of (character: *A Noble Life*), 136–43
Cardross, Helen (character: *A Noble Life*), 139, 140–3
Carey, John, 39
celibacy, 156, 158–60, 161
characters, 6–9, 10–17, 22–6, 75–7; *see also* individual characters
Charisi (Alcharisi), Leonora (Princess Halm-Eberstein) (character: *Daniel Deronda*), 197–200
charity, 35
Chase, Cynthia, 193

Chen, Mia, 120
child-women, 37, 43–5, 51–2
*Clever Woman of the Family, The*
   (Yonge), 160–2
Cohen, Mordecai (character: *Daniel Deronda*), 17, 177, 187, 188, 189–92, 193–6, 198–200, 201
   and James, Henry, 202, 203
Collins, Wilkie, 13, 14, 15–16, 75–8, 234
   *Hide and Seek*, 114n116
   *Man and Wife*, 92
   see also *Law and the Lady, The*; *Moonstone, The*; *Poor Miss Finch*; *Woman in White, The*
Colón, Susan, 153
Conan Doyle, Arthur, Sherlock Holmes, 234–5
Coolidge, Susan, *What Katy Did*, 168n150, 235
Copperfield, David (character: *David Copperfield*), 22
costume, 95
Craik, Dinah Mulock, 13, 14, 16, 105, 235
   and disability, 116–19, 120–2, 184
   and *The Mill on the Floss*, 175–6, 179
   and *A Woman's Thoughts About Women*, 121, 133
   see also *John Halifax, Gentleman*; *Noble Life, A*; *Olive*
Craton, Lillian, 34, 40, 53
Croy, Kate (character: *The Wings of the Dove*), 210–11, 212–15, 216, 219–20, 221, 222–3
crutches, 26, 61, 62, 63, 170n183
Curtis, Rachel (character: *The Clever Woman of the Family*), 160, 161–2
Cvetkovich, Ann, 77, 82

*Daisy Chain, The* (Yonge), 151–61
*Daniel Deronda* (Eliot), 17, 177, 187–202, 203, 211–12

Darwin, Charles, 214
   *On the Origin of Species*, 185, 186, 200
*David Copperfield* (Dickens), 37, 51–2, 53, 59, 60, 131
Davis, Lennard J., 5, 6, 12, 23
   *Enforcing Normalcy*, 10
Denisoff, Dennis, 126–7
Densher, Merton (character: *The Wings of the Dove*), 210, 212, 217, 218, 219, 221–2
Deronda, Daniel (character: *Daniel Deronda*), 17, 187–90, 191, 192–201
desire, 100–1, 179–80
detective fiction, 10, 234–5; see also Collins, Wilkie
Dexter, Miserrimus (character: *The Law and the Lady*), 16, 77, 78, 82, 91–102
Dickens, Charles, 8, 13, 14, 15, 234
   and characterisation, 21–6, 75–6
   and child-women, 51–2
   and heroines, 50–1, 57–8
   see also *Barnaby Rudge*; *Bleak House*; *David Copperfield*; *Dombey and Son*; *Little Dorrit*; *Nicholas Nickleby*; *Old Curiosity Shop, The*; *Our Mutual Friend*
difference, 11, 32
disability, 1–4, 9–11
   and blueness, 106–8
   and celibacy, 158–9
   and characters, 6–9, 11–17
   and Collins, 77–8
   and definition, 4–6, 20n42
   and detective fiction, 234–5
   and Dickens, 24–6
   and disfigurement, 47, 48, 49–50, 70n111
   and femininity, 116–17
   and Gaskell, 173–4
   and *The Heir of Redclyffe*, 144–5, 146, 150–1
   and James, 223–4

and *John Halifax, Gentleman*, 131–5
and *The Law and the Lady*, 91–2, 93–5, 96–7, 98–100
and literary function, 235–6
and *Little Dorrit*, 55–6, 57
and *The Mill on the Floss*, 174–5, 181, 182, 183, 184, 187
and minor status, 22–3, 24
and modernism, 232–4
and *The Moonstone*, 83, 86–7, 88–91
and *A Noble Life*, 136–40, 143
and *Olive*, 122–4, 126–7, 128–31
and personhood, 67n4
and protagonists, 117–18
and religion, 170n183
and Smike, 26–36
and Wegg, Silas, 63–4, 66–7
and Wren, Jenny, 21–2, 58, 59, 61–2
and Yonge, 119–21
*see also* blindness; invalidism; redemptive disability plot; terminal illness
*Dombey and Son* (Dickens), 33, 37, 52, 59
domestic fiction, 16, 105–6, 114n116, 151–2
Dorrit, Amy *see* Little Dorrit
Duborg, Nugent and Oscar (characters: *Poor Miss Finch*), 106–9

Easson, Angus, 30, 36
Edmonstone, Amy (character: *The Heir of Redclyffe*), 144, 146–7, 148, 149, 150
Edmonstone, Charles (character: *The Heir of Redclyffe*), 144–7, 148, 149, 150–1
Edmonstone, Laura (character: *The Heir of Redclyffe*), 147–8, 149
Eliot, George, 8, 13, 15, 16–17
  *Adam Bede*, 10
  *Middlemarch*, 180
  *see also Daniel Deronda; Mill on the Floss, The*

Elwood, Cherry (character: *The Daisy Chain*), 159
eugenics, 12, 186, 215, 234
evolution, 185–6

family chronicles, 144, 149, 151–2, 159–60, 161–2, 168n146; *see also Daisy Chain, The*; domestic fiction
fantasy, 61–2, 64–5
Fasick, Laura, 142, 143
femininity, 25, 30–1, 41–2, 48, 121
  and Collins, 95
  and Craik, 125–6
  and disability, 117
  and *John Halifax, Gentleman*, 131, 132, 133, 134–5
  and Yonge, 157, 158
feminism, 161, 169n173, 232
Finch, Lucilla (character: *Poor Miss Finch*), 102–4, 105–6, 107–10
Fletcher, Phineas (character: *John Halifax, Gentleman*), 131–6
Flint, Kate, 77
Forster, E. M., 22, 23
  *The Longest Journey*, 232–3
*Fortunes of Smike, The* (play), 31
Fosco, Count (character: *The Woman in White*), 79, 80–1
freakishness, 37
Furneaux, Holly, 30, 132

Gagnier, Regenia, 137
Garland-Thomson, Rosemarie, 4, 5, 6, 28, 37, 94
  *Extraordinary Bodies*, 9–10, 11
Gaskell, Elizabeth
  *The Moorland Cottage*, 173–4, 175, 176, 202
  *Ruth*, 10
  'Well of Pen-Morfa, The', 224n5
Gavin, Adrienne E., 64
gender, 30–1, 95, 161–2; *see also* masculinity; women

Gilbert, Pamela, 77
Girard, René, 32
Gladden, Samuel Lyndon, 107
goodness, 215–16, 220, 221
Gordon, John, 48
gothic tradition, 145, 146
Grandcourt, Henleigh (character: *Daniel Deronda*), 192–3
*Great Expectations* (Dickens), 52
grotesque, the, 25, 26, 28, 43, 44
  and Quilp, 37, 39
Guest, Stephen (character: *The Mill on the Floss*), 185–6
Guth, Barbara, 181, 182

Halcombe, Marian (character: *The Woman in White*), 79–82
Halifax, John (character: *John Halifax, Gentleman*), 131–2, 133, 134, 135–6
Hardy, Barbara, 178
Harleth, Gwendolen (character: *Daniel Deronda*), 192–3, 200
*Heir of Redclyffe, The* (Yonge), 105, 144–51
Heller, Tamar, 78
heredity, 186–7, 189, 192, 232–3
heroes, 28, 83–4, 187–8
heroines, 25, 37–9, 47–8, 50–1, 79
Heyns, Michiel, 15, 24
*Hide and Seek* (Collins), 114n116
homoeroticism, 30
Hu, Esther T., 159
Humphrey, Master (character: *The Old Curiosity Shop*), 38, 39
Hutton, R. H., 123, 135

identity, 3–4, 12, 15, 188
illegitimacy, 188–9
illustration, 27–8, 41–5
impairment, 4–5, 15
incapacity, 1–2, 3–4
Indians (characters: *The Moonstone*), 75, 91
Ingham, Patricia, 3, 53

invalidism, 17, 151–2, 153–6, 160, 162, 169n168

James, Henry, 13, 15, 17, 176
  and Craik, 118–19, 223
  and Dickens, 21, 22, 23
  see also *Portrait of a Lady, The*; *Wings of the Dove, The*
*Jane Eyre* (Brontë), 123, 131
Jennings, Ezra (character: *The Moonstone*), 77, 88–90
*John Halifax, Gentleman* (Craik), 119, 122, 131–6
John, Juliet, *Dickens's Villains*, 8, 24, 28
Juckett, Elisabeth, 161–2
Judaism, 189–90, 191–2, 193, 196, 197, 198–200, 201

Kaplan, Cora, 123
Kaplan, Fred, 46
Kappeler, Susanne, 218
Keeley, Mary Ann, 31
Kingsley, Charles, 142, 143
Klages, Mary, 26, 32, 131

Lapidoth (Deronda), Mirah (character: *Daniel Deronda*), 195–6, 199
*Law and the Lady, The* (Collins), 16, 77, 78, 82, 91–102
Lawrence, D. H.
  'The Daughters of the Vicar', 233
  *Lady Chatterley's Lover*, 233
Leavis, F. R., 191, 202
Leavis, Q. D., 119–20
lesbianism, 86–7
Levine, George, 146, 179
Limping Lucy see Yolland, Lucy
Little Dorrit (character), 15, 37–8, 44–5, 52–7
*Little Dorrit* (Dickens), 15, 25, 37–8, 44–5, 52–7
Little Nell (character: *The Old Curiosity Shop*), 25, 37–42, 46, 59
Lonoff, Sue, 78
Lovesey, Oliver, 201

Macallan, Sara (character: *The Law and the Lady*), 92, 95–6, 97–8, 99–100, 101
Maggy (character: *Little Dorrit*), 55–6
Malet, Lucas, *The History of Sir Richard Calmady*, 232
*Man and Wife* (Collins), 92
Mangham, Andrew, 90
Mansel, Henry, 77
Marchioness, The (character: *The Old Curiosity Shop*), 25, 42–4, 45–6
Marcus, Steven, 45
marginalisation, 24, 83–5, 132, 133
marriage plot, 16
　and *Bleak House*, 47, 50
　and *The Clever Woman of the Family*, 160–2
　and *The Daisy Chain*, 155–60
　and *Daniel Deronda*, 187–8, 192–3, 194, 200
　and disability, 118, 121–2
　and *The Heir of Redclyffe*, 144, 147, 148–9
　and *John Halifax, Gentleman*, 133, 134
　and *The Law and the Lady*, 92, 95, 97
　and *The Mill on the Floss*, 181, 183–5
　and *The Moonstone*, 89, 90, 91
　and *Nicholas Nickleby*, 32–3
　and *A Noble Life*, 140–3
　and *Olive*, 127–9
　and *Our Mutual Friend*, 62–3
　and *Poor Miss Finch*, 103, 105
　and *The Portrait of a Lady*, 203–4, 206–7
　and *The Woman in White*, 82
masculinity, 29–30, 131–2, 157, 183
May, Ethel (character: *The Daisy Chain*), 152–3, 156–7, 158, 161
May, Margaret (character: *The Daisy Chain*), 151, 152, 153–7
May, Norman (character: *The Daisy Chain*), 157–8

Mayhew, Henry, 35
　*London Labour and the London Poor*, 1, 2
melodrama, 12–13, 25, 28, 33, 75, 233
Michie, Helena, 50, 61–2
*Middlemarch* (Eliot), 180
*Mill on the Floss, The* (Eliot), 16–17, 173–87, 202, 204, 211–12
Miller, D. A., 16, 77
minor status, 15, 22–4, 25–6
　and *Bleak House*, 46–7, 48–9
　and Collins, 79, 83–4, 92–3
　and Little Nell, 38
　and love, 33
　and Wegg, Silas, 65–6
　and Wren, Jenny, 61
Mitchell, David, 5, 6
　*Narrative Prosthesis*, 9
Mitchell, Sally, 119, 123
　and *A Noble Life*, 136, 137, 140, 143
*Moonstone, The* (Collins), 16, 74–5, 77, 83–91, 92
morality, 16–17, 60, 188–9
　and Eliot, 175, 176–7, 180, 181, 187
　and *The Wings of the Dove*, 221–2, 230n201
Morgentaler, Goldie, 63
Morris, Pam, 23–4
Morville, Guy (character: *The Heir of Redclyffe*), 144–7, 148, 149–50
Morville, Philip (character: *The Heir of Redclyffe*), 149–50
Mossman, Mark, 77
Mowcher, Miss (character: *David Copperfield*), 60
Murphy, Margueritte, 193
Muscular Christianity, 122, 142, 143

Nayder, Lillian, 90
neglect, 124–5
Nell *see* Little Nell
New Poor Laws, 12, 35

*Nicholas Nickleby* (Dickens), 31, 32, 33
  and Smike, 22, 25, 26–36, 134
Nickleby, Kate (character: *Nicholas Nickleby*), 31, 32
Nickleby, Nicholas (character: *Nicholas Nickleby*), 22, 26–30, 134
Nickleby, Ralph (character: *Nicholas Nickleby*), 33
*Noble Life, A* (Craik), 105, 116–17, 119, 122, 133, 136–43
normalcy, 10, 11, 28

O'Connor, Erin, 63–4
*Old Curiosity Shop, The* (Dickens), 25, 36–46, 59
*Olive* (Craik), 105, 119, 122–31
one-leggedness, 63–4
*Our Mutual Friend* (Dickens), 15, 21–2, 26, 33, 52, 57–67, 73n190

Perkin, J. Russell, 131
Phiz *see* Browne, Hablôt K.
*Pillars of the House, The* (Yonge), 105
Pip (character: *Great Expectations*), 22
plot, 3–4, 10–11
  and Collins, 15, 16, 75–6, 78, 101–2, 104–5, 108–9
  and Craik, 123
  and Dickens, 24–5, 26, 32–3, 46–7, 65–6
  and Eliot, 16–17, 180–1, 190–1
  and James, 210–11, 221–2
  and Yonge, 145–6
  *see also* marriage plot; redemptive disability plot
*Poor Miss Finch* (Collins), 16, 78, 82, 92, 102–10
*Portrait of a Lady, The* (James), 17, 177, 202–10, 211–12
Pratalungo, Madame (character: *Poor Miss Finch*), 103–4, 106–7, 108
Price, Martin, 7, 8
prosthesis, 63
Pusey, E. B., 159

Quilp, Daniel (character: *The Old Curiosity Shop*), 36–7, 38, 39–40, 59

racism, 88–9
realist novels, 8, 105, 178–9, 191–2
  and Yonge, 145–6, 153
  *see also* anti-realism
redemptive disability plot, 207, 209–10
  and *Daniel Deronda*, 188, 189, 195, 201
  and Gaskell, 224n5
  and *The Mill on the Floss*, 176
  and *The Portrait of a Lady*, 223
  and *The Wings of the Dove*, 212–13, 220–1
religion, 125, 126, 127, 128
  and disability, 170n183
  and doves, 220, 230n194
  and Malet, 232
  and Yonge, 152–3, 155–6, 157, 158, 159
  *see also* Judaism; Muscular Christianity
Rodas, Julia Miele, 8, 13
Rosenberg, Brian, 21, 24, 55
Rosenman, Ellen B., 192
Rothesay, Olive (character: *Olive*), 122–31, 138
Rothesay, Sybilla (character: *Olive*), 124–5
*Ruth* (Gaskell), 10

Sadrin, Anny, 53
Sanders, Judith, 82
scapegoating, 15, 32
scars, 46, 47, 48, 49–50
Schaffer, Talia, 132, 162, 183–4
  *The Clever Woman of the Family*, 147, 148
  *Romance's Rival*, 20n40, 163n17, 168n139
Schaub, Melissa, 158
Schlicke, Paul, 38

Schor, Hilary, 37, 39, 49–50, 54
    and *Our Mutual Friend*, 57–8,
    62–3, 66
Schramm, Jan-Melissa, 11
self-assertion, 59–60
selflessness, 194–7
sensation, 15–16, 40–1
    and Collins, 75–6, 77, 79–82,
    93, 109
sentimentalism, 25, 122, 134–5, 233
    and Little Nell, 38–9, 40, 42
    and *Nicholas Nickleby*, 26, 28,
    29, 32, 33–6
    and Wren, Jenny, 59, 60
Sewell, Elizabeth, 116
sexuality, 52, 61–2, 233; *see also* desire
shame, 94–5
Showalter, Elaine, 119, 130
Siebers, Tobin, 5, 11
Silver, Anna Krugovoy, 42
Sloppy (character: *Our Mutual
    Friend*), 61, 63, 66, 73n190
Smike (character: *Nicholas Nickleby*),
    22, 25, 26–36, 134
Snyder, Sharon, 5, 6
    *Narrative Prosthesis*, 9
social identity, 3–4, 12
social order, 75, 77, 78, 82
Spearman, Rosanna (character:
    *The Moonstone*), 16, 77, 83–7,
    89, 90–1, 92
Spencer, Herbert, 186, 214
Spenlow, Dora (character: *David
    Copperfield*), 51–2
spiritual insight, 193–4
Steig, Michael, 42
Stephen, Leslie, 185
Stirling, Edward, 31
Stoddard Holmes, Martha, 35, 62, 84,
    128, 162
    *Fictions of Affliction*, 12–13
Sturrock, June, 157, 160
suicide, 91, 92, 101
Summerson, Esther (character: *Bleak
    House*), 15, 37, 45, 46–50

Swiveller, Dick (character: *The Old
    Curiosity Shop*), 43, 45–6
sympathy, 15–16, 35, 188, 194

Tattycoram (character: *Little Dorrit*),
    56
terminal illness, 17, 193–4, 201
    and *Daniel Deronda*, 188, 189–91,
    197–8
    and *The Portrait of a Lady*, 202–4,
    207–8
    and *The Wings of the Dove*,
    211–13, 215–19, 220–1, 223
Theale, Milly (character: *The Wings
    of the Dove*), 17, 177, 211,
    212–21, 223
theatricality, 33–5, 36, 40–2, 93–4
Thomas, Ronald, 16, 76
Thrailkill, Jane, 218
Tiny Tim (character: *A Christmas
    Carol*), 25, 234
Tomalin, Claire, 23
Touchett, Ralph (character: *The
    Portrait of a Lady*), 17, 177,
    202–9, 223
Tractarians, 158, 159
transmission, 194–6, 200
Trent, Nell *see* Little Nell
*Trial, The* (Yonge), 152
Trollope, Anthony, 8, 160
Tulliver, Maggie (character: *The Mill
    on the Floss*), 174–5, 177–87
Twist, Oliver (character: *Oliver Twist*),
    31, 33

ugliness, 83, 86, 92, 95–6

Valeria (character: *The Law and the
    Lady*), 93–9, 100, 101
Verinder, Rachel (character: *The
    Moonstone*), 90–1

Wakem, Philip (character: *The Mill
    on the Floss*), 16, 174–5, 179–86,
    187, 202, 204

Wegg, Silas (character: *Our Mutual Friend*), 15, 26, 58, 63–7
Welsh, Alexander, 90
Wendell, Susan, 2
Wheatley, Kim, 162
Wickfield, Agnes (character: *David Copperfield*), 37, 51–2, 53, 153, 210
Williams, Ermine (character: *The Clever Woman of the Family*), 160–2
*Wings of the Dove, The* (James), 17, 177, 210–24, 232
Woloch, Alex, 15, 23
  *The One Vs. the Many*, 6–7
*Woman in White, The* (Collins), 77, 79–82
*Womankind* (Yonge), 121
*Woman's Thoughts About Women, A* (Craik), 121, 133
women, 116–17, 121, 126–7, 163n18, 176; *see also* child-women; femininity; feminism; marriage plot

Wood, Michael, 224
work, 1, 2, 3, 12
Wren, Jenny (character: *Our Mutual Friend*), 15, 21–2, 26, 57–63, 66–7

Yolland, Lucy (character: *The Moonstone*), 16, 77, 86–7, 90–1
Yonge, Charlotte M., 13, 14, 16, 235
  and *The Clever Woman of the Family*, 160–2
  and disability, 116, 117–18, 119–21
  and *The Pillars of the House*, 105
  and *The Trial*, 152
  and *Womankind*, 121
  *see also Daisy Chain, The*; *Heir of Redclyffe, The*

Zionism, 189–90, 200